W9-CET-350
3 4604 91054 1241

959.704 Tur
Turley, William S.
The second Indochina War : a
concise political and military
history

The Second Indochina War

In Memory of

Lang Bo Tu

From Friends of

Saline District Library

The Second Indochina War

A Concise Political and Military History

Second Edition

William S. Turley

2009

AUG

SALINE DISTRICT LIBRARY
555 N. Maple Road
Saline, MI 48176

ROWMAN & LITTLEFIELD PUBLISHERS, INC.
Lanham • Boulder • New York • Toronto • Plymouth, UK

ROWMAN & LITTLEFIELD PUBLISHERS, INC.

Published in the United States of America
by Rowman & Littlefield Publishers, Inc.
A wholly owned subsidary of The Rowman & Littlefield Publishing Group, Inc.
4501 Forbes Boulevard, Suite 200, Lanham, Maryland 20706
www.rowmanlittlefield.com

Estover Road, Plymouth PL6 7PY, United Kingdom

Copyright © 2009 by Rowman & Littlefield Publishers, Inc.

All rights reserved. No part of this publication may be reproduced, stored
in a retrieval system, or transmitted in any form or by any means, electronic,
mechanical, photocopying, recording, or otherwise, without the prior permission
of the publisher.

British Library Cataloguing in Publication Information Available

Library of Congress Cataloging-in-Publication Data

Turley, William S.
   The second Indochina War : a concise political and military history / William S.
Turley. — 2nd ed.
      p. cm.
   Previously published: Boulder, Colo. : Westview Press, 1986.
   Includes bibliographical references and index.
   ISBN-13: 978-0-7425-5525-9 (cloth : alk. paper)
   ISBN-10: 0-7425-5525-9 (cloth : alk. paper)
   ISBN-13: 978-0-7425-5526-6 (pbk. : alk. paper)
   ISBN-10: 0-7425-5526-7 (pbk. : alk. paper)
   eISBN-13: 978-0-7425-5745-1
   eISBN-10: 0-7425-5745-6
   1. Vietnam War, 1961–1975. 2. Vietnam—Politics and government—1945–
1975.
   I. Title.
   DS557.7.T866 2009
   959.704'3—dc22

                                                            2008031547

Printed in the United States of America

♾™ The paper used in this publication meets the minimum requirements of
American National Standard for Information Sciences—Permanence of Paper
for Printed Library Materials, ANSI/NISO Z39.48-1992.

Contents

Figures, Maps, and Tables

FIGURES

MAPS

TABLES

About the Book

The first edition of *The Second Indochina War* (Westview Press, 1986) was a short history of the conflicts in Laos, Cambodia, and Vietnam which gave equal attention to Communist and non-Communist experiences. In presenting the war as seen by all sides, it was almost unique among books in English, most of which described events in Indochina as backdrop for an essentially American drama. Based on years of research in primary documents and interviews conducted by William Turley in Saigon and Hanoi, it presented an original account of the strategies, perspectives, and internal politics of the Vietnamese Communists. It also drew attention to the Indochina-wide scope of what Americans referred to as the "Vietnam War."

The present, revised edition is more than just an update. While retaining the approach and structure of the first book, it draws upon the avalanche of documentation in the intervening two decades to provide a deeper, more textured analysis of events than was possible before. It also integrates into the narrative the findings of scholars of Cold War history who have had access to Soviet and Chinese archives, and it relies upon the vast outpouring of secondary literature on the war in English and Vietnamese to broaden and deepen the analysis. It is substantially longer than the first edition, but it remains a compact history relative to the scope of coverage.

The book begins by discussing the legacies of colonial rule in Indochina and the origins of the U.S. commitment there. It recounts the development of the Saigon government and explains the bases of revolution in the South, the Communist decision to seek reunification by force, the politics behind the American decision to intervene, the "sideshow" conflicts in Laos and Cambodia, and how North Vietnam survived the bombing. The major military campaigns are clearly described and analyzed, as are the debates over strategy in both Washington and Hanoi, the political maneuvering in Saigon, the negotiations that led to the Paris Agreement, and the stunning Communist victory over the South's army in 1975. The final chapter reviews the limits of American strategy and power, critiques the domino theory, assesses the "lessons," and itemizes the costs. Vietnam is the central focus, but events that unified the conflict in all three countries of Indochina into a single war also receive significant attention.

Concise and clearly written, *The Second Indochina War* is suitable for the general reader, as a text for courses on the war, or as supplementary reading for courses on Southeast Asian politics, U.S. foreign policy, revolutionary conflict, and Asian regional security. Original material on Communist internal debates plus analysis of the politics in Washington, Saigon, and other capitals also make this book a basic reference for any scholar seeking balanced guidance to the war's overarching contours, key issues, and enduring debates.

Preface

Americans have tended to view the "Vietnam War" as an essentially American drama. In popular consciousness, these words are as likely to trigger images of conflict in the U.S. Congress, media, and streets as they evoke images of war in the padi fields of lands far away. If the countries, peoples, and terrain of Indochina have any place in these images at all, it is mostly as dim background against which U.S. soldiers fought valiantly but, in the end, vainly. These images reflect the haunting suspicion that the war's outcome was determined by what happened in the United States, not in Indochina. Thirty-three years after the war's end, Googling "'American experience'–Vietnam" retrieved nearly 3.5 million hits; Googling "'Vietnamese experience'–Vietnam" brought 7,560. Similar searches using the terms "Cambodian" and "Lao" produced derisory results.

The present work grows out of my conviction that what happened in Indochina should be the foreground not background of any general history of the war. The historical momentum of social change and civil conflict in Vietnam, Laos, and Cambodia had its own dynamic, which the United States could influence but not unilaterally reshape to its own liking. The intention here is not to downplay the U.S. involvement, for the U.S. role is partly what sets the second war apart from the first one. U.S. politics, diplomacy, and military actions take up a large part of the discussion. Rather, the intention is to bring the Indochinese and U.S. contexts together in a single brief work. Special attention is paid, moreover, to the viewpoints and strategies of the ultimate victorious parties, particularly the Vietnamese Communists.

The latter emphasis is partly the reflection of the close attention I have given to Vietnamese Communism and the Vietnamese Communist military during thirty-five years of academic research. From habit as well as judgment, I believe these subjects are important and intrinsically interesting. I am also pleased that in the years since the first edition new scholarship has supported certain points that the first edition had to assert against conventional wisdom. New readers probably will not know that "experts" once routinely ascribed Communist strategies, and therefore victories, to the military genius of General Vo Nguyen Giap. But in fact, as the first edition pointed out, Giap was not the grandmaster of strategy for the second war that he was in the first. Hanoi's strategy for the second war was made collectively, with significant civilian as well as military participation. Moreover, Giap was often at odds with the strategies adopted for the war in the South and lost power to influence them as the war progressed.

The first edition was probably less successful attacking the ordinary usage of the terms "Viet Cong" and "VC." The term Viet Cong, originally a contraction of *Viet gian cong san* (Communist Traitor to Vietnam), was a pejorative label that the Saigon government's first premier, Ngo Dinh Diem, afixed to his opponents, Communist or not. With the passage of time, the term came also to be understood among supporters of Saigon as a contraction of *Viet nam cong san*, meaning Vietnamese Communist. Even inhabitants of villages under Communist control might use the term, though clearly not in Diem's sense, and party propaganda twisted it into a badge of honor for people who refused to buckle under the oppression of "American imperialism and its lackeys."[1] The American military used the term to distinguish indigenous Southern revolutionary forces from forces it erroneously called the "North Vietnamese Army." To avoid these terminological thickets, it has seemed best to call organizations as they called themselves, e.g. People's Liberation Armed Force (PLAF) instead of "Viet Cong" and People's Army of Vietnam (PAVN) instead of North Vietnamese Army. Readers also may wish to know that the numbering of plenums of Communist party central committees starts all over with each national congress. The Vietnamese Communists held congresses in 1935, 1951, 1960, and 1976.

I should point out that in Vietnam traditionally and under colonial rule, three, not two, geographic and cultural regions were recognized: the north embracing the Red River delta (*bac bo* in Vietnamese, Tonkin under the French), the center comprising the country's narrow waist (*trung bo*, or Annam), and the south anchored by the Mekong delta (*nam bo*, or Cochinchina). In 1954 the Geneva Agreements arbitrarily created two administrative zones divided at the Ben Hai River and the seventeenth parallel. In the present work, the downcased terms north, center, and south refer to the traditional regions, and the capitalized terms North and South refer to the geographic areas created by the division from 1954 to 1975. To illustrate, a person born in central Vietnam, hence a central Vietnamese by birth, could have been a North or South Vietnamese by political affiliation depending on which side of the seventeenth parallel it was his fate to live during the period of division. I hope this exercise in precision reduces rather than increases confusion.

In acknowledgments, it is customary for authors to absolve others of responsibility, but I wish to pin the blame, at least for conception, squarely on Georges Boudarel and Bui Xuan Quang. It all began with their idea for the three of us to write separate volumes on all three of Indochina's wars (the first, the second, and the one, in 1984, still ongoing) that could be integrated into a single set. Though that idea had to be shelved, it was their suggestion, advice, and encouragement that helped push me toward completion. I sorely missed Boudarel's help with the second edition, as I miss him since his passing.

From a practical standpoint the book owes its existence to the John F. Kennedy Foundation of Thailand and the Fulbright Program, which supported me in 1982–1984 as visiting professor in the American Studies Program of Chulalongkorn University, Bangkok. Due to the extraordinary generosity, kindness, and patience of the American Studies Program director, Professor Wiwat Mungkandi, I was able to devote most of my second year to writing about Indochina, at some expense to his and the program's priorities. I shall be eternally grateful for the hospitality shown me by Professor Mungkandi, the program's deputy director Professor Pratoomporn Vajarasthira and research associate Pranee Thiparat, Professors Kusuma Snitwongse and M. R. Sukhumbhand Paribatra of the Institute of Security and International Studies, and other faculty and staff of Chulalongkorn University too numerous to name, though I should like to mention Prapan Chimwongse, typist of my first draft.

The stay in Bangkok also made it feasible for me to meet frequently with Luu Doan Huynh, then number two in Vietnam's embassy and an historian of the war in his own right, and to make two extremely useful trips to Vietnam, one in March 1983 and another in April 1984, to gather material for several projects among which this book was one. My host in Hanoi was the Institute of International Relations in the Ministry of Foreign Affairs. Through the efforts of the Institute and its director, Mr. Pham Binh, I was able to interview numerous officials and to exchange views with officers in the Military History Institute of the People's Army in Hanoi. More than once did interviews go on longer than planned, and I am grateful for the time that busy individuals found to talk. Except for lodging and travel between Hanoi and Ho Chi Minh City that the Institute provided on my second visit, I made these trips at my own expense.

These visits were my first to Vietnam in a decade. In 1972–1973, I had spent a year in Saigon as a visiting lecturer at Saigon University under the auspices of the Ford Foundation and the Bureau of Education and Cultural Affairs of the Department of State. I conducted a number of interviews with defectors from Communist forces, learned much from the late William C. Gaussman who was then editor of *Viet-Nam Documents and Research Notes*, and had occasional access to U.S. and Saigon government officials. I could not have done my work without the personal interventions of Le Thuc Lan and the assistance of Bui To Loan and Duong Tu Mai. Before then, in 1967–1968, I had used a State Department grant for study in Singapore to support a protracted stay in Saigon, where I had the good fortune to follow Jeffrey Race through some of the research for his book, *War Comes to Long An*, a classic on the war in the Mekong delta. Those years left lasting impressions on my understanding of the war. When I finally got around to writing my own book, William Duiker reviewed the draft and made a number of very helpful suggestions. Sue Davis and Angie Spurlock typed the final manuscript with unfailing good humor.

This second edition is a thoroughly revised, updated, and expanded version reflecting the avalanche of documentation and secondary literature in both English and Vietnamese that has appeared since the first edition in 1986. I was not interested in tackling this project until Keith Taylor revived my interest by inviting me, perhaps unwisely from his point of view, to discuss some papers on the war at a meeting of the Association for Asian Studies in 2005. I then spent a sabbatical semester stewing in the Vietnamese collection of the University of Washington Library, where I enjoyed the help and hospitality of Judith Henchy and Christoph Giebel, and in English-language materials at the University of Cincinnati, where Michelle Vialet gave me direction and a carel. A long list of people have helped by sharing their papers and books or answering my queries through the Vietnam Studies Group use-list: Pierre Asselin, Dorothy Avery, Nayan Chanda, Michael DiGregorio, Dan Duffy, George Dutton, Ronnie Ford, William Frederick, Marc Gilbert, Ang Cheng Guan, Charles Hirschman, Tuan Hoang, David Marr, Ed Moise. Chung Nguyen, Quang X. Pham, Paul Quinn-Judge, Lew Stern, and Vu Tuong. Jennifer Donow and Kevin Davie of Southern Illinois University Carbondale's GIS Services went far beyond the call of their duties in redrawing the maps. None of these good people bear any responsibility for the use or misuse I have made of their comments, sometimes contributed unwittingly. Finally, I will never be able to repay my debt to David Hunt, Adam Fforde, and Brantly Womack, who wrote unbelievably detailed, astute, sometimes argumentative but thoroughly helpful long critiques of the final draft. In dealing with their comments I made literally hundreds of changes on top of the revisions I had already made and added more than a few pages of text. To all of these people, and not least to my wife, Clarisse Zimra, who has been with me each step of the way, I give my thanks.

NOTE

1. Hong Dieu, *Viet Cong la ai?* [Who Are the Viet Cong?] (Saigon-Gia Dinh Zone: NXB Giai-phong, March 1966). Thirty-two page booklet in the Douglas Pike collection, University of California, Berkeley, no. C13, 2953.

Abbreviations

ARVN	Army of the Republic of Vietnam
ASEAN	Association of Southeast Asian Nations
B1, B2, B3, B4	Communist military regions (see Map 4.1 "Communist Military Zones and Regions in South Vietnam")
CIA	Central Intelligence Agency
CIDG	Civilian Irregular Defense Group, RVN
CORDS	Civil Operations Rural Development Support (U.S. office in charge of pacification)
I-IV Corps	ARVN/U.S. military regions (see Map 2.1 "The Republic of Vietnam")
COSVN	Central Office for South Vietnam (of the LDP)
CPSU	Communist Party of the Soviet Union
DMZ	Demilitarized Zone between DRV and RVN
DRV	Democratic Republic of Vietnam ("North Vietnam")
ICP	Indochinese Communist Party
KCP	Kampuchean Communist Party
LDP	Lao Dong (Workers) Party (name of Vietnam's Communist party from 1952 to 1976)
MAAG	U.S. Military Assistance Advisory Group
MACV	U.S. Military Assistance Command, Vietnam
MIA	Missing in Action
MR	Military Region (see Map 4.1 "Communist Military Zones and Regions in South Vietnam")
NATO	North Atlantic Treaty Organization
NLF	National Liberation Front of South Vietnam

NXB	*Nha Xuat Ban* (Publishing House)
PAVN	People's Army of Vietnam
PKI	Partai Komunis Indonesia (Indonesian Communist Party)
PL	Pathet Lao ("Land of Laos," name of Communist Party of Laos)
PLA	People's Liberation Army
PLAF	People's Liberation Armed Force
PRC	People's Republic of China
PRG	Provisional Revolutionary Government of South Vietnam
PRP	People's Revolutionary Party (Southern branch of LDP)
PRU	Provincial Reconnaissance Unit, funded by CIA for the Phoenix Program
RD	Revolutionary Development (also Rural Development) program
RF/PF	Regional Forces/Popular Forces, ARVN
RVN	Republic of Vietnam ("South Vietnam")
RVNAF	Republic of Vietnam Armed Forces
SEATO	Southeast Asia Treaty Organization
USAF	United States Air Force
USSR	Union of Soviet Socialist Republics
VANDPF	Vietnam Alliance of National Democratic and Peace Forces
VNAF	Vietnam Air Force (South)

Chronology

June 28	Secretary of State John Foster Dulles declares that the United States is not a party to the Geneva "armistice agreements."
August 9	Diem government refuses to negotiate with the Democratic Republic of Vietnam (DRV) on elections for reunification.
August 31	Dulles declares support for Diem's position on negotiations with the DRV.
October 23	Fraudulent referendum on whether to establish a republic (98.2 percent of ballots in favor) paves way to depose Emperor Bao Dai and make Diem chief of state.
October 26	Republic of Vietnam (RVN) proclaimed, with Diem its first president.

1956

April 6	RVN declares it is under no obligation to abide by the Geneva Agreements as it is not a signatory, turns down Hanoi offer to negotiate.
April 28	U.S. Military Assistance Advisory Group officially takes over responsibility for training the Army of the Republic of Vietnam (ARVN) from departing French.
July 21	Time limit stipulated by Geneva Agreements for holding referendum on reunification passes.
September	With land reform completed, 10th Plenum of the Vietnam Workers' (Communist) party Central Committee announces "rectification" of land reform "errors;" forecasts "long, arduous, complicated struggle for unification."
December	Instructions from Political Bureau in Hanoi tell Southern cadres to persist in "political struggle" while preparing for "self-defense" and "armed propaganda."

1957

March	Twelfth Plenum of the Central Committee adopts three-year plan to restore production to 1939 level and begin transition to socialism.
May 5–19	Diem visits the United States, addresses joint session of Congress.
October	Communists in the South assemble first battalion-sized armed force from ex-Viet Minh fighters, armed propaganda teams, and sect remnants.

| November 2 | Royal Lao Government and Pathet Lao agree to form coalition government and integrate their armed forces. |
| November 19 | Lao National Assembly chooses Souvanna Phouma to head first neutral coalition government. |

1958

| July 23 | U.S.-supported rightist elements force Souvanna Phouma to resign. |
| August 18 | Pro-U.S. faction in Vientiane forms new cabinet without Pathet Lao and arrests Pathet Lao leaders, ending the first neutral coalition government in Laos. |

1959

January 12–22	Fifteenth Plenum of the Central Committee approves limited armed struggle in the South.
March	Political Bureau authorizes establishment of revolutionary base area in the South's central highlands.
May 6	Diem government issues Law 10/59, which sets up military tribunals to mete out harsh penalties for involvement with the revolutionary movement. U.S. advisers are assigned to ARVN infantry at regiment level, marines at battalion level.
May	Hanoi's Ministry of Defense commissions transportation groups to infiltrate men and supplies in May.
August 28	Party cadres stir ethnic minority dissidence in highlands of Tra Bong district, Quang Ngai province.
August	Group 559 of the People's Army of Vietnam (PAVN) delivers first load of arms to the South.

1960

January 17	Concerted uprisings in Ben Tre province spread across Mekong delta.
January 26	Communist-led forces attack ARVN Fifth Regiment near Tay Ninh city.
August 9	Neutralist military coup restores Souvanna Phouma to power in Vientiane. U.S.-backed rightists counterattack, and Laos slides into civil war.
September 5–19	Third National Congress of the Vietnam Workers' party adopts dual objectives of socialist construction in the

	North and struggle for reunification in the South, chooses new (3rd) Central Committee, elects Le Duan as party first secretary.
November 8	John Kennedy elected president.
December 20	National Liberation Front (NLF) is unveiled at Congress of People's Representatives in the South.
December 31	U.S. military personnel in Vietnam total about 900.

1961

January 1	Pathet Lao and PAVN "volunteers" evict Royal Lao armed forces from the Plaine des Jarres.
February 15	Southern revolutionary armed forces are "unified" to form People's Liberation Armed Force (PLAF), military wing of the NLF.
May 13	Ceasefire in Laos. Three days later, fourteen-nation conference opens in Geneva to restore neutral coalition government.
June 19	Kennedy adviser Dr. Eugene Staley arrives in Saigon to assess Diem's military assistance needs.
October 19–25	Presidential advisers Walt Rostow and General Maxwell D. Taylor visit South Vietnam; plans for enhanced assistance are drawn up on their return to Washington.
December 31	U.S. military personnel in Vietnam total 3,200.

1962

February 8	United States appoints General Paul D. Harkins to head a reorganized military aid mission dubbed the U.S. Military Assistance Command-Vietnam (MACV).
February 16	NLF holds its First Congress.
May	Following rightist military probes, joint Pathet Lao and PAVN forces extend control in Laos; Kennedy dispatches troops to Thailand.
July 23	Geneva conference concludes with signing of treaty to restore the neutrality of Laos.
December 31	U.S. military personnel in Vietnam total 11,300.

1963

| May 8 | Government troops fire on marchers in Hue protesting ban on public celebration of Buddha's birthday, kill nine. |

July 17	Police use clubs to break up Saigon Buddhist demonstration against religious discrimination.
August 21	Special Forces under direction of Diem's brother Ngo Dinh Nhu raid pagodas, arrest 1,400; martial law declared.
August 28	U.S. Ambassador Henry Cabot Lodge recommends Diem's overthrow in cable to Kennedy.
October	Major Generals Duong Van Minh and Tran Van Don request and receive assurance through CIA contact that United States will support a coup.
November 1–2	Military coup ousts Diem; Diem and Nhu are killed.
November 22	Kennedy assassinated; Lyndon Johnson becomes president.
December	Ninth Plenum of the Central Committee in Hanoi criticizes "revisionism," lays basis for increasing Northern involvement in the war in the South.
December 31	U.S. military personnel in Vietnam total 16,300.

1964

January 30	Major General Nguyen Khanh ousts Minh and Don in another military coup; subsequent rivalry and ineptitude of military leaders alienates civilians.
April 25	General William Westmoreland is appointed MACV commander, replaces General Harkins in June.
May 27	Second Lao coalition government collapses; Pathet Lao retake Plaine des Jarres.
July 30–31	South Vietnamese naval forces carry out raids on islands near the coast of North Vietnam.
August 1–2	U.S.-supplied Laotian planes bomb two villages in the North's Nghe An province.
August 2	North Vietnamese patrol boats menace the U.S. destroyers *Maddox* and *C. Turner Joy*; President Johnson orders airstrikes against the patrol boats and their support facilities.
August 7	By a vote of 88-2 in the Senate and 416-0 in the House, the U.S. Congress passes the Tonkin Gulf Resolution allowing the president to use "all necessary steps to prevent further aggression."
December 2	Fighting centered around Binh Gia hamlet begins; PLAF defeats larger U.S.-trained and equipped ARVN force over the next month, demonstrating that American advice would not be sufficient to prevent the ARVN's

	defeat. Fighting ends on Jan. 3, 1965, but Communist operations in the area continue until March 7.
December 8–20	Student and Buddhist demonstrations threaten stability of Saigon's military government.
December 14	U.S. warplanes begin bombing the Ho Chi Minh Trail in Laos.
December 31	U.S. military personnel in Vietnam total 23,300.

1965

February 7	Communist attack on U.S. advisers' compound near Pleiku kills nine U.S. servicemen; U.S. planes make "reprisal airstrikes" against targets in the North.
February 18	Military coup ousts General Khanh.
February 28	U.S. officials reveal that "reprisal airstrikes" on the North will occur on a continuous basis (Operation Rolling Thunder) to pressure Hanoi into a negotiated settlement.
February 29	Hanoi government orders evacuation of the North's cities.
March 9	First U.S. ground combat troops land in Vietnam at Danang.
April 8	Hanoi issues four-point statement advocating peace in the South "in accordance with the program of the National Liberation Front."
June 14	Saigon's ruling committee of generals, headed by Nguyen Van Thieu, chooses Air Vice Marshal Nguyen Cao Ky as premier. Ky's cabinet is the ninth to hold office since November 1963.
November 14–16	U.S. and PAVN units have first major encounter in Ia Drang valley.
December 31	U.S. military personnel in Vietnam total 184,000.

1966

March 10	Dismissal of First Corps Commander Nguyen Chanh Thi sparks demonstrations in Hue and Danang.
March 16	Demonstrations spread to Saigon, spearheaded by Buddhist monks demanding return to civilian rule.
March 23	General strikes occur in Hue and Danang with cooperation of local authorities.

May 15	Ky dispatches two battalions of ARVN marines to seize First Corps headquarters in Danang.
September 11	RVN Constituent Assembly is elected from officially approved slates and denounced by South's Buddhist leaders.
December 31	U.S. force level in South Vietnam reaches 362,000. Contingents from South Korea, the Philippines, Thailand, Australia, and New Zealand total about 50,000.

1967

April	Massive antiwar demonstrations occur throughout the United States.
June	PAVN General Nguyen Chi Thanh presents draft plan for general offensive and attacks on cities in the South.
June 30	Under pressure from other military leaders, Ky withdraws from the presidential race and agrees to run as vice presidential candidate with Thieu.
September 3	Thieu-Ky ticket wins election with 34.8 per cent of the vote.
October	Antiwar rally in Washington concludes with march on Pentagon.
November 21	In a speech to the National Press Club, General Westmoreland claims the end of the war is in sight.
December 31	U.S. military personnel in Vietnam total 485,600.

1968

January 21	Siege of Khe Sanh begins.
January 30–31	Communist forces launch coordinated attacks on the South's major cities and penetrate the U.S. Embassy compound in Saigon.
February 7	PAVN overruns Lang Vei camp near Khe Sanh.
February 24	Communist troops are driven out of Hue after twenty-five days of heavy fighting.
February 27	Joint Chiefs of Staff forward Westmoreland's request for 206,000 additional troops to the president.
February	Senate hearings on the 1964 Tonkin Gulf Incident cast doubt on accuracy of Johnson administration's account of this pivotal event.

March	Clark Clifford replaces Robert McNamara as secretary of defense; General Creighton Abrams replaces Westmoreland as MACV commander.
March 31	Johnson announces he will not seek reelection, suspends bombing of the North except near the demilitarized zone, and calls for peace talks.
May 3	Hanoi and Washington agree to hold preliminary talks in Paris.
May	Weaker, second round of Communist attacks on cities is beaten back in a few days.
October 31	Johnson orders all bombing of North Vietnam halted effective November 1 to meet Hanoi's condition for productive discussions; bombing intensifies in Laos.
November 6	Richard Nixon elected president.
December 31	U.S. military personnel in Vietnam total 536,100.

1969

January 25	Four-party peace talks open in Paris.
February 23	Nixon approves Abrams' request to bomb Communist sanctuaries in Cambodia with B-52s.
March 18	B-52s make the first secret Operation Menu strikes on Cambodian bases. These strikes continue for the next fourteen months.
May 8	NLF unveils ten-point peace plan that demands unconditional U.S. withdrawal and coalition government excluding Thieu.
May 14	With U.S. troop strength in Vietnam at its peak of 543,400, Nixon calls for withdrawal of "all non-South Vietnamese forces" and announces U.S. troops will be gradually withdrawn.
June 10	NLF and allied organizations form Provisional Revolutionary Government of South Vietnam (PRG).
August 4	Henry Kissinger meets Xuan Thuy in Paris to propose compromise.
September 3	Ho Chi Minh dies.
October 15	Nationwide "moratorium" demonstration in the United States. Another is held on November 15. They are the biggest to date.
November 3	Nixon's second major statement on the war conjures vision of disasters that would follow a Communist victory, appeals to "silent majority" for support.

| December | Articles by top PAVN leaders concede Southern revolution is "temporarily" in a defensive position. |
| December 31 | U.S. military personnel in Vietnam total 475,200. |

1970

February 21	Kissinger and Le Duc Tho hold first secret meeting.
February	PAVN and Pathet Lao forces drive Royal Lao, Thai, and CIA-backed H'mong troops off the Plaine des Jarres and Xieng Khoang airfield, enlarging secure logistical corridor through southern Laos,
March 12	With Prince Sihanouk out of the country, Phnom Penh government demands the immediate withdrawal of Vietnamese Communist troops from Cambodian territory.
March 18	Cambodian National Assembly deposes Sihanouk, installs General Lon Nol as chief of state. Sihanouk, in Beijing, forms "national union government" with the communist Khmer Rouge.
March 27–28	U.S.-supported ARVN forces attack Communist base areas in Cambodia.
April 11	Cambodian government troops and police participate in massacres of Vietnamese civilian residents of Cambodia.
April 28	Joint U.S.-ARVN force attacks Communist bases in Cambodian Parrot's Beak.
April 29	Joint U.S.-ARVN force attacks Communist bases in Cambodian Fishhook.
April 30	Nixon reveals U.S. troops are participating in "incursions" into Cambodia. Protests erupt in the United States.
June 24	U.S. Senate repeals the Tonkin Gulf Resolution in vote of 81-0.
June 29	U.S. ground combat troops pull out of Cambodia, leaving ARVN units to continue operations.
June 30	U.S. Senate passes Cooper-Church Amendment barring U.S. military personnel from further combat or advisory roles in Cambodia.
October 7	Nixon proposes standstill ceasefire in all three countries of Indochina.
December 31	U.S. military personnel in Vietnam total 334,600; ARVN total nears one million.

1971

February 8	With U.S. air and logistical support, the ARVN begins Operation Lamson 719 to disrupt PAVN supply lines in southern Laos, but encounters stiff resistance.
March 24	Lamson 719 comes to an end as battered ARVN forces flee or are airlifted out of Laos.
May	Communist party Political Bureau resolves to achieve "decisive victory" in 1972.
August 20	Duong Van Minh withdraws from South Vietnam presidential race, leaving Thieu, after disqualifying Ky, to run unopposed.
October 3	Thieu elected to another four-year term.
December 31	U.S. military personnel in Vietnam total 156,800; ARVN exceeds one million.

1972

March 30	PAVN troops cross the demilitarized zone to launch the largest offensive of the war since 1968; they quickly overrun northern Quang Tri province.
April 6	As Communist forces open a second front close to Saigon, U.S. warplanes resume bombing of the North.
April 7	Loc Ninh falls to PAVN and PLAF troops; An Loc is besieged.
April 15	B-52s join strikes on "military targets" in the North.
May 1	PAVN occupies Quang Tri city.
May 2	In secret meeting with Tho, Kissinger indicates United States is prepared to drop its demand for withdrawal of Northern troops from the South; public talks are suspended on May 4.
May 8	Nixon orders mining of North's harbor and waterways and destruction of all its transportation and communications.
June 28	Behind U.S. aircover, ARVN forces cross the My Chanh River and inch back toward Quang Tri city.
June 30	U.S. military personnel in Vietnam drop to 47,000.
September 16	ARVN retakes Quang Tri city.
October 8	Tho presents Kissinger with "breakthrough" draft peace plan.
October 26	Hanoi reveals contents of tentatively agreed plan; Kissinger proclaims "peace is at hand."

December 13	Further talks concerning changes in peace plan demanded by Thieu break down.
December 18–30	B-52s and tactical aircraft heavily bomb targets in and around the North's major cities.
December 26	Hanoi agrees to resume talks on basis of principles agreed in October.
December 31	U.S. military personnel in Vietnam total 24,200.

1973

January 5	Nixon letter assures Thieu of "continued assistance in the post-settlement period."
January 8	Kissinger and Tho resume negotiations in Paris.
January 16	Nixon threatens Thieu with aid cutoff if Saigon refuses to "close ranks" with Washington on peace agreement.
January 23	Kissinger and Tho reach initial agreement; a separate ceasefire for Laos is concluded.
January 27	Agreement on Ending the War and Restoring Peace in Vietnam is signed in Paris by representatives of the DRV, SRV, PRG, and United States. Ceasefire goes into effect. ARVN continues to reoccupy villages seized by Communist forces just before the ceasefire deadline.
March 29	The last U.S. troops in Vietnam depart for the United States.
April-May	Hanoi, Saigon, and Washington trade charges of ceasefire violations.
June 6–13	Kissinger and Tho meet in Paris, agree on measures to improve observance of ceasefire.
June 29	Compromise legislation passed in the House fixes August 15 deadline for cessation of bombing in Cambodia.
July 10	Thieu launches "administrative revolution" to consolidate his government in the South.
July 14	Air Force Major Hal Knight reveals documents falsified to cover up bombing of Cambodia.
August 26	Pro-Thieu slates win all contested seats in RVN Senate elections.
October	Twenty-first Plenum of the Central Committee concludes that Thieu cannot be made to implement the Paris Agreement, resolves to achieve reunification by military means.

November 7	War Powers Act passes over Nixon's veto.
November 15	Military Procurement Authorization passed by Congress prohibits use of funds for any U.S. military action in any part of Indochina.

1974

January 19	South Vietnam National Assembly special session votes to amend the constitution so Thieu can run for third term; opposition legislators protest.
February	ARVN offensive operations encroach upon areas long under Communist control; Communists retaliate.
March	Heaviest fighting since ceasefire.
April 4	House rejects Nixon administration request for $474 million increase in military aid to South Vietnam, reaffirms cut on May 22.
April 12	RVN withdraws from Paris talks on political reconciliation with PRG.
May 13	PRG delegation withdraws from Paris talks protesting Saigon's withdrawal and ARVN operations in Communist zones of control.
August 6	House cuts military aid appropriation for South Vietnam from $1 billion to $700 million.
August 9	Nixon resigns; Gerald Ford becomes president.
August 11	Ford letter to Thieu reaffirms U.S. commitment, promises "adequate support" for Saigon.
September 20	Antigovernment demonstrations erupt in Saigon following confiscation of newspapers that publish Father Tran Huu Thanh's six-count "indictment" of corruption in the Thieu regime and family.
December 18	Hanoi Political Bureau, in session until January 8, assesses situation as highly favorable, adopts plan for military campaign to defeat Thieu regime in two years.

1975

January 1	Khmer Rouge in Cambodia launch final offensive from siege ring around Phnom Penh.
January 8	Communist forces seize Phuoc Long province north of Saigon.
February 5	General Van Tien Dung leaves Hanoi to take command of offensive in the South.

March 9	PAVN opens offensive with attack on Ban Me Thuot, which falls the next day.
March 14	Thieu orders redeployment to defend Third and Fourth Corps, abandonment of Pleiku and Kontum.
March 15	ARVN retreat from central highlands turns into a rout.
March 22	PAVN crosses the My Chanh River to move on Hue, which falls on March 25.
March 28	PAVN artillery opens fire on Danang airfield; Communist troops enter Danang the next day.
April 1	Marshal Lon Nol leaves for Hawaiian exile as his troops fall back on Phnom Penh.
April 10	Ford requests $722 million emergency military assistance for Saigon. Congressional reaction is overwhelmingly negative.
April 14	Political Bureau gives its approval for Ho Chi Minh Campaign to take Saigon.
April 17	Lon Nol's army collapses; Khmer Rouge enters Phnom Penh.
April 20	PAVN breaks stiff resistance of ARVN Eighteenth Division at Xuan Loc, thirty kilometers from Saigon.
April 21	Thieu announces resignation in televised address, is replaced by Vice President Tran Van Huong.
April 26	Fifteen PAVN divisions plus auxiliaries begin maneuvers for final push on Saigon.
April 28	Duong Van Minh takes over presidency from Tran Van Huong.
April 30	Minh issues radio appeal for ARVN troops to lay down their arms. PAVN advance elements enter Saigon.
December 2	Following local seizures of power by "people's committees" and elections in November, Lao Communists declare the establishment of the Lao People's Democratic Republic.

CHINA

NORTH
VIETNAM Hanoi

Haiphong

Gulf
of
Tonkin

N

Xieng
Khouang

Vientiane

LAOS Hue

THAILAND

Bangkok

CAMBODIA

SOUTH
VIETNAM

Phnom
Penh

Saigon

South
China
Sea

100   0   100   200
Kilometers

Indochina

Introduction

Born in the ashes of World War II, the nascent Democratic Republic of Vietnam (DRV) resisted France's attempt to restore colonial rule, at first by diplomacy and, beginning in December 1946, by arms. Laos and Cambodia were drawn in, and the three countries of Indochina became embroiled in conflict for most of the remainder of the twentieth century. Two breaks in that history, however, divide it into three distinct periods. The first break was the defeat of France in 1954, which marked an end to the First Indochina War but left Vietnam partitioned. The second break was the victory of Communist forces in all three countries of Indochina in 1975 that unified Vietnam and set the scene for confrontation with wary neighbors. In between these two breaks the United States sought to turn back Communist-led struggles for revolution and national reunification by shoring up anti-Communist regimes in Saigon, Vientiane, and Phnom Penh, and by sending more than 2.5 million American soldiers to South Vietnam. Though in many respects a continuation of the first war, the period from 1954 to 1975 was also a distinct phase. This phase should be known as the Second Indochina War.

I prefer "Second Indochina War" to "Vietnam War" because the term identifies the latter as one segment in a longer complex of conflict, it more accurately describes the geographic scope of the fighting, and it avoids focus on a single country. Under this title one is free, indeed obliged, to weave stories from disparate vantage points into a single narrative. To see these stories as a whole, it is helpful to think of the war as a layered conflict. One layer consisted of the purely local revolutionary and nationalist struggles of the Lao, Cambodian, and Vietnamese peoples. A second was the interstate war consisting of American assault on the Democratic Republic and the

1

DRV's support of revolutions in Laos and Cambodia. The contest between the DRV and its Southern rival the Republic of Vietnam (RVN) over the issue of reunification can be viewed as interstate, civil, or both. The third layer consisted of attempts by the United States, the Soviet Union, and China to shape the outcome of the local conflicts and thus win (or not lose) strategic advantage in Asia. Crucially, the layers interacted, as local struggles invited interventions while great power rivalries motivated the United States, the Soviet Union, and China to intervene in ways that intensified the local struggles.

This book moves back and forth between layers of conflict, with special attention to the local struggles, which weighed most heavily in the outcome. However, I do not slight the American role or American obsessions arising from this war. How could one? At the time it ended, this was America's longest war. Major American combat forces fought twenty months longer in Indochina than American revolutionaries fought for independence from Britain. Nearly as many Americans died in combat during the Second Indochina War as during World War I. As of this writing in 2008, the Second Indochina War was also the only significant war that the United States had lost. Understandably, it moved Americans to wonder about the motives of their country's intervention and willingness to spill so much blood without attaining its objective.

One of the enduring puzzles is why the United States involved itself in Indochina in the first place. To someone looking for explanation in the tectonic shifts of world politics, the answer seems obviously to lie in American adjustments to change in the distribution of power during World War II. "Only slowly did it dawn upon us," wrote former Secretary of State Dean Acheson in *Present at the Creation*, "that the whole world structure and order that we had inherited from the nineteenth century was gone and that the struggle to replace it would be directed from two bitterly opposed and ideologically irreconcilable power centers."[1] As Indochina was a place of confrontation between allies of these power centers, the United States could not afford to stand primly aside. To Eurocentric realists like Acheson, the new configuration of world power was such that it was in the interest of America's own strategic security to help France fight the Communist tide in Indochina.[2] A variant of Acheson's view holds that the American interest in Indochina did not reflect concern with the global power balance so much as with access to markets and raw materials needed by Europe and Japan, still recovering from the devastation of World War II.[3]

To Cold War "revisionists," however, the root cause of intervention was internal to the United States. Whether styled as the foreign policy establishment,[4] "National Security Managers,"[5] or civilian and military executives in charge of the world's greatest military machine,[6] the driving force behind American policy in the Cold War revisionist view was an offensive-minded

American bureaucratic elite allied with commercial interests bent on expansion abroad. Explanations can combine variables, as in the argument that it was the great superiority of American power over that of the Soviet Union (a structural feature of the international system) that tempted American foreign policy elites to pressure reluctant presidents (domestic actors) to extend American influence into Indochina, a place previously outside the borders of American attention.[7]

Another puzzle is why did the United States, once it had gotten itself into Indochina, stay so long. The easy answer is that the initial conditions did not change, so neither did the policy. The Cold War continued, therefore so did the national security interest in supporting the French and their Vietnamese "nationalist" successors. The organizational interests of foreign policy and military bureaucracies were constant, therefore elite advisers continued to exert pressure on presidents to intervene. The psychology, commitments, and idiosyncrasies of individuals also played a role. President Dwight D. Eisenhower, it has been argued, maneuvered against people in his own administration to *avoid* deeper entanglement,[8] while Secretary of State John Foster Dulles's self-righteous, moralistic, and inflexible personality sustained a foreign policy of confrontation with Communism during the 1950s.[9] More commonly, however, answers emphasize bureaucratic processes and domestic politics, not personality, as the primary drivers of deepening involvement. "Quagmire" was an early popular image for what resulted from successive presidents approving limited steps to avoid being the first president to lose a war. Daniel Ellsberg revised the quagmire hypothesis into the "stalemate machine," arguing that pressures not to lose a country to Communism yet to win at a cost the American public and Congress would accept caused presidents to do just enough to avoid defeat.[10] Electoral politics and domestic anti-Communism acting in combination were, according to Ellsberg, powerful constraints on rational decision making. If postponement of defeat was what American presidents wanted, that is what they got as soldiers and bureaucrats worked diligently and with some success for two decades to keep South Vietnam out of Communist hands. Insofar as the policy process delivered what presidents wanted, "the system worked,"[11] even if the result was not "victory."

I mention these arguments here to emphasize that the wellsprings of American policy relating to Indochina remain contested ground. This reflects the complexity of the American policy process as much as it does the differences of theory and method among the scholars who study it. If studies of foreign policy decision-making agree on anything, it is that constitutional, bureaucratic, procedural, economic, cultural, electoral, and other factors shape outcomes in ways that frustrate the efforts of presidents to rule their own branch of government.

Actually, no government in this war made policy in the rational, utility-maximizing way imagined in unitary actor models. The Vietnamese Communists were never as unanimous as they seemed and had trouble formulating clear, unambiguous directives. Leaders at the party center often perceived things differently from commanders in the field, who sometimes implemented orders as they pleased or simply ignored them. Although in a few instances the text, for simplicity's sake, refers to actions taken by "the United States" and "the party" as if they were unitary and monadic, they plainly were not.

A simple logic tells people that if the United States, with all its military might, lost to a third rate power the reason must lie in politics. It may be asked, then, what is the point in paying as much attention to military as to political dimensions of the war? Paradoxically, the answer lies in the model of "asymmetric conflict" that explains why conventional military superiority does not necessarily determine the outcome of war. As Andrew Mack observed in a seminal essay published during the war's last year, in every case of successful insurgency against a greater external power "success for the insurgents arose not from a military victory on the ground . . . but rather from the progressive attrition of their opponents' *political* capability to wage war."[12] Insurgents can win against more powerful conventional armies if they fully mobilize their resources in pursuit of a single supreme aim and avoid defeat by not fighting on their enemy's terms. The external power, for whom less is at stake, tires of the expense and distraction that its limited aims do not justify. As Henry Kissinger famously put it, "The guerrilla wins if he does not lose. The conventional army loses if it does not win."[13]

The Second Indochina War was certainly asymmetric in Mack's sense within the layer that pits the United States against the revolutionaries of South Vietnam and their support base in the North. For the Communists, the aims of survival, revolution, and reunification were vastly more important for them than maintaining the South's independence was for the United States, and they mobilized society accordingly. At the war's peak in 1968 the number of American troops in Vietnam was less than 0.25 percent of the U.S. population,[14] while by 1964 the DRV's army had already absorbed 1 percent of the North's population and the sum of army, ready reserves, and village self-defense forces was 20 percent of the population,[15] to say nothing of the mobilization that took place in Southern villages under Communist control during revolutionary high tides. Yet despite their proportionally much greater effort, the Communists posed no threat to the survival of the United States as the U.S. did to the Democratic Republic, and they were utterly incapable of compelling the United States to withdraw by military means alone.

Still, as the logic of asymmetry requires, the insurgents must somehow bend the will of their enemy, and if this cannot be done by peaceful means it must be done by armed force. If the insurgents fight, they must inflict casualties and damage on a continuing basis and in sufficient degree to cause leaders of the external power to revise upward their estimate of the cost of winning. They must inflict casualties and damage as well to generate domestic opposition in the external power's society. They must above all fight to make each new strategy adopted by the external power seem futile, as the appearance that a strategy is succeeding will breed determination in the external power to fight on. And prolongation of war, usually considered the essence of successful insurgency under conditions of asymmetry, may work against the insurgents if it alienates the insurgents' own domestic support or allows time for international circumstances to change in unfavorable ways. Insurgents, too, sometimes find that for political reasons they must hasten the war's end by military means. All of these considerations confronted the revolutionaries in Indochina at one time or another. It is the interplay of politics and war that is crucial, not just one or the other.

It must be borne in mind as well that much of the Second Indochina War was *not* asymmetric. Asymmetry implies a logic that applies to relationships between militarily weak insurgents and militarily strong external powers, not to such relationships as those between the Pathet Lao and Royal Lao Government, the Khmer Rouge and two successive governments of Cambodia, and between Communist revolutionary forces and the RVN. Every one of these relationships involved local contestants and played out to its conclusion after American forces had withdrawn from the field.

Partly because it seemed in retrospect to Americans the quintessential asymmetric conflict, the Second Indochina War acquired powerful and lasting influence as a metaphor in the United States. Every American military intervention abroad since 1975 has been, according to someone, "another Vietnam," although this term has no agreed meaning. Depending on its user, it may mean an inconclusive war in a far away place; a military "quagmire" (to define one metaphor with another); domestic division over national security policy; hippies protesting against American imperialism; a "noble cause" defeated by a spineless Congress and unpatriotic media; and much else. A separate, equally contentious terrain of ambiguity has to do with the "lessons" and their relevance to later conflicts.

No post–Indochina War intervention has evoked more reference to "Vietnam" than the Second Gulf War in Iraq. This was unavoidable. The human mind depends on analogies to make sense of unfolding events, and political leaders will deploy them to mobilize public opinion, rationalize policy choices, score debating points, and intimidate critics. One has only to think of the Munich analogy's impact on the foreign policies of Western nations since World War II, including on the Bush administration's approach to Iraq, to know this is true.

And yet the situation in Indochina circa 1965 was quite worthless as a basis for predicting what would happen in Iraq after March 2003. The differences on the strategic, regional, and local levels of Iraq (unlike those in American domestic politics, policy, and preoccupations) were too great. Communist forces in Indochina had strong backing from the Soviet Union and China; Saddam Hussein's regime and the insurgencies that popped up within days of its defeat had no significant external support, least of all from great powers. The revolution in South Vietnam was entrenched in the villages long before American forces intervened and had a disciplined political organization capable of mobilizing broad popular support; the Iraqi insurgencies were a hodge-podge of sectarian, tribal, ethnic, and criminal militias lacking coordination and unable to organize outside their own communities. Vietnam in particular possessed a sense of nationhood uniting all of the country; Iraqi nationalism was at best a thin gloss on the ethnic/sectarian divisions between Kurdish, Sunni, Shia, and other communities. Anyone who attempted to predict an outcome for the Second Gulf War on the basis of "Vietnam" comparisons should have expected an easy victory and smooth imperium for the United States in Iraq, so much softer a target did Iraq seem. Obviously, the analogy was inappropriate.

Only the defeat of Saddam's army was easy. The Iraqi insurgencies proved to be highly resilient, for reasons that marked the differences not similarities between Iraq and Indochina. Most important was that the social fragmentation that produced multiple Iraqi insurgencies and adulterated Iraqi nationalism also made the country exceedingly difficult to govern, as the British discovered in the 1920s. When the United States withdrew from Vietnam in 1973 and its protégés went down in defeat, the aftermath was peace and stability under a strong government. It was precisely an expectation of the opposite result if American forces withdrew from Iraq that, five years after the invasion, were keeping them in the field. So my advice to readers, as we turn to concentrate on Indochina, is to set aside "Iraq" and focus on the rich complexities of Vietnam, Laos, and Cambodia.

NOTES

1. Dean Acheson, *Present at the Creation: My Years in the State Department* (New York: Norton, 1969): 726.

2. Similar argument is made in James R. Arnold, *First Domino: Eisenhower, the Military and America's Intervention in Vietnam* (New York: Morrow, 1991); Lloyd C. Gardner, *Approaching Vietnam: From World War II through Dienbienphu* (New York: Norton, 1988); and Gary R. Hess, *The United States' Emergence as a Southeast Asian Power, 1940–1950* (New York: Columbia University Press, 1987).

3. Primary exponents of these views are Robert J. McMahon, *Limits of Empire: The United States and Southeast Asia since World War II* (New York: Columbia University

Press, 1999); and Andrew J. Rotter, *The Path to Vietnam: Origins of the American Commitment to Southeast Asia* (Ithaca, N.Y.: Cornell University Press, 1987). A constructivist twist on these themes argues that Washington officials dealt with the new context by interacting dynamically with British and French counterparts, and out of this interaction there emerged a reordering of priorities that ranked cooperation among Western states above the nationalist aspirations of colonial peoples.

4. Gabriel Kolko, *Anatomy of a War: Vietnam, the United States, and the Modern Historical Experience* (New York: Pantheon, 1985).

5. Richard J. Barnett, *Roots of War* (New York: Atheneum, 1972).

6. James William Gibson, *The Perfect War: Technowar in Vietnam* (Boston: Atlantic Monthly Press, 1986).

7. Gareth Porter, *Perils of Dominance: Imbalance of Power and the Road to War in Vietnam* (Berkeley: University of California Press, 2005).

8. Melanie Billings-Yun, *Decision against War: Eisenhower and Dien Bien Phu, 1954* (New York: Columbia University Press, 1988).

9. Townsend Hoopes, *The Devil and John Foster Dulles* (Boston: Little, Brown, 1973).

10. Daniel Ellsberg, *Papers on the War* (New York: Simon & Schuster, 1972).

11. Leslie H. Gelb with Richard K. Betts, *The Irony of Vietnam: The System Worked* (Washington D.C.: Brookings Institution, 1979).

12. Andrew Mack, "Why Big Nations Lose Small Wars: The Politics of Asymmetric Conflict," *World Politics* 27, 2 (January 1975): 177.

13. Henry Kissinger, "The Vietnam Negotiations," *Foreign Affairs* 47 (January 1969): 214.

14. Mack, "Why Big Nations," 179.

15. Nguyen Quoc Dung, "Van de ket hop kinh te voi quoc phong trong 40 nam qua" [The Problem of Coordinating the Economy with National Defense over the Last 40 Years], *Nghien cuu Lich su*, 4 (1985): 12–13.

1

Legacies of Time

On March 29, 1973, the last American combat troops boarded a plane in Saigon, marking the end of U.S. involvement in the Second Indochina War. Although the fighting continued for another two years, the outcome was never seriously in doubt. The United States' intervention was an attempt to reverse historical trends that were firmly established long before U.S. troops arrived. The United States was able to slow these trends but not, without unacceptable cost to itself, to halt them. For the war was not so much a new conflict as it was the resumption of an old, unfinished one. U.S. leaders perceived their involvement on the side of beleaguered regimes as intrinsically different from the preceding French involvement, but entanglement in the three countries' histories was inescapable.

"INDOCHINA"

As popularly told, Vietnam's history is a litany of resistance to foreign domination. Formed in the Red River delta, Vietnam fell under Chinese rule in 208 BCE; the Vietnamese rebelled periodically over the next millennium, achieved independence in 938 CE, defeated another Chinese attempt at conquest in 1077, repulsed Mongol invasions in 1283 and 1287, and successfully resisted yet another Chinese occupation from 1407 to 1427. Out of this experience the Vietnamese fashioned a myth of indomitability in the face of superior force. Historians who debunk this myth point out that the Vietnamese fought more with neighbors to the south and west and among themselves than with China, but the fact remains that the Vietnamese forged a distinctive identity more through interaction with China than with any other country. China was an inescapable presence, alternately menacing and protective, and the only country that threatened Vietnam's independence before the colonial era. Yet, China was also a major source of Vietnam's culture, language, and institutions. A Chinese province for a millennium and a tributary state thereafter, Vietnam had constantly to fear the possibility of absorption into the Chinese empire while participating in an international order that centered on China. Out of this complex association with China and partly in assertion against it, the Vietnamese forged a sense of identity long before Europeans appeared off their shores. A key element of that identity, in addition to a single language, a shared tradition, and a united territory, was an image of heroic resistance to foreign rule. In 1076 the Vietnamese military leader Ly Thuong Kiet roused his troops to repulse the invading Sung with the words, "The Emperor of the South [Vietnam] rules over the rivers and mountains of the southern country. This destiny has been indelibly registered in the celestial book. How dare you, rebellious slaves, come violate it? You shall undoubtedly witness your own and complete defeat."[1] Later generations of Vietnamese would use such materials to construct a "usable past" emphasizing their own defiant peoplehood, though they were not above seeking foreign help when they fell out among themselves.

Another key to Vietnamese identity was the "southward march" (*Nam Tien*) from their homeland in the Red River delta. Squeezed between China to the north, the sea to the east, and mountains to the west, the only way open for the Vietnamese to expand was to the south. The "march" was a process of gradual encroachment by militarized settlements that expunged the Cham empire and was nibbling at Cambodia when westerners arrived on the scene. It did not end until 1834 when Cambodia ceded control of Sa Dec and Chau Doc provinces in the Mekong delta. Much of this expansion took place during two centuries of national division between two aristocratic households, one of which reunited the country with the help of a French missionary and established the Nguyen dynasty in 1802. In the overall scheme of Vietnamese history, the period of division was brief, and neither of the contending factions considered it legitimate. For reasons of geography more than politics, the regional differences that mattered—drawing lines based on accent, cuisine, and mutual stereotypes—corresponded to the ancient Red River delta homeland, the rugged mid-section, and the Mekong delta frontier—north, center, and south or, in Vietnamese, *bac bo, trung bo,* and *nam bo*. Meanwhile, Vietnamese rulers who paid tribute to China fashioned themselves as emperors and exacted tribute from the ethnic minorities and Lao principalities on Vietnam's western flank. Vietnam on the eve of the colonial period was a whole and united country.

Colonial rule began in 1858 with a series of French military thrusts, first at Danang on the central coast of Vietnam and then at Saigon. Ensconced in the Mekong delta, the French in 1863 extended a protectorate over Cambodia, which the Cambodian king accepted to fend off a threatened Siamese invasion. The rest of Vietnam fell under French control in 1883 when the French seized Hanoi to squelch an appeal by the emperor for help from China. Feeling threatened from the west by Siamese penetrations of Laos, the French established a protectorate over that country as well. In "protecting" Laos and Cambodia the French assumed Vietnam's place in the rivalry with Siam for regional dominance, tying Laos and Cambodia into Vietnam's orbit even while preserving them as separate entities. France then set about consolidating its own regional hegemony by creating a federal administrative structure it called the *Union Indochinoise* to rule the region's culturally disparate peoples, employing a term that joined "Indianized" Laos and Cambodia to "Sinicized" Vietnam. Thus "Indochina," which had no previous political, administrative or imagined existence, came into being.[2]

The takeover was resisted at each step, first by the Vietnamese imperial army, later by popularly supported rebellions led by local leaders. A major rebellion under the putative leadership of the boy-emperor Ham Nghi, though instigated by the mandarin class (i.e., the Confucian intelligentsia), broke out in 1885. Significantly, however, these and other uprisings led by traditional elites all failed, and with their failure the institutions and ideology of the Confucian state lost legitimacy. An imperial administration survived and ruled central Vietnam (*trung bo*, which the French called Annam) under French supervision, but traditional economic and community life unraveled under the weight of colonial taxation, an intrusive colonial bureaucracy, the commercialization of agriculture, new patterns of landholding, and urbanization. At the turn of the century, the traditional Vietnamese order was dying, tended by old men who had sat for the mandarinal exams but whose knowledge the young recognized was obsolete.[3] A new generation of the intelligentsia launched a search for other ways to come to terms with the West and Western colonial rule. This search led some to resign themselves to French tutelage, some to study abroad, and some to concoct or adopt doctrines strange to Vietnam, from parliamentary democracy and radical individualism to anarchism and Marxism. Although this search kept the flame of patriotism alive, it also fragmented the elite. Loosely united in a belief that Vietnam should be independent, intellectuals were deeply divided over which person, party, or doctrine should lead the Vietnamese into their postcolonial future.

It was against this background that Ho Chi Minh and a number of other young Vietnamese felt drawn to socialism following the October Revolution in Russia in 1917. Ho at the time was living in Paris, participating with other émigrés in nightly debates on how to achieve national independence and renewal. Russia's grand experiment captivated Ho's circle, which eagerly read the writings of Vladimir Lenin, mastermind of the October

Revolution and now leader of the new Soviet state. Particularly seductive for Ho was Lenin's "Theses on the National and Colonial Question," which moved Ho to burst out: "Dear martyrs, compatriots! This is what we need; this is the path to our liberation!"[4] What Ho found appealing was Lenin's lucid, uncompromising critique of world imperialism. The "thesis" moreover was linked to a larger body of theory on organization, strategy, and tactics as well as to the program of the newly founded Communist Third International headquartered in Moscow. In December 1920 Ho cast his lot with that faction of the French Socialist Party that voted to join the Third International and thus became a founding member of the French Communist Party. Before long he was in Moscow, specializing in peasant affairs for the Communist International (Comintern) and undergoing training for assignment to Asia. In 1924 the Comintern sent him to China, where he coordinated the propaganda and recruitment that culminated in founding the Indochinese Communist party (ICP) in 1930. Thanks to cautious organizational work, a trickle of cadres trained abroad, and escape from the French suppression that weakened rival groups, the ICP would soon become the most effective of all Vietnamese parties and movements opposed to colonial rule. This is not to say that the Communists commanded widespread popular support—no party did. It is only to say that they were better prepared than their rivals to seize the opportunity presented by the outbreak of World War II, when Japan occupied Indochina but left the French nominally in charge.

In 1941 the ICP determined that it would seek independence through armed struggle, and it organized a national united front known as the *Viet Nam Doc Lap Dong Minh* (Vietnam Independence League), or Viet Minh for short. While other nationalist groups ceased activities, fled to China, or collaborated with the French, the Viet Minh prepared for armed resistance. Greatly assisted by the effects of a raging famine and Japan's surrender to the Allies, the Communists rode to power on the crest of a popular uprising known as the August Revolution of 1945. On September 2 Ho Chi Minh declared independence for the Democratic Republic of Vietnam (DRV) encompassing all Vietnamese territory from the Chinese border to the tip of the Ca Mau peninsula.[5]

The August Revolution was a watershed of immense importance, for it destroyed the myth of colonial superiority, regardless whether France restored its rule or not. Equally important, it mobilized a generation—"the generation of '45"—into political activism. Tens of thousands of Vietnam's best and brightest urban youths, swept up in the excitement, rallied to the Viet Minh, providing a critical stratum of educated cadres and potential recruits for party membership. Membership in the party, just five thousand before August, burgeoned. Total armed forces under Viet Minh control grew from five thousand in August to seventy thousand by the year's end.

Ordinary people joined or supported the Viet Minh out of patriotism, not knowing or caring about the central role played by the ICP in the leadership of the Viet Minh or the DRV government. Although other groups contended for leadership, they lacked the Communists' discipline, organizational skills, and focus on mobilizing mass support. The Communists' most potent opponents were protégés of the Chinese *Guomindang* (Nationalist Party), and the Communists scattered them in a spasm of violence. Like it or not, defending Vietnam's newfound independence henceforward meant defending the Communist-led DRV.

The DRV had little time to consolidate this achievement, however, for France withheld recognition and reestablished control over Saigon, the country's largest city. France then entered negotiations with the DRV and agreed in March 1946 to recognize the DRV as a "free state" within the French Union. Further negotiations broke down, however, and fighting erupted in December. In the eight years of war that followed, the Viet Minh grew steadily in political and military strength, especially in rural areas. The victory of the Chinese Communist Revolution in 1949 provided the Viet Minh for the first time with a secure rear and source of training and supply. China also supplied much of the equipment that made possible the Viet Minh's decisive victory over the French at Dien Bien Phu on May 7, 1954.[6] The nine-power Geneva conference, called to end the war in Indochina, held its first session the next day.

ROOTS OF AMERICAN INVOLVEMENT

U.S. policy meanwhile underwent a profound change. Apart from its colony in the Philippines, the United States had never had much interest in Southeast Asia. Occupation of the region during World War II by Japan shattered that indifference by demonstrating the inability of European colonial powers to provide regional order and stability. But the Roosevelt administration had no clearly formed idea what the post-war order should be. Roosevelt himself said more than once that the Europeans, particularly the French, had misruled their colonies and should not be allowed to return, while business interests saw an opportunity to open new areas to American trade. But pressing the Europeans to give up their empires jeopardized cooperation with them in Europe, whose importance far outweighed any other region in American geostrategic perceptions. The U.S. military moreover wished to retain control of the Pacific islands that American armed forces had seized from Japan, making it awkward to demand that France place Indochina under international trusteeship. With the war coming to a close, Roosevelt dropped his insistence on trusteeship for Indochina and in late 1944 reassured the British, French, and Dutch that they could keep their Southeast Asian colonies.

Roosevelt died on April 12, 1945. His successor, Harry Truman, becoming president just two weeks before Germany's surrender, faced more pressing issues than decolonization, on which Truman had no strong position anyway. For Truman and his top foreign policy advisers, securing the cooperation of European allies in building a stable postwar international order was far more important. The administration also soon faced Soviet attempts to extend its influence into Greece, Turkey, and Iran and surging support for Communist parties in several Western European countries, including France. Gaining France's support of establishing the United Nations and securing France's participation in organizing a defense against the Soviet threat were high priorities. To achieve those ends it was necessary, in the estimation of Truman administration officials, to avoid shaking "the precarious balance of French domestic politics to the advantage of the Communist Party," as pressuring France to give up Indochina might do.[7] And so it was that the administration, overriding objections from the U.S. State Department's newly established Southeast Asia Division, reaffirmed French sovereignty over Indochina. Officially neutral toward France's effort to recover Indochina, the United States in late 1945 provided ships to carry French troops to Saigon. In 1946 it began quietly supplying substantial amounts of non-lethal equipment for the French to use in Indochina. France, with Washington's silent consent, also rerouted to Indochina assistance that the United States gave it for use in Europe.[8]

The American purpose, however, was not to help France reestablish colonial rule in its prewar form. The purpose, reflecting both American anticolonial sentiment and a pragmatic belief that France could not win the support of the Indochinese people without satisfying their nationalist aspirations, was to achieve an American objective with a French foil.[9] American strategists wanted France to defeat the Viet Minh but believed that victory was possible only in the context of movement toward national independence. Hence the posture of neutrality while routing through France the military assistance that was meant for Indochina. Meanwhile Washington continued to prod the French to grant self-government to Laos, Cambodia, and Vietnam, using the promise of assistance France desperately needed as a stick. The French reluctantly complied by persuading ex-emperor Bao Dai to head a quasi-independent "State of Vietnam," giving birth to the "Bao Dai solution" in 1949. On March 10, 1949, six months before Mao Zedong proclaimed the People's Republic of China, Truman approved a grant of $15 million in military aid to France for Indochina.[10] So from June 30, 1950, five days after the Korean War began, U.S. aid that had been flowing through France began going directly to Vietnam and to Laos and Cambodia, the other "Associated States" of the French Union.

Although American aid had started to flow independently of events in China and Korea, American perceptions of France's war in Indochina under-

went a fundamental shift in response to them. What to Americans had originally seemed to be an effort by France to restore colonial power gradually
came to be seen as part of the West's larger effort to halt further Communist
expansion. A Viet Minh victory in this updated view would signify a gain for
the communist "bloc." It would destabilize the region, deny commercial access to allies who were economically tied to Southeast Asia, and tilt the global
balance of power. Vice President Richard Nixon put it this way in 1953:

> If Indochina falls, Thailand is put in an almost impossible position. The same
> is true of Malaya with its rubber and tin. The same is true of Indonesia. If this
> whole part of Southeast Asia goes under Communist domination or Commu-
> nist influence, Japan, who trades and must trade with this area in order to exist,
> must inevitably be oriented toward the Communist regime. That indicates to
> you and to all of us why it is vitally important that Indochina not go behind
> the Iron Curtain.[11]

It was "vitally important" to the United States, according to Nixon, that
France defeat the Viet Minh to safeguard Japan's stake in Southeast Asia
and to keep Japan allied with the U.S. Nixon emphasized American strategic security not economic interests, because neither Indochina nor all of
Southeast Asia was economically important to the U.S. From 1955 to 1960,
the entire region accounted for only 3.7 percent of total U.S. trade with the
world, and half of the American trade with Southeast Asia was with the
Philippines; only one-fifth of one percent was with the three countries of
Indochina.[12] Oil had yet to be discovered in the South China Sea. Although
ending colonial trading blocs had long been an American goal and there
was awareness of the region's potential for American interests,[13] security issues took precedence once the Cold War was under way. As the most powerful of the democratic capitalist countries in a bipolar structure of power,
the United States felt obliged to protect the interests of its allies and to help
them recover from the devastation of World War II, the better to face the
new threat of Communism.

The French effort in Indochina thus became, in U.S. estimates, part of
the "free world's" effort to contain Communist expansionism. U.S. aid to
that effort rose to $1.1 billion by 1954; in that year, the United States un-
derwrote 78 percent of France's war expenses.[14] The relationship between
the two countries was not an amicable collaboration, however. At each step
of the way, the French dragged their feet on independence for the Associated States and made the minimum concessions needed to secure the next
tranche of American aid. The French after all fought as much to preserve
their presence in Indochina as to halt Communist expansionism, and many
French officials believed the ultimate American aim was to supplant them.
In the end, American willingness to bankroll the war outlasted the determination of a war-weary France to avoid defeat.

THE GENEVA AGREEMENTS

The United States considered full-scale military intervention but proved unwilling so soon after Korea to take over another land war in Asia. By 1954 the French sought through negotiations at Geneva, Switzerland, only to withdraw, by a face-saving compromise if possible. Fortunately for France, the Soviet Union and China were anxious at that time to avert a confrontation with the United States, and they counseled the DRV to make concessions.[15] DRV leaders, too, feared deepening U.S. involvement. Contrary to their own assessment of what their battlefield victories entitled them, the Communists agreed to a military truce and regrouping of forces on either side of the seventeenth parallel. By a series of undertakings known collectively as the Geneva Agreements, the DRV was confined to territory north of that line, its capital in Hanoi. The State of Vietnam was to occupy the territory south of the line, its capital in Saigon. An International Control Commission (ICC) consisting of representatives of India, Poland, and Canada was to oversee the ceasefire and the regrouping.

The Final Declaration of the conference stipulated that the provisional military demarcation line was for ceasefire purposes only "and should not in any way be interpreted as constituting a political or territorial boundary." Referring to the DRV and State of Vietnam as "representative authorities of Northern and Southern zones of Viet Nam," it provided that in two years a referendum should be held to resolve political issues, particularly reunification. However, of the nine countries that attended the conference, only four (France, Great Britain, the Soviet Union, and China)[16] gave the Final Declaration their unqualified endorsement. The Saigon government denounced the agreement and specifically condemned any provision that might "lead to a direct or indirect partition, final or provisional, in fact or in law, of the national territory."[17] The United States promised to "refrain from the threat or the use of force to disturb" the accords. The United States also expressed a commitment to reunification through free elections supervised by the United Nations and reiterated "its traditional position that peoples are entitled to determine their own future and that it will not join in an arrangement which would hinder this." Diplomacy thus brought a messy end to a messy war, a pause designed to let France withdraw and weakly bound the participants to a lasting settlement.[18] The text of the agreements did *not* establish North Vietnam and South Vietnam as separate sovereign states, and *both* Saigon and Hanoi proclaimed their commitment to maintaining Vietnam's territorial integrity. These undertakings could be interpreted as implying that any conflict between North and South would be an "internal struggle for control of a national society"—in other words, a civil war —in which it would be "inappropriate for a foreign nation to use military power to influence the outcome."[19] A quite different interpretation held that the primary objective in creating two zones was to achieve a military ceasefire, making any use of force by one against the other unlawful, regardless of the status of the demarcation line between them.[20] Political realities overrode the legal disputes, however. Participants at Geneva recognized that the terms of settlement were unrealistic and unlikely to be voluntarily carried out. Saigon and Hanoi violated agreement provisions, and both enjoyed diplomatic recognition by different sets of allies. To Moscow and Beijing, partition was a satisfactory outcome because it stabilized a front line in the Cold War, not unlike the "divided states" of Korea and Germany. Evidence also suggests that the Chinese wanted to halt a Vietnamese drive to dominate all of Indochina, where Beijing wished to exercise paramount influence.[21] Washington, in no mood to take France's place on the battlefield, settled for a chance to halt the Communist advance. These realities confounded attempts to define the legal status of North and South in a definitive way. The United States took the view that the agreements posed no obstacle to recognizing the South's legitimacy and permanence and on these grounds it depicted the second war, when it came, as "aggression from the North."

The Vietnamese Communists, for their part, accepted the agreements with deep bitterness. The declaration gave them uncontested control of only half the country, although they had provided a semblance of legitimate government for all of it from August 1945 to December 1946.[22] Accepting designation of the DRV as nothing more than the "representative authority" of the Northern zone demeaned the August Revolution and Ho Chi Minh's declaration of independence. Moreover, by 1954 the tide of battle had turned in their favor, and if a line were drawn between real zones of control it would not have run between North and South; it would have run around pockets of support from one end of the country to the other. Accepting the seventeenth parallel as a ceasefire line implied a territorial division of power utterly different from the one that actually existed. Moreover, the arrangement gave each "authority" secure control over one half of the country in exchange for abandoning people and territory it controlled in the other. By allowing cadres, fighters, and followers to regroup on either side of the parallel, the agreements guaranteed security to some but left those who stayed behind exposed to retribution by the regime they had fought to overthrow. These provisions applied to both sides, but they deprived the Communists of an imminent victory and allowed their enemies time to retrench. Given the general perception that they would win elections on reunification, it is not surprising that only the Communists expressed an interest in holding them.

The same conference that arranged a ceasefire for Vietnam agreed to neutralize Laos and Cambodia by taking note of the two countries' declarations of intent not to join military alliances, not to request foreign military aid, and not to allow the establishment of bases on their territories by the military forces of foreign powers. The language, however, offered no guarantees. The commitment not to request foreign military aid, for example, could be set aside if aid were needed "for the purpose of the effective defence of their territory." And it was only alliances "not in conformity with the principles of the Charter of the United Nations" that the two countries were obliged not to join.[23] Cambodia and Laos, with governments too weak to defend neutrality against foreign powers bent on subverting it, would be victims of these deliberate ambiguities.

THE WAR TO COME

The United States moved quickly to fill the vacuum left by France's retreat. The U.S. fear, expressed in the "domino theory," was that if the South fell to the Communists, Vietnam's neighbors would fall in succession or at least accommodate Communist influence. China in particular, it was believed in Washington, would realize great strategic gains at the expense of American and, more generally, Western influence throughout Southeast Asia. The United States therefore took steps to make permanent the arrangements that the Geneva conference had declared should be temporary. The Southeast Asia Treaty Organization (SEATO), organized in September 1954, unilaterally offered protection to South Vietnam, which the Geneva Agreements had prohibited from joining military alliances. The United States extended direct military assistance to the Saigon regime (and, secretly, to Laos), including an advisory group whose numbers soon surpassed the limits placed at Geneva on such personnel. In June 1955 Secretary of State John Foster Dulles pointed out that the United States was not a party to the armistice agreements[24] and that it supported Saigon's refusal to consult with Hanoi about elections on the grounds that elections could never be free in the North. In October the United States approved the proclamation of a new constitution that established the Republic of Vietnam (RVN) with a president holding almost dictatorial powers. As they watched the United States stake its prestige on a non-Communist South, the Vietnamese Communists realized, if they had ever doubted it, that reunification might well require them to resume armed struggle.

Communist leaders knew that engaging in such a struggle risked retaliation from the world's greatest military power. That prospect caused some of them to question whether the risk was worth taking. Yet, when the moment of decision arrived, in 1959, they advanced several reasons to believe that the revolution would prevail: (1) the precedent of victory over a modern army in the First Indochina War; (2) U.S. dependence on Saigon for a local ally and the dependence of Saigon on the United States for survival; (3)

the growing strength of socialist countries and of national liberation movements worldwide, which was gradually tipping the strategic balance against the United States; and (4) the ability of politically motivated masses to defeat a technologically superior adversary. The Communists also believed they had no choice but to incur the risk of a U.S. response if they wished to "complete" Vietnam's independence and secure the revolution in the North as well as the South. There was no point in sacrificing those goals to avoid that risk, party leaders believed, because the United States was bent on intervention regardless of what they did. "The American-Diemist plot is to destroy peace, destroy the Geneva Agreements, and divide our country, turning South Vietnam into a colony and military base of the United States to prepare to resume war . . . ," as the party secretariat put it in 1956.[25]

As things turned out, the United States was able to prolong and intensify the war and to strengthen the South Vietnamese regime on whose side it had intervened. But the United States was unable in a few years to reshape what a century of colonial rule had wrought. Those long years of foreign occupation had, by 1954, left Southern Vietnamese society deeply divided—much more than Northern—by sect, class, occupation, and political persuasion. The part of Vietnam that embraced the Mekong delta, what the French called *Cochinchina*, had been the first region to fall under colonial rule. There, the colonial economy made the deepest inroads: it had linked villages to external markets, set the commercial city against the agricultural countryside, sharply increased debt and tenancy, and exacerbated inequalities. Nowhere else in Vietnam had so many people sought security in affiliation with politico-religious and millenarian movements. To these groups were added, in 1954, a sizeable Catholic minority drawn from all three of Vietnam's traditionally recognized regions, the north, the center, and the south. The enlargement of the Catholic minority deepened the divisions in South Vietnamese society. There was no "South Vietnamese" national consciousness in 1954, just as there was no East German or South Korean national consciousness in 1945; there was only a highly fragmented society, arbitrarily separated from its other half to facilitate France's retreat.

As time passed, the diverse fragments of South Vietnamese society sorted themselves into three broad political categories. The core of Saigon's side consisted of the civil servants, military officers, and landlords who had no future under Communism. Political parties seeking power within the Saigon government tended to splinter and then splinter again over differences of region and personality. Some fairly sizeable portion of the South's population also preferred this side to the Communists, though never unconditionally and seldom with enthusiasm. On the revolutionary side, the Communist *Dang Lao Dong* (Lao Dong or Workers' Party, commonly initialized as LDP, with its Central Committee in Hanoi) had broad support in the North and a branch in the South. In rural areas where the Viet Minh had been strong during the war against France, the party enjoyed active support or sympathy. This more encompassing movement of resistance to oppression and demand for change in social relations, "the Southern revolution," also appealed to peasants who perceived themselves as victims of predatory landlords and unjust government policies. Others, such as a smattering of non-Communist intellectuals, monks, and discontented ethnic minorities, aligned themselves with the revolution in reaction against government repression or the U.S. presence.

Between these two groups, in various postures of neutrality, an array of splinter groups dreamt of alternatives to both Saigon and the Communists. These groups articulated what was perhaps the sentiment of the majority of the population, but the groups had no organizational core, no outstanding leaders, and no coherent program. Foreign observers who dubbed these groups and the populations they represented the "Third Force" imputed to them a unity, power, and purpose they never possessed. In the first war the label had been applied to nationalists who opposed both the French and the Viet Minh. In the second it stuck to the amorphous middle, pushed and pulled from both sides by the Saigon government and the Communists.

The war likewise encroached geographically upon all of Indochina. Although Vietnam, with nearly five times the population of Laos and Cambodia combined, was the natural epicenter of conflict, the Communists, the United States, and the Saigon government treated all three countries as a single strategic unit. This perspective had come easily to the French, the colonial masters of the region. It had come later to Vietnamese employed by the French as low-level civil servants in Laos and Cambodia. And it had come perforce to the Vietnamese Communists, beginning with an instruction from the Communist International in Moscow in 1930 to build a single Communist party for all of Indochina. This was an instruction the Vietnamese Communists implemented without much energy or success in Laos and Cambodia and formally abandoned in favor of separate national parties in 1951 (when the Vietnamese party took the name *Dang Lao Dong* [Workers' Party]). But a presumption to mentor the Lao and Khmer persisted among the Vietnamese.[26] War with France, then, made this perspective a military imperative. Attacking Viet Minh redoubts from bases in Laos and Cambodia in 1947, French forces gave the Vietnamese Communists no choice but to see things as the French did. General Vo Nguyen Giap put it this way in 1950:

Indochina is a single strategic unit, a single battlefield, and here we have the mission of helping the movement to liberate all of Indochina. This is because militarily, Indochina is one bloc, one unit, in both the invasion and defense plans of the enemy. For this reason, and especially because of the strategic terrain, we cannot consider Vietnam to be independent so long as Cambodia and

Laos are under imperialist domination, just as we cannot consider Cambodia and Laos to be independent so long as Vietnam is under imperialist rule.

The colonialists used Cambodia to attack Vietnam. Laos and Cambodia temporarily have become the secure rear areas of the enemy and simultaneously their most vulnerable area in the entire Indochina theater. Therefore, we need to open the Laos-Cambodia battlefield resolutely and energetically.[27]

Long before the Second Indochina War, the Vietnamese Communists were treating Laos, Cambodia, and Vietnam as a strategic unit and regarded the denial of Laos and Cambodia to their enemies as fundamental to achieving objectives inside Vietnam. The United States did not have physical bases inside Laos and Cambodia as the French had, and so to strike from the west the U.S. had to develop other ways to penetrate these two countries. Overcoming that constraint led to a "secret" war in Laos, the bombing of Cambodia, and the stationing of fifty thousand American troops in Thailand. The U.S. thus also treated Indochina as a strategic unit, assuring that as the U.S. became more deeply involved in the war the more the war involved all of Indochina.

NOTES

1. Ly Thuong Kiet, "The Principle of Identity," translated in Truong Buu Lum, *Patterns of Vietnamese Response to Foreign Intervention: 1858–1900* (New Haven, Conn.: Yale University Southeast Asia Studies, Monograph Series No. 11, 1967), 47.

2. The term "Indo-China" was coined as early as 1811 by English missionaries to refer to Asia beyond India. A French geographer first used *Indo-Chine* in 1874 in reference to the area approximating today's mainland Southeast Asia, and addition of the modifier *Française* delimited the area to Laos, Cambodia, and Vietnam. The Vietnamese word for Indochina, *Dong–Duong*, did not gain currency until the twentieth century. Christopher E. Goscha, *Vietnam or Indochina? Contesting Concepts of Space in Vietnamese Nationalism, 1887–1954* (Copenhagen, Nordic Institute of Asian Studies, NIAS Report Series, No. 28, 1995), 15.

3. For an evocative analysis of this generational transition, see Hue-Tam Ho Tai, *Radicalism and the Origins of the Vietnamese Revolution* (Cambridge, Mass.: Harvard University Press, 1992).

4. Ho Chi Minh, "The Path Which Led Me to Leninism," in *Ho Chi Minh on Revolution*, ed. Bernard B. Fall (New York: Praeger, 1967), 6; William J. Duiker, *Ho Chi Minh* (New York: Hyperion, 2000), 64–65; and Hue-Tam Ho Tai, *Radicalism*, 69.

5. See David G. Marr, *Vietnam 1945: The Quest for Power* (Berkeley: University of California Press, 1995).

6. Chen Jian, "China and the First Indo–China War, 1950–54," *The China Quarterly*, no. 112 (March 1993): 85–110; and Qiang Zhai, "Transplanting the Chinese Model: Chinese Military Advisers and the First Vietnam War, 1950–54," *The Journal of Military History* 57, no. 4 (October 1993): 689–715.

7. George McT. Kahin, *Intervention: How America Became Involved in Vietnam* (New York: Knopf, 1986), 4.

8. Kahin, *Intervention*, 7–8. For a detailed study of the historical record see Mark Atwood Lawrence, *Assuming the Burden: Europe and the American Commitment to War in Vietnam* (Berkeley: University of California Press, 2005).

9. For development of these themes, see Robert J. McMahon, *The Limits of Empire: The United States and Southeast Asia Since World War II* (New York: Columbia University Press, 1999), 26–42.

10. Kathryn C. Statler, *Replacing France: the Origins of American Intervention in Vietnam* (Lexington: University Press of Kentucky, 2007), 30.

11. Speech delivered in United States on return from a visit to Asia, U.S. Department of State, *Bulletin* 30 (January 4, 1954): 12.

12. International Monetary Fund, *Direction of Trade Statistics*, Geospatial & Statistical Data Center, University of Virginia Library, www.fisher.lib.virginia.edu/collections/stats/dot (accessed September 11, 2006).

13. See Lawrence, *Assuming the Burden*, 46–49, 233–234.

14. Neil Sheehan et al., eds., *The Pentagon Papers* (New York: Bantam, 1971), 10.

15. Qiang Zhai, *China & the Vietnam Wars, 1950–1975* (Chapel Hill: University of North Carolina Press, 2000), 50–63; Ilya V. Gaiduk, *Confronting Vietnam: Soviet Policy Toward the Indochina Conflict, 1954–1963* (Stanford, Calif.: Stanford University/Woodrow Wilson Center Press, 2003), 33–38.

16. The others were the United States, Laos, Cambodia, the Democratic Republic of Vietnam, and the State of Vietnam.

17. "Proposals by the State of Viet-Nam for a Settlement in Viet-Nam: Submitted at the Third Plenary Session, May 12, 1954," in Allan W. Cameron, *Viet-Nam Crisis: A Documentary History, Volume I: 1940–1956* (Ithaca, N.Y.: Cornell University Press, 1971), 265.

18. "[A]n official British source later observed that the Final Declaration 'appears to have the character properly of a statement of intention or policy on the part of those member States of the Conference who approved it.' . . . It is certainly difficult, under accepted rules and practices of international law, to understand how the Final Declaration could be legally binding on any of the participants, much less those who failed positively to indicate their assent to its provisions at the final session of the Conference." Cameron, *Viet-Nam Crisis*, 287n3.

19. Richard A. Falk, "International Law and the United States Role in the Viet Nam War," in *The Vietnam War and International Law*, ed. Richard A. Falk (Princeton, N.J.: Princeton University Press, 1968), 366.

20. John Norton Moore, *Law and the Indo–China War* (Princeton, N.J.: Princeton University Press, 1972), 362–366.

21. Goscha, *Vietnam or Indochina?*, 145–146.

22. The Democratic Republic's actual grip was tenuous and uneven, to be sure. Chinese nationalist and British forces entered Indochina in September 1945 to receive the surrender of Japanese troops. While the Chinese force's predatory behavior probably helped the Communists to mobilize support for the DRV north of the sixteenth parallel, the British commander unleashed French troops south of it to evict DRV and Viet Minh organs from the major cities. Non-Communist groups and parties also contested the DRV's writ in scattered places.

23. "Final Declaration of the Geneva Conference on the problem of restoring peace in Indo-China . . . ," (July 21, 1954).

24. Statement at a press conference, June 28, 1955, quoted in Cameron, *Viet-Nam Crisis*, 378.

25. "Chi thi cua Ban bi thu So 23/CT-TW, ngay 14 thang 4 nam 1956 [Directive of the Secretariat No. 23/CT-TW, April 14, 1956], in Dang Cong San Viet Nam, *Van kien Dang toan tap* [Complete Party Documents (hereafter cited as VKDTT)], vol. 17, 1956 (Hanoi: NXB Ban chinh tri quoc gia, 2002), 146.

26. For further discussion of "Indochina" in the Vietnamese communist policy and strategy, see Gareth Porter, "Vietnamese Communist Policy Towards Kampuchea, 1930–1970," in *Revolution and Its Aftermath in Kampuchea: Eight Essays*, David Chandler and Ben Kiernan, eds. (New Haven, Conn.: Yale University Southeast Asia Studies, 1983), 57–98; Ronald Bruce St. John, *Revolution, Reform, and Regionalism in Southeast Asia: Cambodia, Laos, and Vietnam* (London: Routledge, 2006), 1–19; and William S. Turley, "Vietnam's Strategy for Indochina and Security in Southeast Asia," in *Security, Strategy, and Policy Responses in the Pacific Rim*, ed. Young Whan Kihl and Lawrence E. Grinter (Boulder, Colo.: Lynne Reinner, 1989), 166–171; and Goscha, *Vietnam or Indochina?*

27. Vo Nguyen Giap, "Nhiem vu quan su truoc mat chuyen sang Tong phan cong" [The Military Mission in Transition to the General Counter Offensive] (Ha Dong Committee for Resistance and Administration, 1950), 14, in *Vietnamese Communist Publications*, Library of Congress, Orientalia/South Asia 5 microfilm collection, ed. P.T. Chau, item 40.

2

Between Two Wars

The Geneva Agreements gave combatants three hundred days to assemble in "regrouping zones" and civilians the same amount of time to choose on which side of the seventeenth parallel they wished to live. As French forces regrouped in Northern ports, 928,152 Vietnamese civilians and 120,000 military and paramilitary personnel headed for the South.[1] Eighty-five percent of these regroupees from the North were Catholics, many of whom were humble peasants, led by their priests and egged on by leaflets supplied by the United States that said "Christ has gone to the South" and the "Virgin Mary has departed from the North."[2] More Catholics might have left had DRV authorities not obstructed them.[3] Other evacuees were businessmen and former employees of the colonial administration who could expect to lose wealth and status under Communist rule. Some of the peasants would be settled in hamlets on the outskirts of Saigon to strengthen the capital's security. Ex-colonial civil servants found employment in the Saigon government, buttressing the anti-Communist zeal of the Southern administration. Meanwhile, an estimated 87,000 People's Army troops and 43,000 civilians moved from the South to the North, leaving behind a much larger number of ex-Viet Minh and their families to fend for themselves.[4]

Among those who went north was Do Van Buu.[5] A twenty-year-old platoon commander in 1954, Buu had joined the Viet Minh at age fifteen. On October 26, 1954, Buu's unit and other elements of the People's Army 108th Regiment boarded a Polish ship at Qui Nhon for regrouping in the North. Buu regrouped because his superiors had told him to do so. Besides, he recalled, he had been told that he would be given an opportunity to continue his education and perhaps to meet Ho Chi Minh. Buu expected to return home in two years when elections reunified the country. On this last point, Buu had the personal word of Nguyen Chanh, the popular zone political commissar, who addressed Buu's unit just before it boarded ship: "Comrades," Chanh said, "do not worry! If we do not return by peaceful means we will return by blood, but I assure you we will return to the South!"

Chanh's promise was kept . . . by blood. When Buu returned to the South in 1962, the peace that followed Geneva was long over, if it could be said to have existed at all.

THE RESURRECTION OF NGO DINH DIEM

In 1954 the Communists had reason to be confident, not so much because of the promised elections as because of conditions in the South. What passed for a government was a shambles. The "generals" had only recently elevated themselves from the noncommissioned ranks of French auxiliary forces to command an incompetent army. Regional commanders ignored instructions from the center, while in Saigon a rabble of personal cliques thwarted consensus or decision. The chief-of-staff, General Nguyen Van Hinh, openly vied for power with French encouragement. The bureaucracy, a colonial relic steeped in corruption and lethargy, administered little outside the province and district capitals. Officials who gathered around Bao Dai, the epicurean ex-emperor chosen by France to head the "State of Vietnam" that now ruled the South, had enjoyed lives of comfort and privilege while the Communists had fought to end colonial rule. Wealthy, educated individuals who might have looked for salvation in an anti-Communist regime showed more concern for their property in France. Few people of talent saw much point in making a personal sacrifice for what seemed a lost cause.

Onto the bridge of this sinking ship stepped Ngo Dinh Diem. Born in Hue in 1901 to a Catholic family noted for its Confucian sense of duty to emperor and country, Diem's first ambition had been to be a priest, and he entered government service with a clerical sense of duty.[6] After his graduation at the top of his class in 1921 from the French School of Administration in Hanoi, Diem joined the imperial civil service that administered Annam under French supervision. At the tender age of twenty-eight, he was appointed province chief, and in 1933, Diem leapt over many of his seniors to become minister of the interior to Emperor Bao Dai. In the latter position he worked with uncommon industry and integrity. Frustrated by French obstructionism and court intrigue, however, he soon resigned. Diem then withdrew from public life to read, pray, and prune roses. He sat out World War II, one of the nationalist figures whom the Japanese "protected" from the French, who suspected him of pro-Japanese sympathies. Ho Chi Minh offered him a position in the DRV government in 1946, but Diem, who blamed the deaths of a brother and a nephew on the Viet Minh, refused. In 1950, after four more years of seclusion in Hue, Diem left Vietnam, he claimed, under a Viet Minh death sentence for refusing to cooperate with the Viet Minh and traveled widely before settling at Maryknoll Seminary in Lakewood, New Jersey.

Up to this point, Diem's reputation had rested largely on his service in and resignation from Bao Dai's administration. The resignation in particular had given him standing as a patriot in elite nationalist circles. His subsequent retreat and seclusion were gestures from Confucian tradition, not expressions of modern nationalist ideology. Political leadership to him meant rule by example, precept, and paternalism. His conservative Catholic upbringing reinforced, rather than replaced, the Confucian tendency to base authority on doctrine, morality, and hierarchy. The concepts of compromise, power sharing, and voluntary popular participation were alien to his worldview. One part of him envisioned a uniquely Vietnamese path to modernity that was neither liberal nor Communist, a blend of Confucian moral values and the Catholic reformist doctrines of personalism;[7] the other part was heir to a tradition, instilled by training and experience, that taught him to believe that legitimacy bloomed from his own virtue. Where the Viet Minh represented a rupture with the past in the form of revolutionary transformation, Diem offered an amalgam of continuity and change in the guise of Confucian-*cum*-Catholic modernism.

Whether Diem was the only suitable candidate to lead South Vietnam is a matter of dispute.[8] There were people with more recent experience in government who were as well or better known to Vietnamese.[9] Diem did however enjoy one thing other contenders lacked: the strong support of influential Americans. These included such prominent figures as Francis Cardinal Spellman, Supreme Court Justice William O. Douglas, Senators Mike Mansfield and John F. Kennedy, and ultimately President Eisenhower and Secretary of State John Foster Dulles.

What convinced these Americans that the Catholic Diem should lead an Asian country where only 10 percent of the population was Catholic and the Church was widely seen as a handmaiden of colonialism?[10] Historians offer no single answer. One answer is that Diem's Christianity made him stand out in the eyes of ethnocentric Americans who stereotyped Buddhists as passive and impractical.[11] To the extent that Americans had any impressions of Vietnam, these tended to come from French sources, which reflected presumptions of Western superiority,[12] so a Christian might well have seemed the least unworthy of an inferior lot. Another answer argues that in meetings with Americans Diem concentrated not on his faith but on development and modernization, which resonated with the new American official interest in nation-building.[13] Whatever criteria shaped individual appraisals of

Diem, the unifying element was Americans' paramount concern in the early
1950s with the conjuncture of colonialism's collapse and Communism's
rise. Idealistic Americans across the political spectrum were susceptible
to courting by Third World figures who were both anti-colonial and anti-
Communist, and Diem fit the bill. In partnership with such figures—with
Americans as senior partners—the United States could intervene abroad
to combat Communism without the burden, in American eyes, of association with colonialism. Equally important, Diem sold himself aggressively
through speeches, meetings, and letters, assisted by Wesley Fishel, a young
professor of political science from Michigan State University. No other
prominent Vietnamese nationalist worked so diligently to make himself
known in the United States, and association with well-placed Americans
impressed anti-Communist Vietnamese.

In June 1954, a month before the Geneva Conference wound up its work,
Bao Dai overcame his personal dislike of Diem to appoint him premier. It
was once widely believed that the United States engineered his appointment in a bid to drive out French influence, but no hard evidence has been
found to support this claim. The more plausible thesis is that Bao Dai took
his own counsel, which conceded that Diem was the man best able to secure American support and that he had the support of Vietnamese nationalists as well.[14] Whatever the machinations behind Diem's appointment, the
Americans were not united on how to handle him. His American official
backers at the time were few, and the U.S. mission in Saigon was divided
over whether Diem would make a suitable premier. General J. Lawton
Collins, appointed U.S. ambassador to Saigon in December 1954, frankly
doubted Diem could unite the country behind him, decried the lack of
interdenominational participation in Diem's cabinet, and agreed with the
French High Commissioner Paul Ely that Diem should be jettisoned at the
earliest possible moment.[15] Dulles overruled his ambassador, though still
uncertain that Diem would be able to hold on to power.

At the time he became premier, Diem lacked a political base inside
South Vietnam apart from the elite nationalists organized by his brother,
Ngo Dinh Nhu. Other organizations were rivals if not outright enemies.
For popular support he could count on fellow Catholics around his native
Hue, but it is doubtful that his name and nationalist reputation were widely
known in 1954 among the poor peasants who made up the vast majority
of population in the countryside. The most famous anti-colonialist in the
South as in the North was Ho Chi Minh, and Ho had stature Diem could
never match.[16] Diem needed allies, but American official support was un-
steady. One American official who did commit himself to Diem early was
Colonel (later Major General) Edward G. Lansdale, a former advertising executive and air force officer turned secret agent who had helped Philippine
President Ramon Magsaysay suppress the Huk rebellion of 1945–1948.

Immortalized in *The Pentagon Papers* as the mastermind of a plot to bring Hanoi to a standstill by sugaring its petrol supply, Lansdale was a counter-insurgency expert and skilled intelligence operative. It was Lansdale who headed off one coup against Diem by offering the plotters free trips to Manila; it was Lansdale who arranged to recruit, train, and pay a battalion of palace guards; and it was Lansdale who raised the money to bribe some of Diem's opponents.[17] Lansdale's timely interventions probably helped to stave off Diem's early fall, as did the general impression that Washington stood ready to meddle on Diem's behalf. Even with this help, though, it was a surprise to almost everyone when Diem faced down a challenge from top army officers and then turned on his remaining enemies, chief among them were the politico-religious movements, commonly referred to as "sects."

Large parts of the countryside had remained under the control of these groups since the war. The largest, with an estimated 1.6 million adherents, was the Cao Dai. Founded in 1926 and organized in crude emulation of the Catholic Church, the Cao Dai professed a syncretic religion and controlled the territory west of Saigon with an army of 25,000 men. The Hoa Hao, a Buddhist revitalization movement[18] in existence only since 1939 but with roots in an earlier peasant millenarianism, held sway with an armed force of 15,000 men and perhaps 1.5 million followers in several provinces of the Mekong delta.[19] The French had supplied both groups money and weapons as a counterweight to the Viet Minh and continued to supply them after the war's end. The murky parts of Saigon's economy and administration meanwhile had slid into the hands of a mafia-like gang called the Binh Xuyen. The Binh Xuyen ran gambling, prostitution, opium dens, protection rackets, and the police force under political cover bought by subsidizing Bao Dai's lavish lifestyle. These groups controlled sizeable fiefdoms that their leaders were loathe to relinquish to the new government.

The ability of these groups to operate outside the government's control was evidence of Diem's weakness, not of their strength. What saved Diem were splits among leaders of the groups, the termination of subsidies paid to the Hoa Hao and Cao Dai by the French, and timely U.S. support. With some $8.6 million secretly supplied by the CIA,[20] Diem bought off key Hoa Hao and Cao Dai commanders and absorbed some of their troops into his own army. Then, in March 1955, Diem ordered the closing of the Binh Xuyen's gambling halls, brothels, and opium dens. Deprived of income, the Binh Xuyen precipitated a showdown in the streets of Saigon. Diem's shaky army held, and the Binh Xuyen were defeated. With this collapse of threats to Diem's grip on power, Dulles decided in late April to give him full American backing.

Diem moved quickly to consolidate these victories by organizing a referendum in October 1955 on the question of whether to continue the constitutional monarchy under Bao Dai or to establish a republic under him. Scattered violence and arrests before election day suggested a people divided, but only 1.1 percent of the ballots favored Bao Dai. All the rest went for Diem. A year later, after another rigged election to satisfy U.S. demands for a nod toward democracy, a constituent assembly promulgated a constitution for the Republic of Vietnam (RVN) and installed Diem as president and chief-of-state. (See Map 2.1.)

THE U.S. COMMITMENT

The U.S. aim in supporting Diem was to shore up an anti-Communist regime. The retreat of colonial power had left a vacuum that local Communists, backed by the Soviet Union and, after 1949, China seemed all too likely to fill if the United States did not fill it first. Following closely the conquest and occupation of Japan, this situation presented the U.S. an opportunity disguised as need to act out its "manifest destiny" to emancipate and protect the free peoples of Asia and to tutor them in American models of politics and development. In other words, to engage in "nation-building" as the United States had done, it seemed successfully, in the Philippines. These perceptions led U.S. policymakers to reformulate the strategy of "containment" as resistance to the spread of Communist influence in places the U.S. previously had been content to ignore. In effect, the U.S. sought to preempt Communist expansion by filling the vacuum with states that followed the American path to modernity.[21]

At the time, this strategy did not seem excessively ambitious, as the U.S. military presence in Asia was so superior that successful challenges to its supremacy were difficult to imagine. The commitment it implied also seemed justified by the Chinese Revolution and the Korean War, which had aroused fears that the United States would stand alone if it did not demonstrate firm support for its allies. Meanwhile, at home, U.S. leaders had boxed themselves into virulent anti-Communist postures with the McCarthyite Red scare and their own rhetoric. Such perceptions and pressures cut across party lines, assuring that Democrats and Republicans alike had supported the supply of $3.5 billion in economic and military assistance to the French war in Indochina from 1950 to 1954. No U.S. leader by that war's end or for years to come could have written off the already sizeable U.S. investment in "saving" Vietnam without inviting the charge of being "soft on Communism."

The Eisenhower administration wasted no time in turning South Vietnam into an anti-Communist bastion under American tutelage. To circumvent Geneva's prohibition of military alliances, the Southeast Asia Treaty Organization (SEATO), in September 1954, unilaterally bestowed on Vietnam, Laos, and Cambodia the right to request protection from SEATO in the event

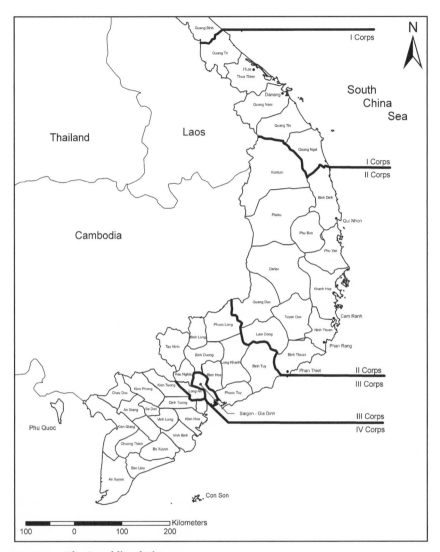

N

I Corps

South
China
Sea

Thailand

Laos

I Corps
II Corps

Cambodia

Quang Binh
Quang Tri
Hue
Thua Thien
Danang
Quang Nam
Quang Tin
Quang Ngai
Kontum
Binh Dinh
Pleiku
Qui Nhon
Phu Bon
Phu Yen
Darlac
Khanh Hoa
Quang Duc
Cam Ranh
Tuyen Duc
Ninh Thuan
Phuoc Long
Lam Dong
Phan Rang
Binh Long
Tay Ninh
Binh Duong
Binh Thuan
Long Khanh
Binh Tuy
Phan Thiet
Hau Nghia
Bien Hoa
Kien Tuong
Long An
Phuoc Tuy
Chau Doc
Kien Phong
Dinh Tuong
An Giang
Sa Dec
Kien Hoa
Vinh Long
Saigon - Gia Dinh
Phu Quoc
Kien Giang
Chuong Thien
Vinh Binh
Ba Xuyen
Bac Lieu
An Xuyen
Con Son

II Corps
III Corps

III Corps
IV Corps

Kilometers
100   0   100   200

Map 2.1.   The Republic of Vietnam

of attack. In October the United States commenced direct military assistance to the Saigon regime. The U.S. army training cycle and field manuals became the standards for Saigon's army. Because the Geneva Agreements had set strict limits on the number of foreign military personnel permitted in either half of Vietnam, the United States augmented its military assistance mission with personnel on "temporary duty" and "loan" that were not clearly proscribed by the Geneva Agreements. A Temporary Equipment Recovery Mission (TERM), ostensibly sent to dispose of surplus material (previously supplied to the French Union forces) with the approval of the International Control Commission, had as its "real assignment to aid in developing an adequate and effective South Vietnamese logistical system."[22] All major South Vietnamese forces had TERM personnel assigned to them for the purpose of developing military training courses, selecting officers for advanced training in the United States, and reorganizing the units along U.S. military lines. By 1956 the U.S. Military Advisory Assistance Group (MAAG), the U.S. military aid mission, plus TERM personnel exceeded the limit placed on foreign military advisers at Geneva by three hundred and fifty.

Parallel to its slow increase of military assistance to Saigon, the United States inserted itself into Laos as well. In 1955 it set up an economic aid office whose "primary focus . . . was defense related."[23] The United States upgraded this activity without appearing to violate the Geneva Agreements by creating a Programs Evaluation Office (not a MAAG) in the embassy staffed by ex-military personnel posing as State Department Foreign Service Officers. These officers worked through the French, who had authorization to maintain a military training mission in Laos. In July 1959, at American suggestion and with French assent, Laos "requested" increased military assistance from the United States. With an increased presence of technicians and Special Forces training teams, the Americans gradually muscled the French aside.[24]

The United States also provided growing amounts of economic, technical, and administrative aid. By 1956 South Vietnam was receiving $270 million per year, which made it the recipient of more U.S. aid per capita than any other country in the world except Korea and sparsely populated Laos. American officials in Washington, however, were too preoccupied with the strategic threat of Communism to care much about how America's client used this aid. Far from strengthening U.S. influence over Diem, the aid encouraged Diem to rule as he saw fit.

Diem gave in easily to his authoritarian and nepotistic instincts. Although his regime needed desperately to broaden its base, he relied for his main support on fellow Catholics, particularly recent arrivals from the North. One brother, Ngo Dinh Can, headed the regime's secretive cadre party; another brother, Ngo Dinh Nhu, served as the president's closest adviser; and still another, Ngo Dinh Thuc, was the archbishop of Vinh Long. Nhu's wife virtually dictated legislation to the National Assembly. An Anti-Communist Denunciation Campaign launched in 1955 to "reeducate" former Viet Minh was a pretext for suppressing dissent from all quarters. The number of politically motivated executions in the South during the 1950s may have exceeded the number in the North.[25] Meanwhile, with U.S. approval, Diem ignored DRV Premier Pham Van Dong's messages proposing consultations on reunification as stipulated at Geneva. By 1956, Diem's personal power was secure, and U.S. support was assured.

THE SOUTHERN REVOLUTION
IN COMMUNIST STRATEGY

The Communists meanwhile had been preoccupied with consolidating their own regime in the North. Though much better equipped than Diem to do this, they too had their problems. The French had gutted basic services and sabotaged or dismantled industries as they withdrew. Many professionals had fled, and party cadres found their guerrilla skills inappropriate for the administration of cities. Cut off from the Mekong delta's rice, the North turned to China for help covering its food shortage. In the hills ethnic minorities who had fought alongside the French held out against the government. Land reform and local administrative reorganization were completed in late 1956, but involved such excesses that the LDP Central Committee felt compelled to offer self-criticism and to unseat the party secretary-general, Truong Chinh.[26] Vo Nguyen Giap made the party's public apology to the people, capitalizing on his popularity as the victor of Dien Bien Phu to placate the victims. Ho Chi Minh, the party's elder statesman, briefly took over as party secretary-general in addition to his largely ceremonial posts of party chairman and president of the DRV. About the same time, Catholic residents of one district in Nghe An province staged a brief rebellion that required suppression by a People's Army division. A group of prominent writers and intellectuals, apparently inspired by de-Stalinization campaigns then under way in other Communist countries, subjected party policies to scathing ridicule in two briefly published journals. This last incident was not negligible, as the critics included individuals, some from the military, who had long supported the revolution.[27] Faced with hunger and turbulence in the North, party leaders must have felt their hands were full and that reunification would have to depend on the elections promised at Geneva.

That certainly was Hanoi's public position, and Hanoi seemed willing to hold the elections if Diem agreed. Behind the scenes, though, Hanoi leaders never placed any real faith in this path to reunification. The Communists were hardly principled proponents of free and fair elections, but that was not the reason for their skepticism. Diem, they calculated, would never agree to an election he expected to lose. By maintaining a public posture of support for the elections, the Communists sought to make Diem seem the obstacle to peace, "democracy," and "unity," isolating him internationally and domestically.[28] Such pressures on Diem's already frail government would make it impossible for him to restore stability and rule effectively. He would have to invite "progressives" into the government who would demand that he implement the Geneva accords. Or the sects might stage a coup and precipitate chaos in which the party and its sympathizers would be able to gain power. If one of these scenarios failed to bring about reunification, there were other options, and by early 1956, it was apparent to party leaders that the time had come to consider these.

The exact role of the Lao Dong Party (LDP) in what subsequently occurred was once a subject of sharp controversy. One theory, popular among critics of U.S. involvement, held that the revolution in the South began as a spontaneous uprising against a repressive regime and that the party only gradually gained predominance within it. The opposed theory, advanced in Washington and Saigon, was that the party masterminded everything from the beginning, and the upheaval was really "aggression from the North." Neither theory was satisfactory. The former properly noted the insurrectionary mood in the countryside but underestimated the LDP's role in giving it shape, coherence, an organizational structure, and leadership. The latter was blind to the well-founded grievances that propelled a revolution in the South and falsely depicted the LDP as a Northern regional organization with a Northern leadership. Today, thanks to massive evidence that includes documents captured in the South, archives opened in Hanoi and Ho Chi Minh City, and scholars' interviews with participants,[29] there are few mysteries about the origins of the Southern revolution or the LDP's role in it.

Somewhat less clear is the role played by the party's Southern membership in making the party's key decisions. Some members who remained in the South after 1954 are known to have opposed the concessions made at Geneva. Those concessions required the Southern branch of the party to bear all the risks of their implementation, while the North advanced peacefully to socialism. When Diem succeeded in eliminating his rivals and opened a vigorous campaign to exterminate Communists, a number of Southern members demanded that the party give higher priority to the "Southern revolution." At no time, however, did the Southern membership constitute a separate Communist party[30] or make policy independently of the Central Committee and Political Bureau in Hanoi.

In 1954 the party organization in the South numbered between 50,000 and 60,000 members, half of them in the Mekong delta. Many took advantage of the provisions of the Geneva Agreements to register with the government and take up a legal existence, while others continued to operate covertly. Natural attrition, a party program to weed out substandard members, and, increasingly, the depredations of Diem's police sharply reduced Southern membership. By 1956 party membership in the South was about 15,000.[31] With numbers falling, morale worsening, and prospects for reunification dimming, the party had very limited ability to shape events in the South. Outside a few old Viet Minh base areas, it was a bystander to the gathering resentments against Diem's rule. Some Southern cadres began to demand a new policy that would permit greater use of armed force. In March 1956 the Nam Bo regional committee (which was responsible for coordinating party activities in the provinces of former Cochinchina) recommended resuscitating Southern armed forces to a level of twenty regular battalions plus provincial and guerrilla units to "support other activities," that is, to provide a shield behind which cadres could continue their work.[32]

The head of the regional committee at the time was Le Duan, a member of the party Political Bureau and longtime specialist in Southern affairs. Born in 1908 in Quang Tri province of southern central Vietnam, Duan had spent much of the 1930s in prison, along with other future party leaders, first in Hanoi and then on the island of Poulo Condore (Con Son). By 1939, he was a member of the Central Committee and may have been implicated, while serving on the Saigon party committee, in the abortive Nam Ky uprising of November 1940 that resulted in the decimation of the hitherto strong southern branch. Returned to prison, he escaped or was released in 1945, resumed activity in the South, and was appointed head of the Central Committee Directorate for the South when this organ was created out of the Nam Bo regional committee in 1951. Although the directorate reverted to regional committee status at the end of the war with France, Duan remained in charge and built a reputation as the "flame of the South" for his ardent advocacy of reunification. In 1957 Ho Chi Minh picked Duan over Vo Nguyen Giap to succeed himself as acting general secretary of the party. Whatever the reasons for this selection,[33] it assured that reunification would rise higher in party priorities. So did the rise of Duan's fellow proponents of a violent path to revolution in the South, Le Duc Tho and Pham Hung. Both men had served as deputies to Duan in the South during the war with France.[34] In 1960 the Central Committee would convert the party's top post to "first secretary" and give it to Duan.

Most party leaders were reluctant in 1956 to alter course significantly, however. They did not wish to jeopardize development in the North, which was then just beginning to show results. Neither did they wish to provoke the United States as long as support from North Vietnam's allies was not assured. In fact those allies were opposed to any effort by Hanoi at that time to achieve reunification by violent means. China was absorbed in its own reconstruction and was not inclined, after the Korean War, to support another conflict on its borders. The Soviet Union opposed revolutionary offensives that might jeopardize its efforts to normalize relations with the West and draw it into confrontation with the United States.[35] The Soviets went so far as to delete Indochina from the agenda of the 1955 Geneva foreign ministers' meeting and advised Hanoi to seek consultations with Diem, even after Diem denounced proposals for a referendum on reunification.[36] In 1957 the Soviet Union was to propose the admission of both North and South Vietnam to the United Nations—a "two Vietnams" policy that directly contradicted Hanoi's wishes and provoked a protest from Hanoi. Russian historian Ilya Gaiduk suggests "that Moscow was even prepared to grant recognition to the Diem regime if the North Vietnamese would not vehemently oppose the idea."[37] According to Gareth Porter, the Communist powers' conscious pursuit of a policy of appeasement was based on recognition of the far greater strategic strength of the United States and "invited the United States to pursue a more aggressive policy in Vietnam."[38] The Vietnamese party stood alone in its advocacy of reunification by any measure outside the Geneva process at that time.

After heated debate, the party reached an awkward compromise. The Central Committee, meeting in April 1956, bowed to the Twentieth Congress of the Communist party of the Soviet Union (CPSU) in allowing that socialism might be achieved by peaceful means, but it made an important reservation: "Where the bourgeois class still possesses a strong military and police apparatus and resolutely uses weapons to suppress the revolutionary movement, a fierce armed struggle to win political power will be unavoidable, so the proletarian class must prepare in advance."[39] A peaceful transition might be possible in some countries, the Vietnamese Communists agreed, but not in all, and it was obvious which situation they felt existed in the South.

The party's Political Bureau, meeting in June, nevertheless made clear that for a time the emphasis was to be on nonviolent action. The task of explaining this decision to Southern cadres fell to Le Duan, Secretary of the Nam Bo region party committee. On returning to the South in August, Duan took up this task in a draft memorandum, which the region committee revised and adopted as "The Path of Revolution in the South."[40] Southern cadres, this document commanded, were to make no immediate attempt to overthrow the Diem regime or to stage armed uprisings. They were to concentrate instead on rebuilding their movement, because a weak movement would be unable to take advantage of favorable political trends. Internal trends were said to be favorable because of growing popular dissatisfaction with the Diem regime. External trends were favorable because of the growing power of the socialist bloc. However, the North needed more time to consolidate itself, the revolutionary movement in the South was still weak, and the Twentieth Congress of the Soviet Communist Party had recently concluded that revolutionary movements could develop peacefully and conflicts should be resolved through negotiations. "The Path of Revolution" therefore instructed cadres to content themselves with exploiting contradictions between Diem's suppressive policies and popular aspirations. They were to do this by strengthening the alliance of workers and peasants, establishing a national front, and agitating for "peace and reunification," "freedom and democracy," and "popular livelihood." The only permissible form of violence was "armed self-defense" when cadres' lives or the survival of party organs were at stake. It was a temporizing decision that papered over intractable differences concerning the priority and means of reunification.[41] One veteran Southern party leader later recalled that some of his colleagues were disappointed by the decision to defer armed offensive, but others perceived "Path" as authorization to "push back against oppression," even though it left higher levels of armed struggle for the future.[42]

For a while, the political struggle seemed to work, thanks as much to Diem as to the party. Propaganda against Saigon's opposition to reunification and dependence on the United States appealed to nationalist sentiment and gained head-nodding support. The party however had more success mobilizing popular support by helping people avoid conscription, police surveillance, controls on movement, fraudulent elections, bureaucratic interference in local affairs, arbitrary uses of police power, and corruption—all of which had increased as Diem had consolidated his power. In rural areas, where roughly one million peasants were tenants,[43] rents took 30 to 50 percent of tenants' crops and landlessness and absentee landlordism were common. The party attacked these inequities, claiming that government reforms did more to preserve them than correct them. One such reform, in 1955, had sought to limit rent by requiring written contracts, but contracts forced peasants to whom the Viet Minh had given land to acknowledge that the land they tilled still belonged to the landlords. Moreover, contracts required peasants to pay rent which, though low, some had not paid while landlords had sat out the war with France in Saigon. In these ways, the reform repealed the much better deal the Communists had given poor peasants earlier.[44] Another reform, in 1956, limited landholdings to 100 hectares (247 acres), a high amount that guaranteed little redistribution would ever take place.[45] The reform had virtually no impact in central provinces where few landholdings exceeded fifteen hectares (about 37 acres). In such a setting, people needed no convincing that the government would never implement a meaningful land reform and would instead continue to represent landlord interests, as the French had done.

Of course the land issue did not give the party equal leverage everywhere. But where landlessness, tenancy, and inequality were high or peasants tilled land the Communists had distributed before 1954, it provided them means of access to peasant communities. As Jeffrey Race wrote about Long

An province, "Land redistribution was an integral part of the Party takeover
. . . ," a means of wresting control from the government at the hamlet level.
Redistributing land to the poorest elements in the countryside upturned
rural power relationships and gave the beneficiaries little choice but to support the revolution. Land and the dignity that went with it, said a former
party member, were things peasants liked. "But if the Communists were to
go and the government to come back, the peasants would return to their
former status as slaves. Consequently they must fight to preserve their
interests and their lives, as well as their political power."[46] Critically, the
Communists' ability to offer the poorer peasants land, a voice in village
government, greater freedom of movement, and militia duties at home
rather than military service far away depended on Saigon's enforcement of
policies that denied peasants these things.

Yet, the Communists were only briefly able to turn this state of affairs to
their advantage. After a period of recovery in 1957 and 1958, the party's
Southern branch headed into what members were to recall as its "darkest
days." This was not the result of more enlightened government policies
but rather of enhanced coercive capabilities. With the sects suppressed and
U.S. assistance growing, Diem had more military, police, and administrative resources to turn against other threats. Gradually his regime penetrated
areas from which it long had been excluded and imposed its will by sheer
physical presence. Law 10/59, promulgated in May 1959 to punish virtually
any kind of involvement with the revolutionary movement, led to sweeping arrests and intimidated the population into avoiding contact with political dissidents of any kind. Cadres not only found it unsafe to carry out
their work or to recruit new supporters but also were themselves arrested
or killed. As a result, many cadres left the party. Some entire party organs
disappeared; most suffered serious losses. Go Vap and Tan Binh districts
just outside Saigon together had 1,000 party members in 1954, 385 in
1957, and only six in mid-1959. Total party membership in the South fell
to about 5,000.[47]

While undeniably effective in temporarily suppressing revolutionary activity, the repression—along with the corruption and authoritarianism of
local officials it exacerbated—"created an atmosphere of terror in the countryside."[48] Popular antagonism toward Diem's regime intensified, rising to
a point that would satisfy almost any definition of a revolutionary situation, with little encouragement or assistance from the party. Party members
generally maintained discipline, and those who did not were more likely
to defect than take up arms. With their numbers falling, members who
remained in the villages had limited ability to shape events. Surveying the
available accounts, Carlyle Thayer concluded that "the rise in highland
violence preceded the Party's ability to control, let alone direct, it."[49] The
situation was equally combustible in the Mekong delta. Nguyen Thi Dinh,

a longtime southern party militant, has written that in her native province of Ben Tre police repression and social inequity drove people and cadres alike to yearn for relief by violent means. In an interview with the author,[50] she claimed that the harsh repression of the Viet Minh and their families in 1958 and 1959 led to the execution of "thousands" and that the party had difficulty containing the popular demand for armed action. The pressure for a change of policy from the party's lower ranks intensified. "Most party members," according to a retrospective on Nam Bo, "wanted to be supplied with weapons."[51] In January 1958, the Nam Bo regional party leadership felt constrained to castigate lower echelons for arguing that the time had come "for the Southern revolution to use violence to defeat U.S.-Diem."[52] Cadres in the field were demanding a change of policy, both to capitalize on the discontent and to save themselves from extermination. David Elliott's meticulous study of this episode in Dinh Tuong province (My Tho in colonial days) concludes: "With the largely spontaneous move toward armed struggle gaining a momentum that threatened a crisis in relations between the impatient southern revolutionaries and the cautious leadership in North Vietnam, the Party finally confronted the issue in early 1959."[53]

The fifteenth plenum of the LDP Central Committee (expanded) met from January 12–22 primarily to discuss the situation in the South. There were two key issues: whether to authorize party organs in the South to inaugurate armed struggle and whether the North should step up its support to the South. On the first issue, the Political Bureau conceded that Southern party members faced a "very difficult and complicated situation" and would never topple Diem with political struggle alone.[54] The plenum resolution also acknowledged that "because the enemy is determined to drown the revolution in blood and fire, and due to the requirements of the revolutionary movement in the South, armed self-defense and propaganda forces have appeared in modest numbers and certain localities in order to support the political struggle. This is essential."[55] With the words "This is essential," the plenum acquiesced to what was already taking place. But it also affirmed that "self-defense and armed propaganda forces must stick to the principle of serving political struggle." Political struggle had to be the priority until preparations had been completed for a transition to armed struggle. Premature transition would risk defeat of the revolution in its infancy. There would be no immediate steps to guerrilla or people's war. Any steps in that direction would require approval from the party center. The deeper message, though, was clear: Southern party organs could now, under restrictive conditions, use arms to protect themselves and their organizational activities.

On the second issue, the plenum recalled that the party had set two strategic tasks: socialist construction in the North and the people's national democratic revolution in the South. Debate over which task should have priority had rippled through the party since 1956 but, the plenum noted, it was an "erroneous tendency" to see them as separate. The South needed the North's help to advance the people's national democratic revolution, while the North could not complete its socialist revolution before the country was reunified. The "DRV," the resolution affirmed, "is the outpost of socialism in Southeast Asia. American imperialism occupies the South and plots to invade the North in order to attack the socialist camp."[56] The North, in other words, would not be secure until the United States had been evicted from the South. The implication was clear: it was in the North's interest to increase its support of the revolution in the South, and time had come to do so.

The full significance of the resolution became obvious in the actions that flowed from it. Meeting in March, the party's Political Bureau issued a directive to establish a revolutionary base in the central highlands, where links could be established to other regions in the South and dissident ethnic minorities could be counted on for support. In this base area party organs were to build armed forces, first to support political struggle and then to advance to limited guerrilla warfare.[57] Around the same time, work began on finding routes and methods to "develop the role of the North in relations to the South."[58] This preceded the official commissioning, in May 1959, of Group 559, a special unit charged with moving people, weapons, and supplies overland from the North to the South. Group 759, for sea infiltration, appeared in July 1959, and Group 959, to supply the Laotian People's Liberation Army and "Vietnamese volunteers" fighting in Laos, came into being in September 1959.[59] These groups took shape slowly, numbering only a few hundred men each at first, and represented a clandestine, limited, even tentative increase in Northern support of the Southern revolution.

Top party leaders resisted an immediate fuller engagement of the North's resources, however much some of them and cadres in the South may have wanted this. The North was not ready to supply the needed support, and the dangers in provoking large-scale U.S. intervention were great. As the party secretariat pointed out, socialist transformation was still underway in the North, and "reactionary forces opposed to socialism" could be expected to collude with "foreign imperialism" in an attempt to reverse the course of revolution. Time was needed to consolidate the socialist system and seal the North against the schemes of "U.S.-Diemist spies, Catholic-exploiting reactionaries, and other reactionary forces."[60] Neither were party leaders prepared just yet to openly contradict Moscow's line on "struggle by peaceful means." Central leaders thus felt constrained in spring 1960 to warn Southern leaders to be "thoughtful and prudent," considering that the revolution's rapid advance might alarm the United States, its lackeys and even "capitalist neutrals" in Southeast Asia into perceiving the Southern revolution as an "offensive by the socialist camp in the region." The crux of the matter was "to correctly assess the balance of forces between us and the enemy on the world stage and in Southeast Asia in order to act in a correct and timely way. . . ."[61] Comrades pressing for a more—or for that matter less—aggressive approach needed to see things in broader context. The constant if waning hope of top leaders was still that the party could attain its objectives by inducing the Saigon government to crumble without having to mount a major military effort backed by the North.

THE ARMED STRUGGLE OPTION

The party in fact had never completely abandoned the armed struggle option. In 1954, the party had left behind in the South enough weapons to arm 6,000 troops and kept intact a few units ranging in size from fifty to two hundred men. These hard-core units, composed almost entirely of party members or members of the party's youth affiliate and well-equipped with a full range of light weapons, led a highly clandestine existence in the mountains of Quang Ngai, the U Minh forest, the Plain of Reeds, and swampy areas of the southeast.[62]

The party kept these forces in reserve, hoping no force of its own would be needed to crumble the regime. Armed action was left to the sects. If sect forces did not overthrow Diem, party leaders had calculated, sect-inspired turbulence would provide a screen for the activities of the party. Although some cadres maintained informal contact with the sects, the leadership apparently considered direct support or cooperation unworkable, even unthinkable.[63] At the beginning of the First Indochina War, the Viet Minh had tried to curb sectarian autonomy, and in 1947 the party had executed Hoa Hao leader Huynh Phu So, incurring the undying wrath of his followers. [64] Sect forces had then allied with the French to fight the Communists. From the party's standpoint the sects were in any case obscurantist, feudal, and unpatriotic. But over the years some sect leaders had developed contacts with the Communists, and when Diem's army attacked sect strongholds in spring 1955 some 2,000 Binh Xuyen and 500 Cao Dai troops scurried into former Viet Minh resistance bases for sanctuary.[65] The flight of sect forces into the arms of the party presented an opportunity for the party to continue harassing the government with minimal involvement by its own armed forces. According to an internal party survey of the period, "the Party planted a number of cadres among the dissident forces and activated armed units equipped with weapons we had hidden."[66]

In late April 1955 the Political Bureau approved a proposal to "win over" the remnants of sect troops and their officers.[67] "Former resistance cadres" began training sect units, and some of these units acquired party members as officers. In late 1956 the party organized a General Staff for these forces along united front lines, that is, combining sectarian and party officials. Operating independently but under loose party guidance, remnant sect units staged a number of violent incidents from December 1956 through mid-1958. However, because its general policy at the time "was to avoid fighting,"[68] the party refused to supply the sect forces from its own caches, to merge them with its own secret units, or to conduct joint operations. Sect forces consequently deteriorated rapidly in the face of repression. "The Resistance army of the religious sects," one semi-official account observed, "dwindled into a mere token force."[69] The party made one last attempt to salvage some sect remnants in late 1958 but concluded that these were too lacking in political reliability, discipline, and determination to serve the party's ends. As sect units disappeared, only a "small number" of sect troops, according to the party's official record, joined the revolutionary armed forces then being assembled in deep secrecy and on a small scale under the party's direct command.[70]

Since June 1956, the Political Bureau had emphasized that political struggle was to "create basic conditions for maintaining and developing armed forces."[71] In response to this policy, the Nam Bo regional party committee had begun organizing "armed propaganda forces" and had authorized the formation of the first battalion-sized unit under party command in the South, Unit 250, which appeared in an old resistance base known as War Zone D northwest of Saigon in October 1957. By that time the party commanded thirty-seven companies scattered widely throughout the Mekong delta, mostly in the west. In mid-1958 the Nam Bo party committee organized an Eastern Nam Bo Command to centralize control over that area's three companies of infantry and one of sappers (commandos with special training in demolitions) whose combined total was approximately three hundred and fifty men.[72]

The party used these forces sparingly. With few exceptions, forces commanded by the party only provided security for cadres engaged in political work, such as "armed propaganda" or "warning" and "punishing tyrants."[73] "Punishing tyrants" could include the "extermination of traitors," or the assassination of people considered hostile to the revolution or dangerous to the party, such as officials who were dedicated, capable, and popular.[74] The general policy was to "Intimidate low-level administrative personnel and spies so that they shrink from their duties" . . . and "conduct more propaganda activities than military activities." This policy "considerably limited the activities of the armed forces."[75] None of these activities met the party's definition of guerrilla war, armed uprising, or people's war.

As we have seen, party members in the South chafed against the restraints on armed action. A scattered few defended themselves with weapons. They also knew the situation was, as David Elliott has written, "explosive." The temptation for Southern party organs to begin armed struggle in anticipation that the center was about to authorize it was no doubt strong. But the practical obstacles to organizing, training, and equipping armed forces without approval or material support from higher authority must also have been great. Party members were few, in hiding, or on the run, and weapons had to be stolen or crude ones made. In early spring 1958 the fifth zone party committee authorized the Quang Ngai province committee to begin launching "uprisings" to throw Saigon's representatives out of hamlets and villages; but uprisings in district seats and the formation of standing armed units under provincial command required prior approval from the zone committee.[76] Local self-defense militia and guerillas began springing up in Quang Ngai in 1958, and standing units appeared in 1959, according to official history. Assembled in March 1959, a 45-man standing unit spearheaded a rash of attacks and demonstrations in Tra Bong district (the "Tra Bong uprising") in August.[77] It took only a "handful of cadres with rudimentary weapons" to spark "concerted uprisings" in "explosive" Dinh Tuong province in early 1960.[78] In Nguyen Thi Dinh's home province of Ben Tre, organized uprisings began on January 17, 1960. Elliott, in his massive study of Dinh Tuong province, concluded that revolutionary forces launched attacks *before* news of the fifteenth plenum reached the delta region, although the regional committee took note of it no later than November 1959.[79]

Cadres, whether they had waited for a new policy with forbearance or had organized armed units and launched attacks without clear authorization, were quick to test that policy's limits. After a kick-off attack on a trainee regiment of the Army of the Republic of Vietnam (ARVN) 5th Division just seven kilometers outside Tay Ninh city on January 26, 1960, the frequency of armed incidents increased rapidly. Typically, small paramilitary units chased out or assassinated local authorities, and party cadres set up new hamlet and village administrations with peasant participation. Whether by demonstrating villagers[80] or handfuls of armed men, government officials were put to flight with astonishing ease. Not only were they unwilling to accept risks that had been the lot of Communist cadres for years, RVN officials also found that they stood alone amidst a rural population, large portions of which regarded them, not the Communists, as the enemy. Sizeable areas quickly fell under the revolution's sway, although the party center in April 1960 judged the balance of forces, particularly on the military side of the equation, still to be decisively in Saigon's favor.[81]

FOUNDING THE FRONT

It was not credible in Vietnam or abroad, however, that such a movement could grow much further on the basis of unorganized mass yearnings alone. A formal organization, nominally independent but in fact under party leadership, was needed to rally popular support while disguising the party's role. Another step taken by the Central Committee fifteenth plenum in January 1959 therefore was to order the establishment of a broadly based national united front in the South.[82] In August the Nam Bo Region Party Committee issued instructions on the selection of delegates, organizational structure and the mobilization of participation in advance of this front's unveiling. [83] The Lao Dong Party's Third National Congress gave its formal approval to these measures in September 1960, noting that "to guarantee a victorious revolutionary struggle in the South under the proper Marxist-Leninist leadership of the worker-peasant classes, the Southern people must set up . . . a broad anti-U.S.-Diem National United Front, with the worker peasant alliance as the base. This front must unite . . . all people who are opposed to the U.S.-Diem."[84]

Here, in party decisions made in Hanoi, were the origins of the National Liberation Front of South Vietnam (NLF), which announced its existence at a Congress of People's Representatives held on December 20, 1960, in eastern Nam Bo (a "liberated area," in fact).[85] Though proclaimed to exist, the NLF did not hold its first formal congress until January 1, 1962. The delay reflected the time needed to create a network of mass associations and village liberation committees, to broaden participation beyond the party and core activists, and to recruit non-party figures of sufficient stature to hold key posts. In the end a suitable candidate for chairman was found in Nguyen Huu Tho, a dissident lawyer (who would later join the party).[86]

The party's Political Bureau reaffirmed the Front's mission in a directive dated January 31, 1961,[87] and laid down basic strategy for a long struggle. In this strategy the balance between political and military struggle would be different in the South's three strategic areas and could shift across time. In jungles and mountainous areas, the military struggle would have higher priority than in other areas; in the lowlands, approximately equal emphasis would be given to political and military struggle; while in urban areas, the principal emphasis would be on political struggle. Activities in the three areas could be coordinated to keep the enemy distracted and off balance. Thus, for example, main forces supported from the North could attack in the highlands to take pressure off political organs and guerrillas in the lowlands, and surges of activity in the lowlands and cities could compel the enemy to spread his forces thinly. Synchronization of struggle by forces-in-place in all three areas was a substitute for mobility. Conceivably, military struggle could become the dominant form in all three areas, but this was not necessary to achieve victory, as had been proved in the war against France. It was more important to develop capacity for coordinated armed and political struggle and on this basis to create conditions for general uprising across the entire country. This had little in common with Mao Zedong's famous dicta on protracted war and stages of war, as Le Duan pointed out: "the Southern revolution will not advance through protracted armed struggle, seizing the countryside to encircle the cities and then using military force to liberate the entire country as China did; rather, Vietnam will follow its own path of partial uprisings, setting up bases, developing guerrilla war, and then advancing to a general uprising, with emphasis on the coordination of political and armed force to win power for the people."[88]

This strategy would be executed in the name of the Front, but the controlling organization, the Front's backbone, was the party. "The party" was the LDP, which renamed its Southern branch the People's Revolutionary Party to divert attention from Hanoi's role.[89] In addition to holding key positions within the Front, party members were, in the words of the party's highest organ in the South, to "lead the front by means of internal education. Party leadership [of the Front] is justified by our party's correct line, the sacrifices and devotion of our party and its members, the open attitude of our cadres in strictly and thoroughly implementing the Front's program, and the correct treatment and helpful guidance we provide our friends in the Front. . . . For the present, public speech and propaganda on 'the party leads the Front' is neither necessary nor advantageous."[90] Parallel instructions from the party's General Military Committee established a "Liberation Army of South Vietnam" as "a part of the People's Army of Vietnam, created, constructed, trained and led by the party."[91] Organized into regular, regional and guerrilla elements and relabeled the People's Liberation Armed Force, the PLAF was subordinate to the PAVN high command in Hanoi.

The unveiling of the NLF in 1960, over a year before its first plenary session, may have been a strategic move by the party to keep pace with events. Certainly the party was under pressure from Southern-based members to step up preparations. Revolutionary armed forces that had numbered perhaps 2,000 in 1959 exceeded 10,000 by the beginning of 1961.[92] The Political Bureau directive cited above noted that there was now "practically no possibility that the revolution will develop peacefully." The party needed the NLF to conceal its role in organizing for the conflict it now regarded as inevitable. Armed struggle henceforward was to be "placed on a par" with political struggle where circumstances permitted.

This still was not a call for "people's war," but it did signal an acceleration of the preparations for one. Events in Laos, as well as in South Vietnam, were forcing the Communists' hand. In Laos, following a mandate of the 1954 Geneva conference, the Royal Lao Government and the LDP-backed Lao Communists (commonly referred to as the Pathet Lao) had reached agreement in November 1957 to form a neutral coalition government. Pathet Lao leaders Prince Souphanouvong and Phoumi Vongvichit had joined the cabinet of the neutralist Prince Souvanna Phouma,[93] Fifteen hundred Pathet Lao troops (one-quarter of their total) had been integrated into the Royal Lao Army, and Pathet Lao-supported candidates had won nine seats in partial elections for the National Assembly.

Up to this point Hanoi approved of these arrangements, which strengthened the DRV's influence and security on its western flank, but this situation deeply perturbed Lao rightists who turned to Thailand and the United States for help. The United States provided encouragement and funds to rightists in the Lao Army, who then ousted Souvanna Phouma in July 1958 and subsequently arrested Pathet Lao members of the government. With Lao neutrality at an end, the Pathet Lao resumed military action, and the country slid into civil war. By August 1959, Thailand, as sensitive as the DRV to instability in Laos, had sent in troops, with U.S. connivance, to help the rightists.[94] A U.S.-inspired coup in December further consolidated the rightists' hold on Vientiane, and the Royal Army attacked Pathet Lao strongholds. These developments, occurring just as the Vietnamese Communists were beginning preparations for armed struggle in the South, presented a serious challenge to Hanoi. The Vietnamese could not afford to permit a U.S.-backed regime in Vientiane to menace access to the Lao mountains through which the North's infiltration routes would pass.

An opportunity to address that challenge arose in August 1960 when paratroop Captain Kong Le, an American-trained officer who had grown thoroughly disgusted with fraudulent elections and the corrupting influence of American aid, seized Vientiane and insisted that the government return to a policy of neutrality. The Soviet Union, anxious to shore up the neutralists in the belief this would stabilize the situation under conditions favorable to the Pathet Lao,[95] began supplying fuel and military equipment to Kong Le while the CIA supplied the rightists under General Phoumi Nosavan in southern Laos. Amidst these maneuvers the Pathet Lao evicted the Royal Army from Sam Neua province in September and from Phong Saly province and the Plaine des Jarres (Plain of Jars) in January 1961. In fact, the Pathet Lao had some help. After war's end a Vietnamese publication openly admitted what had never been much of a secret, namely that "Vietnamese volunteer troops" fought "in coordination with" (actually, at the head or in place of) the Pathet Lao.[96] The effect was to consolidate Communist bases from which to promote revolution in both Laos and South Vietnam. As for Laos, General Phoumi regained control of Vientiane with American and Thai support, but Kong Le's men, transported in Soviet aircraft, linked up with the Pathet Lao to seize the Plain of Jars.[97] President Eisenhower was convinced of Laos's strategic importance but, preparing to leave office, left the festering confrontation for his successor to solve.

Meanwhile, in January 1961, the Nam Bo and Trung Bo party committees merged to form the Central Committee Directorate (or Office) for the Southern Region (*Trung uong cuc mien nam*). Commonly referred to in English as the Central Office for South Vietnam, or COSVN, this body was a forward element of the Central Committee like the one that had run the war in the south against France from 1951 to 1954. As the top ranked party organ in the South, COSVN saw to the implementation of Central Committee and Political Bureau directives and kept the center informed of developments in the South. It could, in "especially urgent circumstances," act with some degree of latitude but was otherwise a Southern field office for the Political Bureau and Central Committee.[98] Nguyen Van Linh, the first secretary of COSVN, was a secret member of the Political Bureau, as were members Vo Chi Cong and Vo Van Kiet.[99] With COSVN in place to represent the party center at a distance from the "rear" in Hanoi, military cadres met on February 15 in War Zone D to assemble all Southern armed units into a single People's Liberation Armed Force (PLAF). The party military committee for the Nam Bo region was designated the Liberation Army Command of South Vietnam.[100] Tran Luong, a COSVN member and full member of the LDP Central Committee, became the command's first head. More Central Committee members, including a clutch of People's Army (PAVN) generals with Southern experience, began arriving from the North in September. By the time the NLF opened its First Congress on February 16, 1962, COSVN exercised control through the Liberation Army Command over about 17,000 PLAF troops.

The party organization in the South recovered remarkably quickly from the "dark days" of 1959. It did this, in large measure, simply by authorizing Southern cadres to protect themselves with armed force and to spearhead "local uprisings" where Saigon authorities were vulnerable. A modest but critical increment in support from the North also helped, as we will see. These steps would not have produced the results they did had it not been for the growing popular resentment of Diem's personal dictatorship in the cities and the social and economic inequities that his regime sustained in the countryside. Diem and his elite landowning and bureaucratic supporters supplied the "contradictions" for the party to exploit, helping the party to attract nonparty supporters, a few of whom appeared in the NLF leadership.

The NLF and the PLAF did not spring like wildflowers from the padi fields, however. And "former resistance cadres" and non-Communists did not come together to found the NLF on their own initiative. Decisions on how to transform a revolt into a revolution, how to organize, arm, and equip it, were made by the LDP Political Bureau and Central Committee. Prior to those decisions and without the support that flowed from them organized and continuous armed struggle was not possible. The NLF was just what its name declared—a front, a coalition of individuals and groups seeking a common goal, but one assembled and controlled by the LDP in perfect conformity with Leninist principles. The NLF and the PLAF were formed and chose leaders in accordance with party directives. Inevitably, disagreements and tensions would crop up between the party center and its delegates in the

South, between leaders focused on development in the North and those who demanded reunification at any price. Haunted by Geneva, Southern cadres in particular tended to fear that if the war became too fierce Hanoi might abandon their cause to protect the North. Nor is it surprising that cadres in the field and central leaders in Hanoi interpreted events differently as the war progressed. Frictions, disappointments, and tussles over strategy were inevitable. Party leaders assigned to COSVN and the NLF could, and did, sometimes disagree with the party center in Hanoi. But party discipline and procedures required members to settle disputes and make decisions through party channels, assuring that the NLF would do the center's bidding throughout the war.[101] As for non-Communists in the Front, what little influence they derived from their usefulness to the party waned as the war grew in scale and victory depended ever more heavily on support from the North.

Ironically, the move to armed struggle reflected party leaders' abiding hope that reunification could be attained by some means short of war. That hope sprang not from anticipation that Diem would accept negotiations and elections, but that a rising tide of popular antipathy to Diem would create new political facts. "Political struggle" would destabilize the regime and lead to a coalition government, an invitation to the United States to leave, and transition to reunification under party rule. The NLF's role in this struggle was to rally the disaffected and campaign across the world for "neutrality," isolating Diem from the many people who wanted no part of American designs for the nation's development and world order.[102]

It was a strategy that sought to reconcile conflicting requirements. On the one hand, Hanoi needed to maintain good relations with a great power ally bent on "peaceful coexistence" and therefore to avoid provoking the United States. On the other hand, the party had to save its Southern branch from extinction if it were to make progress toward reunification under party rule. The risk-minimizing path between these conflicting demands was to increase the North's involvement in gradual, deniable ways while encouraging Southern self-reliance. The party would "prepare" for armed struggle but rely so far as possible on Southern resources to achieve its objectives. A situation similar to what the party envisioned did begin to unfold in 1963, but for reasons party leaders did not foresee.

NOTES

1. Bui Van Luong, "The Role of Friendly Nations," in *Vietnam: The First Five Years, an International Symposium*, ed. Richard A. Lindholm (East Lansing: Michigan State University Press, 1959), 49. The figures from this source are totals for the entire regroupment process and include individuals who found means outside the organized evacuation by sea and air to make their way from North to South. They should be considered approximate despite their precision.

2. Bernard Fall, *The Two Viet-Nams: A Political and Military Analysis* (New York: Praeger, 1967), 153–154. For detailed discussion of the regroupment process by a member of the International Commission charged with overseeing implementation of the Geneva Agreement, see B.S.N. Murti, *Vietnam Divided: The Unfinished Struggle* (New York: Asia Publishing House, 1964).

3. The entire PAVN 305th Division was dispatched to Thanh Hoa province to "persuade" Catholics there to stay, according to a defector who served in the 305th at the time. Some of the confrontations with those seeking to leave were violent. Interview with Dang Anh Kieu, chief of staff, Second Signal Battalion, Second PLAF Division. Douglas Pike Collection, no. 49/70, 11–22, University of California-Berkeley.

4. Murti, *Vietnam Divided*, 224.

5. Do Van Buu is a pseudonym. Interview by the author in Saigon, 1973, on deposit in *Interviews with PAVN and LDP Defectors*, Morris Library, Southern Illinois University Carbondale, 1974.

6. See Denis Warner, *The Last Confucian* (New York: Macmillan, 1963), 84–406; Frances Fitzgerald, *Fire in the Lake* (Boston: Atlantic Monthly Publications, 1972), 80–84, 98–99; and on Diem's wartime role, see Huynh Kim Khanh, *Vietnamese Communism 1925–1945* (Ithaca, N.Y.: Cornell University Press, 1982), 245, 295, 295n9.

7. For analysis of Diem's brand of personalism, see Edward Garvey Miller, "Grand Designs: Vision, power and nation building in America's alliance with Ngo Dinh Diem, 1954–1960" (PhD diss., Harvard University, 2004), 212–227, which aptly describes Diem's political views as "conservative modernism" while conceding that his brand of personalism was "abstract," "dense," and not a coherent guide to action. The leading ideologue of the regime was in any case not Diem but his brother Nhu.

8. For grudging assent by an ex-American diplomat that Diem was the best available candidate, see Paul M. Kattenburg, *The Vietnam Trauma in American Foreign Policy, 1945–75* (New Brunswick, N.J.: Transaction, 1980), 51–52.

9. For a work that questions whether Diem even enjoyed much support among his fellow Vietnamese Catholics see Seth Jacobs, *America's Miracle Man in Vietnam* (Durham, N.C.: Duke University Press, 2004), 4, 12, 57, 59.

10. In the South more than in the North, religious diversity and syncretism were the norm. Buddhism was a pervasive religious identity, but people incorporated elements from other creeds into family rituals and personal beliefs.

11. Jacobs, *America's Miracle Man*, 12.

12. Mark Philip Bradley, *Imagining Vietnam and America: The Making of Postcolonial Vietnam, 1919–1950* (Chapel Hill: University of North Carolina Press, 2000), 45–72, traces the formation of these images before World War II.

13. Miller, "Grand Designs," 69–71.

14. With variation, this is a point on which there is agreement between David Anderson, *Trapped By Success: The Eisenhower Administration and Vietnam, 1953–61* (New York: Columbia University Press, 1991), 52–55; Miller, "Grand Designs," 89–91; and Jacobs, *America's Miracle Man*, 9–11.

15. George C. Herring, *America's Longest War: The United States and Vietnam, 1950–1975* (New York: John Wiley, 1979), 52–53.

16. In Vietnamese, the first name is the family name and the last is the given name, and it is customary to refer only to individuals of exceptional moral or historical importance by their family names. Ho was the only Vietnamese of his time to be widely known by his (pseudonymous) first name. Diem's supporters tried to encourage the use of "President Ngo," but the usage never caught on because Diem lacked the qualities needed to justify it.

17. In his memoir, Lansdale details his maneuvers but denies bribing anyone. Edward Geary Lansdale, *In the Midst of Wars: An American's Mission to Southeast Asia* (New York: Harper & Row, 1972).

18. Hoa Hao adepts rejected the label "reformist" often attached to them, citing the emphasis placed by their founder Huynh Phu So on accommodating orthodox doctrines to their contemporary setting. Nguyen Long Thanh Nam, *Hoa Hao Buddhism in the Course of Vietnam's History*, trans. Sergei Blagov (New York: Nova Science Publishers, 2003), 44–46.

19. Total Cao Dai and Hoa Hao population figures are from Allen E. Goodman, "Government and the Countryside: Political Accommodation and South Vietnam's Communal Groups," RAND Corporation, study P-3924 (September 1968), 11.

20. Bernard Fall, *The Two Viet-Nams* (Boulder, Colo.: Westview Press, 1985), 245–246. In a communication to Fall (p. 246n*), Lansdale claimed money given to sect leaders was for the "back pay" of sect troops.

21. On the balance of Cold War pressures and racialized cultural hierarchies in the American vision of postcolonial Vietnam, see Bradley, *Imagining Vietnam and America*, 172–176. On the role of modernization theory in providing justification and policies for the projection of American power, see Michael E. Latham, *Modernization as Ideology: American Social Science and 'Nation Building' in the Kennedy era* (Chapel Hill: University of North Carolina Press, 2000).

22. James Lawton Collins Jr., *The Development and Training of the South Vietnamese Army, 1950–1957* (Washington, D.C.: Department of the Army, 1975), 4, 7.

23. Timothy N. Castle, *At War in the Shadow of Vietnam: U.S. Military Aid to the Royal Lao Government, 1955–1975* (New York: Columbia University Press, 1993), 15.

24. Castle, *At War*, 18.

25. Alexander Kendrick, in *The Wound Within* (Boston: Little, Brown, 1974), 112, cites a figure of seventy-five thousand for the South. Regarding the North, see note 22. Figures for both North and South are estimates and impossible to verify, however.

26. The errors of excess mentioned in party sources were the result of doctrinaire application of class criteria. Although somewhere between three thousand and fifteen thousand people were executed, some on trumped up charges, the slaughter of five hundred thousand described in anti-Communist propaganda never took place. See Edwin E. Moise, "Land Reform and Land Reform Errors in North Vietnam," *Pacific Affairs* 49 (Spring 1976): 78. Bui Tin, *Following Ho Chi Minh: The Memoirs of a North Vietnamese Colonel* (Honolulu: University of Hawaii Press, 1995), 27, claims the reform "caused the deaths of more than ten thousand people."

27. This incident came to be known as the "Nhan Van–Giai Pham Affair," so named after the titles of the dissident publications. See Georges Boudarel, "Intellectual Dissidence in the 1950s: The Nhan Van–Giai Pham Affair," *Viet Nam Forum* 13 (1991): 154–174.

28. Not incidentally, it was hoped this posture also would placate Southern cadres, who might otherwise have felt abandoned by the party center.

29. The authoritative secondary works are Jeffrey Race, *War Comes to Long An* (Berkeley: University of California Press, 1972); William Duiker, *Communist Road to Power in Vietnam* (Boulder, Colo.: Westview, 1981); Carlyle A. Thayer, *War by Other Means: National Liberation and Revolution in Vietnam, 1954–1960* (Sydney and Boston: Allen & Unwin, 1989); Robert K. Brigham, *Guerrilla Diplomacy: The NLF's Foreign Relations and the Viet Nam War* (Ithaca, N.Y.: Cornell University Press, 1998); and David W.P. Elliott, *The Vietnamese War: Revolution and Social Change in the Mekong Delta 1930–1975*, 2 vols. (Armonk, N.Y.: M.E. Sharpe, 2003).

30. A People's Revolutionary Party (PRP), launched in December 1961, was simply the Lao Dong Party's Southern branch. The name was changed to give the impression that a separate party existed. The PRP was ceremonially integrated into its parent when the LDP adopted the name Vietnam Communist Party (VCP) in 1976.

31. The figure is from an internal party document cited in Carlyle A. Thayer, "Southern Vietnamese Revolutionary Organizations and the Vietnam Workers' Party: Continuity and Change, 1954–1974," *Communism in Indochina: New Perspectives*, ed. J. J. Zasloff and M. Brown (Lexington, Mass.: Heath, 1975), 34. For detailed discussion of the party's fortunes in this period, see Thayer, 33–46; and Race, *War Comes to Long An*, 27–43, 80–104.

32. Department of State, "Working Paper on the North Vietnamese Role in South Vietnam: Captured Documents and Interrogation Reports" (Washington, D.C.: Department of State, May 1968), item 19.

33. See Bui Tin, *Following Ho*, 32; and William J. Duiker, *Ho Chi Minh* (New York: Hyperion, 2000), 499, 503.

34. Tho, a native of the North's Nam Ha province, was deputy to Duan in the Central Committee Directorate for the South during the war against France; Hung, from the South's Vinh Long province, returned to the South in 1955 as PAVN delegate to the International Control Commission set up by the Geneva Agreements.

35. Gareth Porter, "Vietnam and the Socialist Camp: Center or Periphery?" in *Vietnamese Communism in Comparative Perspective*, ed. William S. Turley (Boulder, Colo.: Westview Press, 1980), 225–264.

36. Ilya V. Gaiduk, *Confronting Vietnam: Soviet Policy Toward the Indochina Conflict, 1954–1963* (Stanford, Calif.: Stanford University/Woodrow Wilson Center Press, 2003), 74–75.

37. Gaiduk, *Confronting Vietnam*, 86.

38. Gareth Porter, *Perils of Dominance: Imbalance of Power and the Road to War in Vietnam* (Berkeley: University of California Press, 2005), 32 and 42–44.

39. Plenum resolution quoted in War Experiences Recapitulation Committee of the High-Level Military Institute, *The Anti-U.S. Resistance War for National Salvation 1954–1975: Military Events*, trans. Joint Publications Research Service, JPRS no. 80,968 (Washington, D.C.: Government Printing Office, June 3, 1982), 16.

40. The outline, "De cuong duong loi cach mang mien nam," is in Le Duan, *Le Duan: tuyen tap* [Le Duan: collected works] (Hanoi: NXB Su that, 1987), 75–122. For the revised document as adopted by the Nam Bo regional party committee, see "Duong loi cach mang mien nam," Dang Cong San Viet Nam, *Van kien Dang toan*

tap [Complete Party Documents (hereafter cited as VKDTP)], vol. 17, 1956 (Hanoi: NXB Ban chinh tri quoc gia, 2001), 783–825. The typewritten version in the Jeffrey Race Collection of Vietnamese documents, document no. 1002, Center for Research Libraries, Chicago, is, with minor differences, a copy of the region party committee document. Race analyzes "Duong lo . . ." in *War Comes to Long An*, 75–81.

41. The search for consensus was apparent in differences between drafts. For example, the region party committee's revisions softened some of Le Duan's incendiary language, replacing the South's "revolutionary struggle" with "revolutionary movement" and downplaying the North's need to support it.

42. Tran Bach Dang, "Vai ghi nho ve "De cuong duong loi cach mang mien Nam" [Reflections on "Draft of the Path of Revolution in the South"], *Thanh nien*, August 30, 2006 at www.thanhnien.com.vn/News/PrintView.aspx?!D=160620 (accessed March 15, 2007).

43. Of the roughly one million tenants in South Vietnam in 1955, 600,000 were in the southern region centered on the Mekong delta and 400,000 were in central provinces. An estimated 4 million families were landless, while 2,500 families controlled 40 percent of the country's rice land, most of which was in the southern region. *Land Reform in Vietnam: Working Papers*, vol. I, part 1 (Menlo Park, Calif.: Stanford Research Institute, 1968), 65, 77.

44. Vietnam's postwar government estimated that the Viet Minh distributed about half of the South's cultivated area to "working peasants" during the war against France. Lam Quang Huyen, *Cach mang ruong dat o mien Nam Viet Nam* [The Land Revolution in South Vietnam] (Hanoi: NXB Ban khoa hoc xa hoi, 1985), 73, 113.

45. Race, *War Comes to Long An*, 56–61.

46. Quoted in Race, *War Comes to Long An*, 126, 130.

47. Republic of Vietnam, Joint General Staff J-2 intelligence report, "Study of the Activation and Activities of R" (Saigon, July 17, 1969), 16. Also see Thayer, "Southern Vietnamese Revolutionary Organizations," 42–43; and "Bao cao cua lien khu uy V, Thang 11–1959" [Report of the Zone V Party Committee, November 1959], VKDTT, vol. 20, 1959 (2002), 1007–1031.

48. Elliott, *The Vietnamese War*, vol. 1, 198.

49. Thayer, *War by Other Means*, 147. Also see Pham Thanh Bien, Hong Son, and Do Quang Trinh, "Ve cuoc khoi nghia Tra-bong va mien Tay Quang-ngai mua thu 1959" [The Tra Bong and Western Quang Ngai Uprising in Autumn 1959], *Nghien cuu Lich su* [History Research] (September–October 1972): 19–20; also see Ta Xuan Linh, "Armed Uprisings by Ethnic Minorities along the Truong Son," *Vietnam Courier* (October 1974): 19.

50. Hanoi, March 1983.

51. "Situation of the Nambo Region since 1954 (U)," translation of a document captured by U.S. forces, April 28, 1969. COMUSMACV report 6-028-0130-70 (March 11, 1970), CDEC log no. 01-0533-70, 33. Douglas Pike Collection, Texas Tech Vietnam Virtual Archive, no. 2410604021.

52. "TVBE gui CEB" [Nam Bo Regional Party Standing Committee dispatch to Nam Bo region zone committees], VKDTT, vol. 19, 1958 (2002), 667–668.

53. David W.P. Elliott, *The Vietnamese War: Revolution and Social Change in the Mekong Delta 1930–1975*, vol. 1 (Armonk, N.Y.: M.E. Sharpe, 2003), 227.

54. "Bao cao cua Bo chinh tri tai Hoi nghi Ban chap hanh Trung uong lan thu 15 (mo rong)" [Report of the Political Bureau to the 15th Plenum of the Central Committee (expanded)], VKDTT, vol. 20, 1959 (2002), 1–56.

55. "Nghi quyet Hoi nghi Trung uong lan thu 15 (mo rong) [Resolution of the 15th Plenum of the Central Committee (expanded)], VKDTT, vol. 20, 1959 (2002), 84.

56. "Nghi quyet Hoi nghi Trung uong lan thu 15 (mo rong)," 65–66.

57. "Chi thi cua Bo chinh tri, Thang 3–1959: Ve nhiem vu xay dung can cu cach mang Tay Nguyen" [Directive of the Political Bureau, March 1959, on the task of building a revolutionary base in the Tay Nguyen highlands], VKDTT, vol. 20, 1959 (2002), 250.

58. Phan Huu Dai *et al.*, *Lich su Doan 559, Bo doi Truong Son–Duong Ho Chi Minh* [History of Group 559, Troops of the Trong Son–Ho Chi Minh Trail] (Hanoi: NXB Quan doi nhan dan, 1999), 20.

59. Phan Huu Dai *et al.*, *Lich su Doan 559*, 20.

60. "Chi thi cua ban bi thu, So 186-CT/TW, ngay 17, thang 2 nam 1960" [Directive of the Secretariat, no. 186-CT/TW, February 17, 1960], VKDTT, vol. 21, 1960 (2002), 107.

61. "Dien mat cua Trung uong Dang, So 160, ngay 28 thang 4 nam 1960, Gui xu uy Nam Bo [Cable from the Central Committee to the Nam Bo Region Committee, no. 160, April 28, 1960], VKDTT, vol. 21, 1960 (2002), 290.

62. Race, *War Comes to Long An*, 36.

63. Race, *War Comes to Long An*, 36. Also see Jayne Werner, "Vietnamese Communism and Religious Sectarianism," in *Vietnamese Communism*, ed. Turley, 122–128.

64. For a Hoa Hao leaders' reconstruction of these events, see Nguyen Long Thanh Nam, *Hoa Hao Buddhism*, 68–95.

65. Linh, "How Armed Struggle Began," 21; also see Werner, "Vietnamese Communism and Religious Sectarianism," 122–128.

66. "Situation of the Nambo Region since 1954 (U)," 27.

67. War Experiences Recapitulation Committee, *The Anti-U.S. Resistance War*, 11.

68. "Situation of the Nambo Region since 1954 (U)," 27.

69. Linh, "How Armed Struggle Began," 21.

70. War Experiences Recapitulation Committee, *The Anti-U.S. Resistance War*, 12.

71. Political Bureau resolution quoted in War Experiences Recapitulation Committee, *The Anti-U.S. Resistance War*, 16.

72. Political Bureau resolution quoted in War Experiences Recapitulation Committee, *The Anti-U.S. Resistance War*, 22, 24.

73. "Situation of the Nambo Region since 1954 (U)," 27.

74. The "extermination of traitors" (*tru gian*) program is described in Race, *War Comes to Long An*, 82–83; and Carlyle A. Thayer, *War by Other Means*, 142–145. A more literal translation of *tru gian* would be "fight villains," but within the party it was understood to have the more dire meaning.

75. "Situation of the Nambo Region since 1954 (U)," 27.

76. Pham Thanh Bien, "Ve cuoc khoi nghia Tra Bong va mien Tay Quang Ngai" [On the Tra Bong and Western Quang Ngai Uprising], *Nghien cuu Lich su* [History Research], 12, no. 1 (August 2004), 15. Bien was the deputy province committee secretary in charge of military and cadre affairs in this period.

77. Linh, "Armed Uprisings," 19. See also Bien, "Ve quoc khoi nghia," 16.

78. David W.P. Elliott, *The Vietnamese War*, vol. 1, 209, 212–213.

79. Elliott, *The Vietnamese War*, vol. 1, 229–230, 233–238.

80. David Hunt, *Into the Maelstrom: Vietnam's Southern Revolution, 1959–1968* (Amherst, Mass.: University of Massachusetts Press, forthcoming), chapter 3, details the methods and effects of popular demonstrations.

81. "Dien mat cua trung uong Dang, So 160 . . . ," VKDTT, vol. 21, 1960 (2002), 291–305.

82. "Nghi quyet Hoi nghi Trung uong lan thu 15 (mo rong)," 87–89.

83. "Nghi quyet hoi nghi xu uy Nam bo lan thu V, thang 7 nam 1960" [Resolution of the Fifth Nam Bo Region Party Committee Conference, July 1960], VKDTT, vol. 21, 1960 (2002), 1085–1088.

84. "Bao cao chinh tri cua Ban chap hanh Trung uong Dang tai Dai hoi dai bieu toan quoc lan thu III, Ngay 5 thang 9 nam 1960" [Political Report of the Central Committee to the Third National Congress, 5 September 1960], VKDTT, vol. 21, 1960 (2002), 526.

85. For a personal account of the Front's founding by an insider who was not a party member, see Truong Nhu Tang, *A Vietcong Memoir*, with David Chanoff and Doan Van Toai (New York: Harcourt Brace Jovanovich, 1985), 63–80.

86. Tho would go on to hold the presidency of the unified Socialist Republic of Vietnam after war's end.

87. War Experiences Recapitulation Committee, *The Anti-U.S. Resistance War*, 45–46.

88. Le Duan, "Gui anh Muoi Cuc va cac dong chi Nam Bo" [Letter to Muoi Cuc and Nam Bo Comrades], *Le Duan tuyen tap*, 260–261. Muoi Cuc was Nguyen Van Linh's *nom de guerre*.

89. The LDP Central Committee was explicit about the reasons for the name change: "if the Southern party branch [of the LDP] retains its public name as a branch of the Lao Dong Party under the leadership of the Central Committee in Hanoi, enemies here and abroad will exploit that to falsely slander the North with intervening to overthrow the South and to create difficulties for the North in mobilizing struggle for the South in the sphere of international law." "Chi thi cua Trung uong cuc mien Nam, So 4, nay 27 thang 11 nam 1961" [COSVN Directive no. 4, November 27, 1961], VKDTT, vol. 22, 1961 (2002), 653–654.

90. "Chi thi cua Trung uong cuc mien, Nam, Ngay 16 thang 6 nam 1961" [COSVN Directive, June 16, 1961], VKDTT, vol. 22, 1961 (2002), 638.

91. Vien lich su quan su Viet Nam, *50 nam Quan doi nhan dan Viet Nam* [Fifty Years of the People's Army of Viet Nam] (Hanoi: NXB Quan doi nhan dan, 1995), 168.

92. Figures are from U.S. intelligence sources cited in *The Pentagon Papers*, Senator Gravel edition (Boston: Beacon, 1971), vol. 2, 43.

93. Princes Souvanna Phouma and Souphanouvong, half-brothers united in 1945–1946 against the return of French rule, had gone separate ways after 1949. Souvanna accepted appointment as prime minister in the French-created state, while Souphanouvong worked with the Viet Minh to create a guerrilla organization that became the Pathet Lao.

94. Interview with Major General Pichit Kullawanich, Bangkok, February 21, 1984.

95. Gaiduk, *Confronting Vietnam*, 141.

96. Nguyen Viet Phuong, "Bo doi Truong son va he thong duong Ho Chi Minh" [Truong Son Army and the Ho Chi Minh Road System], *Nghien cuu Lich su* [History Research] (March-April 1979), 22–30.

97. Castle, *At War*, 24–25.

98. "Dien mat cua trung uong gui xu Nam Bo, LKU V, So 28/DM, ngay 14 thang 3 nam 1971 [Central Committee Cable to the Nam Bo Region and Interzone V Committees, no. 28/DM, March 14, 1961], VKDTT, vol. 22, 1961 (2002), 263–265.

99. Vien lich su quan su Viet Nam, *50 nam*, 168.

100. War Experiences Recapitulation Committee, *The Anti-U.S. Resistance War*, 46.

101. This is not to say that the NLF, or rather communist members of the NLF, never suggested policy initiatives and never lobbied for Southern interests. It is to say that the NLF lacked policy autonomy. The distinction is crucial. See Brigham, *Guerrilla Diplomacy*, for analysis that highlights NLF policy initiatives.

102. On the NLF's neutralization proposal, see Brigham, *Guerrilla Diplomacy*, 19–39.

3

Fateful Decisions

The aged monk Quang Duc assumed the lotus position in the middle of a Saigon street. Calmly, without a trace of emotion, Duc sat straight backed while two assistants drenched him with gasoline. Accounts differ as to whether Duc or another monk touched the match to his robes, but the flames instantly bloomed around him, and within a minute he toppled over dead. It was June 11, 1963, a month after South Vietnamese security forces had shot and killed eight students in Hue for defying an order by President Diem banning the display of religious banners. An offering for peace in Theravada Buddhist iconography, Duc's fiery sacrifice made a shocking front page image around the world. In the next two months, four more monks emulated Duc's self-immolation. Combined with protests against religious discrimination, the burnings were the spearhead of mass protest against the tyranny of the Diem regime.

The political turmoil in South Vietnam presented the United States with hard choices. First for lack of alternatives and later with genuine enthusiasm, the United States had embraced Diem as the man to head the government in Saigon. But Diem's regime had developed into a family despotism and he proved to be irritatingly unreceptive to American advice. U.S. policymakers began to view Diem as more of an obstacle than a key to stopping insurgency in the countryside. The Buddhist protest movement of 1963 only revealed in graphic terms what had been fact all along: although Diem did not single out Buddhism for persecution as his detractors claimed, his regime was dominated by Catholics and, like the Catholic colonial regime before it, creed and outlook separated it from the 90 percent of the population that was non-Catholic.

But public hostility was a condition to which Diem and his family seemed oblivious. Diem denounced the Buddhists as Communist-inspired, and Madame Nhu, his sister-in-law, applauded with morbid glee what she called "monk barbeques" (a phrase reported in many news dispatches at the time). American officials in Saigon believed Madame Nhu's husband, Ngo Dinh Nhu, had advised Diem to suppress the Buddhists and would continue to be a poisonous influence so long as Diem was in power. The swirl of protest and plotting taxed American patience with Diem but not with the project of "saving" Vietnam. The American government's commitment was too firm and its reputation too conspicuously on trial to abandon that objective. That, at any rate, was how most U.S. leaders perceived the situation, including the man who succeeded Dwight Eisenhower as president.

KENNEDY'S WAR

John F. Kennedy took office as president of the United States on January 20, 1961. Along with Mike Mansfield, he was one of the senators Justice William O. Douglas had introduced to Ngo Dinh Diem in May 1953 and was among those who had tried to convince the government and media that Diem deserved American backing.[1] A vociferous opponent of assisting the French at Dien Bien Phu, Kennedy had argued at a 1956 conference sponsored by the American Friends of Vietnam, a lobbying group that counted Kennedy as a member, that "Vietnam represents the cornerstone of the Free World in Southeast Asia, the keystone in the arch, the finger in the dike" against the "red tide of Communism." The country was, Kennedy said, a model of "political liberty" and an "inspiration to those seeking to obtain and maintain their liberty in all parts of Asia—and indeed the world."[2] That it was no such thing did not trouble Kennedy, whose words expressed the view, widely held among American politicians, that right-wing autocrats were bulwarks against left-wing revolutions.[3]

American leaders of both parties also assessed Vietnam through the prism of the Cold War, that is, as a battleground in the global confrontation between Communism and Democracy. In this view, Communist-led insurgencies anywhere in the Third World held potential to alter the balance between East and West and therefore had to be resisted. A corollary known as the "domino theory" predicted that if the United States did nothing and South Vietnam "fell," neighboring states would succumb to their own domestic insurgencies or switch allegiance from the West to the Communist bloc. Policymakers understood that the challenges and risks were not clear-cut, but the Cold War and domino paradigms provided the vocabulary and boundaries of discourse on policy alternatives.

On entering office the Kennedy team was aware of tensions in the Sino-Soviet relationship, but it perceived China as the mentor of Communist insurgencies across Southeast Asia that, if successful, would benefit the entire Communist camp. When Soviet Premier Nikita Khrushchev remarked in a speech just two weeks before Kennedy's inauguration that Moscow would support "wars of national liberation," Kennedy's advisers ascribed more importance to this line than to the speech's emphasis on "peaceful coexistence" and concluded that a new Communist global offensive was about to begin. This was a challenge to which the United States, in Kennedy's view and in the view of leaders of both political parties, felt pressed to respond.[4]

The Eisenhower administration, in any case, had already spent hundreds of millions of dollars on the Saigon government, and the new president was under pressure to show resolve. Bowing to the rule that no president, especially a new one, could afford to appear weak, Kennedy told Walt W. Rostow, his personal adviser and an energetic proponent of intervention, "I can't take a 1954 defeat today."[5] Privately, however, the president was having some doubts. Diem's nepotism, dogmatic style, and lack of a common touch were too obvious to ignore. As both head of state and chief executive famous for attention to detail, Diem took the blame for every shortcoming of his regime. An attempted coup just before Kennedy took office underscored Diem's growing isolation. Besides, as president, Kennedy faced an array of foreign and domestic challenges and did not wish to complicate these by expanding American involvement in South Vietnam. Believing U.S. involvement should be limited to providing only the support Diem's government needed to save itself, Kennedy preferred to help Saigon defeat the insurgency without the direct participation of U.S. forces in combat.[6]

With Kennedy, however, came a doctrinal shift that made such involvement more likely, not less. The centerpiece of security strategy during the Eisenhower administration had been massive retaliation, a threat to unleash nuclear war on the Soviet Union if it attacked an American ally. The threat was not credible because it asked allies to believe that the United States would risk its own destruction on their behalf. The strategy also left the United States with no realistic means to cope with "brush-fire wars" in the Third World in which the Soviet Union might be only indirectly involved, if at all. The Kennedy men, particularly the bright young "whiz kids" that Defense Secretary Robert McNamara brought into the Department of Defense, criticized massive retaliation as a muscle-bound strategy. The Kennedy administration therefore adopted the alternative of "flexible response," which General Maxwell Taylor had recommended unsuccessfully to the Eisenhower administration. This doctrine called for the development of an array of options, conventional and irregular as well as nuclear. With Kennedy's blessing, Pentagon strategists, the intelligence services, and the "think tanks" began churning out ideas for "counterinsurgency" against left-wing revolutionary movements in the Third World. The president himself took a personal interest in the creation of the Special Forces, or Green Berets, an elite unit of professionals trained to combat insurgent irregulars by irregular means. The new doctrine, along with the new means and methods, lowered the constraints on waging wars "below the nuclear threshold."

Indochina beset Kennedy even before he settled into the Oval Office. The problem was Laos, where the United States had begun supplying military assistance under the guise of economic aid in 1955. Alarm bells had rung in Washington in late 1960 when neutralist Lao leaders accepted Soviet and Chinese aid and allied with the Pathet Lao and the North Vietnamese helped the Pathet Lao extend its control over much of eastern Laos. The country dominated Eisenhower's briefing of the new president. Almost immediately on taking office, Kennedy set up an interagency task force to develop options, which included the occupation of southern Laos by sixty thousand American troops. Kennedy rejected that option but felt it was necessary to respond in some fashion. In March he authorized the establishment of a helicopter repair and maintenance base under CIA control on Thai soil. This decision, Timothy Castle has written, "inaugurated a policy that would characterize American military activity in Laos for more than a dozen years: extensive CIA paramilitary operations supported by Thailand-based, covert U.S. military agencies."[7] In short order came authorization for the open establishment of a uniformed Military Assistance Advisory Group (MAAG) for Laos, an enhanced U.S. advisory presence in Royal Lao Army units, increased aerial reconnaissance, the creation of a B-26 bomber squadron of a dozen unmarked planes to fly out of Takhli, Thailand, to bomb targets in Laos, and the recruitment of mercenaries from the Hmong ethnic minority in northern Laos. The first combat fatalities and the first captures of U.S. servicemen in Laos duly followed.[8]

In April, however, the other crisis facing the new administration—the failed invasion of Cuba at the Bay of Pigs—made Kennedy wary of schemes hatched in the Pentagon and the CIA. By comparison with Cuba, Laos presented infinitely greater challenges. It was ten thousand miles away not ninety, it was landlocked and therefore a difficult place to send troops, and it shared a mountainous border with China: not a good place to confront an insurgency. Kennedy therefore chose to negotiate. Luckily for him, the Soviet Union and China were more anxious to avoid confrontation in Laos than to help the Pathet Lao and the North Vietnamese overrun the country, which they were poised to do.[9] A Geneva conference on Laos in May–June 1962 agreed to restore a neutral government with participation by all three contending factions and to exclude all foreign military presence from Laotian territory. The agreement soon fell through, though, as North Vietnamese troops did not withdraw, the CIA continued supplying food and ammunition to the Hmong, and the U.S. embassy in Vientiane opened a small office to coordinate military assistance.[10] The "secret war," as it came to be known, was under way.

Kennedy's clandestine action in Laos was firm, but his public diplomacy was soft. Neutralization averted a showdown of the great powers,[11] but it created an inherently unstable local political arrangement and left U.S. allies across the region uncertain about the American commitment to defend non-Communist governments. Kennedy thought he now had to be firm elsewhere. Nowhere did firmness seem more needed than in Vietnam, where leaders in Saigon and Hanoi were weighing American determination in light of events in Laos. Diem refused to sign the agreement on Laos until he received Kennedy's personal assurance that the United States had no plans to neutralize South Vietnam. Thailand, already implicated in American efforts to stem Communist advances in Laos, sought further assurance that the United States would stand by its Southeast Asian allies.[12] Despite his misgivings, Kennedy gave in to assertive advisers like Rostow, who argued that Vietnam was the place where the United States could—and had to—take a stand.[13]

While delegates were assembling in Geneva to discuss Laos, Kennedy quietly sent one hundred more military advisers and four hundred Special Forces into Vietnam. This seemingly small step had immense psychological importance, as it went beyond mere abuse of the Geneva ceiling on the size of military missions that had been set in 1954. Kennedy's action openly breached the accords reached at Geneva. With this move, the administration buried what little was left of the Geneva Agreements and removed a bar to further moves.

Needing opinions on further measures, Kennedy dispatched Vice President Lyndon Johnson to Saigon in May 1961, the economist Eugene Staley a few months later, and the team of Rostow and General Taylor, now Kennedy's personal military adviser, in October. All came back with reports of a deteriorating situation and recommendations to enhance support for Diem. Most important was the Rostow–Taylor report, which recommended placing U.S. advisers at all levels of the Saigon government and military, developing a Civil Guard and Village Self-Defense Corps, and dispatching an 8,000-man "logistic task force" under the guise of flood-control assistance. There were contrary opinions, but Khrushchev's reaffirmation of a commitment to wars of national liberation at the Vienna summit in June 1961 made it difficult for Kennedy to heed his own voice of caution. Rejecting negotiations as a sign of weakness yet averse to sending troops, Kennedy made what a former U.S. diplomat has identified as the first of ten "fateful decisions" that dragged the United States deeper into Vietnam.[14] He authorized an increase of aid and advisers, soon followed by upgrading the Military Assistance Advisory Group (MAAG) to the Military Assistance

Command, Vietnam (MACV). Diem assented with deep misgivings, telling the American ambassador to Saigon that if his government could not win without the help of U.S. forces, "then we deserve to lose."[15] The number of advisers in South Vietnam, less than 800 when Kennedy took office, grew to 3,000 in December 1961 (including an operational U.S. Army helicopter unit) and to 11,000—the equivalent of an army division—in late 1962. With this act, Kennedy tacitly acknowledged that "nation-building" had failed, leaving militarization the only option.

While increasing the number of advisers, Kennedy also weighed a proposal by the Defense Department to use chemical herbicides to clear "firebreaks" on South Vietnam's borders and defoliate the jungle along roads and canals. Though there was concern about world reaction, the State Department did not object. Kennedy approved the idea in principle on November 30, 1961, and for a year afterward all targets required Oval Office approval. Late in 1962 Kennedy yielded to pressure from President Diem to allow limited crop destruction as well and delegated authority over such actions to the U.S. mission in Saigon. Thus began Operation Ranch Hand, which from 1962 through 1971 would spray nineteen million gallons of defoliants (eleven million gallons of Agent Orange) over mostly forested areas of South Vietnam and Laos.[16]

Kennedy's decisions did not live up to his bold rhetoric, however. They were improvisational, incremental, tentative, and temporizing, crafted to keep Diem from collapsing and to silence the critics of inaction. Wanting neither negotiations nor war, Kennedy, like his successors, based his policy on what one of his own advisers was later to describe as "wishful thinking": if this or that reform could be extracted from Diem, if a little more aid were given, if a little more time could be bought, things might get better.[17] "Better" meant reversing revolutionary gains and putting the Saigon regime on a course toward stability and strength. The alternatives of negotiated settlement, neutralization à la Laos, Communist participation in a coalition government, or simply pulling out and leaving Saigon to its fate received only fleeting, dismissive consideration. Desire that Diem should succeed and the view that abandoning Saigon would do irreparable damage to the credibility of U.S. commitments in other parts of the world prevailed over the misgivings.

At the time Kennedy's decisions were not unpopular. The vast majority of Americans had yet to see how the war in Vietnam could disrupt their own lives or that an acceptable outcome would prove elusive. That included youth, who, swept along by the idealist activism of the Kennedy administration, joined the Peace Corps and the struggle for African-American civil rights. Not yet faced with dispatch to the jungles, they largely ignored Kennedy's lurching steps into Laos and Vietnam.

THE COMMUNIST MILITARY CHALLENGE

When Kennedy took office, Indochina's tribulations had yet to enter U. S. consciousness as a war. The Communists devoted a good deal more time to organization and propaganda than to armed attacks. But in September 1961, they did manage to seize a provincial capital just eighty kilometers from Saigon. Revolutionary armed forces grew briskly. U.S. intelligence estimated that the number of regular troops under Communist command grew from 4,000 to 10,000 during 1960 alone. By late 1961 the People's Liberation Armed Force (PLAF), the "main force" of Southerners nominally commanded by the National Liberation Front (NLF), numbered 17,000. These troops were to grow to 23,000 in 1962, 25,000 in 1963, and 34,000 in late 1964. In addition to this body of full-time fighters, village self-defense and regional forces numbered about 3,000 in 1960 and an estimated 72,000 in late 1964. Thus, the total number of revolutionary armed forces, according to U.S. estimates, rose from about 7,000 in 1960 to 106,000 in 1964.[18] A secret assessment by the party's Central Office for South Vietnam (COSVN), the effective command of the revolution in the South, placed the total in January 1964 at 140,000.[19] By either estimate Communist armed forces were growing steadily and rapidly, and with 28 percent of the regulars counted by COSVN as party members, they were firmly under the party's control.

In the beginning most of the units were platoon-sized and took orders from party committees at the district and province levels. Lacking the necessary command elements and training to act in coordination, such units could do little more than mount hit-and-run attacks on isolated outposts and provide security for party organs and roving propaganda teams. By mid-1962, however, three main-force regiments had appeared in the mountainous provinces of central Vietnam designated Military Region 5.[20] The process of grouping independent platoons and companies into larger units then began in earnest.

These units were but the tip of an iceberg. In the Communist strategy, armed forces were to be organized into three categories: guerrilla militias, regional forces, and main forces. In some ways the most important forces were the militias, or the village "self-defense forces," whose duties were to set booby traps, plant punji stakes, dig tunnels, harass patrols and convoys, support nighttime raids on small outposts, collect taxes, and protect local political organs. The militias also provided local party organs with police, intelligence, and a mechanism to recruit and train village youths for "promotion" to the higher force categories. Thus the militias were the foundation of a three-tiered pyramid. They could be lethal in the ambushes and hit-and-run engagements that comprised most of the fighting, and they also were vital to the creation, maintenance, and expansion of the forces above them.

The fact that these forces had to be built largely from scratch made it essential for the Communists to obtain popular cooperation and community sanction, particularly for the formation of village militias. This was done through "political struggle" *(dau tranh chinh tri)* conducted by party and front cadres who worked individually, in teams, and through networks of family and friends to deepen sympathy for the revolution. Their methods went beyond spreading propaganda that demanded reform, justice, and peace to direct personal appeals to individuals who were likely to feel disadvantaged or mistreated by existing political, social, and economic arrangements. People who had fought for the Viet Minh against the French—and suffered because of it under Diem—were the first contacted. In addition to manipulating patriotic sentiment and traditional animosity toward the capital, cadres offered specific benefits (e.g. land, village self-government, education and positions of status for the poor, and intimidation or execution of hated officials and landlords) in exchange for active support. Young people often joined for the chance at upward mobility, the sense of participating with their peers in an historic event, and the excitement. Villagers naturally had to defend the gains thus won and so had reason to make significant sacrifices for the revolution. Political struggle, moreover, extended into the ranks of Saigon's army and bureaucracy in the form of "enemy and military proselytization" *(binh van)* that sought, through propaganda and messages conveyed by intermediaries, to demoralize civil servants and military personnel or to encourage them to desert or defect.

The development of Southern insurgent forces benefited from Northern support as well, but how much was not obvious. Until the Central Committee's fifteenth Plenum in January 1959, as we have seen, party policy was an important factor restraining the use of armed force by the party's Southern branch. The first effect of change in that policy was to unleash forces that were indigenous to the South. However, infiltration of arms and cadres from the North also played a role. Leadership cadres, numbering a few hundred, had shuttled back and forth between North and South ever since 1955. From 1957 to 1958, the party recruited members of ethnic minority groups inhabiting Military Region 5 to improve the lines of communication through the mountains[21] and to guide the small groups of infiltrators that began moving from North to South following the fifteenth plenum.[22] Group 559 of the People's Army (PAVN), introduced in the previous chapter, took over the organization and support of this trickle of infiltrators, which quickly increased. A picture of the first team of infiltrators striding along a jungle trail hangs in Hanoi's Military History Museum, where the guide proudly declares that they were troops of the People's Army marching to the South in May 1959. In January 1960, the PAVN turned its base at Son Tay into a training ground for infiltrators, and shortly thereafter the 324th Division was designated an infiltration training unit.

The division was a fully integrated combat unit of the People's Army. It was not, however, a "Northern" unit in terms of the regional origins of its men, for it was composed of regroupees—Southerners who had "regrouped" in the North after the war with France. The overwhelming majority of people who went South between 1959 and 1964 were from this pool. The regroupees had been born south of the seventeenth parallel and so were best equipped by accent and experience to mingle with the Southern population. Many returned to their home villages to contact families and friends and to resurrect old resistance networks. The regroupees were also an elite group: most held officer or senior noncommissioned officer ranks in the PAVN or were trained political cadres. More than half were party members. More than one-third of the men and women who had regrouped in the North in 1954 returned South from 1959 to 1964, at which point the pool of regroupees still fit for infiltration dried up.[23] The annual number of "confirmed" and "probable" Northern infiltrators estimated by U.S. intelligence and shown in Table 3.1 is broadly consistent with the figure of 40,000 by the end of 1963 provided in the PAVN's official history.[24] Well-trained and yearning to return home, the regroupees supplied an invaluable nucleus of disciplined, skilled cadres. They played a crucial role in the party's recovery from the "dark days" of 1959.

But the regroupees did not supply as much of the movement's rank-and-file as did the South itself. The total number of regroupees sent South amounted to 40 percent of the U.S. estimate and 30 percent of the COSVN estimate of total Southern revolutionary armed forces in 1964. Due to attrition and nonmilitary assignment, the regroupees' actual proportion in this

Table 3.1. "Confirmed" and "Probable" Infiltrators from the North, 1959–1964

1959–60	4,582
1961	6,295
1962	12,857
1963	7,906
1964	12,424
Total	44,064

Source: Working Paper on the North Vietnamese Role in South Viet-Nam: Captured Documents and Interrogation Reports (Washington, D.C.: Department of State, May 1968), introduction, Table 1.

total had to be much lower. The number of combatants recruited in the South up to 1964, as distinct from the regroupees, was at least 60,000 and probably near 100,000. This rapid growth in the number of Southerners bearing weapons for the revolution attested as much to popular readiness for revolt as to the Communists' organizational abilities, although it is highly doubtful that the Southern revolution would have survived suppression by Saigon's army and police but for the discipline, leadership, training, and arms of the regroupees.

The movement from North to South also led inexorably to expansion of the logistical support, or "transportation groups," set up in 1959. One of these, Group 759, was responsible for the maritime route and sent its first ship, the *Phuong Dong I*, to the Ca Mau peninsula in September 1962. From then until February 1965, when its operations were discovered in Phu Yen province, the group's 50- to 100-ton ships carried nearly 5,000 tons of weapons to the South.[25] Unlike the land route, the sea route could reach not only the areas of revolutionary activity in coastal Binh Dinh and Quang Ngai but also the very tip of the Ca Mau peninsula. For awhile it probably was the major channel of arms and equipment to Communist forces in the South.[26]

With the discovery and blockade of the sea route by the U.S. Navy's Operation Market Time, emphasis shifted to Group 559's land route, which western news media quickly dubbed the Ho Chi Minh Trail. This route had followed the communications-liaison lines that had linked Viet Minh bases up and down the Annamite Cordillera during the war against France. In August 1959, Group 559 delivered its first load of weapons, weighing 280 kilograms, in western Thua Thien province.[27] Fear of discovery and clashes with South Vietnamese forces, however, drove the group to map new routes down the western flank of the cordillera, known as the Truong Son range in Vietnamese, inside Laos and Cambodia. The "trail" soon developed into a web of footpaths, roads, and riverine routes down which flowed a steady stream of troops, cadres, equipment, and weapons.

Through the relative security of sparsely settled mountains and triple-canopy jungles, men and women began to wend their way carrying packs weighing up to fifty kilograms and pushing bicycles reinforced to carry 100 to 150 kilograms. One soldier was decorated a Hero of the People's Army for transporting on foot fifty-five tons over a four-year period a distance of 41,025 kilometers, in effect walking around the earth under a load equal to his own weight.[28]

This lightly protected, clandestine movement came under attack by the Royal Lao Army and Hmong irregulars as a consequence of American efforts to maneuver the Laotian government into fighting the Pathet Lao during 1960–1961. These efforts had included the insertion of U.S. Special Forces into Laos's northern provinces to recruit, train, and equip a Hmong guerrilla army. Royal Lao Army and Meo operations inevitably clashed with North Vietnam's construction of the Ho Chi Minh Trail through Laotian territory, triggering a Communist drive to push the Royal Lao Army out of the highlands. The Pathet Lao, stiffened by the PAVN, quickly occupied the eastern half of the country, giving the Vietnamese unimpeded use of the Laotian portions of routes 8, 9, and 12. By the end of 1961, the trail had doubled its capacity, and in June 1962, disregarding Laos's neutralization agreed at Geneva, the Central Military Party Committee issued orders to develop capacity for mechanized transport over new routes still deeper in Laos. Engineering regiments soon joined Group 559 to help build roads, and in 1964 the group moved forty times as much tonnage as in all previous years—51 percent by mechanized means—despite the U.S. bombing of Pathet Lao zones since May of that year.[29] More and more, supplies moved by truck, although cadres and soldiers still walked much of the distance.

It was a hard trip. Infiltrators and supplies reached the jump-off point of Vinh, capital of the North's Nghe An province, by truck and train. From there they proceeded by a route that cut sharply around the western end of the demilitarized zone or by three other routes that swung deeper into Laos. Inside Laos, movement was by foot, oxcart, bicycle, and when the routes extended toward the west, by riverboat. On foot with an occasional short truck ride, the trip from Vinh to the border of South Vietnam took an average of two months (three for those who had to travel the 1,000 kilometers from Vinh to the southernmost way station). Monsoons from May to September turned the trails to mud, slowed motor transport to a crawl, and brought fatigue and disease. An estimated 15–17 percent of the troops moving down the trail fell behind their units, mostly due to malaria.[30] According to an official history, 1.7 percent was killed and 2.99 percent wounded over the seventeen years that the trail was in operation, with the percentage of dying or wounded each year varying between zero and over 9 percent (see Appendix A).

The support system within the trail complex consisted of "military stations" (*binh tram*) about a day's march apart. These stations numbered about sixty in 1969. The typical station staffed by fifteen to twenty people and buried in jungle just off a narrow path to escape aerial detection, provided infiltrators with food, quarters, medicines, and guidance to the next station. When infiltrators reached a trail terminus—usually a base area hard on the border of South Vietnam—they were, in the early years, designated a unit of the People's Liberation Armed Force (PLAF) or assigned to existing PLAF units. In later years they would retain their PAVN designations. Supply convoys were turned over to rear units that would transport them the remaining short distance to the war zone.

Once in the war zone troops could not depend entirely on supply from the North, and regions had to practice more "logistics in place" (growing their own vegetables, for example) the farther they were from a trail terminus. From early 1961 to mid-1965 the logistical branch for B2, the region encompassing the lower half of the South, obtained 72.4 percent of the region's needs on local markets, 13.6 percent from its own production, and 0.7 percent from the enemy. Only 13.3 percent came from the North.[31] Dependency on the North would increase, however. As more units employed heavy weapons, material requirements grew, and the logistical system became more capable.

THE "SPECIAL WAR"

The rapid growth of revolutionary armed forces and Saigon's growing isolation from the countryside did not go unnoticed in Washington. At the same time that he increased the number of U.S. military advisers, Kennedy authorized them to accompany Saigon army units on combat operations down to the company level. Thus began the "special war" advocated by the Johnson, Staley and Taylor-Rostow missions during 1961. As the number of advisers mounted to 11,000 in late 1962, the United States also began providing helicopter transport and air cover. Only one U.S. adviser had died in combat before Kennedy took office; now American deaths and casualties began to occur regularly.

"Special war" strategy held that American military personnel should support and help build Saigon's army while staying in the background, not fighting. On paper this was little more than an extension of the military assistance program that had been in existence for years. By the fall of 1959, thanks largely to U.S. assistance, the Army of the Republic of Vietnam had grown to seven standard divisions, a five-battalion airborne group, eight independent artillery battalions equipped with U.S. guns, and four armored cavalry squadrons. A small air force and navy also had emerged. One of Kennedy's first acts as president had been to offer Diem an additional forty-two million dollars for the expansion and training of the ARVN at the same time that he demanded that Diem introduce political reforms (which Diem quietly failed to do). Subsequent aid allotments helped the ARVN raise its force level by late 1962 to about 220,000 men. Armed, equipped, and trained in the U.S. style, the ARVN was prepared by the United States to meet a Korea-type attack across the demilitarized zone. (The North also had received Soviet and Chinese assistance to reorganize and refit its army and, with the help of a draft instituted in 1960, it had a six-division force of about 200,000 men.)

But "special war" meant more than just enhancing the American advisory role. Kennedy and administration strategists also demanded that priority be given to "counterinsurgency," by which they meant developing capabilities for winning the allegiance of the people and conducting unconventional operations. This demand, in the words of a U.S. Army officer's scathing critique of the army's response, "shook the Army brass. They were, in effect, being told to alter radically the Army's method of operation."[32] To officers fixed on preparing for the "big war" in Europe, insurgencies were just small wars requiring no change in doctrine. "Winning hearts and minds," in their view, was the ARVN's responsibility, if it was a military task at all, and training in unconventional warfare was a diversion from the primary objective of destroying the enemy's regular armed forces. One of these diversions was to send U.S. Special Forces into the central highlands to conduct civic action among the ethnic minorities. Small teams of Green Berets lived among the "montagnards" (French for mountaineers, but referring to a number of quite distinct ethnic minorities) and organized them into Civilian Irregular Defense Groups (CIDG) to attack the Communists in their previously impenetrable mountain redoubts. U.S. military advisers trained not only the ARVN but also supervised the rapid expansion of a village Civil Guard and helped develop programs in psychological warfare, village administration, technical assistance, and propaganda.

The military side of this effort enjoyed some success, thanks in no small measure to the introduction of the armed helicopter, which greatly enhanced the mobility and firepower of ground units. In the spring and summer of 1962, the ARVN went on the offensive and dislodged Communist forces from their most exposed positions. But the Communists quickly adapted to the ARVN's new firepower and mobility. They learned how to bring down helicopters with small arms, how to wait in hiding and destroy the helicopters as they landed, and how to ambush the landing parties at their moment of greatest vulnerability. ARVN commanders reverted to the tactics of caution, refusing to risk troops in battle except behind a barrage of airpower and artillery, methods that drove people into refugee camps or the arms of the revolution.

While "special war" was having mixed results on the battlefield, efforts to overhaul the ARVN from top down had some ominous side effects. One ARVN officer, brought to Fort Benning, Georgia, to design a National Military Academy, recalled a "lack of true cooperation and communication between the Americans and the Vietnamese. I blame both sides: the Americans for their natural superiority complex and the Vietnamese for their natural inferiority complex, a result of so many years serving under the French. The result was, of course, disastrous." The Americans "essentially took charge," emphasizing conventional warfare when it did not seem relevant.[33] The problem, said ARVN General Tran Van Don of the 1950s and early 1960s, was that U.S. preoccupation with invasion from the North deflected attention from "the real threat . . . at village level in the form of . . . highly disciplined guerrilla units where cumbersome conventional units could not operate effectively. The French had already proved this to us. We wondered why we had to repeat the mistake for the Americans." ARVN General Lam Quang Thi cited the American "ethnocentric attitude regarding other countries, which consisted of judging other people by using American customs and standards."[34] Justified in their criticisms or not, ARVN officers often felt pushed aside in their own country. Asked what his military doctrine was, General Cao Van Vien, chief of the ARVN General Staff, told Don, "*As long as the conduct of the war remains an American responsibility, we have no doctrine of our own.*"[35] Of course not all ARVN officers were so critical: many went along quite happily with a program that put them in charge of big units, plentiful weapons, and new technologies of war. But the sense that the ARVN was *their* army and the war was *their* war never came as easily to them as an almost familial loyalty to the PAVN and the revolution came to their Communist counterparts.

This period also witnessed the rise and fall of ambitious state-building projects designed by Diem and his brother Nhu. The first of these was a program, inaugurated in 1955, to relieve population pressure in the crowded lowlands while bringing the central highlands under more effective state control by settling lowland Vietnamese among the highland's ethnic minorities. Ideally, lowlanders and highlanders were to develop the highlands together in a "'fraternal relationship,'" and a detailed study of program documents has found it culturally sensitive in design.[36] But implementation was another matter, and there was no way to control the reactions of the minorities, who often felt pushed off their lands and pressured to change their way of life. The result was an outbreak of ethnic minority dissidence in 1958 that simmered past the war's end.

Highland settlement in its early stages also served as a kind of laboratory for more aggressive schemes to combat insurgency in the lowlands— agrovilles and strategic hamlets. Diem and Nhu, Philip Catton has pointed out, saw these concepts as applications of personalism with its emphasis on the development of local self-sufficiency and communal solidarity.[37] Construction of agrovilles, model settlements designed to concentrate peasants under more direct government control, began in July 1959, but the program soon stalled in the face of popular resistance to the forced labor that was needed to build them. The strategic hamlet program launched in mid-1961 sought to overcome these problems with mildly redistributive reforms, hamlet democracy modeled after traditional councils (which Diem had suspended in 1956), and training peasants to defend their own communities. Ideally the hamlets were to mobilize peasants into active support of the government while denying the revolutionaries access to food, intelligence, and recruits. The hamlets also required fortifying, and in some cases relocating entire rural communities on which insurgents depended for support.

The concept resembled one that the British had used successfully against Communist insurgents in Malaysia in the 1950s, and the mastermind of that plan, Sir Robert K.G. Thompson, offered his advice to Diem and Nhu. There were important differences of structure and scale between the Vietnamese and British plans, however.[38] On taking over the program in late 1961, Nhu ignored Sir Robert's advice to proceed selectively and announced the grandiose objective of organizing between 11,000 and 12,000 strategic hamlets, enough to shelter the entire rural population. Local officials soon had peasants moving their hamlets to new sites or fortifying old ones. The official claim of 7,200 hamlets built by July 1963 was an exaggeration, or at least many of the new hamlets were slipshod affairs, but no doubt a very large number of the South's rural communities did feel some impact of the program.[39]

Well-administered hamlets containing committed anti-Communist populations, like Northern Catholic refugees, could be significant obstacles to the limited scale, politico-military tactics the Communists were then using. COSVN acknowledged that the program enlarged the area under Saigon's control and interfered with cadres' access to the people,[40] and Madame Nguyen Thi Dinh said that for a time in her native Mekong delta province of Ben Tre "it did create some difficulties for us."[41] In nearby Long An province, Jeffrey Race noted that the program "succeeded in stabilizing the situation for a time."[42] Farther north, in Quang Tri and Thua Thien provinces, the Communists acknowledged similar difficulties: "Generally speaking, the Tri-Thien movement developed slowly and weakly [in 1961–1962], as enemy forces were more numerous and stronger than ours; they basically fulfilled their strategic hamlet plan, and pacification was very harsh and maliciously destructive. . . ."[43] Not surprisingly, the Communists set the destruction of strategic hamlets as a top priority.

The program had some serious vulnerabilities for the Communists to exploit. Diem and Nhu were aware of the Malayan precedent, but they did not show much regard for the lessons it held. The Malayan Communist Party was composed mainly of ethnic Chinese, and the Malayan scheme had to separate the insurgents only from about 500,000 ethnic Chinese squatters who were the insurgents' main base of support. The Vietnamese strategic hamlet program, by contrast, attempted to separate the entire rural population from its revolutionary kin by forced draft. Peasants were ordered to move or rebuild their hamlets, without incentive, compensation, or pay, often at a new location far from ancestral graves. On speaking to former residents of the hamlets in Long An province, Race discovered that "those completed were done in form only, with few defensive weapons or obstacles, and with the occupants themselves often forced to buy barbed wire and pickets."[44] Nothing in the program, such as meaningful land reform and redistribution of power to the poor, bound the peasants to their new hamlets or to the government, as such benefits bound peasants to the revolution in areas under Communist control. Much in it, such as curbs on movement and compulsory guard duty, aroused their resentment. The idea that guerrillas could be separated from the people was, in the view of an official U.S. Army history, deluded because in many areas "the two were identical."[45]

COSVN quickly spotted these and other shortcomings: harsh methods of corralling people into the hamlets, the use of coercion rather than positive incentives to secure participation, rapid expansion into areas where Saigon's administrative presence was weak or non-existent, and the inability to organize effective defense of the hamlets once they had been built.[46] By reinstalling Saigon police and administrators, the hamlets made it possible for landlords to collect unpaid rent and restore themselves to local positions of power.[47] Few peasants, and particularly not those who had benefitted from redistributions of land and status while under the revolution's control, had a stake in the hamlets' success. So long as the government maintained a presence in the hamlets, the program could increase the risks to peasants of supporting the revolution, but it could not win their allegiance. As Saigon lacked the means to police every hamlet by force, Communist cadres were able to reestablish contact with the people, especially their relatives. The cadres would then mobilize people to tear down fences and pester guards, provoking a repressive response that would make it easier for the cadres to mobilize people next time, gradually loosening the government's hold.[48] In some places people so resented the program that they welcomed the cadres into their midst more warmly than ever before. In a generally bleak assessment of the balance of forces in mid-1963, COSVN found comfort in "the magnitude of encroachment" by strategic hamlets that exceeded Saigon's control capabilities and created new opportunities to develop mass movements in the enemy's rear, including in the hamlets themselves.[49]

U.S. efforts to save Saigon without sending combat troops began to unravel in the padi fields of My Tho province during January 1963. There, near the hamlet of Ap Bac eighty kilometers southwest of Saigon, an ARVN force of 2,000 men attacked about 300 to 400 entrenched and waiting PLAF troops. The Communists may purposely have baited the trap to demonstrate their strength. Although the ARVN force called in airplanes, helicopters, armed personnel carriers, and U.S. advisers to assist, it suffered 190 casualties and lost five helicopters, while the PLAF claimed to have escaped with twelve dead (the actual number was probably much higher). ARVN troops actually fought rather well, but that did not change the main conclusion drawn by observers and combatants alike. Whatever the tally of bodies, the PLAF had found ways to offset the ARVN's numerical and firepower advantages, proving the inability of American support limited to advice, training, and equipment to save the ARVN from defeat.[50] The U.S. strategy of "special war" stood revealed as a failure.

THE COUP

A change of strategy was more than a year in the future, however. For the rest of 1963, the war in the countryside churned on while attention shifted to the cities. Deeply displeased by political infighting that distracted ARVN commanders from military duties, the Kennedy team was itself divided over what to do. Upon returning from an inspection trip, General Victor Krulak, an expert in counterinsurgency, reported to the president at a meeting of the National Security Council on September 6, 1963, that Diem was a much-loved figure who only needed more U.S. support to win the war. But State Department official Joseph Mendenhall, who had accompanied Krulak, disagreed. According to Mendenhall, Diem was almost universally detested and an obstacle to victory. "You did visit the same country, didn't you?" Kennedy asked.[51]

U.S. frustration with Diem was mounting along with the rise in popular antipathy to his increasingly autocratic rule. Yet, another rigged election in 1959 had produced a National Assembly in which there was only one serious critic of the regime, the genuinely popular Dr. Phan Quang Dan, and Dan soon landed in jail for "electoral fraud." Another coup attempt in 1960 and the bombing and strafing of the palace by two disgruntled air force pilots in 1962 had signaled restlessness in the armed forces. Previously staunch supporters had drifted into opposition, only to be arrested or hounded out of the country. The Kennedy administration had urged Diem to placate his enemies, broaden his government, and crack down on corruption. Instead, Diem placed his trust in an ever narrowing circle of relatives and sycophants. The more the Kennedy administration pressured him, the more Diem cut himself off from its advice.

What Americans saw as Diem's intransigence they attributed to congenital obstinacy, brother Nhu's intrigues, and the justified paranoia of leaders who have real enemies. But intransigence also reflected Diem's belief that he could not survive the appearance of caving in to foreign pressure. This was a legacy of Vietnam's age-old resistance to China, its struggle for independence from France, and, perhaps most poignantly, of Diem's realization that in the contest for legitimacy, his own claim, in contrast to that of the Communists, was weak. For Diem to have accepted U.S. advice would have confirmed his enemy's charge that he was a "puppet" and contradicted his genuinely-held conviction that he was as much a patriot as Ho Chi Minh. To bolster his own claim as a rightful ruler, he had to turn aside his patron's advice, even defy it. By 1963 Diem was so eager to distance himself from the United States that, at French suggestion, he let brother Nhu explore a peaceful accommodation with Hanoi.[52]

Every defect of the regime became a focus of popular resentment: the arrest and torture of prominent people, the silencing of dissent, the replacement of elected village chiefs with ones appointed from Saigon, the appointment of Catholics from central provinces to administer districts in the Mekong delta, the compulsory enrollment of civil servants in brother Nhu's Revolutionary Personalist Workers (*Can Lao*) Party, the construction of a monument to two national heroines carved on orders from Madame Nhu in her likeness, the allocation of government funds for Madame Nhu's personal use, a ban on dancing, Diem's personal inspection of every exit visa application, and the widespread corruption. Americans could be faulted for making unrealistic demands to democratize the country, but many regime actions seemed arbitrary, punitive, or just plain dotty to Vietnamese as well. With Buddhist monks in the vanguard, demonstrations became an almost daily occurrence.

Buddhism, however, was a secondary issue for most of the people who took part in the demonstrations and for many of the monks as well. Although Diem did indeed promote Catholics in government and incorporate Catholic elements into an official state ideology, the monks' cries of "persecution" were contrived to win sympathy more for political than for religious objectives. Protest leaders identified Buddhism with nationalism to capitalize on the growing isolation of the Diem regime. As one monk candidly put it, "The campaign to overthrow the Ngo Dinh Diem regime in 1963 not only succeeded in mobilizing the people to the defense of Buddhism but also awakened the nationalist consciousness of the masses. In every Buddhist the idea of Buddhism and nationalism are intertwined and cannot be easily separated. Many non-Buddhist elements also took part in the Buddhist campaign, not because they wanted to support the Buddhists but because they realized that the Buddhist campaign was consistent with the people's aspirations."[53]

In the name of "defending Buddhism," the monks articulated a broad popular yearning to get rid of Diem, eliminate U.S. influence, restore traditional morality, and recover national harmony. Generally contemptuous of Communism, they saw their movement as an alternative to both Diem and the NLF, a "third force" around which a broad-based coalition government could be formed. Many of them sincerely believed that they and not the Communists possessed ordinary people's hearts and minds and that they could secure this support for a genuinely neutral government of national unity.

The core of the movement was a handful of militant leaders and their followers in and around Hue. Numbering perhaps 100,000 members, this faction owed its dynamism to skillful organization and the charismatic leadership of the bonze Thich Tri Quang. Born, coincidentally, in the same village of central Vietnam as Ngo Dinh Diem, Tri Quang had sided with the Viet Minh against the French and portrayed himself as a revolutionary non-Communist patriot. Tri Quang's rival for influence within the movement was the head of the Institute for Propagation of the Faith, Thich Tam Chau, a pliable moderate based in Saigon. It was Tri Quang's group, though, that set the tone and instigated the protests that degenerated into violent melees between demonstrators and police.

There is evidence that the Communists tried to incite and manipulate the movement, and it would be surprising given their aims, strategy, and methods if they did not attempt it. It also is speculated that Tri Quang was a Communist agent,[54] but his incarceration by the Communists after the war suggests a more complex relationship, if there was one. Diem and Nhu attempted to tar the Buddhists with a Communist brush, but in fact the Buddhists and Communists were rivals for the allegiance of the same constituency. Whatever the Communists' machinations, it is doubtful that they had any effect on the movement, whose demands resonated with popular cravings for peace, reconciliation, and cultural integrity.

Believing repression would fuel even greater opposition, the Americans advised appeasement, but Diem, on the advice of his generals (according to Nhu) or on Nhu's advice (according to his generals), invoked the truncheon. On June 11, 1963, Quang Duc immolated himself, and on August 21, Nhu's Special Forces ransacked the pagodas in Saigon, Hue, and coastal province capitals. Many of the 1,400 people arrested were bonzes.[55] The pagoda raids were a turning point in American discussions whether to keep or jettison Diem. American officials who thought ruthlessness only deepened popular alienation hinted at consequences if those responsible were not punished. Fearing that U.S. military aid could be in jeopardy, Chief-of-Staff Tran Van Don contacted Lieutenant Colonel Lucien Conein, a French-speaking CIA agent whose activities in Indochina dated back to 1944. Don assured Conein that the ARVN had not been involved in the pagoda raids and indicated that planning for a coup was under way.[56]

By chance, Washington had just sent a new ambassador to Saigon to replace Frederick Nolting, who many in the Kennedy administration had come to regard as too "pro-Diem." Nolting's replacement was the enormously self-confident patrician, Henry Cabot Lodge. Lodge carried plenipotentiary powers, and he took his post believing Diem was going to be his main problem. Reports that Diem was in contact with Hanoi through a third party to cut a deal with the enemy [57] and that Nhu was having quiet chats in the palace or at his home in Hue with "Viet Cong" to induce defections as Nolting believed,[58] hardened Lodge's conviction that Diem had to go. On August 24 Lodge received a cable from Washington, drafted by Assistant Secretary of State Roger Hilsman while his superiors were out of town, ordering Lodge to "make detailed plans as to how we might bring about Diem's replacement" if Diem failed to "rid himself of Nhu and his coterie. . . ."[59] Actually, Kennedy and his chief advisers were not yet committed to removing Diem, much less by means of a coup, but Hilsman's cable reflected the drift of discussions taking place in Washington almost every day.

Accounts of what followed differ mainly over the degree of U.S. involvement. According to General Don, the coup plotters kept their plans to themselves until the last moment and acted without prompting from the United States.[60] But it is well established that the generals sought reassurance through Conein that the United States would support a new government. On August 28, 1963, in a cable to President Kennedy, Lodge recommended showing that support: "We are launched on a course from which there is no respectable turning back: the overthrow of the Diem government. There is no turning back because there is no possibility that the war can be won under a Diem administration. The chance of bringing off a generals' coup depends on them to some extent: but it depends at least as much on us. We should proceed to make all-out effort to get the generals to move promptly." Against the advice of General Paul Harkins, the embassy military assistance chief who had argued that Diem should be given a chance to get rid of Nhu, Lodge asserted that "such a step has no chance of getting the desired result and would have the very serious effect of being regarded by the Generals as a sign of American indecision and delay."[61] Kennedy promptly approved Lodge's recommendation, and the cable to Lodge conveying this stated that "the USG will support a coup that has a good chance of succeeding. . . ."[62] Lodge subsequently maintained a conspicuous distance from Diem, but Voice of America broadcast hints of U.S. displeasure with Diem, and on October 5, Kennedy approved a list of aid cuts knowing this would encourage a coup.[63] The generals, who were as dependent on U.S. aid as Diem was, apparently interpreted the threatened aid suspension as a virtual order to stage a coup.[64]

The circle of plotters quickly widened. One key leader, General Duong Van "Big" Minh, had begun his military career under the French and had risen swiftly by commanding the troops that crushed the sects. But he had lost Diem's trust in proportion to his gain in personal popularity, and Diem had divested him of any real authority by making him his personal military adviser. The other key conspirator, General Tran Van Don, had been born in France and had fought for France in Europe during World War II and in Indochina. Swept up with so many other young men in the August Revolution, Don had volunteered to fight for the Viet Minh but had been refused a command because of his French citizenship. He had then salvaged a military career by joining General LeClerc's headquarters staff. When the French created a separate Vietnamese army under Bao Dai, Don had joined what was to become the ARVN. By 1963, as chief of the general staff, he too had earned Diem's distrust. Both Minh and Don were southern Buddhists.

Minh and Don recruited General Tran Thien Khiem, one of the generals most trusted by Diem and commander of the Seventh Division. Other members of the coup group—some of whom one day would mount coups of their own—included Major General Ton That Dinh, commander of the Third Corps around Saigon and a favorite of Diem's brother Ngo Dinh Can; General Nguyen Khanh, commander of the Second Corps and a notorious opportunist; General Do Cao Tri, commander of the First Corps; Colonel Do Mau, chief of military security; Colonel Tran Ngoc Huyen, the devout Catholic commandant of Dalat Military Academy; General Le Van Kim, another ex-Viet Minh who had switched sides in time to carve out a career as an aide to Admiral Thierry d'Argenlieu; Lieutenant Colonel Nguyen Cao Ky, the French-trained chief of a C-47 transport squadron and a northerner; and Nguyen Van Thieu, a Catholic colonel from central Vietnam.

Except for lack of ties to the old aristocratic mandarinate of Annam, the coup group differed little in social background or outlook from other stalwarts of the Diem regime. The officers were mostly products of French education and bourgeois families, holdovers of the colonial system who made up the South's anti-Communist elite. An important hallmark of this elite was a self-serving obtuseness about conditions in which the vast majority of their countrymen lived. General Don believed that most of the land was owned by individuals in small plots "on a highly democratic basis,"[65] although his own father had owned 2,700 lush acres of Long Xuyen province where the average farm holding was five acres and 79 percent of all farm families owned no land of their own.[66] Genuinely repulsed at the beating of Buddhist monks, the officers were piqued at least as much by Diem's efforts to establish his personal control over the army. They had no idea what to do with power once they had seized it.

At 1:30 on the afternoon of November 1, 1963, Colonel Thieu's troops surrounded the presidential palace. At 4:30 p.m., while the palace guards held off the attack, Diem called Ambassador Lodge and the following conversation took place:

Diem: Some units have made a rebellion and I want to know what is the attitude of the USA?

Lodge: I do not feel well enough informed to be able to tell you. I have heard the shooting, but am not acquainted with all the facts. Also it is 4:30 a.m. in Washington and the U.S. Government cannot possibly have a view.

Diem: But you must have some general ideas. After all, I am a chief of state. I have tried to do my duty. I want to do now what duty and good sense require. I believe in duty above all.

Lodge: You have certainly done your duty. As I told you only this morning, I admire your courage and your great contributions to your country. No one can take away from you the credit for all you have done. Now I am worried about your physical safety. I have a report that those in charge of the current activity offer you and your brother safe conduct out of the country if you resign. Have you heard this?

Diem: No. (Pause.) You have my telephone number.

Lodge: Yes. If I can do anything for your physical safety, please call me.

Diem: I am trying to reestablish order.[67]

Diem's isolation was now complete. Later that evening he and Nhu escaped from the palace to the Cercle Sportif, a nearby private sports club. Found hiding in a suburban church the next morning, they were bundled into an armored personnel carrier and shot by one of General Minh's aides.[68] The documentary record suggests that neither Kennedy nor his advisers ever considered what might happen to Diem and Nhu if a coup occurred, and news of their murders shocked him. But his administration had done much to encourage the coup and thereby committed itself to support Minh's Military Revolutionary Council. When Minh himself was overthrown three months later by General Nguyen Khanh (who kept the popular Minh as figurehead chief of state), Washington approved because it believed Minh had "neutralist" tendencies and might seek an accommodation with the Communists.[69] Although Minh's "neutralism" appears to have been little more than a casual interest in French President De Gaulle's proposal for compromise and negotiations,[70] the Americans wanted a leader who would take American advice and prosecute the war energetically. In Khanh they believed they had found him.

Was it a mistake for the United States to abandon Diem? It might seem so. Diem's stubborn independence contradicted Communist propaganda that depicted him as a puppet, and whatever his shortcomings no one disputed his integrity, intelligence, and diligence. The junta that replaced Diem provided a less united, less cohesive, less politically astute, less competent regime. Though more amenable than Diem to American direction, the new regime's weaknesses invited American takeover of the combat effort.[71] In hindsight, it was tempting for Americans to view the Diem years as more promising than the ones that followed. But it was not just a coterie of American officials who wanted to be rid of Diem. Diem, his family, and his government had managed to antagonize a wide swath of Vietnamese society that included more than militant monks and their student followers; it also included the Cao Dai and Hoa Hao communities, union leaders, intellectuals, journalists, tenant farmers, landless agricultural laborers, displaced highland minorities, uprooted residents of strategic hamlets . . . even members of Diem's several cabinets. What was the likelihood that Diem could have overcome the alienation he had helped to create? To be sure, the turmoil was not entirely of Diem's making, but this fact merely highlighted the difficulties any leader acceptable to the United States would face trying to govern South Vietnam. Seen in this light, the American mistake in abandoning Diem—considering what was to follow—may have been to discard an excuse to disengage.

The other assassination in 1963, that of President Kennedy on November 22, made no difference in U.S. policy. Confidantes of the president have said that Kennedy privately expressed misgivings about the war and intended to reduce the American commitment to an advisory role after his re-election,[72] a view strongly endorsed by more than one historian.[73] Fredrik Logevall argues that Kennedy's plan was nothing more than a ploy to pressure Diem, silence critics, and counter the impression that the war was an American affair, but Kennedy would have chosen "some form of disengagement" anyway.[74] This is unlikely. Kennedy often expressed frustration over the war's conduct but was persistent in seeking ways to win it. Moreover, once a president has staked his prestige and credibility on a course of action and powerful bureaucracies have developed interests in implementing it, reversing course is a colossal political challenge. And Kennedy did deepen the American commitment. It was Kennedy who sharply increased the number of American advisors (to 16,000 by the time of his assassination); it was Kennedy who authorized covert raids into North Vietnam; and it was Kennedy, dismayed by Diem's recalcitrance and alarmed by his brother's contacts with the enemy, who acceded to Diem's overthrow. Complicitous in the coup and therefore in Diem's death, Kennedy would have found it politically and morally difficult to withdraw support from the generals Lodge had abetted with Kennedy's approval. Kennedy's planned partial withdrawal, moreover, was contingent on reducing the insurgency to a level the ARVN itself could control—a condition the ARVN would never meet. Finally, nothing in the dual assassinations altered the prevailing belief in Washington that Southeast Asia's future as a non-Communist region hinged on South Vietnam's survival as an independent non-Communist state. Among policymakers, advisors and analysts, pessimism about the prospects of winning was abundant; serious advocacy of alternatives to fighting was nearly inaudible. When Lyndon Johnson took over the Kennedy team, the key players remained in place, still believing that Kennedy's commitment had to be kept, even if that meant expanding U.S. military involvement, and they went on planning accordingly. Johnson too believed in the importance of keeping Kennedy's commitment, of maintaining credibility, but even more he dreaded the domestic political consequences for his "Great Society" reforms that might flow from withdrawal *or* open debate on the probable costs of a deeper commitment.[75]

Johnson did not want a wider war any more than Kennedy did, but both presidents calculated that staying in the war was preferable to getting out.

THE COMMUNIST RESPONSE

The turbulence leading up to Diem's fall diverted attention from the countryside. The construction of strategic hamlets stalled, ARVN units avoided combat, and development programs ground to a halt. The reduced pressure, combined with the crescendo of protest in the South, made it easier for the party to find recruits for its armed forces, tear up roads, and collect taxes. The size of the party's Southern branch grew from the "dark days" of 1959, when it had approached extinction, to nearly 70,000 by late 1963.[76] Although Diem's fall deprived the Communists of a propaganda foil and left them briefly uncertain how to respond, the military governments that followed soon proved to be unstable, fractious, inexperienced, and heavily dependent on the United States. Suddenly it was easier for the Communists to chase Saigon's officials out of hamlets, insert party cadres, and enroll youths in the local militia. In Thua Thien the Communists by their own count had party cells in only 16 percent of hamlets as of late 1963, after which the situation "developed very rapidly."[77] In the Mekong delta, popular support surged and the revolution established "overwhelming military dominance."[78] However, party leaders realized that the generals would be more receptive than Diem to an expanded U.S. role in the war, and that the United States, its prestige on the line, would be more likely to prop up the generals than to seek a political solution. In the event of increased American intervention, the Southern revolution would need increased assistance to maintain its momentum.

The Communists thus faced as much challenge as opportunity when the Central Committee convened its ninth plenum in December 1963, a fluid moment in the South and a perilous one in relations with the Soviet Union and China. The Sino-Soviet dispute had broken into the open, partly over issues that now also divided the Lao Dong Party. If Hanoi placated Moscow by not provoking the United States, it risked displeasing Beijing for aligning with the Soviet Union. And if it increased support for the Southern revolution, heightening chances of U.S. retaliation, it would align its practice with China's rhetoric but alienate the Soviet Union. Vietnamese leaders preferred to stay on good terms with both allies, but with the Southern revolution and reunification at stake a choice had to be made. LDP First Secretary Le Duan made that choice in a keynote speech to the plenum unveiling a decision to increase the North's support to the South.[79]

The move tested the party's unity all over again. Despite the party's decision in 1959 to extend limited support to the Southern revolution, a strong

faction of risk-avoiders had warned ever since against tipping the North further into action that might endanger its development or alienate the Soviet
Union. Debate centered on the regional division of responsibility and the
type of struggle to be waged. In a speech to the Third National Congress of
the party in September 1960, Truong Chinh, a former party general secretary, had emphasized the party's duty "to unite the entire people to strictly
implement the Geneva Agreements," implying that the Southern revolution
too should "uphold peace and achieve national reunification on the basis
of independence and democracy."[80] General Vo Nguyen Giap, minister of
defense, had echoed Chinh and had called for cautious flexibility in dealing
with American plots that "a number of our comrades are not fully aware
of."[81] In contrast, Le Duan had steadfastly argued that national reunification was "not only a task of the Southern people, but also of the entire
people, of the South as well as of the North."[82] In this he had the support of
other leaders who were more confident than Giap of the North's ability to
wage conventional war in the South and in position to make appointments
and promotions in both the party and army.[83] Wrapping his argument in
the unassailable themes of patriotism and the inevitability of victory for a
just cause, Le Duan gradually had gained the upper hand.

In a secret resolution,[84] the ninth plenum adopted a long-range contingency plan for the probabilities of a long war and greater Northern involvement in it. The resolution noted that the symbolic defeat of the "special
war" at Ap Bac left the United States facing a stark choice between further
ARVN defeats or introducing its own ground combat troops. The latter step
would transform the conflict into a "limited war." The Saigon government,
the plenum surmised, might then develop into a neocolonial dependency
able to withstand the pressure of the largely indigenous Southern revolution. This was unacceptable not only because of the obstacle it could pose
to reunification but also because of the threat it would pose to the security
of the North.

Therefore it was necessary, the resolution concluded, to prepare for a
protracted people's war similar to the resistance against France, at least to
begin. Guerrilla warfare was to be the principal mode of attack to start but
main forces were to be built up too for the purpose of "annihilating" regular ARVN units. The strategic key was the "coordinated struggle" of armed
and political movements in the three "strategic zones" of the mountains,
lowlands, and cities. Main forces in mountain bases were to reinforce the
mixed political-armed struggle of the lowlands, from which support could
be extended to a largely political struggle in the cities. All of these struggles
in combination were to divide, distract, deplete, and tie down the materially
superior, more numerous enemy. At a suitable moment, a "general offensive
and uprising" of the urban population coordinated with armed attack by
troops coming from the countryside would "overthrow the enemy's central

government." A separate section of the resolution entitled "The Mission of North Viet-Nam" argued that the North would have to "bring into fuller play its role as the revolutionary base for the whole nation," with scale and timing dependent on U.S. action.[85]

The ninth plenum, Le Duan frankly admitted, was the scene of heated debate. Disunity, he said, had been caused by members who were "influenced by modern revisionism" or "held rightist views."[86] "Revisionism" was code for individuals who feared that open warfare in the South would contradict the Soviet Union's line on peaceful coexistence and placed their faith in a diplomatic solution, as the Soviets preferred. "Rightists" were party members who recoiled from the prospect of provoking American retaliation against the North and questioned the PAVN's ability to defeat U.S. forces. Both revisionists and rightists, said Duan, were wrong. Lieutenant General Tran Van Tra added that the Southern people would bear the greatest hardships in what was, after all, a defense of the entire nation.[87] The North therefore had a moral and practical reason to support the Southern revolution. Another old Southern resistance commander, Major General To Ky, castigated "some people" who exaggerated U.S. tactical power and underestimated U.S. strategic vulnerability.[88] Southerners like Duan and Tra and Northerners like Le Duc Tho who had fought the French in the South were in the forefront, though hardly alone, in calling for war and alignment with China's vociferous anti-U.S. posture.

The ripples of dissent continued to widen as the full implications of the ninth plenum resolution became apparent, prompting the Political Bureau in January 1964 to organize "study and political reorientation" at all levels of the party.[89] "Study" of the resolution was needed because "a few cadres vacillated in the face of the difficulties and complexities of the international workers' and Communist movement, were skeptical of the party's line, propagated points of view that were contrary to that line, and ignored or violated organizational discipline."[90]

Those who "vacillated" were more than a few, and they included some high ranking members of the party. Hoang Minh Chinh, the head of the party school for higher-level cadres, had written a report for the plenum favoring peaceful coexistence, earning him a "revisionist" label. A number of other figures who disagreed too openly with policy or happened to be Moscow-trained landed in prison.[91] Several members of the Central Committee, including ones with ministerial positions in government, lost their posts. Even General Giap fell under suspicion and found himself powerless to protect those who worked under him.[92] DRV students attending Soviet-bloc universities were ordered home for "study" (some refused), and Soviet-bloc diplomats faced new restrictions on their movements and contacts.[93] But debate surged again when the United States began to pour in troops and bomb the North, strengthening the conviction of hard-liners that diplomacy was pointless while confirming the fears of those Duan labeled "rightists" that war would bring destruction upon the DRV.

The military for its part was divided over how to carry out its mission. The PAVN had been engaged since 1958 in a far-reaching program of modernization and reorganization that was intended to strengthen its ability to defend the North by conventional means. Formal ranks and insignia had been handed out, new technical branches had been created, and a draft had been instituted. The training curriculum now included material on modern weapons and tactics, which younger officers interpreted as suggesting that the earlier doctrine of "people's war" was obsolete. Those officers who were loath to pit the semi-modernized PAVN against the United States also opposed reverting to "people's war" in the South. For such officers the Soviet Union was an attractive ally because it could supply modern weapons, equipment, and training that China could not. At least three officers, including a senior colonel named Le Vinh Quoc, reportedly could not reconcile themselves to the doctrinal reversal and requested transfer to the Soviet Union; there Quoc joined the Red Army and attained the rank of major general.[94] Voices of dissent fell silent, though, when Ho Chi Minh, at a special political conference held on March 27–28, 1964, called for unity and commanded the army to prepare for combat.[95]

Ho must have known what was in store. The North had begun strengthening its air defenses in January and preparing for the evacuation of major cities and industrial sites. Since February the CIA had upgraded an earlier program of sporadic commando raids, sabotage, and psychological warfare against the North into one of sustained harassment (the upgraded program was code-named OPLAN-34a). Diplomatic moves had come to naught. In April, Northern-born PAVN regulars, not just Southern regroupees, began special training for the march south.[96] In May, the Political Bureau ordered that the western sub-region of Military Region 5 be converted into a separate "Tay Nguyen Front" (or "B3"; see Map 4.1), a future staging area for main force operations under the direct command of party and military organs in Hanoi.[97] About this time also, the Political Bureau member charged with overseeing the enhanced effort, Nguyen Chi Thanh, reported that war with the United States was unavoidable but that, with the North's support, it could be won. Hanoi thus primed itself for the next U.S. move.

Three separate events that seemed related to leaders in Hanoi must have vindicated those who believed that war with the United States was unavoidable. On August 1 and 2, 1964, U.S.-supplied Laotian T-33 training jets bombed two villages in the North's Nghe An province. About the same time, vessels belonging to the U.S. Navy that had been transferred to the South Vietnamese Navy shelled the islands of Hon Me and Hon Ngu in the Tonkin Gulf. On August 2, a U.S. destroyer, the *Maddox*, exchanged fire with North Vietnamese torpedo boats while gathering intelligence eight nautical miles off the North's coastline (and four nautical miles from its offshore islands). And finally, on August 4, on an extremely dark night and in bad weather, the *Maddox* accompanied by the destroyer *C. Turner Joy* fired on radar objects their commanders believed were attacking them. The captain of the *Maddox* quickly developed doubts that the objects were attack craft, as the evidence of an attack was contradictory. In fact, as a meticulous study by Edwin Moise has shown, the second attack on the *Maddox* never took place.[98] Nonetheless, President Johnson seized on what he probably did believe at the time was a real attack[99] to justify retaliatory airstrikes against the North and to extract special war powers from Congress. Passed with only two dissenting votes,[100] the Tonkin Gulf Resolution authorized Johnson to take "all necessary measures to repel any armed attacks against the forces of the United States and to prevent further aggression." It also authorized him to provide military assistance to any member of the Southeast Asia Treaty Organization (SEATO). Broad in language, the resolution basically ceded to the president the authority to wage an undeclared war. With his approval rating in opinion polls jumping from 42 percent to 72 percent, Johnson claimed to have the support of the American people as well. Facing an election with the foreign policy hard-liner Barry Goldwater, Johnson could let one "incident" pass, but not two.

Unrelated to the resolution but occurring directly after it, Hanoi dispatched the first whole unit of Northern-born regulars to the South. Rather than dispersing among PLAF units as the regroupees had done, this unit stayed together as the independent 808th Battalion, departing the North in August 1964 and entering the South in November, according to American intelligence. The PAVN 95th Regiment departed the North in October and entered the South in December. Three more regiments were detected entering the South between then and May 1965, bringing the number of Northern-born regulars in the South to perhaps 6,500.[101] The PAVN's official history, while vague about the dates of departure, records that "a number of full-strength battalions and regiments" accounted for many of the 9,000 cadres and soldiers who "marched down our commo-liaison route to fight in the South" during 1964.[102] According to a PAVN order of battle published in 1995, the PAVN 95th Regiment left the North's Quang Binh province on November 20, 1964, the first of three regiments of the 325th Division to remain as whole units after arriving in the South. On taking position in the Tay Nguyen highlands, these regiments were designated the 95B, 101B, and 18B.[103]

The party's proponents of reunification by force quite possibly had grown impatient waiting for the United States to make the first move. The PLAF had been overrunning an average of one district capital each week. Of the South's forty-three provinces, the Communists were reckoned to have "significant control" in twenty-two and to "operate widely in all the others," including the eight circling Saigon.[104] COSVN's instructions since shortly after Diem's overthrow had been to destroy the strategic hamlet program, support urban elements demanding democracy, proselytize among disillusioned ARVN officers, and stir up ethnic minority unrest in the highlands. It was making headway on all fronts.[105] But this had not been quite enough to unravel the government in Saigon. Having reached a plateau of military development and lacking a strong organization in the cities, the revolution, according to COSVN's military committee, had been unable during 1964 to "exploit thoroughly the opportunity to create a new situation."[106] Surveying these developments, COSVN nonetheless saw brightening prospects. The "traitor" Khrushchev had been dismissed on October 14, 1964, raising hopes of settling the divisive issue of revisionism. Only two days later China had tested an atomic bomb. And after eight coups it was clear that Diem's overthrow, far from stabilizing the political situation in Saigon, had only made it more "tangled and confused."[107] Still, victory lay just beyond reach. More support from the North would be needed, especially if the United States continued to increase its own involvement.

In February 1965, American aircraft struck the North in reprisal for PLAF attacks on U.S. installations at Pleiku and Qui Nhon, in accordance with plans Johnson had approved two months earlier. In March "reprisal airstrikes" were upgraded to a program of sustained air war known as Operation Rolling Thunder. The arrival that month of two U.S. Marine battalions to protect the airfield at Danang raised the U.S. force level to 27,000. Further arrivals in April and May brought the level to 46,000 and in June to 74,000. U.S. armed forces were ready to fight, and the "limited war" long anticipated by the Communists was about to begin. Believing that the balance of forces in the South was shifting in their favor, the Central Committee authorized an increase in the North's contribution to the South. As this would require expansion of the Ho Chi Minh Trail, increasing support for the revolution in Laos became an "urgent task" as well.[108]

NOTES

1. Joseph G. Morgan, *The Vietnam Lobby: The American Friends of Vietnam, 1955–1975* (Chapel Hill: University of North Carolina Press, 1997), 8.

2. John F. Kennedy, "America's Stake in Vietnam," *Vital Speeches* 22 (August 1, 1956): 618.

3. See David F. Schmitz, *Thank God They're on Our Side: the United States and Right-Wing Dictatorships, 1921–1965* (Chapel Hill: University of North Carolina Press).

4. Nikita Khrushchev's speech delivered on January 6, 1961, appeared in *Pravda* on January 24. For the CIA's summary and analysis of this speech, see Department of State, *Foreign Relations of the United States, 1961–1963*, Vol. 5, *Soviet Union*, document 15 (Washington, D.C., Government Printing Office, 1998).

5. Quoted in Murray Marder, "Our Longest War's Tortuous History," *Washington Post*, January 28, 1973, F2.

6. Howard Jones explores Kennedy's preferences in *Death of a Generation: How the Assassinations of Diem and JFK Prolonged the Vietnam War* (Oxford: Oxford University Press, 2003).

7. Timothy N. Castle, *At War in the Shadow of Vietnam: U.S. Military Aid to the Royal Lao Government, 1955–1975* (New York: Columbia University Press, 1993), 30.

8. Castle, *At War*, 30–40.

9. MacAlister Brown and Joseph J. Zasloff, *Apprentice Revolutionaries: The Communist Movement in Laos, 1930–1985* (Stanford, Calif.: Hoover Institution Press, 1986), 79–80.

10. Brown and Zasloff, *Apprentice Revolutionaries*, 52–53.

11. The Soviet Union, never as committed to supporting the Pathet Lao as the U.S. was to stopping them, terminated its assistance to the Pathet Lao within a year of signing the accords.

12. This reassurance was given outside the SEATO framework in the Rusk-Thanat communiqué of March 6, 1962, which pledged the United States to the defense of Thailand.

13. Jones, *Death of a Generation*, 39–40.

14. Paul M. Kattenburg, *The Vietnam Trauma in American Foreign Policy, 1945–1975* (New Brunswick, N.J.: Transaction, 1980), 108–109.

15. Frederick Nolting, *From Trust to Tragedy: The Political Memoirs of Frederick Nolting, Kennedy's Ambassador to Diem's Vietnam* (New York: Praeger, 1988), 33, 39, 53.

16. William A. Buckingham Jr., *Operation Ranch Hand: The Air Force and Herbicides in Southeast Asia, 1961–1971* (Washington, D.C.: Office of Air Force History, U.S. Air Force, 1982) is an official but scrupulous account.

17. James C. Thompson, "How Could Vietnam Happen? An Autopsy," *Atlantic Monthly* (April 1968).

18. Department of Defense, *United States-Vietnam Relations*, book 2, Table I, LV.A.5 (Washington, D.C.: Government Printing Office, 1971), 25.

19. "Bao cao: tinh hinh mien Nam tu cuoi nam 1961 den dau nam 1964" [Circular on the Situation in South Vietnam from Late 1961 to Early 1964]. In author's possession.

20. War Experiences Recapitulation Committee of the High-Level Military Institute, *The Anti U.S. Resistance War for National Salvation 1954–1975: Military Events*, trans. the Joint Publications Research Service, JPRS no. 80,968 (Washington, D.C.: Government Printing Office, June 3, 1982), 52.

21. Information according to a former PAVN officer who had been attached to the Military Region 5 command staff, interviewed by the author in 1973.

22. Dan Hong, "An Outline History of the Ho Chi Minh Trail," *The Ho Chi Minh Trail* (Hanoi: Foreign Languages Publishing House, 1982), 10.

23. J.J. Zasloff, *Origins of the Insurgency in South Vietnam 1954–1960: The Role of the Southern Vietminh Cadres* (Santa Monica, Calif.: Rand Corporation, RM-5163/2, May 1968).

24. Military History Institute of Vietnam, *Victory in Vietnam: The Official History of the People's Army of Vietnam, 1954–1975*, trans. Merle L. Pribbenow (Lawrence: University of Kansas Press, 2002), 115.

25. War Experiences Recapitulation Committee, *The Anti-U.S. Resistance War*, 32.

26. Christopher E. Goscha, "The Maritime Nature of the Wars for Vietnam (1945–1975)," *Viet Nam Journal* (April 2003). www.vietnamjournal.org/article .php?sid=123&PHPSESSID=447f33e56a6a7ca13f597e6943346e9a (accessed May 10, 2007).

27. Hong, "An Outline History," 14.

28. Hong, "An Outline History," 16.

29. Nguyen Viet Phuong, "Ho doi Truong son va he thong duong Ho Chi Minh" [Truong Son Troops and the Ho Chi Minh Trail System], *Nghien cuu Lich su* [History Research] (March–April 1979): 24.

30. Combined Intelligence Center Vietnam, "North Vietnam Personnel Infiltration into the Republic of Vietnam," Study ST70-05, U.S. Military Assistance Command Vietnam, J-2 (Saigon, December 16, 1970), 24–30.

31. Quan doi nhan dan, *Tong ket cong tac hau can chien truong Nam bo-cuc Nam Trung bo (B.2) trong khang chien chong My* [Review of Logistical Work in the B2 Theater in the Anti-U.S. Resistance War] (Hanoi: Tong cuc hau can, 1986), 35. This volume is stamped "Secret: internal army distribution."

32. Andrew F. Krepinevich Jr., *The Army and Vietnam* (Baltimore: Johns Hopkins University Press, 1986), 36.

33. Tran Ngoc Chau with Tom Sturdevant, "My War Story: From Ho Chi Minh to Ngo Dinh Diem," in *Prelude to Tragedy: Vietnam, 1960–1965*, ed. Harvey Neese and John O'Donnell (Annapolis, Md.: Naval Institute Press, 2001), 187–188.

34. Lam Quang Thi, *The Twenty-Five Year Century: A South Vietnamese General Remembers the Indochina War to the Fall of Saigon* (Denton: University of North Texas Press, 2001), 170. Thi adds, however, that relations between ARVN unit commanders and U.S. counterparts in the field were generally positive. See Ronald H. Spector, *After Tet: The Bloodiest Year in Vietnam* (New York: The Free Press, 1993), 112–116, for a summary of American views.

35. Tran Van Don, *Our Endless War* (San Rafael, Calif.: Presidio Press, 1978), 150. Emphasis is in the original.

36. Stan B-H Tan, "Dust Beneath the Mist": State and Frontier Formation in the Central Highlands of Vietnam, the 1955–61 Period" (PhD diss., Canberra, The Australian National University, 2006).

37. Philip E. Catton, *Diem's Final Failure: Prelude to America's War in Vietnam* (Lawrence: University Press of Kansas, 2002), 117–140.

38. On Thompson's advice and Vietnamese response to it, see Catton, *Diem's Final Failure*, 96–97.

39. See Milton E. Osborne, *Strategic Hamlets in Viet Nam* (Ithaca, N.Y.: Cornell University Southeast Asia Program Data Paper no. 55, April 1965), 32–35.

40. "Nghi quyet cua Trung uong cuc mien Nam, thang 7 nam 1963" [COSVN Resolution, July 1963], Dang Cong San Viet Nam, *Van kien Dang toan tap* [Complete Party Documents (hereafter cited as VKDTT)], vol. 24, 1963 (Hanoi: NXB Chinh tri quoc gia, 2003), 866–867, 870–871.

41. Interview with the author, Hanoi, March 30, 1983.

42. Jeffrey Race, *War Comes to Long An* (Berkeley: University of California Press, 1972), 133.

43. Ban tong ket chien tranh chien truong Tri-Thien-Hue, *Chien truong Tri-Thien-Hue trong cuoc khang chien chong My cuu nuoc toan thang* [The Tri-Thien-Hue Theater in the Anti-U.S. National Salvation Struggle] (Hue: NXB Thuan Hoa, 1985), 75.

44. Race, *War Comes to Long An*, 133.

45. Jeffrey J. Clarke, *Advice and Support: The Final Years, 1965–1973* (Washington, D.C.: Center for Military History, 1988), 15.

46. "Nghi quyet cua Trung uong cuc mien Nam, thang 7 nam 1963" [COSVN Resolution, July 1963] VKDTT, vol. 24, 1963 (2003) 868–869.

47. Lam Quang Huyen, *Cach mang ruong dat o mien Nam Viet Nam* [The Land Revolution in South Vietnam] (Hanoi: NXB Ban khoa hoc xa hoi, 1985), 148.

48. "Kinh nghiem chong fa ap chien luoc cua dong bao xa H (Khu II)" [Experiences struggling against the strategic hamlet of compatriots in village H (zone II)], ca. October/November 1962, Pike document VCD-35.

49. "COSVN Standing Committee Directive Discussing the Tasks for the Last Six Months of 1963." September 1963. Douglas Pike Collection, Texas Tech University Virtual Vietnam Archive, no. 2320109003.

50. Mark Moyar, *Triumph Forsaken: The Vietnam War, 1954–1965* (New York: Cambridge University Press, 2006), 186–205, pins much of the blame for this battle's outcome on the principal American adviser, John Paul Vann. Whether that argument has merit or not, it ignores the fact that the PLAF demonstrated an unexpected ability to upgrade its weaponry and tactics in ways that nullified improvements in the American-trained and equipped ARVN.

51. There are a dozen variants of this quote in as many sources. This one is found in Roger Hilsman, *To Move a Nation: the Politics and Foreign Policy of the Administration of John F. Kennedy* (New York: Doubleday, 1967), 501.

52. Marianna Sullivan, *France's Vietnam Policy: A Study in French-American Relations* (Westport, Conn.: Greenwood, 1978), 67–69.

53. Thich Nhat Hanh, *Vietnam: Lotus in a Sea of Fire* (New York: Hill and Wang, 1967), 45.

54. Moyar, *Triumph Forsaken*, 217–218.

55. Don, *Our Endless War*, 72.

56. Don, *Our Endless War*, 91.

57. On Diem's contacts with Hanoi, see Ellen Hammer, *A Death in November: America in Vietnam, 1963* (New York: E.P. Dutton, 1987), 223–224; Mieczyslaw Maneli, *War of the Vanquished*, trans. Maria de Gorgey (New York: Harper & Row, 1971), 112–152; and Truong Vinh-Le, *Vietnam, où est la vérité* (Paris: Lavauzelle, 1989), 91, 316–317. Diem's contact was Mieczyslaw Maneli, head of the Polish delegation to the International Control Commission. French Ambassador Roger Lalouette carried Diem's messages to Maneli.

58. Nolting, *From Trust to Tragedy*, 118.

59. *State-Saigon Cable 243*, August 24, 1963, National Security Archive, George Washington University, www.gwu.edu/~nsarchiv/NSAEBB/NSAEBB101/index.htm (accessed March 5, 2007). See discussion by John Prados at www.gwu.edu/~nsarchiv/NSAEBB/NSAEBB101/index.htm#doc2.

60. Don, *Our Endless War*, 98.

61. *The Pentagon Papers*, Senator Mike Gravel edition (Boston: Beacon, 1971), vol. 2, 738–739.

62. *State-Saigon Cable 272*, August 29, 1963, www.gwu.edu/~nsarchiv/NSAEBB/NSAEBB101/index.htm (accessed March 5, 2007).

63. Roger Hilsman, a Kennedy aide, cited in George C. Herring, *America's Longest War: The United States and Vietnam, 1950–1975* (New York: John Wiley, 1979), 104.

64. Michael Maclear, *The Ten Thousand Day War* (London: Thames Methuen, 1981), 81.

65. Don, *Our Endless War*, 25.

66. Race, *War Comes to Long An*, 58–60.

67. *The Pentagon Papers*, 268.

68. The assassinations were carried out on orders from Minh, according to Don, *Our Endless War*, 112. Also see Jones, *Death of a Generation*, 435.

69. *The Pentagon Papers*, 304–305.

70. Don, *Our Endless War*, 134–135.

71. For an analysis of the RVN as a "recalcitrant ally" no matter who its leaders were, see Lawrence E. Grinter, "Bargaining between Saigon and Washington: Dilemmas of Linkage Politics During War," *Orbis* 17, no. 3 (Fall 1974): 837–867.

72. A notable exception is Kennedy's secretary of state, Dean Rusk (as told to Richard Rusk), *As I Saw It*, ed. Daniel S. Papp (New York: Norton, 1990), 441–442.

73. Howard Jones, *Death of a Generation*, 377–406, 452–456. Also see John Newman, *JKF and Vietnam: Deception, Intrigue, and the Struggle for Power* (New York: Warner, 1992); David Kaiser, *American Tragedy* (Cambridge, Mass.: Harvard University Press, 2000); and Neese and O'Donnell, *Prelude to Tragedy*.

74. Fredrik Logevall, *Choosing War: The Lost Chance for Peace and the Escalation of War in Vietnam* (Berkeley: University of California Press, 1999), 69–73, 395.

75. Francis M. Bator, "No Good Choices: LBJ and the Vietnam/Great Society Connection," an Occasional Paper of the American Academy of Arts and Sciences, Cambridge, Mass. (2007). Bator was Johnson's deputy national security adviser.

76. "Bao cao: tinh hinh mien Nam tu cuoi nam 1961 den dau nam 1964."

77. Ban tong ket . . . , *Chien truong Tri-Thien-Hue*, 75n1.

78. David W.P. Elliott, *The Vietnamese War: Revolution and Social Change in the Mekong Delta 1930–1975*, vol. 1 (Armonk, N.Y.: Sharpe, 2003), 617–619.

79. "Mot vai van de trong nhiem vu quoc te chu Dang ta" [Problems Concerning Our Party's International Tasks], *Lich su Dang Cong san Viet Nam, Trich van kien Dang* [History of the Vietnam Communist Party: Excerpts from Party Documents] (Hanoi: Marx-Lenin Textbook Publishing House, 1979), vol. 3, 265–313.

80. Truong Chinh, "The Party's Ideological Work," in *Third National Congress of the Viet Nam Workers' Party: Documents, vol. III* (Hanoi: Foreign Languages Publishing House, 1960), 10–11.

81. Vo Nguyen Giap, "Strengthening National Defence and Building up the People's Armed Forces," *Third National Congress, vol. II*, 54. In the same speech, Giap argued that if the United States attacked the North, "our compatriots in the South would certainly rise up as a single man to stop them. . . . However, this is no reason why we should underestimate the enemy, and disregard their plots."

82. Le Duan, "Leninism and Vietnam's Revolution," in *On Socialist Revolution in Vietnam*, vol. 1 (Hanoi: Foreign Languages Publishing House, 1965), 48.

83. Bui Tin, *Following Ho Chi Minh: The Memoirs of a North Vietnamese Colonel*, trans. Judy Stowe and Do Van (Honolulu: University of Hawaii Press, 1995), 46.

84. A copy of this resolution, captured in the South, is translated in *Viet-Nam Documents and Research Notes,* no. 96 (Saigon: U.S. Mission, July 1971). The Vietnamese text was published after the war in *Mot so van kien cua Dang ve chong My, cuu nuoc, Tap I (1954–1965)* [Some Party Documents on the Anti-U.S. National Salvation Resistance, Vol. I] (Hanoi: NXB Su That, 1985), 159–210.

85. *Viet-Nam Documents and Research Notes,* no. 96.

86. Talk by Le Duan at the ninth plenum, *Hoc Tap* [Study and Practice] (February 1964), translated in *Viet-Nam Documents and Research Notes,* no. 96.

87. Tran Van Tra, speech commemorating the third anniversary of the NLF, *Quan doi nhan dan* [People's Army], December 19, 1963, 1.

88. *Quan doi nhan dan,* December 21, 1963, 4.

89. "Chi thi cua Bo chinh tri So 74-CT/TW, ngay 27 thang 1 nam 1964 [Political Bureau Directive no. 74-CT/TW, January 27, 1964], VKDTT, vol. 25, 1964 (2003), 42–49.

90. Ban tu tuong-van hoa trung uong, *So thao luoc su cong tac tu tuong cua Dang cong san Viet Nam, 1930–2000 (du thao)* [Draft Outline History of the Ideological Work of the Vietnam Communist Party, 1930–2000] (Hanoi: NXB Chinh tri quoc gia, 2000), 243.

91. Lien-Hang T. Nguyen, "The War Politburo: North Vietnam's Diplomatic and Political Road to the Tet Offensive," *Journal of Vietnamese Studies* 1, no. 1–2 (February/August 2006): 17.

92. Bui Tin, *Following Ho,* 54–55.

93. For discussion of this affair based on dispatches from East Germany's embassy in Hanoi, see Martin Grossheim, "'Revisionism' in the Democratic Republic of Vietnam: New Evidence from the East German Archives," *Cold War History* 5, No. 4 (November 2005): 451–477.

94. Lu Tuan (pseud.), *Mien Bac Ngay Nay* [The North Today], unpublished ms. in author's possession, ca. 1972. Quoc was the political officer for Military Region 3 and sought "political asylum in the Soviet Union," according to Bui Tin, *Following Ho,* 54.

95. "Bao cao tai Hoi nghi chinh tri dac biet" [Statement to the Special Political Conference], *Lich su Dang Cong san Viet-Nam,* vol. 3, 214–231.

96. The month can be inferred from Ho's March speech and the publication of articles on a new training method in the army newspaper *Quan doi nhan dan* in May. The articles included, on May 26 and 28, 1964, a translation from Chinese of "Kuo Hsing-fu's Training Method" extolling political motivation as a means to overcome fear of sophisticated weaponry and minimize reliance on foreign assistance.

97. War Experiences Recapitulation Committee, *The Anti-U.S. Resistance,* 62; and Vien lich su quan su Viet Nam, *50 nam Quan doi nhan dan Viet Nam* [Fifty Years of the People's Army of Viet Nam] (Hanoi: NXB Quan doi nhan dan, 1995), 195.

98. Edwin E. Moise, *Tonkin Gulf and the Escalation of the Vietnam War* (Chapel Hill: The University of North Carolina Press, 1996). According to Hanoi's official account, two PAVN Naval Command torpedo boats and a "command vessel" attacked the Maddox on August 2, and Vietnamese naval, antiaircraft and local popular forces thwarted operation "Pierce Arrow" (retaliatory strikes against petroleum storage facilities and torpedo bases) on August 5. But nothing took place on August 4 other than American naval maneuvers that the Johnson administration misinter-

preted to provide a pretext to bomb the North. Vien lich su quan su Viet Nam, *50 nam Quan doi nhan dan Viet Nam* [50 years of the People's Army of Vietnam] (Hanoi: NXB Quan doi nhan dan, 1995), 196; Giap Van Cuong et al., *Lich su Hai quan nhan dan Viet Nam* [History of the People's Navy] (Hanoi: NXB Quan doi nhan dan, 1985), 91–100; and Thuong vu Dang uy va bo tu lenh quan khu 3, *Quan khu 3 lich su khang chien chong My cuu nuoc (1954–1975)* [Military Region 3 in the Anti-U.S. National Salvation Resistance] (Hanoi: NXB Quan doi nhan dan, 1995), 87–89.

99. Moise, *Tonkin Gulf*, 210.

100. These were cast by senators Wayne Morris of Oregon and Ernest Gruening of Alaska. Senators and representatives cast their votes without detailed information about the incidents or the covert operations, which the Johnson administration withheld.

101. Combined Intelligence Center Vietnam, U.S. Military Assistance Command J-2, "Update: The NVA Soldier in South Vietnam," Research and Analysis Study ST76-013 (Saigon, October 18, 1966), 2.

102. Military History Institute of Vietnam, *Victory in Vietnam*, 127.

103. Vien lich su, *50 nam*, 199. Also Pham Gia Duc, *Su Doan 325 1954–1975* (Division 325, 1954–1975), vol. II (Hanoi: NXB Ban Quan doi Nhan dan, 1986).

104. "Toward the Showdown?" *Time* (August 7, 1964).

105. "Nghi quyet hoi nghi TWC lan thu hai, So 2/NQ, thang 3 nam 1964" [Resolution of the Second COSVN Conference, no. 2/NQ, March 1964], VKDTT, vol. 25, 1964 (2003), 693–771.

106. "Nghi quyet quan uy mien Nam 1-1965" [Resolution of the Party Military Committee, Southern Region, January 1965]. In author's possession.

107. "Nghi quyet hoi nghi Trung uong cuc lan thu ba, So 2/NQ, thang 1 nam 1965 [Resolution of the COSVN third conference, no. 2/NQ, January 1965], VKDTT, vol. 26, 1965 (2003), 669–670, 676.

108. "Nghi quyet: Hoi nghi lan thu 11 (dac biet) cua ban chap hanh trung uong Dang (khoa III) [Resolution of the 11th (Special) Meeting of the Third Party Central Committee], *Mot so van kien cua Dang ve chong My, cuu nuoc, Tap I (1954–1965)*, 216, 218.

4

Americanization

"America seemed omnipotent then," Philip Caputo, a former U.S. marine, wrote of 1965. "The country could still claim it had never lost a war, and we believed we were ordained to play cop to the Communists' robber. . . . We saw ourselves as the champions of a cause that was destined to triumph."[1] Such were the convictions of just about every American involved in the war, from President Johnson down to the lowliest grunt. Many believed that the Communist revolution in Vietnam would dissolve before the mere display of U.S. power. If it did not, most Americans were confident that the United States could crush the revolution with overwhelming armed might. Two world wars and the Korean War had proved that no country on the planet could match America's capacity to apply high volumes of firepower and sophisticated technology to battle. How could the United States not prevail again?

Although the American conceit ignored how Indochina's Communists might respond, it was not entirely fanciful. When a unit of U.S. combat marines landed near Qui Nhon, Vietnam, in June 1965, the squad of local guerrillas that had been sent out to observe them, unbeknownst to the marines, turned and ran. Every revolutionary from the lowliest guerrilla to the party first secretary knew that victory could not come by pushing U.S. soldiers into the sea. Nor could it come just by surviving the onslaught. The United States had to be made to withdraw of its own accord. This, the Communists knew, could only be done by thwarting the U.S. expectation of success, forcing Washington to admit the bankruptcy of each option in a dwindling set, until only withdrawal remained.

In the beginning, however, U.S. intervention rescued Saigon from a desperate situation. Just as the Communists' decision in 1959 to send "regroupees" and arms to South Vietnam rescued the Southern revolution from its "darkest days," so did the U.S. intervention almost certainly save the Army of the Republic of Vietnam (ARVN) from collapse. That intervention also transformed the terminal stages of a revolutionary and civil conflict that had grown out of colonialism's unfinished business into a multi-layered international war. The conflict between the Saigon government and Communists plus sympathizers inside the South was civil. So were the conflicts between local Communists and the governments of Laos and Cambodia. The conflict between the Saigon and Hanoi governments was also civil if one held, as both governments did, that the seventeenth parallel was a temporary dividing line between two zones of a single country; it was an international conflict if, as successive American administrations argued, the line had become in reality a boundary between two states. American attacks on the North and on the operations of its People's Army of Vietnam (PAVN) in Laos and Cambodia were acts of interstate warfare, while Soviet and Chinese support of the North and American support of the South added the dimension of a proxy conflict. The essence of this war in all its complexity defied capture in a simple expression or single sentence.

GOING IT (ALMOST) ALONE

Key allies resisted American pressure to join the fight. French President Charles De Gaulle maintained on the basis of France's experience that the issues were essentially civil and no amount of foreign military intervention would settle them. De Gaulle was determined in any case to carve out an independent role for France and to curry favor in the Third World, where U.S. interventionism was unpopular.[2] Britain gave a little help with intelligence, training, and advice in the early 1960s and then reduced its support to rhetoric and diplomacy, in keeping with its reduced global role. The British shared French skepticism about a military solution, and Prime Minister Harold Wilson faced strong opposition to U.S. policy in Vietnam from the left wing of his own Labour Party.[3] Wilson flatly refused Johnson's request to send a military contingent, however small. Europeans generally thought that the United States was preoccupied with Asia at the expense of Western security and doubted that a stable government would ever emerge in Saigon. Japan was prohibited by its constitution from sending troops and allowed the United States to use bases in Japan as staging areas only because the U.S.–Japan security treaty required it to do so. Tokyo tepidly endorsed American actions, hoping to soften trade frictions with the United States and regain control over Okinawa. Many Japanese recalled how their own soldiers had become bogged down in China during World War II and feared the security treaty would drag them into the conflict if the U.S. effort faltered.[4] In all of these cases, domestic public opinion ran against U.S. actions, limiting the support governments could give, had they wished to give it.

To avoid the appearance of acting unilaterally, the Johnson administration asked friends and allies in the region for military aid and combat troops. Only Australia and New Zealand responded voluntarily, though not with equal enthusiasm. Desperate to show "many flags" in South Vietnam, the administration offered in December 1964 to pay all the costs of any combat unit a country would dispatch to the war. None immediately accepted, although South Korea, the Philippines, and Thailand did eventually accept what one study calls a "bribe" of additional aid to send troops.[5] In all of these countries the decision to participate was unpopular, and in the Philippines it was deeply, lastingly divisive. Just five nations sent military forces to fight alongside the United States, and the modest contributions of non-military aid by more than thirty other countries to "Free World Assistance" did little to change the impression that this was an American war. None of this help came as a result of effort by the Saigon government, which lacked the material and diplomatic resources to extract help from its neighbors. To be sure, anti-Communist leaders in the region feared that leftist sentiment would spread in their own countries if the United States failed in Vietnam, but the political weakness that made them fear the left also made them reluctant to give overt material support without strong inducement from the United States.

HANOI'S ALLIES

The administration also had to consider the possible reactions of the Soviet Union and China. The Soviet Union was constrained by geography and its wish to avoid major conflict, but both Communist powers, and particularly Vietnam's neighbor China, opposed an extension of American power in Asia. Would Moscow and Beijing increase the supply of weapons to Hanoi, and would they allow these weapons to be used in the South? If the war grew in scope and intensity, at what point would Beijing send its own troops into combat, as it had done in Korea? One thing was certain: Sino-Soviet rivalry for leadership of the world Communist movement would give both Moscow and Beijing reason to support Hanoi's war aims. Washington would not soon get help finding a diplomatic solution in the two Communist capitals. Moreover, the Sino-Soviet rivalry would cause Moscow and Beijing to increase support to Hanoi if the latter came under attack. Less clear was how much and what forms of pressure the United States could apply without provoking Chinese intervention or Soviet troublemaking in other parts of the world. Advised that China might intervene if the United States endangered the existence of the government in Hanoi,[6] Johnson granted the military's request for a major buildup in the South but authorized only "graduated" steps to apply pressure on the North. As Secretary of State Dean Rusk put it, "The possibility of Chinese intervention definitely influenced how we fought this war."[7]

The fear that increased American involvement would provoke responses from the USSR and China, stimulated by the Korean War analogy, was not unfounded. Moscow agreed to supply Hanoi antiaircraft equipment soon after the Gulf of Tonkin incident, and Soviet Premier Alexey Kosygin visited Hanoi in February 1965 to declare that the Soviet Union was "ready to give the Democratic Republic of Vietnam all necessary assistance if the aggressors dare to encroach on its independent sovereignty."[8] Surface-to-air missiles, radar equipment, MIG fighters and IL-28 light bombers began flowing from the USSR to the Democratic Republic of Vietnam (DRV) in substantial quantities. Meanwhile, in December 1964, Hanoi and Beijing concluded a secret agreement permitting 300,000 Chinese troops[9] to enter the DRV's northern provinces to build roads, protect rail lines, and man antiaircraft batteries, a deployment that freed Northern troops for dispatch to the South.[10]

There was never any question that China would serve as the DRV's strategic rear in the event of an expanded war. China already, from 1956 to 1963, had supplied the DRV with 270,000 rifles, more than 10,000 artillery pieces and 2.02 million shells, 1,000 trucks, 28 naval vessels, 15 airplanes, and assorted other equipment and uniforms.[11] And China promised more. Several times during 1964, Mao Zedong, who exercised great influence over China's foreign policy at the time, assured DRV leaders that they could count on China to send troops to fight if the United States invaded the North.[12] In August China initiated closer military cooperation with Hanoi and began beefing up its air, antiaircraft, and naval assets along their common border.[13] In October Mao emphasized Vietnam's responsibility to meet an American invasion on its own but assured Hanoi that "so long as the green mountain is there, how can you ever lack firewood?"[14] Not intimidated by American retaliatory strikes in spring 1965, Liu Shaoqi, China's president and deputy party chairman, replied to LDP first secretary Le Duan's request for "volunteer" pilots and soldiers by saying, "We will offer what you are in need of and we are in a position to offer."[15] In May Zhou Enlai, China's premier, told a visiting delegation from the National Liberation Front of South Vietnam (NLF) that "We will go to Vietnam if Vietnam is in need, as we did in Korea,"[16] reaffirming a message he had transmitted to the United States via President Ayub Khan of Pakistan.[17] In October 1965 Zhou Enlai and Pham Van Dong, DRV premier, discussed the "complicated" issue of "international volunteers going to Vietnam."[18] Detailed discussions on exactly when and in what manner China would participate in the defense of the North went on through the last half of 1965.[19] Throughout these meetings the Chinese were careful to stress that they would take no initiative to provoke a war with the United States and would dispatch combat forces only in response to an American invasion of the North. The Chinese clearly did not want to become directly engaged in a fight with the United States, but by word and deed they made it equally clear that they would not allow their ally to be crushed.[20] The Great Proletarian Cultural Revolution subsequently caused Beijing's attention to turn inward and soured relations with Hanoi, but in 1965 these events lay in the future. Uncertain about China's intentions or for that matter the extent to which other Communist countries might come to Hanoi's aid, Johnson's advisers recommended that he concentrate American forces in the South and use only airpower against the North.

WESTMORELAND'S STRATEGY

"It was apparent," a senior U.S. military adviser would later write, that in 1964 "the South Vietnam government could not prevent the enemy from taking over the country."[21] No sooner had Diem been ousted than Saigon's new military rulers had fallen to bickering among themselves. The ARVN's morale, never good, went into steep decline. The government, already shaky and unpopular, was reluctant to enforce the draft that had been in effect since 1957. In 1964, 73,000 men deserted. Paramilitary and auxiliary units, the fruits of U.S. advice and assistance during the preceding four years, were disbanding or defecting. The government formally dissolved the strategic hamlet program, conceding that "only a small percentage of the hamlets still remained in friendly hands."[22] The U.S. advisory mission admitted in mid-1964 that the initiative had passed to the revolution.

Weighing the choices of escalation and withdrawal, Johnson and his top advisors (Robert McNamara, McGeorge Bundy, and Rusk—all Kennedy appointees) succumbed to the "credibility imperative" and opted to avoid defeat.[23] The decision, to apply graduated pressures rather than overwhelming force, assumed that a "signal" of U.S. determination would be sufficient to dissuade Hanoi from supporting the revolution in the South. Incrementalism would minimize the risks of a response from China, avoid a commitment too deep to terminate, and allow Johnson to stay focused on getting his Great Society reforms enacted. This was to be a "limited war," fought for limited objectives, without placing the nation on a war footing or disrupting Americans' lives, and without arousing popular emotions that might prove hard to control.[24] At the time, Johnson and his chief advisers feared losing the ability to keep the war limited as much as they worried about maintaining public support.

The one group of advisers who should have presented a coherent and professional military point of view, the Joint Chiefs of Staff, was too hampered by interservice rivalries to do so, according to H.R. McMaster's influential study, *Dereliction of Duty*.[25] However, there was no consensus in the officer corps that more aggressive action would be successful, and more than a few senior officers opposed sending a large American force into another ground war in Asia.[26] The one thing on which civilian and military strategists seemed to agree was that "winning" required compelling the Communists to terminate the insurgency or at least reducing it to a scale that would no longer require a "substantial" presence of U.S. forces.[27] Planning began in late 1964 to launch air strikes against the North and to build up American ground combat troops in the South.

The man chosen to implement these plans, Lieutenant General William C. Westmoreland, was descended from men who had fought for the South in the U.S. Civil War. A graduate of West Point in 1936, an artillery officer in North Africa and Europe, a regimental commander in Korea, with a silver mane and a jutting jaw, "Westy" was a general by predestination. He was also the creature of the new U.S. Army, a vast bureaucracy in which management skills and respect for routine counted more than a grasp of strategy or tactical brilliance. Westmoreland had risen steadily thanks to influential patrons and the skillful use of talented staff assistants. Deputy commander of the U.S. Military Assistance Command/Vietnam (MACV) since January 1964, Westmoreland took over full command from General Paul Harkins in June.

Compared to the Pollyannish Harkins, Westmoreland was a grim realist. Told to request whatever he needed to win the war, he outlined a two-phase plan. In the first phase (at last through 1965), he proposed to build a logistical base for a large force. In the next phase, U.S. forces would search out and destroy the Communists' main units, especially in remote or thinly inhabited areas where U.S. firepower and mobility could be brought to bear against PAVN base areas and troop concentrations. Meanwhile the ARVN, strengthened by an enhanced assistance program, would concentrate on pacification in the more densely populated lowlands. The combination, Westmoreland theorized, would give the PAVN no choice but retreat if it wished to avoid defeat, leaving the ARVN to take care of what Southern revolutionary forces remained. Though reluctant to fix a timetable for victory ("incredible," he said of an earlier Harkins' prediction of six months), Westmoreland ventured to suggest that if his requirements were met, it might be possible to begin withdrawing U.S. troops by late 1967.[28]

The Westmoreland strategy relied partly on the sheer magnitude of U.S. resources. American forces in South Vietnam rose from approximately 80,000 men in 1965 to a peak of 543,000 in 1969. (Australia's contingent peaked at 7,672, New Zealand's at 552, Thailand's at 11,568, the Philippines' at 2,020, and South Korea's at 50,003. At the height of aggregate allied involvement, also in 1969, the total strength of allied troops including tiny contingents from Spain and Taiwan was 68,889).[29] A vast complex of infantry support bases sprang up all over South Vietnam. Some 2,000 aircraft (exclusive of helicopters) were posted to Guam, the Philippines, Thailand, and aircraft carriers. A seemingly endless supply of artillery, tanks, jeeps, trucks, and other equipment crossed the Pacific.

The combination of these resources gave Westmoreland his strategic equation: mobility + firepower = attrition. A network of fortified hilltop "firebases" covered almost every nook and cranny with artillery fire. Under that protection, infantry patrols fanned out to engage the enemy. Battalion-strength reaction forces stood ready to join the fray by helicopter and, with the help of artillery and airpower, to pulverize the enemy at low cost in casualties to themselves. The war would reach a "crossover point" when these tactics caused more enemy casualties than the enemy could replace. Westmoreland thus hoped to inflict losses on the Communists that they would find intolerable while keeping U.S. losses at a level that the U.S. Army—and the American people—would accept.

The intended targets of "search and destroy" were the Communists' armed forces, particularly their main-force units. Effective attack required finding the exact location of an elusive enemy, for which purpose the United States had developed technology and techniques never before tested in counterinsurgency warfare. Portable radar, infrared spotting scopes, and urine-detecting "people sniffers" were deployed to pinpoint trails, bivouac sites, and units on the move. Fifty thousand tons of herbicides were dumped on millions of hectares, clearing away half of the South's jungle cover. In areas declared "free-fire zones" and presumably devoid of civilian inhabitants, no authorization was needed to bomb and shell suspected enemy supply lines. By a combination of both well-aimed and random shots Communist forces were to be kept on the move, on the defensive, and run to ground.

Westmoreland preferred to fight in thinly inhabited border regions, but some of the largest revolutionary bases were in the Mekong delta and along the coast where Communist combatants and cadres mingled with a dense civilian population. Combat was unavoidable in these areas, which held 80 percent of the population and where tactics suited to "search-and-destroy" were sure to harm civilians. Bombs and artillery shells would fall on hamlets in the path of sweeps, aircraft would strafe black-clad peasants who looked like "VC" (Viet Cong), and "free-fire zones" were not always devoid of population. "Harassment and interdiction fire," the random shelling of areas suspected to contain enemy troops, could as easily fall on civilians, houses, and crops. If guerrillas shot at aircraft or Communist troops were spotted passing through a village, shelling the nearest hamlet would become the common response. The ARVN, tasked with policing hamlets and villages, was particularly inclined to retaliate with air and artillery. Inevitably, people would leave their homes to find refuge in safer areas.

The heavy reliance on superior technology and abundance of equipment and weaponry was not simply the "American way of war" inherited from past wars. It also minimized American casualties, a desirable aim in itself but especially so in a war for limited objectives. American soldiers would be sent for short tours of duty, not for "the duration" as was the case for their enemy. While Communist regulars endured open-ended deployment under extraordinarily harsh conditions and Communist militia lived in their home villages, the American military would rely on massive applications of firepower, logistical abundance, and a promise of a return home in twelve months to dampen the domestic political repercussions.[30]

Westmoreland not unreasonably considered coping with the immediate military threat to be his first priority. However, his strategy imposed a U.S. design on the war. Control over resources gave the United States the decisive voice in planning, and technology shaped American choices about strategy and tactics that the ARVN could not emulate. The leaders and army the United States came to rescue were shunted aside. "Americans in late 1965 abruptly took over the war, shoved aside the Vietnamese counterparts, and executed the war unilaterally," as one former ARVN general bitterly recalled years later.[31] The desire to "win hearts and minds" and build a viable government was often declared, but in practice these efforts were relegated to "the other war," a term that aptly located them on the periphery of Westmoreland's perceptions, a bias the general shared with the large majority of his fellow officers. Like French commanders before him, Westmoreland's instinct was to try to force the enemy to fight on American terms, for these were the terms on which the United States held an overwhelming advantage. Pushed far enough, however, Westmoreland's strategy had potential to confront the Communists with a far greater challenge than anything they had faced before.

HANOI'S SOUTHERN COMMAND

As Westmoreland prepared to put U.S. forces into combat, the Communists set their own plans in motion. Up to that time, the Central Office for South Vietnam (COSVN), the Central Committee's forward element in the South, had been headed by Nguyen Van Linh, a native of Hanoi who had spent almost his entire revolutionary career in the South. Linh's principal assistants were Vo Van Kiet, a native of Vinh Long province deep in the Mekong delta who had led Viet Minh forces there before and after 1954, and Vo Chi Cong, a native of central Vietnam's Quang Tri province who was vice chairman of the NLF and later party commissar to Military Region 5.

All three men had been secretly elected to the Central Committee in 1960. Other figures who assumed important posts in the South around 1965 were Tran Bach Dang, a Southerner who took charge of propaganda among the Saigon intelligentsia; Mai Chi Tho, brother of Le Duc Tho; and Tran Nam Trung, commander in chief of the PLAF. Because the political struggle was paramount, COSVN's small military section consisted of personnel who had led guerrillas against France and formed the Eastern Interzone Command in 1956.

To prepare COSVN for the coming armed struggle, the Central Committee assigned Lieutenant General Tran Van Tra to the office. A native of Quang Ngai province and a party member since 1938, Tra was appointed commander and political officer of the Saigon-Gai Dinh special zone and southern regional commander in 1950. He regrouped to the North in 1954, became a deputy chief of the PAVN general staff in 1955, and was said by defectors to have gone abroad for training. Taking over as head of COSVN's Central Military Committee in 1963, Tra began to organize a command staff for the lower half of the South (or B2) that fell under COSVN's jurisdiction.[32] Just to the north, another regroupee general from Quang Ngai, Nguyen Don, arrived about the same time to set up a command reporting directly to Hanoi for Military Region 5 (B1), a strip of coastal provinces where people had strongly supported the Viet Minh. (See Map 4.1.)

Meanwhile, as described in the previous chapter, Hanoi was gearing up to provide greater support, including whole PAVN units composed of Northern draftees. The Central Committee acknowledged that if the United States introduced more troops and intensified pressure on the North, "it can cause us much more damage and our people's patriotic struggle may become more difficult, complicated, and protracted. . . ."[33] Although some officers had wanted to avoid confrontation with the United States so long as the PAVN was at a severe firepower disadvantage and Soviet support was tepid, they now had no choice. Means to fight a superior army had to be found. As Northern-born regulars began training for infiltration in April 1964, the army adopted a new training regimen. Based on a Chinese model, the training stressed the superiority of human factors over material ones to convince the troops that politically–motivated revolutionary soldiers could prevail over U.S. weapons.[34] The party's Political Bureau also sent one of its own members who had conspicuously identified himself with this approach on a clandestine mission to the South to draft a strategic plan. Upon his return, the Political Bureau approved his recommendations, and in October 1964 he crossed back into the South to implement them.[35]

If Westmoreland was predestined to be MACV commander, Nguyen Chi Thanh was even more the inevitable COSVN chief. Born in 1914 to a poor peasant family in Thua Thien province, Thanh participated in strikes by tenant farmers at age seventeen and joined the party in 1937. A year later

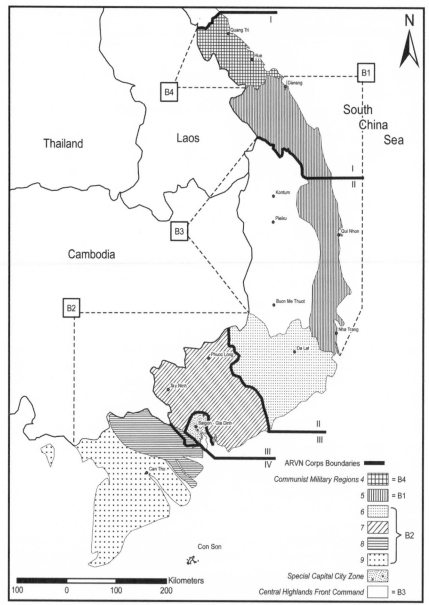

N

I
Quang Tri

B1

B4
Hue

Danang

South
China
Sea

Thailand   Laos

I
II

Kontum

Pleiku

B3   Qui Nhon

Cambodia

Buon Me Thuot

B2

Nha Trang

Da Lat
Phuoc Long

Tay Ninh

II
III

Saigon - Gia Dinh

III
IV   ARVN Corps Boundaries

Communist Military Regions 4   = B4

5   = B1

Can Tho   6
                                             7   } B2
                                             8
Con Son   9

Special Capital City Zone

Kilometers
100   0   100   200   Central Highlands Front Command   = B3

Map 4.1.   Communist Military Zones and Regions in South Vietnam, 1973–1975
Source: Based on a map in Lt. Gen. Tran Van Tra, *Nhung chang duong cua "B2-Thanh dong." tap V. Ket*
thuc chien 30 nam (Ho Chi Minh City: Van Nghe Publishing House, 1982); and fn. 1, p. 7.
Note: Consolidation and adjustment of Communist regions took place several times during the 1960s.

he was elected secretary of the party committee in Thua Thien province. A commanding presence, an infectious enthusiasm, and organizational talent soon brought him to the attention of party leaders, who invited him to the party conference at Tan Trao in 1945, elected him to the Central Committee, and placed him in charge of the resistance in central Vietnam. In 1950 Thanh was appointed head of the army's General Political Directorate (GPD), and he won a seat in the Political Bureau a year later. Thanh was given in 1959 the PAVN's highest rank, general-of-the-army (*dai tuong*), an honor that by law only the president, Ho Chi Minh, could bestow, and which made him the sole equal in rank of Vo Nguyen Giap, the minister of defense. Perhaps due to disagreements with Giap, Thanh left the GPD in 1961 to concentrate on preparations for the unification struggle. He was one of the party's most vehement spokesmen for reunification at any price and more sanguine than Giap about confronting the Americans in main force, "big-unit" warfare. With Giap shunted aside in the controversy over revisionism, control over strategy was firmly in the hands of Party Secretary General Le Duan supported by Le Duc Tho, Pham Hung, and Nguyen Chi Thanh.

Accompanying Thanh on the journey south were PAVN Brigadier Generals Tran Do (an alternate member of the party Central Committee), Le Trong Tan, Nguyen Hoa, and Hoang Cam. All were veterans of the war with France and were chosen for their experience in main-force combat.[36] Also present were "many high- and mid-level cadres experienced in building main forces and commanding large assaults" with whose help Thanh was to set up a Southern regional military command.[37] On arriving at COSVN headquarters in late 1964, Thanh took over as first secretary of both the party and military committees, with Do serving as his deputy. Other PAVN officers and subordinates followed to flesh out the military command structures in COSVN headquarters and in regional organs.

The influx of PAVN officers into the South invited speculation that the North and Northerners were taking over the Southern revolution. In fact, promoting the Southern revolution was an objective of the Lao Dong Party, which had members from all regions and defined its mission in national not regional terms. (A People's Revolutionary Party, unveiled as an ostensibly separate Communist party for the South in 1963, was simply a name given to the party's Southern branch. The PRP was ceremonially "reunified" with the parent party in 1976 and never mentioned again). Moreover, the first PAVN generals sent from the North, with few exceptions, were either Southern regroupees or Northerners who had fought in the South during the first war. Northerners without Southern experience began to join these in significant numbers only when the supply of regroupee officers ran out during 1964, which was about the same time that requirements for officers trained in conventional warfare increased. Thanh's insertion above Nguyen

Van Linh and Tran Van Tra in COSVN's top posts merely reflected Thanh's higher party rank. The dispatch of high-ranking cadres from the North reflected the raised status of reunification in party priorities, not a takeover by Northerners.

The essence of Thanh's recommendation was to proceed with the strategy outlined at the ninth plenum. The PLAF had been unable during 1964 to deal the ARVN a "decisive blow" despite the latter's "involvement in seven coups d'état," as a chagrined COSVN military affairs committee noted.[38] Yet the ARVN's steady weakening presented opportunities for attack that were not to be passed up. At the same time, any of the three options contemplated by the United States—attacking the North, intensifying the "special war," and transforming the conflict into a "limited war" by introducing "hundreds of thousands" of U.S. troops—could create difficulties. To maintain momentum and tie down the United States in a war confined to the South, the Communists decided it was necessary to accelerate the formation of main forces in the lowlands and proceed with infiltration of regular PAVN units from the North. Both of these moves required increasing supply over the Ho Chi Minh Trail into the central highlands.

As far back as November 1953, party leaders recognized that "only by developing into the central highlands is it possible to obtain the most strategic position in the South."[39] The highlands' jungled mountains afforded cover for the supply depots and staging areas that the PAVN would need to engage in regular warfare and support the PLAF. So the Political Bureau came easily to the decision in May 1964 to elevate the western subregion of Military Region 5 into a separate headquarters, or front command. Four months later, a detachment from Region 5 set up a Central Highlands Front Command (B3) to build bases where major supply trails spilled into the South's hilly midriff.[40]

BINH GIA

But the war intensified first in the lowlands. There, the PLAF had begun to form mobile units and to receive new weapons during 1964. Having depended for most of its weapons and ammunition on what it captured from the ARVN, the PLAF began that year to receive AK-47 assault rifles, 7.63-mm machine guns, RPG-2 rocket launchers, 82-mm mortars, and 57-mm and 75-mm recoilless rifles. Most of the weapons were made in China. Some PLAF foot soldiers soon had a firepower advantage over their ARVN counterparts whom the United States had equipped with surplus from World War II. Standardization of equipment also facilitated the formation of larger units.

By late 1964 COSVN felt ready to launch a campaign with units of battalion and regimental size, some of them equipped with mortars, recoilless rifles, antiaircraft machine guns, and pack howitzers recently delivered from the North. Beginning the night of December 2 (or the third or fourth—Communist sources disagree, but American sources say the fourth), two PLAF regiments of the newly formed Ninth Division and assorted local forces came together to attack targets in Phuoc Tuy province southeast of Saigon. Centered on Binh Gia, a "strategic hamlet" built by Northern Catholic refugees, the attacks drew a strong response from ARVN ranger and marine units on helicopters, but the PLAF held its ground. With feints, withdrawals, and help from local forces, the PLAF lured the ARVN into ambushes, frustrated ARVN attempts to concentrate for counterattack, and chewed up ARVN reinforcements.[41] After the fighting subsided around January 3, it appeared that a Communist force of about 1,500 had killed 10 percent of the 2,000–man ARVN force, shot down three helicopters, and wounded six U.S. crewmen while losing perhaps 140 of its own troops.[42] American advisors on the scene conceded victory to the PLAF. Although the largest and best reported PLAF victory thus far, Binh Gia was by no means an isolated incident. In this and similar actions across the country, the ARVN was losing an average of one infantry battalion each week, and senior U.S. officials believed that they saw evidence of a shift to the "third stage" of "mobile warfare" prescribed in the military writings of Mao Zedong.[43]

They were wrong. The Communists disagreed among themselves on the relevance to Vietnam of Mao's strategy. To skeptics the Chinese formula seemed simplistic, mechanistic, and ill-adapted to Vietnam's geography and to combat with a vastly more powerful enemy than the Chinese had faced. This was a conclusion PAVN generals had drawn from the campaign in the Red River delta in 1951–1952, in which Viet Minh forces suffered debilitating casualties in futile onslaughts on heavily fortified French positions. Lacking a vast territory in which to maneuver and facing an enemy that enjoyed airpower in abundance and supply from abroad, revolutionary forces could not melt into the countryside and gradually build strength in a remote base as the Chinese Communists had done against the Japanese and the Guomindang. For the same reasons, they could not afford to abandon the cities and populated lowlands, allowing the enemy unimpeded use of the country's most valuable resources. The Vietnamese had to maintain a presence in the enemy's rear and on rural "fronts" by political and military means. Only in this way could they keep their more powerful enemy off balance. The image of interlocking teeth and the expression "our rear is in front of us" captured the idea. All forms of war and struggle needed to be developed from the beginning to the end of the conflict. Parallel to military actions, efforts had to be made to disrupt the enemy's administrative apparatus, spread propaganda, recruit new members, and intimidate civilian opponents.

The Binh Gia "campaign," as the Communists styled it, did not conclude until March 7, 1965. Until then the Communists conducted armed propaganda and claimed to have instigated "uprisings" in half a dozen nearby hamlets.[44] Yet, what impressed the U.S. command was the battle, which convinced American military observers that only U.S. troops could cope with the new "stage" the war had entered. The real significance of that perception, however, was not that the war had entered Mao's "third stage," but that the strategy of "special war" was dead. "Limited war" was about to begin. The real "stages" of the war were not fixed by Communist strategy but by American designs that the Communists calculated they had only to thwart in order to win.

RESCUE MISSION

As the United States mulled over its options during the spring of 1965, few doubted that Saigon was headed for defeat. The new military leadership of Air Vice Marshal Nguyen Cao Ky and General Nguyen Van Thieu, in power since Ky and Thieu had ousted General Khanh in February, inspired no more confidence than its predecessors. The two men were rivals not collaborators, who had been forced into an alliance by the exasperated Americans. The rising number of desertions in the armed forces (a total of 113,000 in all troop categories in 1965, an increase of more than 50 percent over the previous year)[45] had dashed U.S. hopes of setting the ARVN quickly on its feet. Even earlier, in January, Defense Secretary Robert McNamara and National Security Adviser McGeorge Bundy had advised President Johnson to consider sending U.S. troops into action, and a powerful group within the administration, headed by Westmoreland, the Joint Chiefs of Staff, and Walt Rostow, was pushing for intensification of the air war against the North. Sustained air attacks began in March but failed to force Communist concessions or to weaken the Communist offensive in the South.

At a meeting in Honolulu in April, the Joint Chiefs, McNamara, and Lodge's replacement as ambassador, General Maxwell Taylor, agreed to increase the number of troops to 82,000 in order to protect airbases and, if things went badly, hold "enclaves" along the coast. But the 27,000 U.S. troops in Vietnam already had permission to go on combat patrols, and neither Westmoreland nor the ARVN generals could see the sense of a purely defensive U.S. role. "The Communists," said General Thieu, "controlled 75 percent of the countryside. We controlled only the chief towns. We had the impression we would be overrun. There was a crucial need for American troops."[46] Ambassador Taylor was reluctant to approve a much larger presence for fear this would only further reduce the ARVN's will to fight, but by mid-year, he too agreed there was no alternative. In July, Westmoreland submitted a request for 179,000 troops, and President Johnson announced on the twenty-eighth that the force level would rise to 125,000 troops.

By August, the U.S. command felt ready to begin offensive operations. To kick off the campaign with a big victory, the command sought a Communist stronghold that would be susceptible to complete destruction. The area chosen was the Batangan peninsula, twenty-five kilometers south of the U.S. Marine base at Chu Lai. The villages of the peninsula had supported the Viet Minh during the resistance and had been a revolutionary base for at least two years before the marines arrived. Three of the villages, anchored by a hamlet called Van Tuong, were tightly organized guerrilla communities, riddled with tunnels, concrete reinforced bunkers, trenches, mine fields, and food and weapons caches. The terrain, marked by rocky hills and terraced padi fields, completed this fortress, defended by a well-organized local militia and an estimated 2,000-man PLAF regiment.

The peninsula seemed to afford the U.S. command an opportunity to bottle up a sizeable Communist force and to exterminate it with overwhelming firepower. Opening Operation Starlite on August 18, a battalion of marines on helicopters cut the peninsula at its neck, three companies made an amphibious landing on one shore, and a blocking force took up positions on another. Nearly 6,000 marines pressed the defenders against the sea while Phantom and Skyhawk jets, two destroyers, and ground artillery saturated the cordoned area with napalm, rockets, and bombs.

As a display of firepower, the attack was impressive. In its wake the marines claimed to have found 599 "VC" bodies (or 700, or 964, depending on the source) and to have taken 122 prisoners. But they reluctantly revealed that they had 45 dead and 203 wounded of their own, and they had difficulty persuading reporters that all of the Vietnamese bodies were "VC." Despite capturing only 127 Communist weapons and the escape of three-quarters of the PLAF regiment, General Westmoreland cited the battle as proof that U.S. troops could defeat "any Viet Cong or North Vietnamese forces they might encounter."[47]

COSVN's General Thanh, however, pointed to the battle as evidence that "the Southern Liberation Army is fully capable of defeating U.S. troops under any circumstances, even though they have absolute superiority of . . . firepower compared with that of the liberation army."[48] Bluster aside, Thanh was making a serious point. An account of the battle reported years later in the PAVN newspaper, *Quan doi nhan dan* (People's Army), focused on how the defenders had taken advantage of the rough terrain to set up cross fires that offset the marines' firepower superiority and then had broken out of the encirclement. What counted to the Communists was not so much the tally of bodies as the fact that the PLAF and local guerrillas had engaged

U.S. troops at a time and place chosen by U.S. commanders, yet had lived to fight another day. Survival was more important than winning in tactical situations. Indeed, almost as soon as the marines withdrew, the Batangan peninsula reverted to the status it had held before Operation Starlite.

Years later, long after the Batangan villages had witnessed a succession of efforts to "pacify" them, a U.S. civilian official filed a confidential report that read in part:

> For more than five years the Batangan Peninsula has symbolized VC influence in Quang Ngai and has posed a threat not only to the people of Binh Son and Son Tinh districts but to neighboring districts including the city of Quang Ngai itself. It provided a source of supply, recruits, food and weapons to the 48th main force battalion as well as other VC units. While it is true that U.S., Korean and ARVN forces conducted periodic operations in this area, the VC merely faded away until the operation terminated and then returned to their base which remained virtually intact.[49]

The report went on to call the efforts toward establishing control over the peninsula since 1968 a "success story" of the war. But it acknowledged the continued operation of the PLAF Forty-Eighth Battalion and that U.S. support was still needed if the ARVN were to keep the area "pacified."

After Starlite the center of U.S. attention turned to the highlands, where it was feared that the Communists were preparing to "cut the country in two." Actually, all major links except air had been cut long ago, and only the Communists moved on the ground at will. What the Communists decided to do was meet the United States head on, and this implied a need to seize strategic positions and push supply lines beyond the lower end of the Ho Chi Minh Trail. The only existing road link between the Cambodian bases and road networks in the lower highlands, Route 19, passed through the Ia Drang valley on its way to Pleiku. There in the Ia Drang, on October 19, 1965, the PAVN 304th Division attacked ARVN camps and outposts of the montagnard Civilian Irregular Defense Group (CIDG) at Plei Me, hoping to lure American forces into battle where PAVN commanders thought they held an advantage. And indeed, the U.S. First Cavalry Division, an entirely airmobile unit that had just recently established a base at nearby An Khe, rushed to the rescue. The fighting soon turned into a series of bloody clashes that continued until November 20.

U.S. troops swept around the valley in their helicopters, chasing, blocking, surrounding, and engaging any PAVN units they could find. The PAVN adapted by focusing fire on helicopter landing zones, attacking only at close quarters or at night, and cutting up small U.S. detachments. In the words of a former CIA analyst, PAVN claims to have annihilated a U.S. battalion were "not entirely without foundation," but the U.S. military estimated that the PAVN lost more than 3,500 while U.S. forces lost 305. In this outcome

American commanders saw proof of the effectiveness of helicopter-assault tactics and the strategy of attrition, while the Communists disputed the numbers and concluded that they could stay in the fight despite the Americans' huge technological edge.[50]

As 1965 came to a close the Communists could point to success in attacking the Danang airfield and mounting assaults against outposts all over the South. They also succeeded in grouping PLAF regiments into two divisions (the Ninth and Fifth) in the Mekong delta and two more (the Third and Second) in the populous central provinces. In March 1966 a PAVN force overran the Special Forces CIDG camp in the A Shau valley and turned the valley into a major base for infiltrating personnel and supplies from the North through Laos into Thua Thien province. But the Communists had been unable to prevent U.S. forces from gaining a foothold in the highlands or from penetrating some areas where revolutionary forces previously had been safe from attack. Mixed results and heavy losses sowed doubt about the wisdom of big-unit warfare, forcing Thanh to defend his strategy. In a speech to COSVN cadres in mid-1966, Thanh admitted that the United States had only begun to tap its potential, but he maintained that big-unit warfare, at least in the highlands and other remote areas, was necessary if the revolution were to stay on the offensive. Dispersing into guerilla formations in all regions would sacrifice all that had been won and be tantamount to defeat. "If we want to take the defensive position," he said, "we should withdraw to India."[51]

On the question of tactics, Thanh also held strong views. Many PAVN commanders had come south with their heads full of conventional doctrine, some of it learned from Soviet manuals and from training abroad. But tactics developed by the Soviet Army for use in Europe were irrelevant to a much less technologically sophisticated army fighting in the jungles of Indochina. Better, he said, to find a "special way of fighting the Americans," "the way a tiger leaps at his prey"—in other words, force the enemy to fight "our way" by mounting short, swift, surprise assaults at close quarters and then disengaging rapidly to avoid the full impact of U.S. firepower. No battle should last more than twenty minutes, no campaign more than five days. Of course political struggle among the people and within the enemy's armed force would continue, and so would the effort to build guerrilla forces in lowland villages. But under no circumstances was he willing to slacken the mainforce offensive or adopt a solely guerrilla-based strategy.[52]

THE BIG SWEEPS

Despite American successes and relentless build-up, a few Congressional leaders began to express doubts about the candor and accuracy of administration statements. Senator J. William Fulbright (D-Ark.), who had managed the Tonkin Gulf Resolution on the Senate floor as chairman of the Senate Foreign Relations Committee, said he felt "hoodwinked" by the administration's manipulation of Congress, and he organized hearings in January–February 1966 to grill Secretary of State Dean Rusk. Response to the hearings, historian Robert D. Schulzinger observes, revealed "public anxieties about the course the country followed, yet the depth of public concern did not lead to concrete alternatives to the Johnson administration's policies."[53] Neither did that concern cause General Westmoreland to alter his plans.

By mid-1966 Westmoreland completed his support base and begun the campaign of attrition. The number of U.S. troops in Vietnam stood at 350,000, which combined with 315,000 ARVN regulars and an equal number of auxiliaries brought the total number of armed personnel on Saigon's side to more than one million. On the revolutionary side, there were 114,000 main forces (including 46,300 PAVN regulars) and 112,000 guerrillas for a total of 225,000, according to estimates by the U.S. command. In fact those numbers were low, as concern about political reactions in the United States caused Westmoreland to demand conservative estimates.[54] A CIA estimate that added hamlet-level militia, service troops, and political cadres to the mix yielded a total of 600,000, sparking debate that would fester until war's end about the military relevance of hamlet "self-defense" militia and political cadres.[55] The Communists for their part counted 320,000 people in guerrilla and local militia for a total of 435,000 in all troop categories.[56]

No set of figures could accurately reveal the strengths and weaknesses of the two sides, however. The Communists' regular forces in 1966 were well-equipped with light arms, and their logistical "tail" was small by comparison with the U.S. Army, whose support elements were at least eight times larger than combat forces. The Communists put a higher proportion of their troops into the fight.[57] But the Communists lacked the heavy weapons, armed vehicles, transport, and airpower that the United States and its allies enjoyed in abundance. Village guerrillas (*du kich*) were armed with rifles and hamlet militia (*tu ve*) might, if they were lucky, have grenades, but the critical function of these categories apart from local defense, digging tunnels, setting booby traps, and collecting taxes was to serve as a recruitment pool for the regular forces. This structure allowed Communist regular units to reconstitute themselves quickly despite devastating losses, to the consternation of American commanders trying to "attrit" them. It also gave them forces in place that could appear at a moment's notice, compensating for the lack of air and motorized mobility. Nonetheless, when all was said and done, Communist forces' raw destructive capacity was only a fraction of the allies'. By the reckoning of the Pentagon's own statistician, "from 1965 on, the allies always outnumbered the Communists by at least three to one. . . . If the additional allied advantages of mobility, firepower, and combat support are taken into account it is even more difficult to understand how the Communist army survived."[58]

Communist strategy sought to redress the uneven military balance with adaptive tactics and a favorable political environment. Not even the prospect of more U.S. troops perturbed dialecticians who saw in the growing U.S. presence an opportunity to whip up a patriotic backlash. Anticipating a rise in anti-U.S. sentiment in the South, a Central Committee twelfth plenum in December 1965 had called for a "people's war of national resistance." In addition, the plenum had reaffirmed support for General Thanh's main-force offensives in order to deliver a "decisive victory in a relatively short period of time."[59] The war would proceed on two levels, with conventional "big-unit" attacks to convince the United States that Westmoreland's strategy could never produce an acceptable outcome (thus delivering a "decisive victory in a relatively short period of time"), while "people's war" waged by guerrillas, political cadres, and the masses supplied support and a strategic option if "big unit" attacks resulted in excessive losses.

One of the party's fondest dreams seemed about to materialize in the spring of 1966 when Prime Minister Ky dismissed Nguyen Chanh Thi, the popular Buddhist commander general of the ARVN First Corps, and thus provoking another wave of Buddhist dissidence in Hue and Danang. Rallying to Thi's defense, demonstrators demanded free elections and a return to civilian rule. ARVN units clashed for control of Danang in a virtual civil war within the civil war, and South Vietnamese aircraft fired on U.S. Marines. Although they had done nothing to create this upheaval, which had roots in festering grievances against Diemist holdovers in the local administration, the Communists saw the opportunity and rushed to exploit it.[60] The PAVN 324B Division slipped into Quang Tri province, and a new military region covering Quang Tri and Thua Thien provinces (the Tri-Thien Region, or B4) under Hanoi's direct command (not COSVN's) appeared in April.[61] Thinking that Hanoi was preparing to seize these two provinces, the United States installed a string of combat and fire-support bases all along Route 9 from Dong Ha to the Laotian border. (See Map 4.2.) Work began on an anti-infiltration system, popularly known as the McNamara Line or Electric Fence, which consisted of a strip of sensors, infrared intrusion detectors, electronic warning devices, and minefields. Pitched battles within range of PAVN artillery and antiaircraft weapons raged at Con Thien, Gio Linh, Camp Carroll, Rock Pile, and Khe Sanh. Bitter fighting left U.S. and ARVN troops in control of the high ground, and the U.S. command claimed to have held off the "invading North Vietnamese."[62]

The Communists had flexible objectives, however, and the military seizure of the two provinces came second to diverting attention from the Tri-Thien lowlands and loosening Saigon's hold over Hue and Danang so that

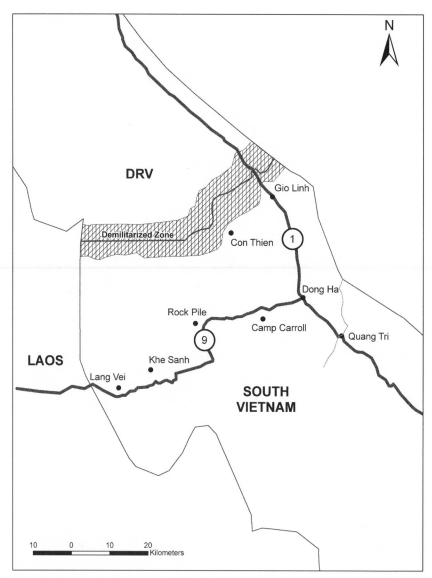

Map 4.2.   Route 9

the wave of dissent could erupt into mass uprising. But party organs in the cities were too weak to exploit the situation. "We lost an opportunity to win an even greater victory," Le Duan was to say.[63] Meanwhile the offensive in these provinces also sought to drain resources away from Westmoreland's accelerating campaign of attrition farther south.

There, for the "Iron Triangle" thirty-five kilometers northeast of Saigon, a staging area adjacent to the Cambodian border (War Zone C), the United States planned the largest "search-and-destroy" operation of the war. The area also contained COSVN headquarters. Believing the Communists were preparing to swarm out of these bases and attack population centers, U.S. and ARVN forces launched probes into War Zone C during April 1966. These forces stumbled into the PLAF Ninth Division (whose presence was suspected but whose location was unknown) and the PAVN 101st Regiment. An operation code-named Attleboro was mounted to exterminate the Communist forces. Attleboro involved 22,000 U.S. and ARVN troops, 1,600 tactical air sorties, and the dropping of 12,000 tons of bombs (one-third by B-52s). U.S. commanders credited Attleboro with a very favorable "kill ratio" of nearly fourteen enemy killed for every friendly loss; the capture of large stocks of rice, weapons, and supplies; and the foiling of Communist plans to attack the major population centers near Saigon and the Mekong delta.[64]

The PLAF command, however, noted with approval that, in what it called "the Tay Ninh Campaign," elements of Ninth Division and auxiliaries fought one hundred different engagements over a period of nearly two months.[65] Despite some "depletion," revolutionary forces escaped extermination and put up resistance until the last enemy troops had withdrawn. The PLAF assessment conceded that airborne U.S. and ARVN troops had been able to seize strong tactical positions, but it scoffed at them for not following through with infantry assaults. Aerial bombardment had an insignificant effect, and Attleboro neither exterminated Communist forces nor denied them the use of War Zone C, the Communist command claimed. Even the United States had to admit that it had not found COSVN headquarters.

Nevertheless, Westmoreland's team thought it had hit upon an effective technique and mounted a similar operation, Cedar Falls, against the Iron Triangle in January 1967. This operation, immortalized in Jonathan Schell's book, *The Village of Ben Suc*,[66] sought to destroy forever a complex of tunnels, bunkers, and "combat hamlets" that reputedly were home to the PLAF 272nd and 165th regiments and administrative headquarters for the Saigon-Gia Dinh Military Region.

Ben Suc, a Viet Minh base during the first war, had been an outpost for an ARVN battalion from 1955 to 1964. The PLAF had routed the battalion, and Ben Suc, to the evident satisfaction of its 6,000 inhabitants, had become a solid NLF village. Fearing a breach of security, the United States did not inform South Vietnamese authorities of Operation Cedar Falls until it was about to be launched. The population was evacuated, aircraft and artillery bombarded the dense jungle, and sixty-ton Rome Plow bulldozers cut giant swaths through the brush. Tunnel and bunker complexes were blown up. Finally, the plows flattened Ben Suc. U.S. Army engineers planted 10,000 pounds of explosives in the tunnels underneath and blew what remained of Ben Suc from the face of the earth.

Like Operation Attleboro, Cedar Falls produced a large number of "VC" bodies and substantial quantities of confiscated supplies. According to the U.S. general in command, the operation was "a decisive turning point in the Third Corps area . . . and a blow from which the VC in this area may never recover."[67] In fact, Cedar Falls did demolish the area's physical structures and remove its population. But it missed the bulk of Communist main forces headquartered there—they had slipped away as soon as the operation began—and left enraged villagers sweltering in hastily constructed refugee camps.

With barely a pause, U.S. and ARVN forces returned to War Zone C to search for the Communist forces that Attleboro supposedly had crushed three months earlier. Operation Junction City also sought to destroy COSVN headquarters (again) and make the area permanently insecure for the Communists. It, too, relied on sudden helicopter deployments, large infantry sweeps, and lavish use of firepower. It, too, ended with the announcement of a high "body count" and large quantities of seized weapons, supplies, and documents. The PLAF's assessment, however, claimed that the majority of engagements had occurred at Communist initiative or on terms that Communist units had been willing to accept. Four regiments, it noted, had been able to attack continuously throughout the entire period of the operation,[68] and COSVN and PLAF Ninth Division headquarters remained as elusive as ever.

In the end, the three operations failed to deny the use of War Zone C and the Iron Triangle to the Communists. Lacking sufficient forces to occupy either area permanently, U.S. commanders had to admit that Communist troops and cadres soon returned to their positions.[69] But the operations did inflict heavy losses and showed that the Communists no longer enjoyed unimpeded use of what had been secure base areas.

STALEMATE

By mid-1967 the situation was in a strategic stalemate. With 425,000 troops and an enormous logistical base, U.S. forces were too powerful for the Communists to evict; they had also pushed some PAVN support facilities into Laos and Cambodia. U.S. pressure of quite a different kind had put an end to coups in Saigon and paved the way in September for the election of Nguyen Van Thieu as president and Nguyen Cao Ky as vice-president. The ARVN, deployed mainly in static defense but acquiring better weapons and maneuver units, was no longer on the verge of collapse.

On the other hand, revolutionary forces retained the capability for offensive action. The PAVN still roamed the mountains, and a growing volume of matériel was moving over an improved Ho Chi Minh Trail. In provinces directly below the demilitarized zone, U.S. camps were under almost continuous attack by PAVN units supported by heavy artillery and antiaircraft weapons fired from across or within the DMZ. Guerrilla and regional forces, undiminished in size, were still able to hit outposts and ambush convoys in most parts of the countryside at times of their choosing. While the revolution had lost control of territory and people to U.S. and Saigon forces, its capacity to outlast American patience was undiminished.

Against this background, General Westmoreland returned to Washington in November to reassure a restive Congress that although the Communists had not been defeated, the end was in sight. The United States and its allies were making "tremendous progress," according to Westmoreland. Actually, the flaws of his strategy were increasingly apparent. The vast size of the U.S. presence and the destructiveness of U.S. tactics may have seemed necessary to cope with an emergency and to limit U.S. casualties, but they had self-defeating side effects. The big sweeps and lavish firepower that produced a high "body count" also caused civilian casualties, drove peasants off their land, and sowed resentment. American money and bases created jobs, but they also exacerbated corruption and immorality, to the abhorrence of Vietnamese middle classes and intellectuals. U.S. assistance helped to train, equip, and expand the ARVN, but it deepened ARVN dependence on the United States for everything from bullets, trucks, and artillery to the will to fight.

Moreover, Defense Secretary McNamara had concluded in late 1966 that the United States simply was not able to kill or capture enemy forces at a rate exceeding their replacement. As of mid-1967 the North had sent less than 2 percent of its male labor force into combat. The Communist political organization in the South was still able to find recruits for local guerrilla and regional forces, if not as easily and as widely as before. Communist forces were able to control their loss rates by evading combat or reverting to small-scale attacks when set-piece battles would prove too damaging, a fact that revealed which side really held the initiative.[70] The number of Communist troops, by the Americans' own count, was growing not shrinking. Even Westmoreland's intelligence chief routinely ended his briefings by saying "The North Vietnamese and Viet Cong have *the will and capability* to conduct a protracted war of attrition at current levels of activity *indefinitely*."[71] Westmoreland's "crossover point" was a moving target and beyond reach. Meanwhile the United States was spending two billion dollars per month on the war, and with more than 5,000 U.S. soldiers dead in 1967 alone, the toll was rising. "'Westy just doesn't get it," General Frederick C. Weyand, the U.S. commander of Third Corps, told two reporters on condition of anonymity. "'The war is unwinnable. We've reached a stalemate and we should find a dignified way out.'"[72] (Weyand would go on to serve as the last MACV commander in 1972–1973 and Army chief of staff in 1974–1976.)

While the big-unit battles soaked up attention and resources, U.S. officials largely ignored the political dimensions of the conflict. As suggested earlier, this was partly a consequence of the army's institutional investment in conventional warfare. A coherent "new model" pacification program did not get under way until mid-1967. This program sought to achieve territorial security by reforming the administration at the hamlet level, stimulating economic revival, and gradually turning responsibility for protecting the rural population over to local forces recruited from the population itself. However, aside from its late inception, the promised new order suffered in comparison with the one that many peasants already knew well—that of the revolution. It was administered from "outside" the village by officials at the district and provincial levels, not by local people; its incentives (medical care, educational facilities, a police presence) demanded no particular response in return; and it did not (until 1970) include land reform.[73] In fact embassy officials opposed radical land reform on the grounds that this would antagonize the government's main social base (see chapter 7). The battle for "hearts and minds" was going nowhere, even though suppression was having effects that the U.S. command judged to be favorable.

A new political front also had appeared within the United States itself. Dissent, after gestating in pacifist and civil-rights groups, had broken out on university campuses in 1965. An antiwar movement of diffuse aims and no formal leadership had spread outward from the few elite universities where it had begun. The vast majority of dissenters abhorred the destruction committed in their country's name and wanted to withdraw from a war in which they could see no vital U.S. interest at stake. By no accident, the stridency of the movement rose in proportion to demands of the draft. Although the movement provoked the antipathy of older, conservative segments of society, by 1967 it also was attracting support from establishment figures.

Perhaps more importantly, and quite apart from the movement, the war had begun to corrode the willingness of ordinary citizens to give unconditional support to their government in time of war. The problem, as many saw it, was not with U.S. purpose or decency, but with policies that held little promise of quick and decisive victory. Major newspapers that had supported the war shifted to critical stances. Public-opinion polls showed popular support for the war dipping below 50 percent in mid-1967. By October, only 28 percent of the American people supported the way President Johnson was conducting the war, and the percentage who thought it had been a mistake to enter the war in the first place had risen to 45 percent. Inside the administration, McNamara registered his disillusionment, recommended lowering objectives, and quietly announced he would depart at a future date. But Johnson remained determined to see the war through and dug in to fight his critics. In this he had the support of his field commander, General Westmoreland, who assured Johnson and the nation that the enemy's hopes were "bankrupt" and the war was entering the phase in which "the end begins to come into view."[74]

The Communists observed this sharpening of "contradictions" within the American administration and society with satisfaction. The military stalemate, bearable to them, was unacceptable to the United States. As a global power the United States had obligations elsewhere that ruled out endless involvement in an inconclusive war. Under conditions of stalemate, or interminable war, the United States eventually would have to withdraw. To the Communists, though, a standoff was sufficient to turn the tide in their favor. Communist forces had retained the initiative despite a firepower handicap, and they were steadily upgrading their own conventional warfare capability. While the U.S. effort was approaching its peak, the Communist effort had room to grow. So long as Communist forces held their own in the military struggle and socialist allies remained committed to supporting them, Hanoi had no reason to seek a peaceful settlement through compromise.

Yet, through 1967, the dominant voices within Johnson's administration remained confident that the U.S. could prevail over what they regarded as a fourth-rate power. These advisors did not perceive the situation as a stalemate and believed, like Westmoreland, that the tide had shifted in Saigon's favor. The United States moreover still had capacity to increase its effort. The problem for the Communists, therefore, was to discredit the Johnson administration "hawks" by demonstrating that a stalemate did indeed exist and that there was little the United States could do to break it. That, they concluded, would require intensifying the "coordinated struggle," bringing the war right into the enemy's most secure rear areas.[75]

NOTES

1. Philip Caputo, *A Rumor of War* (New York: Holt, 1977), xii.

2. Marianna P. Sullivan, *France's Vietnam Policy: A Study in French-American Relations* (Westport, Conn.: Greenwood, 1978), 71–75.

3. Sylvia Ellis, *Britain, America, and the Vietnam War* (Westport, Conn.: Praeger, 2004), 1–36. On the early 1960s, see Peter Busch, *All the Way with JFK? Britain, the US, and the Vietnam War* (Oxford: Oxford University Press, 2003).

4. Thomas R. H. Havens, *Fire Across the Sea: The Vietnam War and Japan, 1965–1975* (Princeton, N.J.: Princeton University Press, 1987), 5, 25.

5. Robert M. Blackburn, *Mercenaries and Lyndon Johnson's "More Flags": The Hiring of Korean, Filipino and Thai Soldiers in the Vietnam War* (Jefferson, N.C.: McFarland, 1994), 24–30.

6. "Probable Consequences of Certain US Actions with Respect to Vietnam and Laos" (SNIE 50-2-64) and "Probable Communist Reactions to Certain US Actions" (SNIE 10-6-65), in *Estimative Products on Vietnam 1948–1975*, ed. National Intelligence Council (Washington, D.C.: Government Printing Office, April 2005, CD-ROM version).

7. Dean Rusk (as told to Richard Rusk), *As I Saw It*, ed. Daniel S. Papp (New York: Norton, 1990), 456–457; Lyndon Baines Johnson, *The Vantage Point: Perspectives of the Presidency 1963–1969* (New York: Holt, Rinehart and Winston, 1971), 119, 149, 369, 370.

8. *Keesing's Contemporary Archives* (London: Keesing's Limited, 1965), 20761.

9. At their peak in 1967, Chinese troops in the DRV numbered one hundred and seventy thousand.

10. Ilya V. Gaiduk, *The Soviet Union and the Vietnam War* (Chicago: Ivan R. Dee, 1996), 16, 20, 24. In August 1966 the CIA detected elements of two railway engineering divisions and one antiaircraft division of the Chinese People's Liberation Army numbering from 25,000 to 45,000 operating in the DRV along the main railway lines from China. "The Vietnamese Communists' Will to Persist, 26 August 1966," Memo 26, 95, in *Estimative Products on Vietnam*.

11. Chen Jian, "China's Involvement in the Vietnam War, 1964–69," *The China Quarterly*, no. 142 (June 1995): 359–360.

12. Yang Kuisong, "Changes in Mao Zedong's Attitude toward the Indochina War, 1949–1973," trans. Qiang Zhai (Washington, D.C., Cold War International History Project, Working Paper No. 34, February 2002), 28–29; Qiang Zhai, *China & the Vietnam Wars, 1950–1975* (Chapel Hill: University of North Carolina Press, 2000), 130–135.

13. Chen Jian, "China's Involvement," 364.

14. Mao Zedong and Pham Van Dong, Hoang Van Hoan, Beijng, October 5, 1964, in "77 Conversations between Chinese and Foreign Leaders on the Wars in Indochina, 1964–1977," ed. Odd Arne Westad et al. (Washington, D.C.: Cold War International History Project, Working Paper No. 22, May 1998), 76.

15. Liu Shaoqi and Le Duan, Beijing, April 8, 1965, in "77 Conversations," 85. In the end, China did not send pilots, but the Soviet Union and North Korea did. Kim Yong Nam, chairman of the North Korean Supreme People's Assembly, said on a visit to Hanoi in 2001 that eight hundred North Korean pilots had flown North Vietnamese planes in the war. Don Kirk, "North Korean and Vietnamese Trade Compliments," *International Herald Tribune* (July 16, 2001), 5.

16. Zhou Enlai and Nguyen Van Hieu, Nguyen Thi Binh, Beijing, May 16, 1965, in "77 Conversations," 86.

17. Zhou Enlai and Pakistan President Ayub Khan, Karachi, April 2, 1965, in "77 Conversations," 80, 83.

18. Zhou Enlai and Pham Van Dong, Beijing, October 9, 1965, in "77 Conversations," 90.

19. Chen Jian, "China's Involvement," 369.

20. Chen Jian, "China's Involvement," 366. It takes some bending of the evidence and discounting of the consensus among Cold War historians with access to Chinese archives to conclude, as American proponents of invading the North have done, that China told Hanoi it would *not* send troops. For an updated version of the pro-invasion argument, see Mark Moyar, *Triumph Forsaken: The Vietnam War, 1954–1965* (New York: Cambridge University Press, 2006), 321–322 and 480n60.

21. James Lawton Collins Jr., *The Development and Training of the South Vietnamese Army, 1950–1972* (Washington, D.C.: Department of the Army, 1975), 47–48.

22. Richard A. Hunt, *Pacification: The American Struggle for Vietnam's Hearts and Minds* (Boulder, Colo.: Westview, 1995), 25.

23. Fredrik Logevall, *Choosing War: The Lost Chance for Peace and the Escalation of War in Vietnam* (Berkeley: University of California Press, 1999), 388.

24. The Johnson administration's attempt to implement "limited war" doctrine is the subject of George Herring, *LBJ and Vietnam: A Different Kind of War* (Austin: University of Texas Press, 1994).

25. H.R. McMaster, *Dereliction of Duty: Lyndon Johnson, Robert McNamara, the Joint Chiefs of Staff, and the Lies That Led to Vietnam* (New York: HarperCollins, 1997).

26. Robert Buzzanco, "Division, Dilemma and Dissent: Military Recognition of the Peril of War in Viet Nam," in *Informed Dissent: Three Generals & the Viet Nam War*, ed. Dan Duffy (Chevy Chase, Md.: Vietnam Generation and Burning Cities Press, 1992), 9–16.

27. William Conrad Gibbons, *The U.S. Government and the Vietnam War, Executive and Legislative Roles and Relationship, Part III: January–July 1965* (Princeton, N.J.: Princeton University Press, 1989), 359–361.

28. William C. Westmoreland, *A Soldier Reports* (New York: Doubleday, 1979), 149–150 and Westmoreland, *Report on the War in Vietnam* (Washington, D.C.: Government Printing Office, 1968).

29. Stanley Robert Larsen and James Lawton Collins Jr., *Allied Participation in Vietnam* (Washington, D.C.: Department of the Army, U.S. Government Printing Office, 1985), 23.

30. One-year tours were widely believed responsible for weak unit cohesion and "short-timer's fever," or anxiety and risk aversion as the end of one's tour approached. For an informed comparison of Communist and American troop motivation, morale, training, and tactics, see Ronald H. Spector, *After Tet: The Bloodiest Year in Vietnam* (New York: The Free Press, 1993), 46–91.

31. Speech by ex-ARVN Lieutenant General Lu Lan at Texas Tech University, *Friends of the Vietnam Center* 13, no. 2 (Spring 2006): 3.

32. I am indebted to Nayan Chanda and Paul Quinn-Judge for help in locating biographical information on Linh, Kiet, and Tra,

33. "Nghi quyet hoi nghi Trung uong lan thu 11 (dac biet), Ngay 25, 26, 27 thang 3 nam 1965" [Resolution of the 11th plenum of the Central Committee (special), March 25, 26, 27, 1965], Dang Cong San Viet Nam, *Van kien Dang, toan tap*, [Complete Party Documents (hereafter cited as VKDTT)] vol. 26, 1965 (Hanoi: NXB Ban chinh tri quoc gia, 2003), 106.

34. *Quan doi nhan dan* [People's Army], 26 and 28 May 1964.

35. Vien lich su quan su Viet Nam, *50 nam Quan doi nhan dan Viet Nam* [Fifty Years of the People's Army of Vietnam] (Hanoi: NXB Quan doi nhan dan, 1995), 198.

36. Hoang Van Thai, "The Decisive Years: Memoirs of Vietnamese Senior General Hoang Van Thai," *Saigon Giai Phong* (13 March–14 May 1986), 3, trans. Joint Publication Research Service, JPRS-SEA-87-084 (Springfield, Va.: National Technical Information Service, June 23, 1987), 48.

37. Vien lich su, *50 nam*, 198–199.

38. "Nghi quyet quan uy mien Nam-1-1965" [Resolution of the Party Military Committee, Southern Region, January 1965]. In author's possession.

39. Statement of the party military committee, quoted in War Experiences Recapitulation Committee of the High-Level Military Institute, *The Anti-U.S. Resistance War for National Salvation 1954–1975: Military Events*, trans. Joint Publications Research Service, JPRS no. 80,968 (Washington, D.C.: Government Printing Office, June 3, 1982), 62.

40. War Experiences Recapitulation Committee, *The Anti-U.S. Resistance War*, 62.

41. "Chien dich Binh Gia, 4-12-1964-3-1-1965" [The Battle of Binh Gia, 4 December 1964–3 January 1965, *Quan doi nhan dan* [People's Army] (2 November 1972), 2. Also see Vien lich su quan su Viet Nam, *Lich su Quan doi nhan dan Viet Nam* [History of the People's Army of Vietnam], vol. II (Hanoi: NXB Quan doi nhan dan, 1988), 251n1.

42. *New York Times* (December 30, 1964), 1; and *New York Times* (January 10, 1965), 1.

43. *New York Times* (January 2, 1965), 1; also Westmoreland, *A Soldier Reports*, 95.

44. Vien lich su Quan doi nhan dan Viet Nam, *Lich su nghe thuat chien dich Viet Nam trong 30 nam chien tranh chong Phap chong My 1945–1975* [Vietnam's Art of the Military Campaign in 30 years of War against France and the U.S. 1945–1975], (Hanoi: NXB Quan doi nhan dan, 1995), 282–287.

45. In the regular army, the increase in the number of desertions from 1964 to 1965 was 120 percent. Jeffrey J. Clarke, *Advice and Support: The Final Years, 1965–1973* (Washington, D.C.: U.S. Army Center of Military History, 1988), Table 3, 43. For a comparison of the Communists' efforts to make their military wing seem "a logical extension of the family and village" with the ARVN's "modern" bureaucratic rational approach, which assured a high level of desertion, see Robert K. Brigham, *ARVN: Life and Death in the South Vietnamese Army* (Lawrence: University Press of Kansas, 2006), 1–18.

46. Quoted in Michael Maclear, *The Ten Thousand Day War* (London: Thames Methuen, 1981), 127–128.

47. Westmoreland, *Report on the War*, 102.

48. Secret speech given in March 1966, in Department of State, *Working Paper on the North Vietnamese Role in South Vietnam: Captured Documents and Interrogation Reports* (Washington, D.C.: Department of State, May 1968), item 302.

49. "Status of Batangan," DCF Ill MAF/PSA, Quang Ngai, May 6, 1969. Uncatalogued document, Carlisle Barracks, Pennsylvania.

50. Merle L. Pribbenow, "The Fog of War: The Vietnamese View of the Ia Drang Battle," *Military Review* (January–February 2001): 96, 97.

51. Notes of a cadre who attended Thanh's speech, in Department of State, *Working Paper,* item 65.

52. Department of State, *Working Paper,* item 65.

53. Robert D. Schulzinger, *A Time for War: The United States and Vietnam, 1941–1975* (New York: Oxford University Press, 1997), 222.

54. As Westmoreland admitted in testimony given for his lawsuit against CBS News in November 1984. A good review of this controversy is Edwin E. Moise, "Why Westmoreland Gave Up," *Pacific Affairs* 58, no. 4 (Winter, 1985–1986): 663–673.

55. The "numbers controversy" flared anew when former CIA analyst Sam Adams accused MACV of undercounting in "Vietnam Cover-up: Playing War With the Numbers," *Harper's* (May 1975): 41–73. For rebuttal, see James J. Wirtz, "Intelligence to Please? The Order of Battle Controversy during the Vietnam War," *Political Science Quarterly* 106, no. 2 (Summer 1991): 239–263. Also see Jake Blood, *The Tet Effect: Intelligence and the Public Perception of the War* (London: Routledge, 2005). Adams elaborated on his argument in a posthumously published book, *War of Numbers: An Intelligence Memoir* (South Royalton, Vt.: Steerforth Press, 1994).

56. Department of State, *Working Paper,* item 65.

57. "In 1967, out of a total U.S. force of 473,000 in Indochina, only 49,500 (10.46 percent of the total) were rifle-carrying grunts of the infantry. . . . In that same year the NVA/VC could put an estimated 63,000 combat troops into the field." Micheal Clodfelter, *Vietnam in Military Statistics: A History of the Indochina Wars, 1772–1991* (Jefferson, N.C.: McFarland, 1995), 238.

58. Thomas C. Thayer, *War Without Fronts: The American Experience in Vietnam* (Boulder, Colo.: Westview, 1985), 39–40.

59. War Experiences Recapitulation Committee of the High-Level Military Institute, *The Anti-U.S. Resistance War for National Salvation 1954–1975: Military Events,* trans. Joint Publications Research Service, JPRS no. 80,968 (Washington, D.C.: Government Printing Office, June 3, 1982), 85.

60. American official and media claims to see a Communist hand behind this particular instance of Buddhist dissent remain unsubstantiated. See Robert J. Topmiller, *The Lotus Unleashed: The Buddhist Peace Movement in South Vietnam, 1964–1966* (Lexington: University Press of Kentucky, 2002), 58–60.

61. War Experiences Recapitulation Committee, *The Anti-U.S. Resistance War,* 89.

62. Willard Pearson, *The War in the Northern Provinces, 1966–1968* (Washington, D.C.: Department of the Army, 1975), 3–9.

63. From a letter written a year later to the Saigon-Gia Dinh party organization, quoted in War Experiences Recapitulation Committee, *The Anti-U.S. Resistance War,* 87–88.

64. Bernard William Rogers, *Cedar Falls-Junction City: A Turning Point* (Washington, D.C.: Department of the Army, 1974), 11–12.

65. PLAF Tactical Operations Center, "Tay Ninh Campaign (3 November–30 December 1966)," February 1, 1967. Translated captured document in author's possession.

66. Jonathan Schell, *The Village of Ben Suc* (New York: Vintage, 1967).

67. William E. DePuy, quoted in Rogers, *Cedar Falls-Junction City,* 78.

68. PLAF Tactical Operations Center, "Tay Ninh Campaign."

69. Rogers, *Cedar Falls-Junction City*, 158.

70. Thayer, *War Without Fronts*, 89–91.

71. Brigadier General Joseph A. McChristian, quoted in Blood, *The Tet Effect*, 31.

72. Quoted in Murray Fromson, "Name That Source," *The New York Times* (December 11, 2006), identifying Weyand as the anonymous source of R.W. Apple's story, "Vietnam: The Signs of Stalemate," *The New York Times* (August 7, 1967).

73. The Communists claimed to have raised the proportion of the South's land redistributed or otherwise "put under the peasants' control" from 50 percent at the end of the war with France to 70 percent in 1965. Lam Quang Huyen, *Cach manh ruong dat o mien Nam Viet Nam* [The Land Revolution in South Vietnam] (Hanoi: NXB Ban khoa hoc xa hoi, 1985), 102, 113.

74. Gareth Porter, ed., *Vietnam: A History in Documents* (New York: New American Library, 1981), 352, 354.

75. See article by Truong Son (pseud. for Nguyen Chi Thanh) in *Visions of Victory*, ed. Patrick J. McGarvey (Stanford, Calif.: Hoover Institution Press, 1969), 119–149; and Van Tien Dung, *May van de nghe thuat quan su Viet-nam* [Problems of Vietnamese Military Art] (Hanoi: NXB Quan doi nhan dan, 1968), 127–193.

5

Air War

Stalemate in the South paralleled a different kind of impasse over the North, Laos, and Cambodia, where U.S. and RVN aircraft rained bombs and missiles for ten years. Begun ostensibly as reprisal for Communist attacks on American targets in the South, the air war quickly broadened into an attempt to force a compromise on Hanoi and to interdict Northern logistical support of revolutionary forces all over Indochina.

The most authoritative account of munitions expended by all American aircraft (including helicopter gunships and C-130 transport planes) was presented during hearings in the U.S. House of Representatives on the impeachment of President Nixon. (See Table 5.1.) The RVN Air Force (RVNAF) and small contingents of Australian and New Zealand air forces expended about 1.4 million additional tons,[1] making the total dropped by all forces on all of Indochina about eight million tons. This figure was more than twice the total dropped by all aircraft in all of World War II. The U.S. Air Force alone dropped three times what it had dropped in all theaters of that war and thirteen times what it had dropped in Korea.[2] One-third of the tonnage fell from B-52s, some of them modified to carry up to 27,000 kilograms (60,000 pounds) of bombs. From altitudes of more than 10,000 meters, a "cell" of three B-52s could carpet a "box" one kilometer wide and three kilometers long.

The data make it immediately obvious that most of the bombing took place inside South Vietnam, followed by Laos, then the DRV, and Cambodia. Including non-U.S. bombing, approximately four million tons of bombs or half the total fell on the South, principally in thinly populated areas and in tactical support of ground combat. The extraordinarily heavy aerial bombardment, not to mention lavish use of artillery, left the South

Table 5.1.   U.S. Aerial Munitions (tons)

	DRV	RVN	Laos	Cambodia	Total
1964	154	3,250	36	0	3,440
1965	40,554	118,360	15,607	0	174,521
1966	128,904	237,332	73,620	0	439,856
1967	246,328	473,038	127,902	0	847,268
1968	227,331	793,663	238,233	0	1,259,227
1969	659	633,562	515,035	70,500	1,219,756
1970	2,467	237,968	453,256	94,207	787,898
1971	2,683	113,395	447,449	63,514	627,041
1972	215,631	551,453	144,127	53,412	964,623
1973	15,397	40,931	78,035	257,465	391,828
Total	880,108	3,202,952	2,093,300	539,098	6,715,458

Source: House of Representatives, Committee on the Judiciary, Hearings, pursuant to H. Res. 803, "A Resolution authorizing and directing the Committee on the Judiciary to investigate whether sufficient grounds
exist for the House of Representatives to exercise its constitutional power to impeach Richard M. Nixon,
President of the United States of America," Book 11: Bombing of Cambodia, May–June 1974, Appendix
D, 90–103.

pock-marked from sea to mountains. Parts of Laos and Cambodia where
the PAVN had logistical facilities were even more heavily cratered. In the
North, the targets were military, transportation, and industrial sites, although under the policy of "graduated pressures" the choicest targets were
not the first hit, in the hope that Hanoi would make concessions to save
them. Bombing of the North was lighter than in the South but geographically more concentrated and more disruptive of economic activity. The
release of a million tons of bombs over the DRV is often cited as the most
intensive campaign of strategic bombing in the history of warfare, but that
distinction may belong to the South if driving people out of the countryside
by bombing and shelling is also considered strategic.[3]

STRATEGY IN SEARCH OF A RATIONALE

The failure of the covert operations to deter Hanoi triggered the Tonkin
Gulf incident and then turned American strategists to the wider use of
bombing.[4] U.S. bombing outside the South began on December 14, 1964,
with eight sorties a week against the Ho Chi Minh Trail in Laos. Communist
attacks on U.S. installations at Pleiku and Qui Nhon in February provided
a pretext to strike the North directly. From "reprisal airstrikes," it was a
short step to sustained bombing. By late March 1965, Operation Rolling
Thunder was sending aircraft against the North daily. From 25,000 in 1965,
the number of sorties grew to 79,000 in 1966 and 108,000 in 1967.[5] The
program continued, with "halts" and "pauses" (nineteen altogether) related

to negotiation offers, until formal peace talks began in November 1968. Begun on the assumption that bombing would change Hanoi's behavior in a few weeks or months, advocates "did not foresee that the program would last several years."[6]

In the beginning the bombing concentrated on military targets in the panhandle south of Hanoi, largely for fear of provoking Chinese intervention. But as that fear waned and panhandle targets were destroyed, restrictions loosened on bombing farther north, near but not in major cities, and in the Red River delta. In mid-1966 petroleum storage facilities all over the country were added to the list of targets. A year later U.S. airplanes were attacking industrial targets and electrical production facilities as far north as the Chinese border, and by late fall 1967 they had destroyed or damaged all but a very few targets of military or industrial value. Aside from rail lines and bridges (repaired many times over), few targets were worth hitting again once they had been bombed.

The initial rationale was to coerce Hanoi into suspending its support for the revolution in the South. American officials believed that Hanoi could not be so deeply committed to reunification that it would jeopardize the economic progress of the North in order to achieve that goal. "Graduated pressures" or "phased escalation" could be coupled with an offer to halt operations in return for concessions in negotiations, or so American policymakers hoped. This calculation was not fanciful, for as we have seen an important faction within the Hanoi leadership had been reluctant to commit the North to large-scale support of the Southern revolution precisely because it feared such a commitment would result in destruction of the North's economic and social gains. U.S. estimates quickly proved erroneous, however, as party leaders refused to bargain away what they all agreed were basic national rights guaranteed by the Geneva Agreements.

Another rationale was to curtail the flow of men and supplies over the Ho Chi Minh Trail into the South. The North, in fact, was able to increase the flow,[7] so the rationale shifted in mid-1965 to limiting the flow's increase. However, success in forcing the North to divert resources into keeping the Trail open also drew more PAVN troops into Laos and more support of the Pathet Lao.[8] The flow of supplies down the trail, in any case, was not the main support of Communist forces in the South until 1968 because the majority were still Southerners who drew on their villages for supply.[9] Yet another argument, made by Secretary of Defense Robert McNamara, was that the bombing had raised morale in the South, and to discontinue it would have a demoralizing effect there.[10] Thus did McNamara make psychological impact on the South,[11] rather than the North, the primary rationale for bombing.

As for effect on the North, unlike Germany in World War II it possessed neither munitions plants nor industries vital to its war effort, as it depended on the Soviet Union and China for most of its weapons, heavy equipment, and sophisticated manufactured goods. Its army did not depend until late in the war on a huge logistics tail but on a relatively primitive transportation system that could, if necessary, be reduced to human porters and oxcarts moving over dirt trails. Political considerations forbade targeting population, dams, dikes, and ports. The bombs had to fall on roads, bridges, fuel dumps, military installations, and transportation complexes. Such targets could be quickly repaired, replaced, moved, or circumvented and so had to be bombed again and again. Air Force General Curtis Lemay advised, "We should bomb them into the stone age."[12] McNamara thought otherwise and told the president in October 1966 that "To bomb the North sufficiently to make a radical impact upon Hanoi's political, economic, and social structure would require an effort which we could make but which would not be stomached either by our own people or by world opinion, and it would involve a serious risk of drawing us into war with China."[13]

Bombing advocates argued that the North could be pushed to some sort of psychological "breaking point." But just what that point was and how much bombing it would take to push the North over it were questions U.S. strategists never answered.[14] Nor was it explained, if it was considered, why the North Vietnamese would succumb to pressures that Germans and Japanese had survived in World War II. In Germany and Japan, bombing, which included terror bombing of cities, reduced confidence in victory, but this had occurred in countries that were already losing and were not engaged in wars of national resistance. To be sure, "graduated" intensification of the bombing gave Hanoi time to brace for attack while pauses gave it respites in which to recover, suggesting to American advocates of airpower that political restrictions on the air campaign made it ineffective. This was a conclusion, however, that ignored the massiveness of the bombing and the measures taken by the North to survive it.

RESURRECTING THE RESISTANCE

The society against which the United States threw its latest technology of war was one of the world's poorest. In a population of nineteen million, three-quarters were cultivators. The Red River delta was one of the world's most densely populated regions, and per capita income was among the world's lowest. Despite some recent improvements in farming techniques, agricultural methods were largely the same as they had been for a millennium. Agricultural production had stagnated from 1958 to 1965, the period during which the government cajoled 90 percent of rural families to join cooperatives.[15] Although some families had joined reluctantly, the cooperatives were based on the communities to which almost all Vietnamese felt a primordial attachment, and they assured an egalitarian distribution of benefits. Furthermore, a large majority of these communities had given their support to the Viet Minh during the resistance against France. (Five thousand out of seven thousand in the Red River delta alone had done so, according to French General Henri Navarre.) Since the bombing began only ten years after the first war's end, these communities were prepared to respond almost reflexively to a call for measures to assure, as their leaders put it, "national salvation."[16]

In December 1964 People's Army propaganda teams began fanning out across the Northern countryside to organize "civilian-military unity days" in every hamlet and village. With skits and storytelling, the teams evoked the powerful imagery of national resistance, then organized people to repair roads, ferry troops across rivers, and assist the army in every way.[17] Work also was stepped up on "combat hamlets and villages" modeled after the fortress communities of resistance-era liberated zones. Each hamlet became, or was supposed to become, a self-sufficient "basis of lasting struggle" with its own arsenal, underground bunkers and storehouses, outlying defenses with connecting trenches, and well-trained militia.[18] Combat hamlets and villages provided territorial defense and mobilized the rural labor force to fix roads and bridges, repair irrigation canals, watch for enemy agents, and maintain agricultural production. Militia forces grew to two million, roughly 10 percent of the population. Although these measures were carried out most urgently along the coastline below the twentieth parallel, much of the countryside was organized to keep supplies moving to the "front," repair bomb damage, and build a dense thicket of popular self-defense against ground attack.

Meanwhile, on February 29, 1965, just two days before Rolling Thunder began and a day after U.S. officials announced that "reprisal airstrikes" would be extended, the North Vietnamese government issued an order to evacuate children and old people from major population centers. Vinh, the assembly point for the Ho Chi Minh Trail, quickly emptied. (See Map 5.1.) About fifty thousand residents of Hanoi left the city by the fall. A second evacuation order in April 1966 extended to everyone who was not "truly indispensable." Government agencies relocated outside the city, factories were dismantled, and the ration cards of "nonessential personnel" were invalidated. People literally had to follow their meal tickets to the countryside. Hanoi's population dropped by half. When raids killed two hundred around Hanoi in November 1967, the city's population fell to two hundred and fifty thousand, one-quarter of its pre-bombing total. Except in the port of Haiphong, the evacuation of cities that lacked Hanoi's importance was even more thorough.[19]

Dispersal of the economy followed the evacuation of the people. One objective was to move industrial targets, such as they were, away from

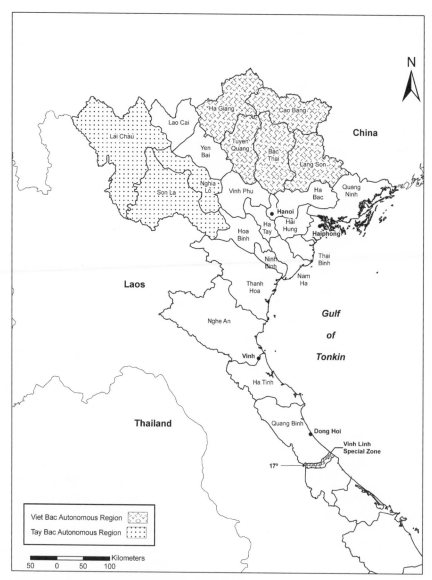

Map 5.1. The Democratic Republic of Vietnam

population centers and aerial detection; another was to increase local economic self-sufficiency. A plan devised in mid-1965 envisioned the development of every province into an integrated, self-sustaining economic unit able to carry on resistance in the event of invasion or destruction of other provinces, just as revolutionary bases had struggled in isolation during the war against France.

The Thai Nguyen iron works and the Haiphong cement factory could not be moved. But pharmaceutical factories, machine shops, textile mills, and other enterprises were knocked down and carted off to the mountains, in some cases to be reconstructed in caves.[20] Some factories hid their machinery in huts scattered through a village and others had to relocate repeatedly to escape detection. Efficiency plummeted of course, and by 1967, many factories were producing less than half of their planned output. But home handicrafts and private production in tiny cottage industries sprang up to help fill the gap in basic consumer needs. Central planning gave way to local initiative,[21] and local party cadres submitted to public criticism. Through decentralization and "direct democracy," the party sought to "recreate the resistance spirit of unity."[22]

Nowhere were these measures more severely tested than in the panhandle provinces through which men and supplies funneled toward the Ho Chi Minh Trail. Hit worst of all was the area just north of the demilitarized zone, which was beginning to recover from some of the most savage typhoons on record when the bombing began. Yet, people seemed more willing to sacrifice the more they were bombed. In Vinh Linh Special Zone, the area just north of the DMZ where even party members had shirked militia duty before the war, 42 percent of the entire population was enrolled in the militia by 1969.[23] On average, it was claimed, every village in the mountains had one hundred militiamen and every village in the plains had three hundred, helping to "maintain security in areas at peace and ready to fight or support the army in the event of war."[24] In Quynh Luu district of Nghe An province, a dike that would have taken more than forty years to complete at prewar rates was said to have been built in six months.[25]

Such reports may have been concocted to shore up confidence, but they played to popular pride in the aptitude of Vietnamese villages to engage in collective action when threatened. Northern (and central) Vietnamese society had been formed in an unremitting struggle with nature. The annual cycle of drought and flood had made individual security dependent on cooperation with others. On an almost yearly basis, peasants had fallen back on village-based cooperation to survive natural calamity, and many times their rulers had done so to thwart a foreign invasion. So it was this time, even to the point of digging vast underground galleries in heavily bombed areas and preparing to fight entirely with local forces, as had been done in the Scholars' Revolt of the 1880s. Against this background, the bombing—like flood, drought, typhoon, or Chinese invasion—appeared as just one in the succession of disasters that it had been the region's lot to endure. Thus it is not surprising that the regime, which had come to power partly on the strength of village-based patriotism, was able to extract enormous sacrifices from people who made them, for the most part, without complaint.

As a Communist state on the Stalinist/Maoist model, the DRV did not rely solely on people's goodwill to guarantee order and security. On the contrary, it possessed highly effective institutions of control that penetrated every corner of society. The family registration system (*ho khau*) required everyone to carry an identity card and families to maintain residence permits. Block captains in towns and cities; vigilance committees in factories, schools and government offices; and "hardcore" citizens in rural hamlets formed a popular movement that provided eyes and ears for the state's security service, the *Cong an*. This organization intensified its work when the air war began. A description of some wartime order and security activities in Ha Bac, the province that extends eastward from Hanoi and where thirty-five hamlets were judged to present a "complicated political situation," is worth quoting at length:

> The movement helped the struggle for security in a timely fashion against counterrevolutionaries and criminals. . . . In January 1965 we smashed a newly formed reactionary organization in the area between Viet Yen, Tan Yen and Hiep Hoa districts of which Nguyen Van Dai (AKA Ly Vien) in Viet Tien (Viet Yen) village was the leader. Nguyen Van Dai was a wicked village bully landlord we had jailed but who on release still refused to submit to reform and who took advantage of the American attacks on our province to organize the "True Vietnam Restoration Party." This fellow issued a program and guidelines for action while waiting for the opportunity of the American/puppet "Northward march" to overthrow our revolutionary government. His organization had 21 members but had no time to go into action before we seized them. . . . [W]e punished many different reactionaries, among which were reactionary followers of Christianity. Generally speaking, our Catholic compatriots are industrious workers who energetically contribute to defense and construction of the nation, but counterrevolutionary groups often influence them to oppose the state. Struggling against Catholic reactionaries takes place in a complicated way, but under the correct leadership of the party committee and aided by the masses, the province people's security organization scored many victories. In 1965, of 115 hamlets having Catholics, we were able to build order and security movements in 72. . . .[26]

In addition to suppressing "counterrevolutionary groups," the Ha Bac *Cong an* in 1967 "warned 51 people for listening to enemy radio, verified whether information was true in 103 cases and checked out 64 anonymous letters sent to cadres and people with the purpose of undermining unity and sowing doubt about our party's leadership."[27] The North clearly was not a seamlessly unified, ideologically unanimous society, but it had discipline and resilience that its enemy in the South lacked.

Conditions of daily life were hard, and not just in the worst-hit regions. Villages that escaped destruction of a road, bridge, or buildings nonetheless suffered from the disruption of markets and the decline of essential supplies. Only large infusions of aid from China and the Soviet Union kept the people fed at a barely adequate level, as population growth outpaced production. Ingenious and strenuous measures maintained health care and education, but the quality of both declined. Yet the party apparently had little difficulty persuading the people to blame their hardships on U.S. aggression.[28] More for inspirational than practical effect, the government distributed handheld weapons to peasants and militia with instructions to set up networks of fire in which to ensnare low-flying planes.

The bombing actually appears to have helped the party promote some of its political and social objectives. Before the war, only 31 percent of all Catholic families in Nghe An province had joined cooperatives, but after just two years of bombing their 80 percent membership was near the national rate.[29] Increased demand for labor to repair roads, rebuild bridges, and serve as porters reduced rural underemployment, helping the government to achieve one of its major goals in the countryside. Ethnic minorities who made up 15 percent of the North's population and straddled sensitive borders found themselves the object of accelerated effort to secure their loyalty to Hanoi. Women not only came to dominate the rural work force but also were catapulted into positions of responsibility and power.[30]

There were signs of discontent, to be sure. No less a figure than Truong Chinh grumbled openly about survival measures that had the effect of repealing socialism. A decree on punishment of "counterrevolutionary crimes" issued in November 1967 hinted at discontent that was broader than just a handful of "revisionists." The state's centralized administrative control weakened as villages assumed responsibility for their own survival and governance. But despite all these signs of stress, none suggested imminent collapse. The reason was that party leaders, government officials, and ordinary people, on the whole, perceived the stakes to be nothing short of national survival, and they believed they were winning. Even after defecting to the West, Bui Tin, a former journalist for the PAVN newspaper, wrote that "although we . . . suffered heavy destruction . . . we still stood surprisingly firm. . . . Factories collapsed, bridges were broken, roads torn to bits, schools and hospitals razed to the ground. But all this only raised the level of bitterness and hatred at being attacked so inhumanely, and conveyed new purpose to our combatants. Our traditional patriotism was strengthened. It inspired us to affirm our fundamental sense of nationhood."[31]

THE LIMITS OF BOMBING

President Johnson declared an end to the bombing on October 31, 1968. Reflecting a fundamental shift in U.S. estimates of the prospects for success, the decision also was tacit acknowledgment that the United States could not go on pulverizing a society so much smaller, weaker, and poorer than itself without provoking moral outrage at home and abroad. U.S. strategists boasted that the campaign was "precise" and "discriminating," but they could not tell where bombs would fall when pilots jettisoned ordnance to evade attack or missed their targets. Fifteen months before the bombing ended, McNamara himself had guessed it was inflicting 1,000 civilian casualties a week and declared the spectacle disgusting.[32] Evidence that the bombing had influenced Hanoi's negotiating position was nil. Evidence that it had staunched the southward flow of men and equipment was unconvincing, prompting proposals to construct an anti-infiltration barrier just below the DMZ and across the Ho Chi Minh Trail in Laos.[33] Besides, 818 U.S. airmen had died and 918 aircraft had been shot down as a result of fire from the North's 6,000–7,000 antiaircraft batteries and nearly 200 SA-2 missile sites. Time and again, the American air force and navy had developed tactics and electronic-warfare technology that nearly overwhelmed the North's air defenses, but each time the North, with Soviet and North Korean assistance, had found ways to counter these improvements.[34] The bombing had indeed found a "breaking point," but it had turned out to be the limit of U.S. will to bomb for dubious gain.

The North was still in ruins when U.S. planes returned during 1972 to carry out the most devastating raids of the entire war. Later, the Communists would reveal that the bombing over the course of the war had destroyed virtually all industrial, transportation, and communications facilities built since 1954, blotted out ten to fifteen years' potential economic growth, flattened three major cities and twelve of twenty-nine province capitals, and triggered a decline in per-capita agricultural output.[35] Perhaps just as debilitating, the economy had become structurally dependent on inputs obtained through foreign aid without much regard to cost, producing chronic inefficiencies and waste.[36] Still, the North had survived, or as party leaders put it "defeated" the U.S. "air war of destruction" and so was able to go on serving as the "great rear" for the war in the South, frustrating Washington's attempt to impose its preferred solution by force.

NOTES

1. Estimate derived by subtracting figures in Table 5.1 from the totals of all allied air forces from 1965 to 1971 provided in *The Air War in Indochina*, ed. Raphael

Littauer and Norman Uphoff (Boston: Beacon, Cornell University Program on Peace Studies, 1972), 279, and adding the annual average of non-U.S. munitions expended (142,585 tons) for the years 1972–1974.

2. Carl Berger, ed., *The United States Air Force in Southeast Asia, 1961–1973* (Washington, D.C.: Office of Air Force History, 1977), 366.

3. I am indebted to David Hunt for pointing out this ambiguity in the meaning of "strategic bombing." Personal communication, January 15, 2008.

4. James Clay Thompson, *Rolling Thunder: Understanding Policy and Program Failure* (Chapel Hill: University of North Carolina Press, 1980), 27–28.

5. "Sorties" included flights devoted to suppressing antiaircraft fire, protecting the planes that carried the bombs, aerial reconnaissance, etc., which accounted for perhaps half of the total flown. The number of sorties thus reflects only the general magnitude of the increase of bombing.

6. Thompson, *Rolling Thunder*, 29.

7. A study produced by the PAVN's logistical branch indicates that in 1965–1968 Group 559 delivered 49 percent of "planned" supplies to the South, with losses due as much to weather and accidents as to U.S. bombardment. Nonetheless, the tonnage delivered in 1968 was 12.6 times as great as the tonnage delivered in 1965. From 1966 to 1972, the average annual loss of trucks (measured in tonnage) was 50.8 percent, yet the Group managed to increase the number of "active" trucks on the trail and the efficiency per truck in each year except two (1969 and 1971). Quan doi nhan dan Viet Nam, *Van tai quan su chien luoc tren duong Ho Chi Minh trong khang chien chong My* [Strategic Military Transport on the Ho Chi Minh Trail in the Anti-U.S. Resistance War] (Hanoi: Directorate of Logistics, 1988), 57, 64, 80n2, 377.

8. Ronald B. Frankum Jr., *Like Rolling Thunder: The Air War in Vietnam 1964–1975* (Bolder, Colo.: Rowman & Littlefield, 2005), 118, 121, 131.

9. A U.S. Air Force study in 1966 estimated that of the three hundred and eighty tons of supply needed per day by a Communist battalion in the South, only thirty-four tons came from outside the South. Mark Clodfelter, *The Limits of Air Power: The American Bombing of North Vietnam* (New York: The Free Press, 1989), 134–135. In 1965–1968 "communist troop strength in the south increased seventy-five percent, the number of their attacks grew by 500 percent, and their overall activity went up 900 percent. These figures demonstrate that the U.S. air offensive had only a minimal impact on the warmaking capabilities of the communists in the south." Micheal Clodfelter, *Vietnam in Military Statistics: A History of the Indochina Wars, 1772–1991* (Jefferson, N.C.: McFarland, 1995), 222.

10. Thompson, *Rolling Thunder*, 45.

11. Presumably McNamara was referring to the morale of Southern leaders, not of ordinary people.

12. Quoted in David Halberstam, *The Best and the Brightest* (New York: Random House, 1969), 560.

13. *The Senator Gravel Edition of the Pentagon Papers* (Boston: Beacon, 1972), vol. 4, 125–126.

14. The answer lay beyond the grasp of U.S. strategists because they wrongly believed that the war pitted the North against the South and the "North's" goal was not central to its continued existence or to top party leaders' hold on power.

For an academic analysis that ably surveys the American puzzlement yet makes the same errors about the Vietnamese, see John E. Mueller, "The Search for the 'Breaking Point' in Vietnam," *International Studies Quarterly* 24, no. 4 (December 1980): 497–519.

15. Chu Van Lam, "45 nam nong nghiep Viet Nam" [45 years of Vietnamese agriculture], *45 nam kinh te Viet Nam (1945–1990)* [45 years of Vietnam's economy, 1945–1990], Dao Van Tap, ed. (Ban Khoa hoc xa hoi, 1990), 100–101.

16. An excellent if somewhat romanticized study of the Northern countryside by a first-hand observer is Gerard Chaliand, *The Peasants of North Vietnam* (Baltimore, Md.: Penguin, 1969).

17. *Quan doi nhan dan* [People's Army], January 9, 1965, 1, 2.

18. *Quan doi nhan dan* [People's Army], November 14, 1964, 2.

19. See William S. Turley, "Urbanization in War: Hanoi, 1964–1973," *Pacific Affairs* (Fall 1975): 370–397.

20. For a comprehensive survey of these measures, see Jon M. Van Dyke, *North Vietnam's Strategy for Survival* (Palo Alto, Calif.: Pacific Books, 1972), 189–215.

21. On the manner in which economic management of the industrial sector became "fundamentally chaotic and certainly not 'planned,'" see Adam Fforde and Suzanne H. Paine, *The Limits of National Liberation* (London: Croom Helm, 1987), 84–99.

22. Editorial, *Nhan dan* [The People], August 30, 1967, 1. For discussion of the war's impact on political participation in the DRV, see William S. Turley, "Political Participation and the Vietnamese Communist Party," in *Vietnamese Communism in Comparative Perspective*, ed. W.S. Turley (Boulder, Co.: Westview, 1980), 182–189.

23. Tran Dong, *Hoc Tap* [Study and Practice] (March 1969), 19.

24. Nguyen Quoc Dung, "Van de ket hop kinh te voi quoc phong trong 40 nam qua" [The Problem of Coordinating the Economy with National Defense over the Past 40 Years], *Nghien cuu lich su*, 4 (223) (1985), 43.

25. Ho Dinh Tu, *Hoc Tap* [Study and Practice] (August 1967), 30.

26. *40 nam chien dau xay dung va truong thanh cua Cong an nhan dan Ha Bac (1945–1985)* [Forty Years of Struggle, Construction and Maturation of the Ha Bac People's Security Service], ed. Nguyen Quynh and Pham Khac Thieu (Ha Bac: Cong an tinh Ha Bac, for internal distribution only, 1985), 88–89.

27. *40 nam chien dau xay dung va truong thanh cua Cong an nhan dan Ha Bac*, 88–89.

28. Chaliand, *The Peasants*.

29. Chaliand, *The Peasants*.

30. See William S. Turley, "Women in the Communist Revolution in Vietnam," *Asian Survey* (September 1972): 793–805.

31. Bui Tin, *Following Ho Chi Minh: The Memoirs of a North Vietnamese Colonel* (Honolulu: University of Hawaii Press, 1995), 63–64.

32. On McNamara's change of attitude see Halberstam, *The Best and the Brightest*, 765–770.

33. James J. Wirtz, *The Tet Offensive: Intelligence Failure in War* (Ithaca, N.Y.: Cornell University Press, 1991), 120–124; Thompson, *Rolling Thunder*, 52–53.

34. Merle L. Pribbenow, "The -Ology War: Technology and Ideology in the Vietnamese Defense of Hanoi, 1967," *The Journal of Military History*, no. 67 (January 2003): 175–200.

35. Vietnam Communist Party, Central Committee Political Report, Fourth Party Congress, December 1976; and *Vietnam: Destruction, War Damage* (Hanoi: Foreign Languages Publishing House, 1977), 28.

36. Fforde and Pain, *The Limits*, 128.

6

Tet

At midnight on January 31, 1968, a million tiny explosions roared across the city. The bright flashes of firecrackers glowed and flickered against the buildings and rising smoke. It was Tet in Saigon, the beginning of the New Year, a sacred time of reunion and renewal, kicking off *Tet Mau Than*, the Year of the Monkey. Two and a half hours later, an old Renault taxi and a small truck crept through the now silent streets and stopped in front of the U.S. Embassy. Nineteen sappers piled out, blew a hole in the compound wall, and rushed in. Meanwhile, some 84,000 Communist troops moved toward their targets in five municipalities, thirty-six province capitals, and sixty-four district seats. The "Tet Offensive" was under way.

For weeks the Communists had meticulously stocked weapons, ammunition, and food in the homes and businesses of urban sympathizers. Vegetable carts bound for market had carried rifles. A ship from Hong Kong had unloaded crates of ammunition marked "firecrackers" onto a dock in Saigon. Combatants and agitators had trickled into the cities one by one or in small groups aboard buses, bicycles, and on foot. Others had gathered at secret locations on the outskirts of the cities. Political cadres had made discreet contact with urban dissidents. And civilians who observed these movements said nothing about them, suggesting that if people did not support the Communists, they at least feared them or were indifferent to the fate of the Saigon authorities.

Not every movement went undetected, and by late January the usual whispering had changed tone, if one listened carefully. But rumors of uprising had been heard before, and the evidence hinted at something too audacious to be believed. The attacks achieved almost complete surprise, not in their occurrence but in their coordination, extent, and intensity.

Despite three years of massive U.S. involvement, the Communist offensive was bigger and more complicated than any before, and it struck the very centers of previously inviolable cities. The bulk of the assault forces were indigenous Southern irregulars, and the preparations for the offensive required at least the passive collusion of many urban residents who the U.S. and its allies supposed were its victims. No matter how the fighting ended, U.S. claims of military victory would not be able to erase the impression among the American people that all the blood and expense had been, and always would be, for naught.

GENESIS OF AN URBAN-RURAL STRATEGY

The Tet strategy was hardly a new idea for the Vietnamese Communists. Its germ was the August Revolution, in which the Communists had provided a nucleus of armed force for the popular uprisings that had brought the party to power in 1945. Party leaders ever since had debated whether surrounding the cities with rural revolution, as Maoists advocated, was sufficient for victory in Vietnam. The problem was that if cut off from the countryside, the cities could still hold out with support from the "imperialist" hinterland. Moreover, given Vietnam's cramped geography, enemies who controlled the cities could launch powerful attacks into liberated areas if not distracted by turbulence in their own rear. The strategic solution, called "general offensive and general uprising" (*tong cong kich/tong khoi nghia*), was to mount simultaneous armed attacks and popular uprisings at many geographical points. Armed forces would enter towns and cities to shield political organs and mass demonstrations that would demand a new government. Even if this plan did not sweep the revolution to power, the Communists theorized, it would destroy the enemy's illusion of progress, jolt him into searching for an exit, and thus constitute a "decisive victory."

The idea exercised a powerful hold on revolutionaries who saw themselves as ordained to lead a small, impoverished nation in resistance against more powerful foes. It was especially popular among party members whose revolutionary careers had begun amidst the patriotic fervor that had seized the cities in August 1945. Many believed that the proper stimulus could make the cities explode again. Party leaders had never neglected the cities in their plans and had considered attack in the enemy's most secure areas, in coordination with region-wide popular uprisings, as their ultimate weapon. If such an offensive could be mounted successfully in the South, it would reaffirm the party's legitimacy as well as bring victory. The Central Committee's resolution 9 in 1963 had foreseen the need for a "general offensive and general uprising," and in 1964, the party's Central Office for South Vietnam (COSVN) had drawn up tentative plans, selected targets,

and subdivided Saigon into five "lines of attack."[1] Fairly detailed planning
was under way by mid-1966.[2]

The Communists realized that they could not simply replay the August
Revolution, however. The United States and the "puppet" Saigon regime
presented a much more formidable obstacle than the shaky Japanese-
installed administration that urban insurrections and a few thousand Communist partisans had overwhelmed in 1945. Much more military power
would have to be projected into the cities and coordinated with popular
uprisings to have great effect. But unlike the situation in 1945, power was
now available and securely based in the North. The party also had a large
organization in the South that leaders believed controlled nearly four million people.[3] If they bypassed U.S. positions, revolutionary forces stood a
chance of destroying the "puppet."

Why did Hanoi decide upon this course at this time? The conjuncture
of several factors made a "decisive blow" appear desirable, at least in the
view of Le Duan, Le Duc Tho and other radical re-unifiers who dominated
the party's leadership. First and foremost was stalemate on the battlefield,
which the Communists recognized but the Americans, or at least Johnson
administration "hawks," did not. American leaders, so far as the Communists could tell, still believed that they could win at acceptable cost or
negotiate their way out of the war on favorable terms. So long as "hawks"
were in charge of American war strategy, the war would continue. The
second factor was the 1968 elections in the United States, which would
put pressure on American leaders to end the war by force or negotiations.
The Johnson administration had begun to make secret diplomatic contacts
with Hanoi, suggesting the onset of new challenges and opportunities.[4]
Third was the Sino-Soviet rift, which motivated both Moscow and Beijing
to support Hanoi's war aims. As time passed, however, Moscow and Beijing had begun to regard each other as the primary threat and the United
States as a potential balancer. Moscow viewed Hanoi's war as an obstacle
to détente with the West and encouraged Hanoi to negotiate. Beijing
preferred that the Vietnamese bleed the U.S. in a protracted guerrilla war,
out of which China could emerge as the dominant power in Asia. China's
acquiescence in Hanoi's determination to mount big offensives and win
"decisive" battles (for which Hanoi needed Soviet weapons and supplies)
was rapidly ebbing.[5] Dependent on foreign suppliers with limited patience
and facing a dangerous enemy, Hanoi could not assume its allies would
continue indefinitely to provide unconditional support. Moreover, Hanoi
had to confront the fact that revolutionary forces inside the South were
no longer growing (for the situation in B2, see Appendix B). Breaking the
stalemate would take more than merely continuing as before. And though
hard to confirm, there is reason to surmise that Le Duan pushed for a
"decisive blow" as a way to weaken his rivals in advance of the succession

struggle that was expected to occur after the death of a now seriously ailing Ho Chi Minh.[6]

Preliminary planning began in April 1967 at a meeting of the Political Bureau and Central Military Committee, which ordered the General Staff to assess the requirements of achieving a "decisive victory." After consulting field commanders,[7] Nguyen Chi Thanh traveled to Hanoi in June to present a draft plan for attacking the cities. Party leaders were receptive. Leaders whose priority was to save the North from the air war's destruction and those who wished to strengthen the North's capacity to support the war in the South could at least agree on the urgent need to drive the Americans out of the war. New difficulties would arise if the United States prolonged its involvement or invaded the North.[8] In instructions to COSVN in June, the Political Bureau pointed out that the United States had the means to increase attacks on the Democratic Republic of Vietnam (DRV) from air and sea, blockade the port at Haiphong, destroy the North's dikes and crops, dominate the area directly south of the demilitarized zone (DMZ), and cut lines of communication and transport to the South. The Americans could be expected to "squeeze us to negotiate on conditions favorable to them so that they can withdraw from the war before their elections in 1968." But if that effort failed the war could "continue within its present sphere, or may widen to engulf the entire country and all of Indochina." It was imperative therefore to deliver a shock that would force the United States to negotiate on terms favorable to the revolution. This required destroying the confidence of American leaders. To keep up the pressure past the offensive's opening blows, it would be necessary as well to disrupt the pacification program and recover control in the countryside in order to sustain "fighting-while-negotiating" from a position of strength for what might prove to be quite a long time.[9]

Thanh's proposal for an all-out effort met stiff resistance. General Vo Nguyen Giap, for one, expressed doubt that Southern irregulars could do the job unaided and resisted substituting regulars of the People's Army of Vietnam (PAVN) for fear this would provoke even higher levels of American involvement.[10] Giap's longstanding position was that the North's first responsibility was to consolidate socialism in the North, preserving itself as a secure rear base, while the South should liberate itself.[11] Such objections, according to historian Lien-Hang T. Nguyen, reopened the contest between "North first" and "South first" factions that had smoldered ever since the ninth plenum in 1963. The dichotomy oversimplifies the debate,[12] but there is no doubt that the Le Duan/Le Duc Tho group seized on it to suppress rivals. "[W]aves of arrests took place in Ha Noi in what has been called the 'Revisionist Anti-Party Affair.' . . . The alleged infiltration of saboteurs was supposedly widespread: cabinet ministers, high-ranking officers in the PAVN, Central Committee members, National Assembly delegates, government leaders, distinguished veterans, intelligentsia, journalists, doctors, and professors were," according to those in the South-first faction, "all part of a massive conspiracy to overthrow the government." Hoang Minh Chinh, labeled a revisionist for supporting the Soviet line on peaceful coexistence in 1963, wrote a paper four years later on "Dogmatism in Vietnam." For this he was imprisoned and later placed under house arrest until long after war's end. As in 1964, members of Giap's staff (but not Giap himself) also found themselves under arrest.[13]

Nguyen Chi Thanh's death on July 6, 1967, may have cleared the way for an agreement on a scaled-down version of his plan.[14] In an article serialized in the party newspaper *Nhan dan* (The People) during September, Giap signaled his grudging approval but warned against expecting quick victory. Orders went out to Southern command organs the same month. Units with the People's Liberation Armed Force (PLAF) and Southern irregulars, those orders made clear, were to bear the main burden of attacking the cities while the PAVN created diversions or stood in reserve.

What, then, did the Communists hope to achieve? The goal was never outright military victory. The Central Committee's formal authorization in January 1968 set the aim no higher than to "smash the aggressive will of the Americans, forcing them . . . to cease war operations against the North, while we protect the socialist North and achieve the paramount objectives of the Southern revolution, which are independence, democracy, peace, neutrality, and national reunification." To the latter end the Committee approved setting up a second front parallel to the National Liberation Front of South Vietnam (NLF) to attract broader popular participation and accelerated efforts to build "people's organs of revolutionary power" in villages, towns, and cities. Uprisings led by these new organizations, the committee hoped, would lead to the formation of a new government more amenable than President Nguyen Van Thieu's to the objectives of the Southern revolution.[15] Party leaders held different expectations of success but agreed it should be possible to jolt the war into a new phase leading toward, if not immediately causing, U.S. withdrawal. The most optimistic hope was that the offensive would paralyze the Thieu regime's military and administrative apparatus, generate popular demand for Thieu to step aside, and end in coalition government. Deprived of the "puppet" on whom the United States depended to justify intervention, the Americans would have no choice but to fix a date for their withdrawal. Somewhat less sanguine was the hope that if the offensive did not achieve this aim quickly, at least it would convince American leaders of the futility of their "limited-war" strategy and the necessity to begin negotiating on Hanoi's terms.

ISLANDS OF PEACE

The cities up to this time had experienced a few terrorist incidents, but never had the fighting in the countryside intruded much upon the daily lives of urban residents. A person born in Saigon, Hue, Danang, or Can Tho could have reached maturity without feeling any direct effect of the war. For many urbanites, U.S. intervention brought jobs and higher pay, not pain and suffering. The only sound of combat audible in Saigon was the low rumble of B-52 strikes thirty kilometers away. City youth also were more likely than rural youngsters to qualify for student draft deferments or to have families with the financial or political means to arrange avoiding military service altogether. Urbanites were largely oblivious to the terror endured by peasants in contested areas and could, if they wished, regard the war as someone else's misfortune.

However, rural insecurity, the destructiveness of U.S. tactics and economic distortions, and "normal" causes of urbanization had contributed to a migration toward the cities. The proportion of the total population living in the country had dropped from 80 percent to about 70 percent since 1960, a trend that would continue, lowering the percentage of rural population a further five percent by 1970.[16] Bombing and shelling that caused civilians to flee contested areas, often to district towns and refugee camps, threatened to shrink the Communists' main base of support. American analysts who noticed the trend were "both troubled and excited to realize that the United States might finally have hit on a strategy to defeat the enemy."[17] The thought occurred as well to General William Westmoreland, who wrote in a memo on the "refugee problem" that relocating people "into areas that will facilitate security and prevent communist control apparatus from re-entering the community" might be quicker and cheaper than trying to drive the "communists and their political control" out of populated areas.[18] "Draining the water to catch the fish" had become *de facto* a major component of American strategy, and it had potential to undermine the Communists' ability to wage a "people's war" from bases in the countryside. But it also gave the Communists reason to hope that they might find an enlarged pool of urban supporters in the shantytowns spreading on the outskirts and along the back streets of Saigon, Danang, Hue, Qui Nhon, Cam Ranh, My Tho, and a dozen lesser provincial capitals.

Noteworthy, too, was the changing political scene in Saigon. The era of revolving-door juntas had ended, and Thieu was safely ensconced in Independence Palace. On the surface it seemed that a new elite—younger, more career-oriented, and more attuned to American ways than the haughty Francophiles it displaced—had consolidated a firm hold on power. Thieu certainly typified the new group. Born a Buddhist in 1923, he was from a modest, provincial background. Emerging from the first war as a major in the French Army, Thieu transferred to the Army of the Republic of Vietnam (ARVN) and trained in the United States in 1957. The next year, at the height of the Diem era, he married into a wealthy Catholic family and converted. With his wife's connections, the right patrons, hard work, and a knack for adroit maneuver, Thieu was admirably equipped to rise in the armed forces but not to inspire a people.

The consolidation of the Thieu regime began with elections for a Constituent Assembly in 1966 when Thieu as chief of state still shared power with Premier Nguyen Cao Ky. Elections for village councils and hamlet chiefs followed in spring 1967, a genuine if fragile accomplishment that laid a basis for the rehabilitation of Saigon-sponsored local government.[19] At the top, however, Thieu and Ky parted over which of them should run for the new office of president. Leaders of opposing cliques, they threatened to split the military once again. Only when it became clear that the majority of senior officers and the United States supported Thieu did Ky agree in June 1967 to run for vice president on Thieu's ticket.

Attention then shifted to culling the civilian candidacies, partly to reduce their exorbitant number but also to remove some genuine electoral threats. Maneuvers in the Constituent Assembly disqualified General Duong Van "Big" Minh, who had announced his intention of returning from exile on the tennis courts of Bangkok. The popular, former minister of economics, Au Truong Thanh, who had dared to withhold a gold sales distributorship from the chief of police, also was eliminated. Further manipulations pared down the number of slates to eleven. Of these, the best known of the civilian tickets was headed by Phan Khac Suu and Dr. Phan Quang Dan, both of whom had gained fame by spending time in Diem's jails. Another ticket, headed by Tran Van Huong and Mai Tho Truyen, could count on the aging Huong's prominence as a lay leader of the Southern Buddhist Association to win support among Buddhists in the deep south. A third slate consisting of Truong Dinh Dzu and Tran Van Chieu lacked personal distinction but captured attention by calling for negotiations to end the war, apparently at the instigation of the NLF.[20] The Dzu-Chieu slate was promptly dubbed the peace ticket.

The campaign was to have begun with a tour of the provinces by all eleven slates of candidates. But Thieu and Ky refused to join, and the air force C-47 that was to carry the other candidates to their first destination delivered them to the wrong airport. Huong claimed that "the government purposely arranged the trip to humiliate us and make clowns out of us."[21] The tour fell apart, and though a second was arranged, the civilians held the military responsible for irregularities that continued down to the end of the campaign. Thieu and his associates, however, were constrained from blatantly rigging the election by the realization that such a sham would create insurmountable problems in Washington and that the election would take place under the scrutiny of a huge foreign press corps and other observers. On September 3, 1967, according to the published results, 83.8 percent of the South's registered voters cast ballots. The Thieu-Ky ticket won, but with only 34.8 percent of the votes. The pattern of local results suggested that Thieu and Ky did best where the military felt most free to help; they lost in Hue, Danang, and Saigon. If the results were at all accurate, it was clear that not one of the slates was the first choice of any significant segment of the electorate. The Dzu-Chieu "peace ticket" took 17 percent of the vote, sufficient along with Thieu's weak showing to encourage the Communists to believe that the urban population could be won over.

U.S. officials naturally pointed to the turnout as evidence that most South Vietnamese preferred a non-Communist government. But the election did little to confirm the stature of Thieu as the man to head it. Moreover, it had taken U.S. pressure to assure that elections were held and to unify the military. It was also obvious that civilian elites, once united in opposition to Diem, were now antagonistic to the military government, and the elections had helped to sharpen that antagonism. These elites were also deeply divided among themselves. The threat of collective defeat by the revolution was no more sufficient in 1967 than in 1964 to restrain the personal ambitions and venality of people who could not be sure how long any state, least of all one held together by American cajoling, would last. Although the city scene was changing, none of this change suggested any worsening of prospects for the Communists.

KHE SANH

Communist strategy called for luring U.S. forces away from population centers, and so the Tet Offensive began neither at Tet nor in the cities. It started with probes in the central highlands in October 1967 and then shifted to Khe Sanh, the outpost of a rifle company of U.S. Marines near the western end of Route 9. Located on an open plateau, the marine camp and nearby Khe Sanh village faced peaks more than 850 meters high, behind which forested hills rolled into Laos and the demilitarized zone. There, the marines found the PAVN 325c Division digging into the peaks during the spring of 1967.[22]

The small marine camp was highly vulnerable. Though supported by artillery at the Rock Pile and Camp Carroll, it was just fourteen kilometers from the terminus of an improved road over which the PAVN could move heavy equipment. The marines therefore sent in two battalions of reinforcements. After a few sharp engagements the PAVN division shifted eastward to join other units in feints and jabs along Route 9. Infantry assaults on strong points, then artillery barrages, made northern Quang Tri province once again a major focus of U.S. attention.

The PAVN 325c was accompanied by the 304th Division when it returned to the Khe Sanh area in December 1967. More marine reinforcements plus an ARVN battalion brought the number of base defenders up to 6,000 Finally, on January 21, the two PAVN divisions broke the suspense with attacks on hilltop outposts and a massive artillery barrage that destroyed the base's largest ammunition dump, cratered the runway, and damaged a dozen helicopters. The "siege" of Khe Sanh had begun.

Reports of PAVN divisions maneuvering in the hills around Khe Sanh conjured up the spectre of Dien Bien Phu, the French outpost overrun by the Viet Minh in 1954. Welcoming the chance to confront Communist regular forces in a set-piece battle, just as the French had welcomed a show-down at Dien Bien Phu, the U.S. command pulled 15,000 elite troops from all over the South's five northern provinces to reinforce the Route 9 combat bases. Soon a total of 50,000 U.S. troops were tied down at Khe Sanh or in its support. By the end of January, as Communist assault forces assembled on city outskirts, attention in Saigon and Washington was riveted on the mountains. For days after the Tet attacks in the cities, Westmoreland and Thieu believed Khe Sanh was the "real" target and the city attacks the diversion, such a hold did Dien Bien Phu have on their thoughts.

PAVN commanders surely would have been happy to overrun Khe Sanh if the opportunity had arisen. But the victors of Dien Bien Phu could not have been less aware than Westmoreland of the differences between the two battlefields. In the first place, Khe Sanh was not remote, as Dien Bien Phu had been. It was barely fifty kilometers from the sea and thirty minutes by air from the huge airbase at Danang. The French, by contrast, had bottled themselves up in rugged mountains more than 300 kilometers from their support in Hanoi. Compared to the 325 assorted aircraft available to the French Union force, the United States could draw from 2,000 aircraft including big C-123 and KC-130 transports to provide Khe Sanh with almost constant aerial cover and supplies. Neither was Khe Sanh in a valley ringed by mountains. On a plateau, it faced hills on only one side, and the marines held several of the peaks. The possibility of encircling the base from high ground did not exist as it had at Dien Bien Phu. Finally, although it used more firepower at Khe Sanh (122-mm artillery, 122-mm rockets, 120-mm mortars, and Soviet-built PT-76 light amphibious tanks) than in any single engagement up to that time, the PAVN faced Khe Sanh's ample artillery, the 175-mm guns of Camp Carroll, and massive, all-weather aerial bombardment. By the time the siege eased in mid-April, U.S. aircraft had dropped more than 100,000 tons of bombs (including 60,000 tons of napalm) on a battlefield of a dozen square kilometers.

The 20,000 PAVN troops deployed at Khe Sanh were less than half the number used at Dien Bien Phu, a deployment indicative of PAVN strategists' true objectives, although the PAVN had tripled in size since 1954. U.S. estimates of PAVN casualties were less than half the 23,000 suffered in the earlier battle. The PAVN attempted to dig siege trenches, as it had done at Dien Bien Phu, but it was a belated effort, and the Communists never tunneled beneath marine positions as required for an all-out assault. The level of effort was sufficient to sustain a credible diversion, but not to mount a realistic attempt to overrun the base so long as the United States was determined to hold it.

The deputy editor of *Quan doi nhan dan* (People's Army) newspaper affirmed in an interview in 1984 that Khe Sanh was never intended to be another Dien Bien Phu. The earlier battle took place after seven years of war had worn down the French, he said, whereas the United States in 1968 was at the peak of its military power. Another Dien Bien Phu at Khe Sanh would have been "impossible." Rather, he said, the Khe Sanh battle, aside from providing a strategic diversion, was a test of the U.S. reaction to the PAVN's use of the DMZ. The PAVN command wanted to determine how the United States would respond if the PAVN staged attacks from the zone, specifically whether the United States would sent troops into the North.[23]

Hanoi derided the Western preoccupation with the Dien Bien Phu analogy as it applied to Khe Sanh. Communist commentators pointed instead to Lang Vei, a Special Forces/Civil Irregular Defense Group (CIDG) camp eight kilometers east of the besieged marines. Led by eleven PT-76s, PAVN forces on February 7, 1968, completely overran the camp, killing 250 montagnard and twenty-four U.S. defenders.

THE ATTACKS ON THE CITIES

While the PAVN was hitting Khe Sanh and several other highland targets, assault forces slipped around lowland outposts to penetrate the cities. Some struck prematurely at Qui Nhon, Kontum, Pleiku, Darlac, and Nha Trang on January 29, but U.S. and ARVN intelligence missed the attacks' significance. More than half of the troops in the ARVN were on leave for Tet. If a skittish American commander had not pulled several U.S. battalions closer to Saigon in early January, the city would have been almost completely devoid of reaction forces. Westmoreland and his staff anticipated an attack in the northern provinces, not in the cities. According to Westmoreland's chief intelligence officer, General Phillip B. Davidson, there was uncertainty about timing, but "no responsible American or South Vietnamese official believed that the enemy would throw himself at the heart of Allied Strength—the cities. The result of such rashness—a devastating enemy defeat—was predictable, and thus, intellectually unacceptable to General Westmoreland and to the other military professionals on his staff."[24] And so in the wee hours of Tet, after the firecrackers had ceased popping, the celebrations had died down and people had gone to bed, the cities were protected thinly or not at all.

The estimated 67,000 maneuver forces and 17,000 hastily recruited guerrillas that attacked the cities had been led to believe that final victory was at hand. Instructions to local party cadres spoke of annihilating Saigon's administrative apparatus and organizing the masses to help consolidate revolutionary power.[25] At higher levels, however, it was understood that these were maximum objectives. During an interview in 1973, the ex-PLAF Colonel Tran Van Dac, who helped plan the attack on Saigon-Cholon, remarked that "the party did not say certain places had to be held for so long, but that what could be occupied should be held as long as possible, the longer the better. Any occupation for some length of time was in some measure a success, a victory."[26]

The wave of attacks that broke on January 31 was the first of three violent surges planned for 1968. The assault on the U.S. Embassy, which resulted in the deaths of five U.S. Marines and all of the attackers, was but the tiny if symbolically devastating kickoff. An estimated 4,000 troops joined in the attacks on Saigon, hitting Tan Son Nhut airfield, the ARVN general staff compound, government ministries, and Independence Palace. Battalion-sized forces invested several neighborhoods in Cholon, Saigon's heavily ethnic Chinese quarter. Tanks and helicopter gunships, sent to evict them, reduced entire city blocks to rubble. Forces that seized large portions of several delta towns were destroyed along with the buildings they occupied. In the large majority of cases, the attacks were beaten back in a few days. However stunning they seemed to the defenders, the attacks would have been more powerful and better coordinated with political demonstrations but for two things: Westmoreland shortened the Tet ceasefire, forcing the Communists to move the date forward at the last minute, and calendars disagreed on what was the first day of the lunar new year.[27]

Only in Hue did attacking forces hold out longer. The estimated 7,500-man assault force, one of the few consisting largely of uniformed PAVN regulars, entrenched itself behind the walls of the old city and fought until February 24. Roughly two-thirds of the attackers and nearly 500 ARVN and U.S. Marines died in bitter door-to-door fighting, artillery shelling, and aerial bombardment that left 100,000 civilian refugees. In the aftermath, 2,800 bodies were found in mass graves, and another 2,000 people were missing, stirring a hot dispute about the causes and implications were the Communists ever to win.[28] Since the war, Communist sources have obliquely admitted that at least some of the killings were deliberate. As the PAVN's official history put it, "Under the leadership of Party organizations the people established a revolutionary governmental apparatus and numerous mass organizations. They organized self-defense forces and eliminated tyrants and traitors."[29] Other sources have described secret organs that helped to "fight dishonest people and eliminate traitors"[30] and ordinary citizens who guided "traitor elimination teams" (*doi tru gian*) to the homes of Saigon government officials, army officers, and "reactionaries."[31] A history published in Hue after the war for limited distribution also noted the "important contribution" made by "armed security and special action units in eliminating traitors . . ." and the "revolutionary atmosphere" that moved people in one district to rise up and chase down, seize and flog (*trung tri*) "reactionaries, thugs, and spies. . . ."[32] The Communists were not alone in executing civilians, though. The journalist Don Oberdorfer learned that as the tide of battle shifted "a South Vietnamese government intelligence unit employed the confusion to send out 'black teams' of assassins to eliminate some of those believed to have aided the enemy."[33] And the numerous "missing" included people who died in bombing and cross fires plus an unknown number of activists who went North with retreating Communist forces. Lethally chaotic, the three-week occupation of Hue was the nearest the Communists came to taking over and holding a city.

The first wave of attacks spluttered to an end with mortar and rocket barrages against several cities. Although U.S. and ARVN forces held the streets, half of all U.S. maneuver battalions were tied down in the First Corps. The ARVN had pulled back into defensive positions, leaving the countryside undefended and the Communists free to reestablish or expand liberated zones. On April 20 a handful of dissident intellectuals presented themselves to the public through clandestine radio broadcast and leaflets as the Vietnam Alliance of National Democratic and Peace Forces and declared adherence to the NLF. The non-Communist founders and their friends in the NLF may well have seen the alliance as a counterweight to the party center's domination of the NLF,[34] but the Central Committee four months earlier had authorized creation of the alliance as the "second front" to attract the support of "patriotic" professionals, the "national bourgeoisie," and anti-Thieu officers and officials of the "puppet army and administration."[35]

A second wave of attacks in early May attempted to keep allied forces off balance and disrupt pacification, but, lacking surprise, the attacks were quickly beaten back, although fighting in a few cities including Saigon was heavy and deadly. A third wave featuring some big-unit battles below the DMZ brought the offensive to a close in August. Cadres who had freely entered rural communities during the first wave when ARVN and U.S. forces withdrew to defend the cities found themselves exposed when those forces pushed back out into the countryside to resume pacification.

Despite initial panic, neither the ARVN nor the Saigon government collapsed. Students and sympathizers helped to form a "revolutionary administration" in Hue and Tra Vinh, but the urban population mostly had taken to shelter when banner-waving activists appeared in the streets. Uprisings were more widespread than most observers supposed in areas where the ARVN and U.S. fall back reduced the risk for civilians to participate,[36] but the gains were not lasting. In the Mekong delta's Dinh Tuong province, "nearly the entire rural population . . . was immediately and effectively mobilized in support of the offensive. . . . In short a *rural* uprising did take place." But the General Uprising did not materialize in the province capital, and when the offensive sputtered out villagers returned to the everyday survival tactics of passivity and evasion.[37]

Communist leaders may have overestimated their support in urban centers, possibly due to inaccurate reporting from the field and a tendency to see signs of anti-Americanism as evidence of sympathy for the revolution.[38] Due perhaps to miscalculation, the Communists allocated less military force to the cities than to the diversions (e.g., Khe Sanh), which may unintentionally have aided in deceiving the U.S. and its allies.[39] The outcome was nonetheless costly. An estimated 40,000 communist soldiers died in the attacks,[40] compared with 1,100 Americans and 2,300 for the ARVN. As communist battalion-sized attacks tapered off, Washington and Saigon claimed a military victory.

THE AMBIGUITIES OF DEFEAT

But the military balance hardly mattered and was in any case difficult to assess. As the fighting subsided in Hue, General Westmoreland claimed that the Communists had used up all of their "military chips" in one last "throw of the dice." Now weakened and overextended, he said, they were vulnerable as never before, and their vulnerability presented a "great opportunity" to go for the kill. With the agreement of the Joint Chiefs, Westmoreland proposed an "amphibious hook" around the demilitarized zone to destroy bases and staging areas, attacks on sanctuaries in Laos and Cambodia, and intensified bombing of the North. Westmoreland requested more than two hundred thousand additional troops to carry out his plan, an increase that would require mobilizing the reserves.[41]

Westmoreland's request was submitted in a report by General Earle G. Wheeler, chairman of the Joint Chiefs, which presented a bleak prospect if the request were not granted. Though crafted to shock, the report, dated February 27, 1968, was more realistic than many that had preceded it. Reproduced in *The Pentagon Papers*, it made the following points:

- The current situation in Vietnam is still developing and fraught with opportunities as well as dangers.

- There is no question in the mind of MACV [U.S. Military Assistance Command, Vietnam] that the enemy went all out for a general offensive and general uprising and apparently believed that he would succeed in bringing the war to an early successful conclusion.
- The enemy failed to achieve this initial objective but is continuing his effort. Although many of his units were badly hurt, the judgment is that he has the will and the capability to continue.
- Enemy losses have been heavy; he has failed to achieve his prime objectives of mass uprisings and capture of a large number of the capital cities and towns. However, with replacements, his indoctrination system would seem capable of maintaining morale at a generally adequate level. His determination appears to be unshaken.
- The enemy is operating with relative freedom in the countryside, probably recruiting heavily. . . . His recovery is likely to be rapid; his supplies are adequate; and he is trying to maintain the momentum of his winter-spring offensive.
- The structure of the GVN [Government of Vietnam, i.e., Saigon] has held up but its effectiveness has suffered.
- The [ARVN] held up against the initial assault. . . . However, ARVN is now in a defensive posture around towns and cities and there is concern about how well they will bear up under sustained pressure.
- The initial attack nearly succeeded in a dozen places, and defeat in those places was only averted by the timely reaction of U.S. forces. In short, it was a very near thing.

The report then came to its sober conclusion:

> MACV has three principal problems. First, logistic support north of Danang is marginal owing to weather, enemy interdiction and harassment and the massive deployment of U.S. forces into the DMZ/Hue area. Opening Route I will alleviate this problem but takes a substantial troop commitment. Second, the defensive posture of ARVN is permitting the VC to make rapid inroads in the formerly pacified countryside. ARVN, in its own words, is in a dilemma as it cannot afford another enemy thrust into the cities and towns and yet if it remains in a defensive posture against this contingency, the countryside goes by default. MACV is forced to devote much of its troop strength to this problem. Third, MACV has been forced to deploy 50 percent of all U.S. maneuver battalions into I Corps, to meet the threat there, while stripping the rest of the country of adequate reserves. If the enemy synchronizes an attack against Khe Sanh/Hue-Quang Tri with an offensive in the Highlands and around Saigon while keeping the pressure on throughout the remainder of the country, MACV will be hard pressed to meet adequately all threats. Under these circumstances, we must be prepared to accept some reverses.[42]

If the report sought by means of candor to alarm the president into expanding the war, it backfired. Coming less than three months after West-moreland had said the end of the war was in sight, it only confirmed the pessimism of the new secretary of defense, Clark Clifford, and caused the president to turn to dovish civilians for advice.[43] Disclosure of the troop request on March 10 in the *New York Times* provoked a public uproar. The official optimism of years past suddenly seemed proof of incompetence or deception. Moreover, no one could be certain that even with the additional troops the United States could impose a military solution or intimidate Hanoi into submission. Something messier, riskier, and as inconclusive as past events seemed just as likely.

The Senate Foreign Relations Committee meanwhile had held hearings on the Tonkin Gulf Incident that cast doubt on Johnson's version of that pivotal event. Congressional support for the war, which until then had been solid, began to ebb away. In mid-March, Senator Eugene McCarthy (D-Minn.), the Democrat's "peace candidate" for the presidential nomination, took 42 percent of the vote in the New Hampshire primary, inspiring Senator Robert Kennedy (D-N.Y.) to join the race on an antiwar platform. Although Johnson beat McCarthy in New Hampshire, the president sensed impending defeat. If he stood for reelection, the campaign would divide the nation; if he won, his presidency would be ineffectual. So, on March 31, 1968, Johnson announced that he would not seek the nomination for another term. He also declared a bombing halt over the North except for a narrow strip above the demilitarized zone and called on Hanoi to agree to peace talks. Hanoi accepted on condition that the talks begin by discussing a complete bombing halt. The United States agreed, and formal talks opened in Paris in May.

The Tet Offensive demolished the credibility of officials who had claimed to see "light at the end of the tunnel." Dovish opinion gained respectability within the administration itself. In large measure, it was Lyndon Johnson who had defeated both himself and his policies by refusing to make hard choices. A consensus-seeking, centrist politician, he had sought to hoard the capital of his 1964 landslide victory by antagonizing no one. Fearful of the right, he had refused to "sell out" Saigon and withdraw. Reluctant to antagonize the left, he had given the Joint Chiefs less than what they asked. Above all, needing support for ambitious domestic reforms (civil rights and the "Great Society" programs to combat poverty), he had dreaded becoming the first U.S. president to lose a war. At each moment that called for decision, Johnson had chosen only to stave off defeat. But absence of defeat was a recipe for stalemate, and endless war was acceptable to no one.

THE PATIENT PUBLIC

American public support for the war was about what it had been for the Korean War, though less favorable than support for World War II and a good

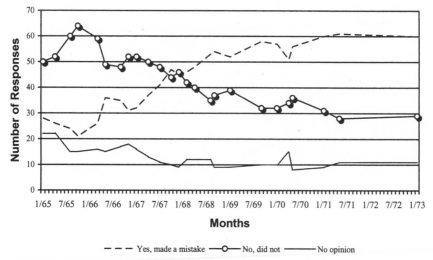

Figure 6.1.   U.S. Public Support for the War
Source: Survey by Gallup Organization, January 1965–January 1973, iPOLL Databank, The Roper Center for
   Public Opinion Research, University of Connecticut, www.ropercenter.uconn.edu/ipoll.html (accessed
   December 30, 2006).
Note: The question was, "Do you think the U.S. made a mistake sending troops to fight in Vietnam?," except for January, April, and October 1965, when it was "Some people think we should not have become
   involved with our military forces in Southeast Asia, while others think we should have. What is your
   opinion?" Markers on the "yes, made a mistake" (= no, we should not have become involved) line indicate
   months the poll was taken.

deal more favorable than support for World War I. Support began strong
as American troops entered the war in Vietnam then slowly fell in response
to the rise in casualties and the inconclusiveness of the fighting (see Figure
6.1). Support (indicated by the response, "no, did not make a mistake") actually increased slightly right before the Tet Offensive while the administration was trumpeting American successes and enemy losses. The percentage
of people expressing belief that the United States was making "progress"
also shot up seventeen points from July to November 1967 before it fell
back during 1968.[44] This pattern has been cited as evidence that the contrast
between official optimism before the offensive and media reports of defeat
afterward caused the public to turn against the war, making it impossible
for Johnson or his successors to prosecute the war effectively.[45] But doubt
whether victory was attainable had begun to spread *before* the offensive,
and Tet's primary impact on policy was to alter the balance of influence
among policy advisors. As the rise in public support during the Republican
National Convention in August (hard on the heels of resumed bombing)
and, later, during the invasion of Cambodia suggests, people were as ready
to support continued belligerency after Tet 1968 as they had been before
it. The proportion of people approving the president's handling of the war

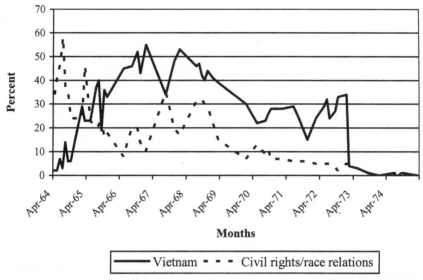

Figure 6.2. Issue Salience in U.S. Public Opinion: percent of respondents ranking "Vietnam" or civil rights and race relations as "most important"
Source: Public Opinion Online, Roper Center at University of Connecticut, Lexus-Nexus. Retrieved December 30, 2006.
Note: The question was, "What do you think is the most important question facing the country?"

reached its lowest point (29 percent) in September 1967 and rose modestly *after* the offensive began. After Richard Nixon's election, it exceeded 50 percent for most of his presidency, spiking regardless whether Nixon made a gesture toward peace or ordered more bombing.[46] People supported action if they believed it would move the war toward a conclusion. It was the cost and promises without result that annoyed them. By shattering the illusion of progress, the Tet Offensive caused people to reflect about the war's aims and costs, but it did not cause them to turn suddenly against continued involvement. Declining support for the war was a gradual, long-term trend, more closely associated with the length and rising costs of war than with any specific event.[47]

As support declined, so did the war's priority as a public issue. The other issue that commanded significant attention was the combination of civil rights and race relations (see Figure 6.2). Asked to name the most important problem facing the United States, the largest percentage of Americans from February 1965 to August 1971 said Vietnam. Civil rights and race relations came second. The one time a third issue beat Vietnam for first place was in May 1970, when "student unrest" was a trope for "Vietnam." The war's salience spiked at the very beginning of the Tet Offensive (though no more than in January 1967) but settled back to pre-Tet levels within a few months. After that public attention declined in rough parallel with declines in American casualties and levels of American military activity. Tet was pivotal for the Johnson administration, but not because of any surge in public pressure to end the war.

Contrary to common belief, support for the war was stronger among young people than older Americans. The antiwar movement had the appearance of a youth crusade because young people were more visible in demonstrations. Both Johnson and Nixon feared obsessively that foreign Communists would exploit the youth movement, and both pressured executive branch agencies to gather information on antiwar activists. They need not have worried. The antiwar community was "too diverse and freewheeling to be under anyone's control."[48] The leading student of U.S. wartime public opinion credits the antiwar protest movement with electing Nixon twice: once in 1968 by withholding votes that would have given victory to Hubert Humphrey, who steadfastly defended Johnson's war policies, and once in 1972 by capturing control of the Democratic party and nominating antiwar candidate George McGovern, "the worst presidential candidate [in terms of electability] any party has put forward in modern times."[49]

Counting from the first day of Tet in 1968, American participation in the war would continue for five years and fifty-seven days, about twice the time that had passed since U.S. Marines hit the beach in 1965. Thirty thousand more American soldiers would die. To be sure, Americans would grow weary of war and divided over what to do, but only a minority wanted peace at any price. Constraints on presidential action based in Congress, the Senate, and the administration itself would be stronger than any imposed by the broad public.

THE COMMUNIST VICTORY

How did the Communists view Tet and its aftermath? The first COSVN assessment on January 31, 1968, claimed success in "paralyzing" the Saigon administration, confusing the U.S. command, and inflicting heavy damage. But efforts to seize "primary objectives" and to "motivate the people to stage uprisings and break the enemy's oppressive control" were disappointing.[50] The Communists realized from the start that they were unlikely to achieve their maximum aims.

In March, a fuller COSVN assessment directed attention to the successful disruption of the enemy's "two-pronged tactic" of military action and rural pacification. U.S. and ARVN forces, the assessment accurately observed, had been forced to withdraw from the countryside to defend the towns, cities, and lines of communication. In consequence, "additional wide areas in the countryside containing a population of 1.5 million inhabitants" had been liberated. The revolution had gained access to "immense resources of manpower and material." But the offensive had failed to eliminate much of the enemy armed force; the urban attacks had "not created favorable conditions for motivating the masses to arise"; and recruitment was insufficient to sustain "continuous offensives and uprisings."[51]

Seeking something grander than talks in Paris, the Communists proceeded in May with their second wave of planned attacks. "The Americans," *Quan doi nhan dan* (People's Army newspaper) editorialized, "have not given up, so our people will have to suffer more before we can win final victory." In fact, Southern cadres had begun to question why they should do all of the suffering to obtain relief for the North alone; others wondered why, if negotiations had begun, they had to go on fighting. General Van Tien Dung, the PAVN chief of staff, replied to the carping by pointing out that a bombing halt was essential if the North were to strengthen its role as the "great rear area" for the Southern revolution,[52] and a COSVN directive dated January 10 castigated cadres who had thought the campaign would be a "one-blow affair."[53]

The U.S. agreement to an unconditional bombing halt and NLF participation in four-party talks allowed party leaders to claim a satisfactory outcome. As explained to lower-ranking cadres, the United States had been forced to de-escalate, cease bombing the North, and join Hanoi at the conference table.[54] Final victory was conceded to lie in an indeterminate future, but the "limited war" strategy had been discredited. U.S. plans to escalate had been preempted, and the war had entered the penultimate phase of "fighting-while-negotiating."[55] The battlefield result was a disappointment, but it opened up political opportunities. As PAVN General Tran Do put it, "In all honesty, we didn't achieve our main objective, which was to spur uprisings throughout the South. . . . As for making an impact on the United States, it had not been our intention—but it turned out to be a fortunate result."[56]

The party's official history describes the Tet Offensive as a great victory, and in the only sense that mattered—impact on the enemy's calculus of cost relative to objectives—it was. But many cadres had hoped to turn the tide of battle inside South Vietnam and ruefully questioned the price they had paid for mere negotiations and a bombing halt in the North. According to wartime leaders in Southern Trung Bo (Communist Military Regions 5 and 6), "numerical strength diminished greatly, stores of weapons and ammunition were empty, food was insufficient, and production in the rear collapsed. In some armed units the ration per soldier per day was only 200 grams of cooked rice. . . ." Dependent on prepositioned supplies, units scattered before U.S. and ARVN counterattacks and pacification drives when supplies ran out.[57] Other regions were no better off. Former PLAF leader Madame Nguyen Thi Dinh described in an interview the post-Tet period as an "especially difficult time."[58] Communist histories are virtually unanimous in using the word "difficult" to depict the period from late 1968 through 1970. Just why it was difficult has been explained in bitter detail by one of the offensive's planners, General Tran Van Tra, in a book that was suppressed soon after publication:

> In Tet 1968, we did not correctly assess the concrete balance of forces between ourselves and the enemy. Nor did we fully realize that the enemy still had considerable capabilities while ours were limited. Consequently, we set requirements that exceeded our actual strength. That is, we based our action not on scientific calculations or careful weighing of all factors but, in part, on an illusion which arose from subjective desire. Although the decision was wise, ingenious and timely . . . and created a significant strategic turning point in Vietnam and Indochina, we suffered heavy losses of manpower and matériel, especially of cadres at various echelons, which caused a distinct decline in our strength. Subsequently, we not only were unable to preserve all the gains we had made but also had to endure myriad difficulties in 1969–70 so that the revolution could stand firm in the storm. While it is obvious that the road to revolution is never a primrose path . . . in Tet, 1968, had we considered things more carefully and set forth correct requirements in conformity with the balance of forces between the two sides, our victory would have been even greater, our cadres, troops and people would have spilled less blood, and the subsequent development of the revolution would have been much different.[59]

While careful to blame an anonymous "we," Tra articulated the belief that when the party leadership made mistakes it was always the Southern revolution that paid for them. In this he was not alone. Cadres posted to the South tended to believe that things would have been different if Nguyen Chi Thanh had lived. He, many believed, would have kept the more cautious high command in Hanoi from scaling down his plan, and his genius for mass organization would have guaranteed a better popular response in the cities. The first wave of attacks would have been more powerful, touching off uprisings that would have made the second wave more powerful still. Each successive surge of violence would have been stronger than the last. As it was, complained one former regroupee captain, the campaign had "an elephant's trunk and a snake's tail": it started big and tapered off to nothing.[60] Behind such views lay the firm conviction that what had prevented the masses from rising to support the revolution was fear of reprisal. If the enemy's "oppressive apparatus" had been broken, the people would have flocked to the revolution's banner. A short leap of faith sustained Southern cadres' confidence that more force and better organization would inspire greater uprisings next time. As General Tra wrote, "Tet 1968 was an extremely valuable practical experience."[61]

NOTES

1. Tran Van Tra, *Nhung chang duong cua "B2-Thanh dong": tap V, Ket thuc cuoc chien tranh 30 nam* [Stages on the Road of the B2-Bulwark, vol. V, Concluding the 30 Years War] (Ho Chi Minh City: Van Nghe, 1982), 144.

2. See the letter from comrade Ba (Le Duan) to the Saigon regional party committee, *Viet-Nam Documents and Research Notes*, no. 102, part 1 (Saigon: U.S. Mission, February 1972).

3. Tra, *Nhung chang duong*, 128.

4. Ronnie E. Ford, "Intelligence and the Significance of Khe Sanh," *Intelligence and National Security* 10, no. 1 (January 1995): 148–152.

5. John Garver, "The Tet Offensive and Sino-Vietnamese Relations," in *The Tet Offensive*, ed. Marc Jason Gilbert and William Head (Westport, Conn.: Praeger, 1996), 46–52, ably describes the doctrinal dispute between Hanoi and Beijing but misses a material basis for Beijing's concern in Hanoi's dependency on the Soviet Union for the conventional armament needed to wage big-unit warfare.

6. Bui Xuan Quang, "Vietnam: Tet 1968, la déchirure," *Cosmopolitiques* (March 1988): 41.

7. Vien lich su quan su Viet Nam, *Lich su Quan doi nhan dan Viet Nam* [History of the Vietnam People's Army] (Hanoi: NXB Quan doi nhan dan, 1988), vol. II, 369–370.

8. See planning documents for attacks on Saigon-Cholon, *Viet-Nam Documents and Research Notes*, no. 45 (October 1968), 10.

9. "Chi thi cua Bo chinh tri ban chap hanh trung uong gui Trung uong cuc (trich)" [Directive of the Political Bureau to the Central Office (excerpt)], in *Mot so van kien cua Dang ve chong My, cuu nuoc, Tap II (1967–1970)* [Some Party Documents on the National Salvation Resistance against America] (Hanoi: NXB Su That, 1986), 49–52.

10. Vo Nguyen Giap, *May van de duong loi quan su cua Dang ta* [Some Problems of our Party's Military Line] (Hanoi: NXB Su That, 1970), 325–384.

11. For discussion of Giap's views and conflicts with other leaders, see Cecil Currey, "Giap and Tet Mau Than 1968: The Year of the Monkey," in *The Tet Offensive*, ed. Gilbert and Head, 73–88.

12. Any attempt to identify clear-cut, stable factions in Hanoi's politics is destined to fail. Some leaders who were anti-revisionist, making them "pro-China" in 1963, were supporters of big-unit warfare and against China's preference of protracted war by 1967; and General Giap, who was about as consistent as any leader in supporting the Chinese preference for protracted war found himself, in both 1963 and 1967, lumped with the "pro-Soviet" revisionists. Other issues besides the war faced the leadership, and these caused shifting, cross-cutting alliances. That the Anti-Party Affair resonated across the years suggests an element of personal rivalry as much as disagreement over strategy, ideology, or policy. For a nuanced discussion, see Sophie Quinn-Judge, "The Ideological Debate in the DRV and the Significance of the Anti-Party Affair, 1967–68," *Cold War History* 5, No. 4 (November 2005): 479–500.

13. Lien-Hang T. Nguyen, "The War Politburo: North Vietnam's Diplomatic and Political Road to the Tet Offensive," *Journal of Vietnamese Studies* 1, no. 1–2 (February–August 2006): 25, 26, 128–129n.

14. Thanh's official obituary, written by Bui Tin, the PAVN journalist who later defected, said he died of heart failure in Hanoi. See Bui Tin, *Following Ho Chi Minh: The Memoirs of a North Vietnamese Colonel* (Honolulu: University of Hawaii Press, 1995), 61–62. U.S. intelligence claimed he died in a B-52 strike in Binh Duong province (or in Hanoi from wounds suffered in such a strike). Hoang Van Hoan, a member of the Political Bureau who defected to China in 1979, claimed in his memoirs that Thanh was murdered, but the plot could never be exposed because of the damage it would do to the reputation of Le Duan, the party's general secretary. Hoang Van Hoan, *Giot nuoc trong bien ca* [Tears in an Open Sea] (Beijing: Ban Tin Viet Nam, 1986), 420. Tin stuck by his account after leaving Hanoi for exile in the West.

15. "Nghi quyet hoi nghi lan thu 14 cua ban chap hanh trung uong Dang (khoa III) [Resolution of the 14th plenum of the Third Central Committee], January 1968, in *Mot so van kien cua Dang ve chong My, cuu nuoc, Tap II (1967–1970)* [Some Party Documents on the National Salvation Resistance against America] (Hanoi: NXB Su That, 1986), 70.

16. See Allen E. Goodman and Lawrence M. Franks, "Dynamics of Migration to Saigon, 1964–1972," *Pacific Affairs* 48, no. 2 (Summer 1975): 199–214. Survey research showed that for people migrating to Saigon, "the war was only one of a number of reasons" for their decision, according to Goodman and Franks, "Between War and Peace: A Profile of Migrants to Saigon," Southeast Asia Development Advisory Group (New York, n.d.), 1. For people fleeing contested areas to towns and camps, however, the war was clearly the major motivating factor.

17. See David Hunt, *Into the Maelstrom: Vietnam's Southern Revolution, 1959–1968* (Amherst: University of Massachusetts Press, forthcoming), chapter 7.

18. Westmoreland memorandum titled "The Refugee Problem" dated January 4, 1968, quoted in David W. P. Elliott, *The Vietnamese War: Revolution and Social Change in the Mekong Delta 1930–1975*, vol. 2 (Armonk, N.Y.: Sharpe, 2003), 1133.

19. For a hopeful assessment of prospects for creating "political community" through elections, see Allen E. Goodman, *Politics in War: The Bases of Political Community in South Vietnam* (Cambridge, Mass.: Harvard University Press, 1973).

20. Robert K. Brigham, *Guerrilla Diplomacy: The NLF's Foreign Relations and the Viet Nam War* (Ithaca, N.Y.: Cornell University Press, 1998).

21. *Saigon Post* (August 8, 1967), cited in Charles A. Joiner, *The Politics of Massacre: Political Processes in South Vietnam* (Philadelphia: Temple University Press, 1974), 126; also see 97–171 for detailed analysis of this election.

22. Background on Khe Sanh may be found in Willard Pearson, *The War in the Northern Provinces, 1966–1968* (Washington, D.C.: Department of the Army, 1975), 29–80; and in Bernard C. Nalty, *Air Power and the Fight for Khe Sanh* (Washington, D.C.: United States Air Force History, 1973). On the Communist view of this battle, see Ang Cheng Guan, *The Vietnam War from the Other Side: The Vietnamese Communists' Perspective* (London and New York: RoutledgeCurzon, 2002), 129–130.

23. Interview with Colonel Nghiem Tuc in Hanoi, April 23, 1984.

24. Phillip B. Davidson, *Vietnam at War, The History: 1946–1975* (Novato, Calif.: Presidio, 1988), 478–480.

25. See the directive of November 1, 1967, from the party's southern province-level standing committee in *Vietnam: The Definitive Documentation of Human Deci-*

sions, ed. Gareth Porter (Stanfordville, N.Y.: Earl M. Coleman Enterprises, 1979), 477–480.

26. Interview with Colonel Tran Van Dac (aka Tam Ha), Saigon, February 23, 1973, on deposit in *Interviews with PAVN and LDP Defectors,* Morris Library, Southern Illinois University Carbondale, 1974.

27. Ronnie E. Ford, "Tet Revisited: The Strategy of the Communist Vietnamese," *Intelligence and National Security* 9, no. 2 (April 1994): 272–273.

28. See Douglas Pike, *The Viet Cong Strategy of Terror* (Saigon: U.S. Embassy, February 1970); Don Oberdorfer, *Tet! The Story of a Battle and Its Historic Aftermath* (Garden City, N.Y.: Doubleday, 1971); Steve Hosmer, *Viet Cong Repression and Its Implications for the Future* (Lexington, Mass.: Heath, 1970), 28; D. Gareth Porter and Len E. Ackland, "Vietnam: The Bloodbath Argument," *The Christian Century* (November 5, 1969): 1414–1417; and Gareth Porter, "U.S. Political Warfare in Vietnam—The 1968 Hue massacre,'" *Indochina Chronicle* (June 1974).

29. The Military History Institute of Vietnam, *Victory in Vietnam: The Official History of the People's Army of Vietnam, 1954–1975,* trans. Merle L. Pribbenow (Lawrence, Kan.: University Press of Kansas, 2002), 218.

30. Tong Hoang Nguyen, "Ky niem khong quen" [Unforgettable Memories], in *Hue Xuan 68* [Hue, Spring '68] (Hue: Thanh Uy Hue, 1988), 204.

31. Le Thi Mai, "Tro lai mua xuan" [Going Back to Spring], in *Hue Xuan 68* [Hue Spring '68] (Hue: Thanh Uy Hue, 1988), 296–297. As noted earlier, in the party's internal discourse and documents the term *tru* usually implied "exterminate," but "eliminate" is probably closer to the intended meaning in works meant for public consumption.

32. Ban tong ket chien tranh chien truong Tri-Thien-Hue, *Chien truong Tri-Thien-Hue trong cuoc khang chien chong My, cuu nuoc toan thang* [The Tri-Thien-Hue Battlefield in the Anti-U.S. National Salvation Resistance] (Hue: NXB Thuan Hoa, 1985), 142, 147.

33. Oberdorfer, *Tet!,* 232.

34. Brigham, *Guerrilla Diplomacy,* 89.

35. "Nghi quyet hoi nghi lan thu 14 cua ban chap hanh trung uong Dang (khoa III) [Resolution of the 14th plenum of the Third Party Central Committee], January 1968, in *Mot so van kien cua Dang ve chong My, cuu nuoc, Tap II (1967–1970)* [Some Party Documents on the National Salvation Resistance against America] (Hanoi: NXB Su That, 1986), 70.

36. As Ngo Vinh Long argues in "The Tet Offensive and Its Aftermath," in *The Tet Offensive,* ed. Gilbert and Head, 89–105.

37. Elliott, *The Vietnamese War,* 1044 and chapter 19 *passim.*

38. James J. Wirtz, *The Tet Offensive: Intelligence Failure in War* (Ithaca, N.Y.: Cornell University Press, 1991), 82–83.

39. Wirtz, *The Tet Offensive,* 83–84.

40. For a debunking of higher estimates that suggest that Communist casualties might well have been lower than the widely accepted one give here, see Ngo Vinh Long, "The Tet Offensive . . . ," 105–108.

41. John B. Henry, "February 1968," *Foreign Policy* (Fall 1971): 17, 21.

42. *The Pentagon Papers,* Senator Mike Gravel edition, vol. 2, (Boston: Beacon, 1971), 546–547.

43. See Clark Clifford, "A Viet Nam Reappraisal," *Foreign Affairs* (July 1969): 601–622.

44. *Survey by Gallup Organization, January 1967–July 1969*, iPOLL Databank, The Roper Center for Public Opinion Research, University of Connecticut, www .ropercenter.uconn.edu/ipoll.html (accessed December 30, 2006).

45. See Jake Blood, *The Tet Effect: Intelligence and the Public Perception of War* (London: Routledge, 2005).

46. *Survey by Gallup Organization, September 1964–February 1973*, iPOLL Databank, The Roper Center for Public Opinion Research, University of Connecticut, www.ropercenter.uconn.edu/ipoll.html (accessed December 30, 2006).

47. As it was in the Korean War, which "followed to a remarkable degree the same trend pattern and was a function of the logarithm of the number of American casualties." John E. Mueller, *War, Presidents and Public Opinion* (New York: Wiley, 1973), 266.

48. David Maranis, *They Marched into Sunlight* (New York: Simon & Schuster, 2003), 199.

49. John Mueller, "Reflections on the Vietnam Antiwar Movement and on the Curious Calm at the War's End," *Vietnam as History*, ed. Peter Braestrup (Washington, D.C.: University Press of America, 1984), 153.

50. "Circular from Central Office of South Vietnam," *Visions of Victory: Selected Vietnamese Communists Military Writings, 1964–1968* ed. and trans. Patrick J. McGarvey (Stanford: Hoover Institution Publications, 1969), 252–256.

51. "Requirement and Purpose of Study of the Sixth Revolution of Nam Truong," notes of a cadre, *Viet-Nam Documents and Research Notes*, no. 38 (July 1968).

52. *Quan doi nhan dan* [People's Army], June 17, 1968, 1–3.

53. Captured document released to the press by the U.S. Mission, Saigon, August 21, 1968, in *Vietnam: The Definitive Documentation*, ed. Porter, 512–516.

54. Captured document released to the press by the U.S. Mission, Saigon, November 8, 1968, in *Vietnam: The Definitive Documentation*, ed. Porter, 517–519.

55. Cuu Long (pseud.), in *Quan dol nhan dan* [People's Army], January 15, 1969, 2–3.

56. Quoted in Stanley Karnow, *Vietnam: A History* (New York: Viking, 1983), 523.

57. Hoi dong bien soan lich su Nam Trung bo khang chien, *Nam trung bo khang chien (1945–1975)* [The Southern Trung Bo Resistance, 1945–1975] (Hanoi: Vien Lich su Dang, 1992), 403, 406.

58. Interview with the author, Hanoi, March 30, 1983.

59. Tra, *Nhung chang duong*, 57–58.

60. Interviewed in Saigon in 1973.

61. Tra, *Nhung chang duong*, 57–58.

7

The Road to Paris

On Sunday afternoon October 8, 1972, Henry Kissinger had his "most thrilling moment in public service." The venue, no. 108 avenue de General Leclerc in Gif-sur-Yvette, was the one-story cottage that cubist painter Fernand Léger had bequeathed to the French Communist party. Seated across the green baize table, Political Bureau member Le Duc Tho was repeating over and over. "This is what you yourself have proposed. . . . It is the same proposal made by President Nixon himself—ceasefire, release of prisoners, and troop withdrawal. . . . As to the internal political and military questions of South Vietnam we agree on principles. . . . This new proposal is exactly what President Nixon himself proposed." Kissinger, President Richard Nixon's national security adviser, instantly recognized Tho's words as the breakthrough he had long desired. Eighteen days later, Radio Hanoi unveiled what four years of secret negotiations had wrought, and Kissinger announced that "peace is at hand."[1]

But peace was still three months away. The war continued as it had during the four years of talks, bloody as ever. For the United States, getting out of the war proved to be more difficult than getting in. For Nixon and Kissinger were determined to withdraw at no cost to U.S. prestige, and the Communists demanded withdrawal on terms four American presidents had vowed never to accept. Groping for "peace with honor," the United States' only options were to impose a solution by some massive spasm of violence or to shift the burden to their South Vietnamese allies. In the end Nixon exercised both options, obtained peace for the United States, and left the Vietnamese to continue the fighting.

With thrusts into Cambodia and Laos and resumed bombing of the North, Lyndon Johnson's successor sought to wring concessions from Hanoi while turning over vast amounts of equipment to a growing, improving Army of the Republic of Vietnam (ARVN). But the inevitability of U.S. disengagement, declared by American leaders themselves, gave the Communists reason to hold out for their maximum terms. "Fighting while negotiating," the Communists coordinated military with diplomatic struggles in an effort to deepen the "contradictions" in the enemy camp. The central contradiction, according to the Political Bureau, was that the United States could not withdraw any faster than the ARVN was ready to take over. Yet, withdrawal once begun was not something that could be reversed. The Americans' hand in the negotiations could only weaken.[2]

THE NIXON-KISSINGER STRATEGY

Richard Nixon was an unlikely peacemaker with Communists, especially where Indochina was concerned. As a junior congressman in the 1940s, he had built a reputation battling the specter of domestic Communism. As vice president in the Eisenhower administration, he had recommended that the United States intervene to rescue the French at Dien Bien Phu, and Lyndon Johnson, then leader of the Democratic Party majority in the Senate, had denounced "Nixon's war." In 1967 Nixon had vigorously defended the U.S. involvement in Vietnam on the grounds that it had contained China and bought time for "free" Asian nations to build themselves.[3] But on taking office as president in January 1969, he declared a "war for peace." To an aide, he said: "I'm not going to end up like LBJ [Johnson], holed up in the White House afraid to show my face in the street. I'm going to stop that war. Fast."[4]

In Henry Kissinger, the German-born Harvard professor and strategist of global power, Nixon found an improbable ally. Nixon had a reputation for being vindictive, aloof, and insecure; Kissinger loved to charm and jest. Prior to his appointment by the moderate conservative Nixon, Kissinger had associated with Republican moderates and had run diplomatic errands for Johnson. But, like Nixon, Kissinger disdained bureaucracy and savored intrigue. Although Kissinger had equivocated about U.S. involvement in Vietnam at the beginning, as a theorist of Realpolitik it was crucially important to him that commitments at least appear to be kept. Consummate courtier and cunning bureaucratic infighter, Kissinger was abundantly willing and superbly qualified to supply the shape for Nixon's wish. On taking office, the two men were optimistic that a fresh start and new approaches could break the negotiating deadlock.

But huge gaps in perception and principle still divided the two sides. Hanoi's terms had not changed since April 8, 1965, when Premier Pham Van Dong had enunciated "four points" based on the 1954 Geneva Agreements: (1) recognition of Vietnam's national right to peace, independence, sovereignty, unity, and territorial integrity, and the cessation of all U.S. military activity in both the North and South; (2) strict implementation of the 1954 proscription against military alliances with foreign countries and foreign military bases "while Vietnam is still temporarily divided into two zones"; (3) settlement of South Vietnam's internal affairs "in accordance with the program of the South Vietnam National Front for Liberation" (NLF); and (4) peaceful reunification by the Vietnamese people in both zones without foreign interference.[5] The third point required the establishment of a coalition government composed of the NLF and partners sympathetic to its program. Hanoi also demanded acceptance of the NLF as the only true representative of the people of South Vietnam, prefiguring a demand that the Front participate in negotiations on an equal footing with Saigon. Agreement to hold four-party negotiations had come in November 1968 only after the Johnson administration secured Nguyen Van Thieu's consent by threatening to negotiate without him.

American leaders, ironically, had been no less enthusiastic than Communist leaders in professing fidelity to the Geneva Agreements. Washington's "fourteen points" of January 7, 1966, had listed the agreements in first place as "an adequate basis for peace in Southeast Asia." But Lyndon Johnson also had said in a speech at Johns Hopkins University on April 7, 1965, that the United States was committed "to help South Vietnam defend its independence." This implied that South Vietnam was a sovereign independent state with the sole right to fix the terms on which it would consider reunification with the North.

Accordingly, the Johnson administration had insisted on withdrawal of North Vietnamese troops in advance of U.S. withdrawal and had refused to discuss political arrangements except in terms of the South's "self-determination." Nixon and Kissinger supported these positions. To get talks moving, Kissinger persuaded Nixon to propose a mutual troop withdrawal and "restoration" of the demilitarized zone as a boundary. But this proposal, by implying that North Vietnamese as well as U.S. troops were "foreign" to South Vietnam and that Vietnam was two countries, ran directly counter to Hanoi's non-negotiable position that Geneva had affirmed Vietnam's juridical unity.

The Nixon-Kissinger proposal required Hanoi to accept an independent and non-Communist South Vietnam as a prerequisite of U.S. withdrawal. What happened later would be for the Vietnamese to decide, but no one doubted President Nguyen Van Thieu's determination to oppose reconciliation with the North. The United States also insisted that withdrawal had to occur under circumstances that could not be construed as an American defeat. U.S. credibility with allies in Europe and as a counterweight to Soviet power in Asia was at stake. To those who urged Nixon to imitate French

President Charles De Gaulle's pullout from North Africa, Kissinger pointed out that the general had taken four years to extricate France from Algeria precisely because it had been crucial to keep his nation's "cohesion and international stature intact." This had required De Gaulle to withdraw "as an act of policy, not as a collapse, in a manner reflecting a national decision and not a rout."[6] Nixon and Kissinger intended to do the same.

Their strategy rested on the insight that without the support of Moscow and Beijing, Hanoi would be unable to withstand American force or to defeat the ARVN. And since Moscow was in a mood for détente, the U.S. could play to Moscow's interest in return for Moscow's help in getting Hanoi to compromise. In an exercise of "linkage," Nixon and Kissinger would offer the Soviets increased trade, strategic arms limitation, and participation in Mideast peacemaking in exchange for progress on issues of importance to the U.S., including the war. The U.S. would play a similar game with Beijing, calculating that neither of the two Communist rivals would allow the other to be the exclusive beneficiary of improved relations with the United States.

As for tactics, Kissinger had conceded before his appointment that military means alone were incapable of producing victory. Therefore, he had written, military operations should be geared solely to negotiating objectives, and the responsibility for conduct of the war should be turned back to the South Vietnamese. The United States should negotiate only on military issues, leaving political questions to the Vietnamese. If Hanoi proved intransigent and the war dragged on, Kissinger concluded, "we should seek to achieve as many of our objectives as possible unilaterally."[7] The final element in the U.S. strategy was supplied by Nixon's "madman theory of war." "They'll believe any threat of force Nixon makes because it's Nixon," the president explained to an aide. "We'll just slip the word to them that, for God's sake, you know Nixon's obsessed about Communism . . . and he has his hand on the nuclear button."[8] Fearful of that "madman Nixon," Nixon calculated, Hanoi would gladly negotiate with the good Dr. Kissinger. Such, then, was the Nixon plan for "peace with honor" for the United States. To the Communists, however, a plan for withdrawal that left the South firmly in the hands of an anti-Communist government looked like a plan for peace through U.S. victory, and this they had sworn to resist.

WIDENING THE WAR

Nixon and Kissinger soon had a chance to test their ideas. Although Johnson had stopped the bombing unconditionally, he believed he had Hanoi's promise to cease attacks on major cities and across the demilitarized zone. A pullout from the South by a few units of the People's Army of Vietnam

(PAVN) in the summer and fall of 1968 seemed to confirm Hanoi's assent to the "understanding." But Nixon had no sooner settled into office than he received evidence that Hanoi had begun to infiltrate more troops and to prepare for a new offensive. Rather than resume the bombing of the North, which might provoke a public outcry, the president turned his attention to the Communist sanctuaries in Cambodia.

The thirteen sanctuaries were a string of staging areas, supply dumps, and rear-echelon headquarters scattered from Laos to the Gulf of Thailand just inside or straddling Cambodia's border with Vietnam. Since the massive "search-and-destroy" operations on South Vietnam's side of the border in 1966, the Communists had relied increasingly on the sanctuaries, with the reluctant consent of Cambodia's Prince Norodom Sihanouk. Routinely described as "mercurial" in the Western press, Sihanouk was Cambodia's charismatic ex-king. An intelligent despot and a wily diplomat, he was passionately dedicated to preserving Cambodia's independence with himself as chief of state. To peasants and the uneducated, Sihanouk was the person who came to mind when they heard the traditional dictum, "A country without a king cannot exist."

In the early 1960s Sihanouk tried but failed to insulate Cambodia from the gathering storm by seeking international guarantees of his country's neutrality. Unable to deny use of Cambodian territory by the belligerent parties and resigned to a Communist victory in Vietnam, he severed diplomatic relations with the United States in May 1965 and strengthened ties with China. He also allowed the Vietnamese Communists to use the port of Sihanoukville as a back door to eastern Cambodia. With the connivance of the Royal Cambodian Army, the Hak Ly Trucking Company hauled supplies from Sihanoukville to bases in the Parrot's Beak, a salient of Cambodian territory that jutted toward Saigon. According to historian Christopher Goscha, weapons for 50,000 soldiers passed through Sihanoukville between 1965 and 1967. In addition to arms and supplies imported through Sihanoukville, the Communists purchased or procured a roughly equal tonnage of rice, petrol, and other supplies from inside Cambodia.[9] Arranged only months after the U.S. Navy shut down the coastal operations of Group 759, access to Cambodia gave Hanoi a secure way to move supplies to within fifty kilometers of Saigon.

In return for his cooperation, Sihanouk demanded recognition of the existing Vietnam-Cambodia border, which the National Liberation Front of South Vietnam (NLF) granted in 1967. (The Hanoi government demurred, pointing out that it did not have a common border with Cambodia). Collusion with Sihanouk also required the Vietnamese to limit the support they were giving to the Cambodian Communists, or Khmer Rouge ("Red Cambodians") as Sihanouk called them. For Hanoi, leaving Sihanouk in power, at least for a time, was vastly preferable to his most likely immediate replacement, a cabal of anti-monarchist and anti-Vietnamese military figures who would cooperate with the United States. Supporting a Khmer Rouge armed struggle would have jeopardized an arrangement Hanoi needed to supply forces in South Vietnam. Le Duan explained this to Khmer Rouge leader Saloth Sar (Pol Pot) in June 1965, basically asking the Cambodian Communists to put their revolution on hold while the Vietnamese war was in progress. Through the rest of the 1960s, Hanoi did little to help the Khmer Rouge, who turned their main effort to agitation among discontented peasants. These efforts began to pay off in 1967, when peasants in the western Cambodian province of Battambang resisted Cambodian army enforcement of compulsory rice sales to the state.[10] Further uprisings under tighter Khmer Rouge control in 1968 marked the beginning of a sustained armed struggle. Hanoi, however, counseled restraint, deepening Khmer Rouge suspicions about Hanoi's long-range intentions and widening the rift between the two parties.[11] Meanwhile, the Vietnamese Communists had gone on importing supplies through Siha-noukville and building support facilities at locations just inside Cambodia's border with South Vietnam.

Although the U.S. military command in Saigon considered these bases a menace, recommendations to attack them had clashed with Washington's political scruples. Cross-border operations had been limited to sporadic ARVN "hot-pursuit" intrusions and highly clandestine forays by montag-nard mercenaries under Green Beret officers.[12] But Nixon wanted to pre-empt Communist offensives, and in the absence of more attractive alterna-tives, bombing the sanctuaries gained appeal. So did the idea of signaling to Hanoi that Nixon was prepared to take unprecedented steps to break the negotiating deadlock.

Into this receptive environment, General Creighton Abrams, who re-placed General William Westmoreland in mid-1968, sent a cable on Febru-ary 9, 1969, claiming to have located the Central Office for South Vietnam (COSVN) headquarters in Base 353, five kilometers inside Cambodia, and requesting authority to attack with B-52s. On March 17, Nixon approved.

Thus began the secret bombing of Cambodia. On March 18, following procedures that had been carefully contrived to conceal their targets,[13] forty-eight B-52s dropped their long strings of bombs into a patch of Cam-bodian territory covering twenty-five square kilometers. The U.S. military report after the bombing indicated that the strike had taken place in South Vietnam rather than in Cambodia. The mission, code-named Operation Breakfast, went unnoticed in the United States. After Breakfast came opera-tions Lunch, Snack, and Dinner. Over a period of fourteen months, 4,308 B-52 sorties dropped bombs on all but two of the sanctuaries in operations known collectively as Menu.

The secret, revealed in the *New York Times* on May 9, aroused no public interest. Nixon, however, rushed to plug the leak with taps on the telephones of key officials. Lacking a judicial warrant, this action violated U.S. law—the first such abuse of power that would lead to Watergate. What did the administration want so desperately to keep secret? Given that the Communists had openly compromised Cambodia's neutrality, Washington might have seen benefit in making its riposte public. American diplomats also had interpreted signs from Sihanouk the year before that indicated he would acquiesce to the bombing,[14] and, indeed, Sihanouk denied knowing about the action for months after it began. The ostensible reason for secrecy was, as Kissinger put it, "to avoid *forcing* the North Vietnamese, Prince Sihanouk . . . and the Soviets and Chinese into public reactions they might not be eager to make."[15] But the administration also did not seek congressional approval or allocation of funds for any American military activity in Cambodia, activity that was, regardless of the justification, an act of war that expanded the fighting just as sentiment in Congress was building to end it. Not until June was a full briefing given to congressional leaders, and it was limited to individuals who could be counted on to support military action. Just four months later, closed hearings on the "secret war" in Laos by the Senate Committee on Foreign Relations led eventually to what some observers believed the secrecy was really intended to avoid: media nosiness, congressional scrutiny, and legislation to cap U.S. aid.[16]

In Cambodia, where most Khmers detested the Vietnamese and educated urbanites resented Sihanouk's autocratic nepotism, the bombing emboldened republican nationalists opposed to Sihanouk and to his truckling to Hanoi. In April 1969 war goods ceased to pass through Sihanoukville or were held up in Royal Cambodian Army depots.[17] Diplomatic relations with the United States, suspended since 1965, resumed in June. Of these developments, a cadre in the People's Liberation Armed Force's (PLAF) headquarters wrote in early fall that "due to the confusing political situation in Cambodia . . . we have met many difficulties in our diplomatic relations with Cambodia from the Central down to the local levels." The United States, he predicted, "will attack deep in the border areas to pressure Cambodia. They will try to . . . undermine the solidarity of Cambodia and our country. As for Cambodia, insurmountable difficulties will arise if she demands aid from the U.S."[18]

The whole delicate arrangement by which Sihanouk had kept his country out of the war, and the Khmer Rouge at bay, was unraveling. Hanoi needed to compensate for the loss of access to Sihanoukville to continue moving large quantities of supplies to the Mekong delta. Suddenly it was in Hanoi's interest to support the Khmer Rouge armed struggle as a screen for extension of the Ho Chi Minh Trail into northeastern Cambodia. Setting aside past disagreements with Pol Pot, the Vietnamese invited the Cambodian Communists to cooperate, welcomed Cambodian party delegations to set up permanent quarters near COSVN and in Hanoi, and began supplying weapons and equipment to the Cambodians.[19] Some of the few thousand Cambodian Communists Hanoi had taken in for training and study in previous years also returned to Cambodia around this time. Parallel to these steps, the Lao Dong (Workers) Party (LDP) Central Committee in January 1970 ordered work to begin on pipelines for petroleum and upgrading land routes in the trail complex. "Special attention," the plenum added, should be paid to coordination with "Laotian soldiers and people in central and southern Laos."[20]

The Operation Menu bombing damaged the sanctuaries and triggered political instability in Phnom Penh. It and the more widespread bombing that followed also "gave the Khmers Rouges a propaganda windfall which they exploited to the hilt."[21] But it did nothing to modify the Vietnamese Communists' stand in negotiations. The NLF unveiled "ten points" on May 8 that reiterated demands for unconditional U.S. withdrawal and a coalition government excluding Thieu. A month later came the creation of a Provisional Revolutionary Government of the Republic of South Vietnam (PRG) headed by Huynh Tan Phat, chief of the People's Revolutionary Party, actually the Communist party's Southern branch. NLF President Nguyen Huu Tho, a party member since 1963, became chairman of the PRG's council of advisers. The Democratic Republic of Vietnam (DRV) National Assembly recognized the new structure as the "legal government and true representative of the people of South Vietnam."[22] By this device, and intimations of willingness to hold just the sort of exercise in electoral self-determination that resonated with American principles, Hanoi sought to stimulate opposition to the war and increase the pressure on the Nixon administration to be more flexible. The Soviet Union and its allies soon accorded the PRG full diplomatic recognition, thereby signaling support of a political settlement but on Hanoi's terms. Many non-aligned nations—Algeria, Syria, Egypt, India, Sudan, Mali, etc.—followed suit.[23]

Perceiving no basis for compromise, Nixon and Kissinger proceeded unilaterally with gradual troop withdrawals and accelerated strengthening of the Army of the Republic of Vietnam (ARVN). The first step, they calculated, would silence domestic criticism and deprive Hanoi of the hope that the American people would press for peace on the Communist's terms; the second would lay a basis for eventual, total withdrawal in circumstances acceptable to the United States, whether Hanoi agreed or not. Nixon announced the first withdrawal of 25,000 troops in June 1969 and a month later, in what came to be known as the Nixon (or Guam) Doctrine, he stated that in future the United States would "look to the nation directly threatened to assume the primary responsibility of providing manpower for its defense."[24] In limited wars, the United States would furnish military and economic aid to its allies but it would not send troops. He also made known his desire to improve his relations with Moscow—if Moscow would help wring concessions from Hanoi. Kissinger then sought a secret meeting with DRV plenipotentiary Xuan Thuy, through the assistance of Jean Sainteny, the former French delegate general in Hanoi. Meeting with Thuy in Sainteny's Paris apartment on August 4, Kissinger suggested compromise.

This was not the first time that Hanoi and Washington made surreptitious contact. Indirect contact was made through representatives of the Canadian, French, British, Italian, Polish, Romanian, Norwegian, Soviet, and Chinese governments at various times, beginning as early as June 1964. The first official direct contact took place between the U.S. ambassador and the DRV consul general in Rangoon, Burma, in December 1965; another such channel opened briefly between the United States and DRV embassies in Moscow in January 1967. Kissinger, himself, while still professor of government at Harvard, joined with two Frenchmen, Herbert Marcovich and Raymond Aubrac, the latter a personal friend of Ho Chi Minh, to convey messages between Washington and Hanoi. Marcovich and Aubrac made a trip to Hanoi in July 1967 with the blessing of both the French and U.S. governments, and from then until October, they served as conduits for a spate of exchanges with Kissinger. But these contacts were only preliminaries, not negotiations of substance, and they came to naught. So too had the secret meetings that took place, once the Paris talks opened, between the heads of the DRV and U.S. delegations. In meeting Thuy, Kissinger could only hope that a new mix of carrots and sticks, spelled out in a new context, might lead eventually to an exchange of concessions. But Thuy, though he agreed to continue secret discussions at a higher level, was impervious to Kissinger's pleas for compromise.

Afraid of losing public support if he did not soon break the negotiating logjam, Nixon ordered the National Security Council to draw up plans for "savage, punishing blows"—an order that was deliberately leaked to the press in the hope of softening Hanoi's stance. Work began on contingency plans code-named Duck Hook, a mining and bombing operation that Nixon said should be of such intensity that it would push the North or its government to, but not quite over, the brink of total collapse. Faced with such a prospect, Nixon and Kissinger calculated, Hanoi surely would compromise. Memos from Kissinger and an attachment to the National Security Council's report raised the possibility of using nuclear weapons. Presumably after reflecting on the repercussions of actually carrying out such a threat, however, Nixon cancelled further planning for Duck Hook and settled instead for a worldwide nuclear alert in the last half of October to signal resolve and preserve his "madman" reputation.[25]

None of this bluster made any impression on Hanoi. The antiwar movement displayed undiminished vigor in demonstrations on October 15, 1970. Barely a month later, the massacre of unarmed civilians by American soldiers in My Lai hamlet broke into public view, sullying the army's reputation and sharpening the moral edge of opposition to the war.[26] Troop withdrawals did not win back support for the forces that remained but rather fueled demand for more withdrawals. Abandoning plans for "savage, punishing blows," Nixon was left with no policy save the rather vague idea of turning the war over to the South Vietnamese.

The disappointment made Nixon combative. In a speech on November 3, he conjured up a specter of the bloodbath that would follow "precipitate withdrawal," pinned the blame on the protesters, and appealed for support from the patriotic "silent majority." Opinion polls showed that the majority of the U.S. population believed entering the war had been a mistake, but approval of Nixon's handling of it shot up dramatically (to 64 percent in January 1970).[27] The U.S. public wanted out of the war, the polls said, but on Nixon's terms. Nixon was pleased. "We've got those liberal bastards on the run now," he told an aide.[28] But all he really had done was to buy time to consider his options, among which "savage, punishing blows," though not nuclear ones, remained very much alive.

THE LULL

The temptation to strike was irresistible, partly because Nixon's own program of withdrawals had set a limit on how long U.S. power would be available for that purpose. Moreover, the Communists had suffered setbacks and seemed vulnerable. Under the combined pressure of 500,000 U.S. troops, a growing ARVN, and accelerated pacification, the Communists had been unable to recover from losses suffered in the 1968 Tet Offensive. A revolution that once had promised rural youths adventure and advancement was now known to be filled with hardship and death. There was "no point in drafting more people," one local party organ complained, "because they will desert anyway."[29] Northern regulars increasingly filled in PLAF units and sometimes found themselves having to share even their food with local forces, an inversion of the "people's war" principle that local forces should be self-sufficient.[30]

U.S. intelligence estimates showed Communist armed forces in the South declining from 250,300 in 1968 to 197,700 in 1971.[31] With the number of PAVN troops in the South during those years fairly stable at 80,000 to 90,000,[32] the decline in the Communist armed forces had come largely from the depletion of Southern ranks. General Abrams, charged with fighting a rearguard action anyway, abandoned Westmoreland's big-unit, "search-and-destroy" strategy of attrition. In its place the former tank commander and protégé of General George Patton ordered his officers to place less emphasis on "body count," more emphasis on small-unit patrolling and territorial security, and to integrate combat operations with pacification. In one notable exception, a brigade of the U.S. 101st Airborne Division entered the A Shau Valley in May 1969. There, not far from where the Communists had overrun a Special Forces camp in 1966 and then developed an infiltration corridor, the brigade engaged a PAVN regiment on Ap Bia mountain, known to Americans as Hamburger Hill, in ten days of bloody combat. When they finally took the hill, the Americans counted more than 630 Communist dead at a price of seventy dead of their own. Although they abandoned the hill after the battle, sparking debate at home over the point of it all, U.S. forces stayed in the valley.

The Communists felt the pressure. General Tran Van Tra recalled bitterly that in this period many local party organs and cadres were "lost." In heavily populated Long An province, the independent main force 320th Regiment, sent to obstruct pacification, had to disperse into platoons and squads and take over the work of defunct political organizations. "Sending a concentrated main-force unit to operate in such a dispersed manner," wrote Tra, "so one could say it no longer operated as a main-force unit, was something we did most reluctantly, but there was no alternative under the circumstances at that time."[33] Lengthy articles by the PAVN's top brass in December 1969 obliquely acknowledged that the Southern revolution was "temporarily" in a defensive posture. A study years later by the PAVN Military History Institute described units and civilian supporters in some regions "from the end of 1968 through 1970" as becoming "irresolute, vacillating, lacking in confidence, and shrinking from struggle with the enemy." "Many localities," the Institute observed, "advocated changing the orientation of attack, taking the countryside as the main arena, and regrouping to thwart the enemy's 'rural pacification strategy.'"[34] Or as another study put it, "Our basic-level political organs were almost all exposed in the Tet offensive and uprisings, allowing the enemy to suppress them. Revolutionary forces were thus significantly weakened. . . . This difficult situation extended into early 1970 before things could be reestablished and stabilized." Uncertainty and disagreements in Hanoi about the true state of affairs in the South delayed the formulation of an effective response.[35]

The revolution was not disintegrating, however. Communist cadres did not all die or defect; some went into hiding. The sacrifice of main forces in protecting the political infrastructure and guerrilla movement in the Mekong delta was done to preserve a foundation on which to rebuild in future.[36] In 1970, according to the party's figures, the Southern Trung Bo regional party organization lost 3,233 non-military members but gained 5,800 new ones.[37] Farther north, along the seam between the central highlands and coastal provinces, ARVN shifts from territorial defense to attack left voids for local Communist organs to fill. Although U.S. officials pointed proudly to TV antennas sprouting from tiled roofs as proof that the "other war" for hearts and minds was being won, popular attitudes changed very slowly. Military power could increase the risk of supporting the revolution and force the Communists to revert to small-unit warfare, but it could not impose a new set of loyalties. The substantial portion of peasants whose political allegiances had jelled during the war against France had no affection for a Saigon government they regarded as aloof, corrupt, and careless in the way its armed forces used firepower. The ARVN undercut its own cause by helping absentee landlords collect rents in newly "secure" areas around Saigon. [38] James Trullinger has described how one community near Hue, literally in the shadow of the U.S. Army 101st Airborne Division encampment, remained sympathetic to the revolution behind a "pacified" facade.[39] Using American records to study pacification in Hau Nghia province on Saigon's western edge, Eric Bergerud concluded that military pressure and attrition depleted Communist political and armed forces, but "efforts to change the fundamental attitudes of the people of Hau Nghia toward the GVN [Saigon] failed. . . ."[40]

Equally revealing, although U.S. combat deaths were declining, those of the ARVN were running at twice their pre-1968 levels and rising. The "lull," as it was called in the United States, referred only to the big-unit warfare and the trend in U.S. casualties. American military losses in 1970 were half what they had been the year before, and though nearly the same as in 1966, the probability of an American soldier dying in Vietnam would decline sharply. Down in the villages and hamlets, the Communists still initiated most of the combat contacts and were exacting a fearful toll among their fellow Vietnamese (see Figure 7.1). Casualties among ARVN Regional and Popular Forces (RF/PF) and paramilitaries were accounting for 60 percent of Saigon forces killed in Communist attacks, while these irregulars were inflicting about a third of all Communist casualties.[41] The real war was in the villages, in skirmishes too small to capture press attention. But there was no denying that both the Communist political "infrastructure" and armed forces in the South had been weakened. If U.S. estimates can be believed, Communist battle deaths in 1970 were two-thirds as high as in 1969 but 3.7 times as high as the combined deaths of forces from the United States, the Republic of Vietnam, and allied nations. During what was a respite mainly for the American forces, the United States sought to back out, leaving Vietnamese—and Cambodians and Lao—to carry on the war.

VIETNAMIZATION

While acknowledging the rising political pressure to end the war, a study by U.S. Military Assistance Command, Vietnam (MACV) in January 1969 argued that a "reduction of American forces is required, not simply as a ploy to 'buy' time, but also as a necessary method of compelling the South

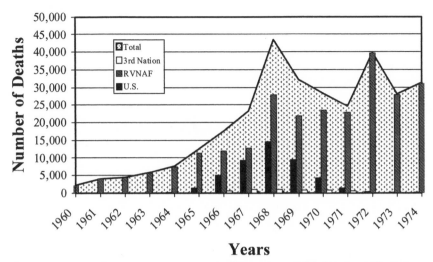

Years

Figure 7.1.   Annual U.S., RVNAF (RVN Armed Forces), and Third Nation (Allied) Combat Deaths
Source: Jeffrey J. Clarke, *Advice and Support: The Final Years, 1963–1973* (Washington, D.C.: Center for Military History, 1988), 275; and *The Air War in Indochina*, ed. Raphael Littauer and Norman Uphoff, (Ithaca, N.Y.: Cornell University Program on peace Studies, 1972), 267–272.

Vietnamese to take over the war. They must! Even ignoring the objectives of the GVN [the Saigon government] the attainment of US objectives is dependent upon the performance of the South Vietnamese government and its armed forces. Hence, an orderly turnover of the war effort is mandatory."[42] The time to withdraw had arrived, in this assessment, for reasons that were unrelated to what was happening inside the United States. "Turning over the war" was the only way the South Vietnamese could be made to stand on their own, which was precisely the U.S. objective. In March, MACV reported to the National Security Council that the situation in Vietnam had improved to the point where the United States could soon begin to "de-Americanize" the war. "I agree," said Defense Secretary Melvin R. Laird, "'but not with your term 'de-Americanizing.' What we need is a term like 'Vietnamizing' to put the emphasis on the right issues."[43]

In fact Vietnamization had begun improvisationally in 1968 with a general mobilization that had raised the total armed forces under Saigon's command to more than 800,000, of which 380,000 were in the regular army. Triggered by the Tet offensive, Saigon's buildup began in the same year that American troop strength peaked and continued as American troops began to withdraw. By 1970 the total was near one million; more than half those troops were irregular territorial defense forces (see Table 7.1).

ARVN firepower also increased as departing U.S. units left behind their arms and equipment. The ARVN by 1970 was amply equipped with the

Table 7.1. Republic of Vietnam Armed Forces (RVNAF) Strength

Year	Army	Air Force	Navy	Marine Corps	Total Regular	Regional Forces	Popular Forces	Total Territorial	Grand Total
1954–55	170,000	3,500	2,200	1,500	177,200	54,000[a]	48,000[a]	102,000	279,200
1959–60	136,000[b]	4,600	4,300	2,000	146,000	49,000[b]	48,000	97,000	243,000
1964	220,000	11,000	12,000	7,000	250,000	96,000	168,000	264,000	514,000
1967	303,000	16,000	16,000	8,000	343,000	151,000	149,000[b]	300,000	643,000
1968	380,000	19,000	19,000	9,000	427,000	220,000	173,000	393,000	820,000
1969	416,000	36,000	30,000	11,000	493,000	190,000	214,000	404,000	897,000
1970	416,000	46,000	40,000	13,000	515,000	207,000	246,000	453,000	968,000
1971–72	410,000	50,000	42,000	14,000	516,000	284,000	248,000	532,000	1,048,000

Source: James Lawton Collins, Jr., The Development and Training of the South Vietnamese Army, 1950–1972 (Washington, D.C.: Department of the Army, 1975), appendix D, 151.

Note: All figures are approximate.

[a]Civil Guard (later Regional Forces and Self-Defense Corps (later Popular Forces) were official authorized only in 1956.

[b]Decline due to increased desertions and recruiting shortfalls.

latest U.S. small arms and was beginning to acquire sophisticated heavy artillery (e.g., 175-mm self-propelled guns), tanks, trucks, aircraft, and communications equipment. The value of U.S. arms transfers to Saigon rose from $725 million in 1968 to $925 million in both 1969 and 1970. (North Vietnam's arms transfers from Communist countries fell from $525 million in 1968 to $200 million in l970.)[44] U.S. units began cutting back on offensive patrols, leaving these to the ARVN. Figures on the Third Corps near Saigon showed the ARVN accounting for only 20 percent of enemy killed-in-action in the fall of 1969 but 32 percent and rising six months later.[45] The Communists' charge that the aim of Vietnamization was to "change the color of the corpses" was crude but accurate.

Turning over weapons and missions to the ARVN would achieve little, however, if more were not done to restore the Saigon government's authority in the countryside. The "other war" finally got its chance. Seeing an opportunity in the Communists' post-Tet fallback, the U.S. mission had launched a three-month accelerated program in November 1968 and then prolonged it as fixed policy. "Accelerated pacification" (i.e., a push to "clear and hold" territory where the Communist hold had weakened) shifted the emphasis from "search and destroy" and "body count" to security of population and "nation-building." It also coordinated and updated programs that previously had functioned separately and at a low level of priority. One program, financed by the CIA and headed by former Viet Minh officer Nguyen Be, trained 59-man teams to spearhead "rural construction." Rural development, or RD, had antecedents in Saigon government civic-action programs headed by other ex-Viet Minh commanders going back to 1955, and it represented a conscious attempt to emulate the Communists' focus on the local level. In RD, teams were sent out to help reorganize village administration, start construction projects, and train villagers to defend themselves. Another program, the Chieu Hoi, or Open Arms amnesty program, offered defectors (called ralliers) a new life on the government side. Perhaps most controversial was the Phoenix Program. This program sought to coordinate a variety of intelligence organizations and their operations so they could more effectively identify members of the Communists' political organization. Specially trained "provincial reconnaissance units" were then sent to arrest or "neutralize" these operatives. When integrated with other pacification programs, "RD" and Phoenix (called *Phuong Hoang* in Vietnamese after a mythical bird of prey) became parts of a single "Pacification and Development Plan."

The broader political framework came in for reform as well when President Thieu, realizing his survival depended on enlarging his political base before the United States withdrew, agreed to village elections and administrative decentralization in 1969. The other critical step needed to contend for the allegiance of the peasantry—land reform—proved harder to secure.

Ever since President Ngo Dinh Diem's limited reforms in the mid-1950s, which had ceded credibility on this issue to the revolution, pressure in Saigon for adoption of more effective measures had been weak. Nothing got done because landed interests dominated the National Assembly and had strong ties to the governing class, and American officials feared that land redistribution would alienate an important constituency of the central government.[46] Senior AID officials were so hostile to the idea of redistribution that in 1968 they stripped the mission's one vigorous advocate of reform of his staff and transferred him to South Korea.[47] It took the shock of Tet 1968 to jolt the embassy into supporting reform and urging it upon Thieu, who had to then overcome stiff landlord opposition in 1970 to win passage of legislation authorizing a sweeping Land-to-the-Tiller Law. This law recognized peasants' ownership of the land given them by the Communists, set up procedures to liquidate remaining tenancy, and reduced the maximum landholding to fifteen hectares in the south and five in the center. Peasants received deeds for the land they tilled, which was a guarantee of private ownership that the Communists would never offer. The amount of cropland tilled by tenant farmers fell from 60 percent to 10 percent in three years (in Saigon's books) as large numbers of tenants and farm laborers became landowning farmers.

Even if it did nothing more than give legal sanction to redistributions the Communists had already made, the law removed an incentive for peasants to support the revolution. Not incidentally, Thieu hoped the reforms would make the peasants grateful to him. For most peasants, though, the reforms merely repealed Saigon's past sins and were little more attractive than the reforms (equalization of holdings, pooling of labor and tools, substitution of taxes for rent, mutual assistance in management of irrigation, and canal-building) that the Communists had been offering for years.[48] But, combined with the pacification programs and decentralization, Thieu's reforms constituted Saigon's first serious attempt at a comprehensive political strategy.

The measures mimicked Communist techniques without the Communists' rootedness in the countryside, and they came late in the day. The 59-man RD teams had to recruit outside the villages they were supposed to help. Staffed heavily with urban youth avoiding the draft, the teams remained outsiders to the villages they were sent to rescue. When the teams moved on, the Communists moved back in. The Chieu Hoi program claimed more than 47,000 "ralliers" in 1969 alone and a total of 194,000 by late 1972, but many were in fact pro-Saigon civilians who "rallied" at the instigation of Chieu Hoi officials for a share of the reward.[49] William Colby, the U.S. pacification chief (later head of the CIA), estimated that of the 79,000 guerrilla defectors reported in 1969 and 1970, only 17,000 were genuine.[50] Very few high-ranking cadres defected, noted a report for the Pentagon, and "it is they whom the GVN must win to its side if the political war is to be won."[51] The Communists, moreover, used the program to recycle their own cadres into a legal existence and to infiltrate Saigon's territorial forces. And individuals used the program for personal reasons: a pregnant woman interviewed in 1973 who had "rallied" to get better medical care rejoined her husband in the maquis as soon as her baby was born.[52] Of course there were deserters as well as defectors from Communist forces, but figures on these have uncertain accuracy and meaning. Desertions from Saigon's side continued at an annual net rate of more than 10 percent for all forces and about 30 percent for regular ARVN combat units.[53]

As for Phoenix, the sharpening of Saigon's police and intelligence work had effect. COSVN in January 1971 credited it with achieving "temporary results," contributing to the "sacrifice and difficulty" imposed by pacification.[54] But the program was difficult to administer and susceptible to abuse, as Colby admitted.[55] American advisors could not assure that Saigon police always used Phoenix instruments as intended, particularly after CIA supervision ceased in 1969. The program's defenders bridled at the characterization of the provincial reconnaissance units (PRU) as "hit teams" and "bump-off squads," but even CIA agents sometimes used these terms.[56] The units did chase down and arrest Communist cadres, but they sometimes failed to discriminate between activists and sympathizers. Some observers believed the program was more helpful than harmful to the Communists because it alienated people whose only crime had been to live in a Communist-controlled zone.[57] The Republic of Vietnam (RVN) anyway lacked an adequate judicial system and detention facilities to run the program as the Americans designed it.[58] The Pentagon's monthly statistical summary credited Phoenix with the "violent deaths" of 26,369 Vietnamese from 1968 through 1972; "many of whom were probably only marginally involved in the insurrectionary movement. . . ."[59] To the extent that Phoenix was successful it may have added incentive for Hanoi to send reinforcements to the South,[60] but the Communists' political "infrastructure" tended to bounce back after local campaigns ended anyway.[61]

Thieu's land reforms sharply reduced officially recorded tenancy in the Mekong delta, and elected village councils gained a measure of control over local affairs in "secure" areas, but profiteering and abuse increased in both programs when U.S. interest declined.[62] A computerized measure of security, the Hamlet Evaluation Survey, fixed the "contested portion" of the population (that portion not under the control of either side) at just 5 percent in 1970, but the figures, biased to show "progress" in any case, could not measure political allegiance or the intensity of popular commitment. Much of the increase in "secure" population was the result of movement from the countryside to the cities, not the extension of government "control" into the hamlets.[63]

Despite the uncertainties, American officials took the numbers as signs of progress in the "other war," and Communist sources bear them out. By the Communists' own count, the number of people living in liberated zones of the B2 Theater (Nam Bo), stable at four to five million from 1961 through 1966, declined a million in 1967–1968 before plummeting to 1.5 million in 1969 and to just 229,000 in 1971 (see Appendix B). Another source, also speaking of B2, observed that agricultural "production in liberated zones and base areas declined considerably and people's lives encountered many difficulties, especially in families with dead or wounded and cadres and soldiers away from home."[64] People did not leave Communist-controlled areas to escape the revolution so much as the bombing and shelling that made the physical risk and economic cost of staying in them too high. The Communists held their own in the balance of armed forces, but the popular base was shrinking, increasing the Southern revolution's dependency on support from the North.

Meeting in late April 1969, the Political Bureau acknowledged the gravity of the situation. Armed forces in the South were encountering problems of supply, morale, and recruitment; mass associations had lost members; the enemy's intelligence gathering had improved; and so forth. There was also the risk that "de-Americanization" might allow the United States to remain involved in the war in sufficient force to prolong it. That prospect suggested two scenarios: (1) the U.S. might be forced to withdraw via a political settlement that would leave the revolution to face a continuing "complicated" struggle; or (2) "if our attacks are not sufficiently strong and the U.S. temporarily overcomes its difficulties," the United States might try to protract the war and "de-escalate from a position of strength." In either case, there was risk that the United States would resume bombing the North or expand the war into Laos and Cambodia.[65] The Bureau's great worry was that a protracted war would allow the U.S. to strengthen the Saigon government to a point that would make the RVN and its army hard to defeat. Although some organs in the South advocated shifting to a rural-based, counter-pacification strategy,[66] the dominant concern was to prevent the RVN's consolidation. There was to be no slackening of effort or change in general strategy, no shift to an exclusively rural orientation, no downgrading of political or armed struggle in any form. Southern forces were to prepare for a prolonged struggle but could expect to fight in the near future to shorten it. Circulated in the South in modified form as COSVN resolution 9, the Bureau's instructions were explicit that "We should be determined not to let the movement stand still at a low form of struggle."[67] Thus did Hanoi order forces in the South to prepare for the unwanted possibility of protracted war while striving to avert one.[68] This was a highly controversial decision whose equivocal nature suggested a compromise between leaders who felt it was urgent to force a conclusion and those who favored a strategy of protracted war.[69]

Meanwhile, the American mission in Saigon assessed the pacification, Phoenix and land-reform programs as bases for hope that the Saigon government and armed forces would be able to stand on their own as American forces withdrew. The United States and its allies began to think that they, not the Communists, now held the keys to victory, provided that Thieu and his generals gained confidence and took responsibility into their own hands.

UNIFYING THE INDOCHINA BATTLEFIELD

Believing things were going well, Nixon and Kissinger in late 1969 requested another round of secret negotiations with Hanoi. On February 21, 1970, Kissinger had the first in a series of clandestine meetings with Le Duc Tho. Seconded to Hanoi's Paris delegation as "special adviser," Tho was in fact the fifth-ranked member of the Political Bureau, the sole civilian member of the Central Military Party Committee, and, after Le Duan, the party's chief strategist on Southern affairs. Reunification had been his specialty since serving as COSVN deputy secretary under Le Duan from 1951 to 1954. Scion of a wealthy family, Tho brought a convert's zeal to his job as head of the party's Political Organization Committee, whose tasks included enforcement of the party's ideology. To Kissinger, Tho epitomized the stony graduate of colonial prisons, a rigid catechist of Leninism, a Vietnamese chauvinist, and a xenophobe.[70] To Tho, Kissinger seemed bellicose, arrogant, deceitful, and, like Nixon, "unworldly" (*niais* in French) while supposing himself "the master of 'political realists.'"[71]

Kissinger tried to put Tho on the defensive with evidence of U.S. public support for Nixon and of Communist reversals on the ground. Tho retorted: "Before, there were over a million U.S. and puppet troops, and you failed. How can you succeed when you let the puppet troops do the fighting? Now, with only U.S. support, how can you win?" Kissinger had to admit that the question already had begun to torment him,[72] though Tho might have had doubts about the strength of his own hand, too. Additional meetings in March and April ended inconclusively. Neither side felt compelled to make major concessions; each counted on further fighting to sway the other.

In fact the Political Bureau had decided more than a month before the two men first met to brace for a widening of war by coordinating advances all over Indochina.[73] The United States had enjoyed considerable success raising a mercenary army in Laos under H'mong tribal leader "Marshal" Vang Pao, and along with Thai "volunteers" (up to twenty-seven infantry and three artillery battalions paid for by the U.S.),[74] these forces had begun in 1969 to menace PAVN supply lines deep inside Laos. In February 1970 the Vietnamese and Pathet Lao struck back, pushing Royal Lao forces out of the Plaine des Jarres and off the Xieng Khoang airfield. The PAVN went on to seize Attopeu and Saravane provinces for the Pathet Lao. The real objective, though, was to protect and expand the logistical corridor running through southern Laos that had gained importance due to the "complicated" situation in Cambodia.

The final collapse of Cambodia's tattered neutrality was now just days away. On March 12, 1970, while Prince Sihanouk was on a diplomatic mission abroad, the Cambodian government demanded the immediate withdrawal of Vietnamese troops from Cambodian territory. The Vietnamese did not budge, and the Cambodian army attacked, with support from Saigon army artillery. Finally, on the eighteenth, after a coup d'état, the National Assembly deposed Prince Sihanouk and designated Lieutenant General Lon Nol as chief of state. The Saigon government promptly pledged to help Lon Nol stamp out Communist activity on the border, while in Beijing, Sihanouk declared the formation of a "national union government" that included his erstwhile enemies, the Khmer Rouge.

The United States did not plot Sihanouk's ouster, although Nixon welcomed it. Kissinger denied an American hand behind the coup, citing the CIA's failure to predict the event.[75] The coup was in fact a mixed blessing for the United States. The Operation Menu bombing had damaged but not destroyed the Communists' sanctuaries, and Sihanouk's ambivalent diplomacy seemed an obstacle to doing more. But, with Lon Nol determined to push Communist Vietnamese forces out of the sanctuaries, a new war might shape up in Cambodia just as the United States was trying to extricate itself from Vietnam. It was also clear that the conservative leaders now heading the Cambodian government would not be able to survive without U.S. support. If Sihanouk returned to power on Communist shoulders, all of Cambodia would be enemy territory, outflanking South Vietnam. On balance, though, the coup strengthened the temptation to clean out the sanctuaries and, for Nixon, as he confided to aides, to "show who's really tough."

With ARVN generals impatient to seize the initiative, the United States decided in late March 1970 to support South Vietnamese "incursions" into Cambodia. Battalion-sized forces backed by U.S. helicopters crossed the border on March 27 and 28. Tactical air strikes code-named Patio supported this move up to eight miles into northeastern Cambodia. Vietnamese Communist forces countered on April 3 by spreading out from their sanctuaries and pushing westward, turning weapons and equipment over to the Khmer Rouge as they went. Ostensibly to "save" Phnom Penh and defend U.S. citizens remaining in South Vietnam, Nixon ordered what was in fact an attempt to crack the Communists' Cambodian stronghold, an order he issued without consulting Lon Nol.

On April 28, U.S. advisers and air support followed an ARVN force into the Parrot's Beak, and on the twenty-ninth, a joint U.S.-ARVN force of

20,000 men pushed into the Fishhook (another salient of Cambodian territory, north of Parrot's Beak). Meeting only rearguard resistance, U.S. and South Vietnamese forces uncovered sprawling complexes of living quarters, mess halls, training sites, and storage depots. Thousands of weapons, millions of rounds of ammunition, tons of rice, and hundreds of vehicles were seized. But the PAVN already had trucked much greater quantities of equipment deeper into Cambodia. The bases, it was found, did not hug the border as believed but "extended far into Cambodia, often serviced by unknown roads and trails built specifically for the purpose."[76]

Military logic suggested pursuit, but Nixon limited ground intervention to sixty days and thirty-five kilometers into Cambodia to deflect domestic and international criticism. The gesture meant nothing to the antiwar movement, however, and the most violent demonstrations of the entire war broke out in the United States. Congress proceeded to repeal the Tonkin Gulf Resolution and prohibited U.S. combat or advisory activity in Cambodia. After leveling the Fishhook towns of Snoul and Mimot, U.S. troops pulled out on June 30. Air strikes code-named Freedom Deal supported Lon Nol government troops up to fifty miles inside Cambodia until mid-August, and 34,000 ARVN troops stayed behind to mop up.

ARVN troops and their commanders unfortunately were in no mood to be well-behaved visitors in their neighbor's country. One of the Lon Nol regime's first acts was to unleash a pogrom against Vietnamese residents in Cambodia, and their bloated bodies floated down the Mekong River into South Vietnam. Ordered to attack the sanctuaries, the ARVN went on a vengeful spree, and ARVN commander General Dang Van Quang organized the theft of everything from civilian valuables to the equipment of the Royal Cambodian Army for distribution among his fellow officers.[77]

The ARVN's revenge was oil on the Cambodian fire. Once content to protect its sanctuaries and supply lines, the PAVN evicted the Royal Cambodian Army from much of the northern and eastern interior. As the ARVN rampaged through the countryside, the Communists placed their own troops under strict orders to avoid contact with the civilian population.[78] Specially trained teams then set to work with Khmer Rouge cadres to strengthen the indigenous revolutionary movement. With the charismatic prince on their side and the ARVN crashing about on the other, this was not hard to do. Under the banner of Sihanouk's Front Unifié National Kampuchean (FUNK), the teams exhorted the Khmer to defend themselves against the U.S.-South Vietnamese "invaders." Hamlet-level FUNK committees began recruiting troops for the Khmer Rouge guerrilla army. By June, Hanoi's Political Bureau could declare that North Vietnam had become "not only the common rear area for the great front line in the South, but . . . also the common rear area of the Laotian and Kampuchean revolutions."[79] In late September, PAVN-supported Khmer Rouge closed several of the highways leading into Phnom Penh.

The opening of a new front did more than extend the war spatially. It triggered a new war, and the trigger was Hanoi's attempt to bolster the Khmer Rouge in the hope that they would help protect operations in Cambodia as the Pathet Lao were doing in Laos. In mid-1970 Hanoi dispatched Cambodian cadres who had been living in the DRV since 1954 and insisted that they be assigned to command positions in the Khmer Rouge eastern military region. Fearing that this foreshadowed Vietnamese domination, the Khmer Rouge leadership in July 1971 named Vietnam the main enemy of the Cambodian revolution. Khmer Rouge aligned with Pol Pot began purging and executing "Hanoi Cambodians," and skirmishes between Khmer Rouge and PAVN units broke out in July 1973.[80] Even before the Second Indochina War came to an end, a third one thus began to take shape. For the moment, though, the Khmer Rouge mostly faced Phnom Penh, leaving the Vietnamese free in northeastern Cambodia, the southern terminus of the Ho Chi Minh Trail.

DETOUR INTO LAOS: LAM SON 719

In 1970 President Thieu seemed unperturbed by the sprawl of war around him. Encouraged by the ARVN's performance in Cambodia, he suggested invading North Vietnam. American policy and domestic politics ruled out supporting the ARVN on a "northward march," but U.S. commanders shared Thieu's belief that the ARVN was ready to take on the PAVN in direct, large-scale combat. With restraint lowered by the Cambodian incursion and attention habitually focused on logistical lines, the MACV and ARVN staffs zeroed in on the Ho Chi Minh Trail in southern Laos.

The trail complex was an enticing target. B-52 bombardment had only slowed the crawl of men and equipment through the jungle, yet PAVN dependence on the trail had grown tremendously since the closure of the supply route through Sihanoukville. In late 1970 U.S. intelligence detected a twofold increase in the rate of PAVN infiltration and an accumulation of supplies in one of the trail's key hubs near the Laotian town of Sepone. A drive from the Vietnamese border to Sepone during the Communists' peak resupply effort, the MACV-ARVN command calculated, would blunt PAVN initiatives for a year to come. Such was to be the objective of Operation Lam Son 719.

Overconfident that forces that had penetrated Cambodia would romp across Laos, the U.S. and South Vietnamese commands ignored some crucial differences. The PAVN's Laotian installations were not remote sanctuaries but the core of its logistical lifeline. The Sepone area bristled with nineteen PAVN antiaircraft battalions, twelve infantry regiments, a tank regiment, an artillery regiment, and elements of five divisions. Reinforcements were only a few days' march away in nearby North Vietnam and other parts of Laos. Here, unlike in Cambodia, the PAVN was close to home, in control of terrain it could not afford to lose, and in a country where U.S. troops were prohibited by Congress from entering. The ARVN would have to attack alone.

On February 8, 1971, 5,000 ARVN troops set out to march down Route 9 into Laos. The United States provided logistical support from Khe Sanh. Ten kilometers into Laos, the attack stalled until reinforcements brought the force up to 21,000. Behind a shield of B-52 bombers, the ARVN pushed forward, reaching the outskirts of Sepone on March 6 and destroying PAVN supply dumps. But by then ARVN units were strung like threaded beads across forty kilometers of PAVN-infested jungle. Heavily reinforced, the PAVN struck back at the ARVN "tail" on Route 9, assaulted outlying firebases, shelled Khe Sanh, and set up a network of antiaircraft fire. As bad weather closed in, withdrawal turned into a rout. What MACV-ARVN spokesmen called an "orderly retreat," newsmen captured in images of terrified ARVN troops dropping from the skids of overloaded helicopters. On March 24, a day ahead of schedule, the ARVN pulled its last troops out of Laos, admitting to 1,200 dead, more than 4,200 wounded, and 107 helicopters shot down. Whether the ARVN would soon be able to fight alone was suddenly in doubt.

The Communists suffered heavily too. It appears moreover that they had to revise their timetable for recovering the "strategic offensive position," that is, resuming major main-force offensive action and entering the "decisive period" in 1971.[81] But the Sepone base was back in service only days after Lam Son 719 ended, and the southward flow of supplies and equipment quickly resumed. More important, the Communists perceived the battle as an indicator of future possibilities. "It was proof," a PAVN military historian said, "that the PAVN could defeat the best ARVN units. We had not been certain we could do this. 'Vietnamization' did create a strong ARVN, and in the battles of 1969–1970 we did not defeat the ARVN, which left us doubtful and apprehensive. Our army had to learn how to organize large-scale battles. So 1971 was a big test."[82] The geographical expansion of the battlefield also played into the Communists' hands. For as the United States withdrew, Saigon was left, in effect, to do more with less.

SPRING OFFENSIVE

In May 1971 the Political Bureau resolved to make 1972 the year of "decisive victory."[83] The need to bring the war to a swift conclusion or at least to achieve strategic superiority in a definitive way was urgent. Hanoi leaders could not be sure how American détente with the Soviet Union and China would affect them, and they feared the consequences of the growing enmity between Moscow and Beijing. For years Hanoi had pleaded for bloc unity, but as time passed and the United States reduced its role in Vietnam, Beijing came to see Moscow as more of a threat than Washington. The Soviet invasion of Czechoslovakia in August 1968 aroused Chinese fears of Soviet "social-imperialism," and the two Communist powers engaged in major military skirmishes across their common border in 1969. Although neither Beijing nor Moscow could afford openly to sell out the Vietnamese, Beijing believed the war gave Moscow an opportunity to gain a foothold on China's southern flank. The more Hanoi depended on the Soviet Union for high-tech weaponry and heavy equipment for aerial defense of the North and to mount main-force offensives in the South, the more Chinese leaders criticized Hanoi's strategy and friendliness with Moscow.

Hanoi dispatched NLF delegations in an attempt to keep Beijing sweet, but the Chinese were not fooled.[84] These years, moreover, were the high tide of the Cultural Revolution (1966–1969), which the Chinese unsubtly pressured Hanoi to emulate. Relations between the two, once as close as "lips and teeth," had taken a turn for the worse with the 1968 Tet Offensive, whose design contradicted Chinese advice. Beijing was also displeased with Hanoi's decision to negotiate, which Hanoi apparently made without informing Beijing.[85] To show displeasure with Hanoi's impudence, China began reducing its aid to Hanoi in the spring of 1968. Chinese armed forces were sent to protect the DRV's rail lines and help with coastal and antiaircraft defense. Number 170,000 at their peak, they were completely withdrawn by July 1970.[86] Chinese leaders also suggested to the Vietnamese that Vietnam's reunification should be a prolonged process.[87]

But China, too, was in a predicament: while improving relations with the United States to counter the Soviet threat, it needed to avoid pushing Hanoi further into Soviet arms. That latter fear caused Beijing in 1971 to approve Hanoi's negotiating strategy and to increase economic (not military) assistance.[88] But Chinese suggestions that Hanoi should soften its demand to exclude Thieu from a postwar coalition government[89] and Nixon's visit to China in February 1972—which Hanoi asked Beijing to cancel—stoked Vietnamese fears of abandonment by an essential ally. The Soviet Union meanwhile also began reducing its military assistance, hinting at a commitment to the DRV's defense but not to Vietnam's reunification by force. Troubling shifts of stance by Moscow and Beijing, along with the approach of the U.S. election year and nearly complete withdrawal of U.S. forces from ground combat, suggested to Hanoi that a pivotal moment had arrived. "A decisive victory," said the Politiburo, was now needed to force the United States "to end the war by negotiating from a position of defeat."[90]

Le Duc Tho detailed the Bureau's thinking in a memo to Southern commanders. "The advantageous time to solve our problems on all battlefields as well as in negotiations," wrote Tho, "is after we win victory in spring-summer-fall and before the American general elections begin." The point was not to sway the electoral outcome but to get a settlement before Nixon was re-elected and might stiffen his terms, or worse. To do this required "to basically defeat Vietnamization," that is, demonstrate that this strategy too had failed. Tho did not say Vietnamization was succeeding, but reversing its progress was clearly a major objective. "If a few large main-force divisions, the backbone of 'Vietnamization,' are eradicated then the balance of forces on the battlefield will shift greatly." At the same time, it would be necessary to roll back the ARVN presence in the countryside and reestablish liberated areas so that "the political movement in the cities can expand and leap forward. Eradicating the enemy, liberating the countryside and rising up in the cities are intimately related to one another in an organic way," Tho wrote, although he acknowledged the weakness of the urban movement. Whatever the course of battle, however, Tho vowed that negotiations would not conclude as they had in 1954, with revolutionary forces withdrawn from the South. There could be a coalition government, but it would have to provide for a political process culminating in "a people's democratic government that we lead." Absent that assurance, "we will not rule out a return to war. . . ."[91]

The Communists thus aimed to defeat the ARVN in main-force battle, roll back pacification, and revitalize the guerrilla movement. If this were done, and the United States withdrew, the situation would be no worse than it had been before the United States intervened—when Communist forces were pushing Saigon nearly to the point of collapse.[92] If things went well, Communist forces would seize and hold the South's northern provinces and dictate terms for a "transitional government at the upper level" and a "three-segment coalition government" that could include anyone but Thieu.[93]

Shades of 1968, but with a difference. This time the Soviet Union had supplied a threefold increase in arms, including T-54 medium tanks, armed personnel carriers, 57-mm antiaircraft batteries, SA-7 hand-held missiles, and a vast array of artillery from 76-mm through 130-mm field guns. Supplies were pre-positioned near targets in sufficient quantities to sustain combat for weeks. Though still much inferior in firepower to the ARVN (which enjoyed a twenty-to-one advantage in artillery shells and could call on U.S. airpower in emergency), the PAVN would not again pull its punches. With the U.S. force level down to 95,000 (of which only 6,000 were combat troops and the rest were support troops), Communist strategists assumed they had only to contend with the ARVN. Although the ARVN had an overall numerical advantage, many ARVN troops were tied down providing security at military bases, public buildings, bridges, and the like. Pentagon estimates of regular-force manpower available for offensive combat showed the Communists, for the first time, to have the greater strength.[94]

In early 1972, while Washington and Hanoi dithered over revisions of their negotiating proposals, all but three of the PAVN's thirteen combat divisions moved toward targets in the South. Including PLAF units (reinforced by Northern troops), the assault force numbered up to 200,000 men. Their assignment was to attack on widely separated fronts, draw the ARVN away from populated areas, break up Saigon's outermost ring of defense, and help local forces in the lowlands carry the attack into the enemy's "secure rear areas."

In the dawn of March 30, 1972, under cover of clouds and rain, three divisions supported by several artillery regiments crossed the demilitarized zone.[95] It took them just two days to overrun all twelve of the bases and outposts that U.S. Marines had turned over to the ARVN Third Division. The division's 56th Regiment defected, the rest of the division began to disintegrate, and the entire northern half of Quang Tri province fell under Communist control. Further south, in Thua Thien province, PAVN and local regional forces seized the approaches to Hue.

The PAVN 320th Division opened a second front in the western highlands. Behind tanks and antiaircraft weapons that had just moved down newly constructed roads, the division attacked more than a dozen ARVN outposts southwest of Kontum and blocked Route 14 and Route 19.

A third front, opened on April 2 in northern Binh Long province, quickly forced the ARVN to withdraw from outlying positions in order to defend the province capital. On the fifth, two regiments of the PLAF Fifth Division fell on Loc Ninh, where they were joined by twenty-five tanks the next day. Radio contact with Loc Ninh ceased on April 7. Even as Loc Ninh's survivors fled toward An Loc, nineteen kilometers in the direction of Saigon, An Loc felt the first probes of the PLAF Ninth Division. Suddenly, the PLAF Seventh Division blocked Route 13 about twenty-five kilometers south of An Loc, and the town's five ARVN regiments and ten thousand civilians found themselves under a siege that would last until June

The fourth front was the Mekong delta. Here the U.S.-ARVN pacification program had made the deepest inroads, and the Communists desperately needed to recover access to rice and manpower. Waiting until the ARVN Twenty-First Division had departed to join the relief of An Loc, a PAVN infantry regiment moved out of Cambodia into Kien Tuong province where it linked up with other infantry regiments and a sapper regiment to attack lightly defended ARVN and regional force outposts. Masked by more than one hundred guerrilla-style attacks, more PAVN units infiltrated the delta (particularly Dinh Tuong province) and forced suspension of the pacification program.

The rapidly deteriorating military situation placed the United States in a difficult position. Washington could not stand aside while everything the country had worked twenty years to accomplish came apart. But neither did Nixon and Kissinger, on the brink of major breakthroughs in détente with Soviet Union, wish to jeopardize the Moscow summit planned for May 22,1972. Would the Soviets cancel the summit if the United States retaliated against Hanoi? What would happen to relations with China, just reestablished by Nixon's dramatic visit to Beijing in February? Nixon and Kissinger had counted on détente with Moscow and Beijing to isolate Hanoi, but now their own hopes restrained them.

Hanoi's leaders had calculated correctly that Nixon would not return U.S. ground forces to combat, and they professed not to fear tactical use of U.S. airpower in the South. But they underestimated the lengths to which Nixon was prepared to go in an election year to prevent an outright defeat while America's reputation was still at stake. On April 6, U.S. fighter bombers raided military targets 100 kilometers north of the demilitarized zone. Meanwhile, a massive strike force of B-52s and other aircraft was readied at Utapao in Thailand, at Danang in South Vietnam, on Guam, and aboard six aircraft carriers. Uncertainty about Moscow's reaction stayed Nixon's hand, but evidence that Hanoi had committed its forces to the complete destruction of the Saigon government and was succeeding overcame Nixon's hesitation. For three days starting April 15, Nixon sent B-52s over the North for the first time since 1969. Aimed at military targets in Hanoi and Haiphong, the raids also damaged four Soviet vessels. The protest over the bombing, however, was greater in the U.S. Congress and the media than it was in Moscow. China's ping-pong team went ahead on April 18 with a call on Nixon at the White House, signaling that the bombing would have no effect on relations with China. China also refused to allow Soviet aid to pass through Chinese territory instead of the North's mined ports.[96] Kissinger, returning from a secret trip to Moscow, reported that the Soviets were not ready to help end the war, but they would acquiesce in "pushing [North Vietnam] to the limit."[97] Both Moscow and Beijing continued to support Hanoi materially, but neither of them was willing to put improved relations with the U.S. in jeopardy by doing more. Neither, however, did they pressure Hanoi to discontinue the offensive.

In late April, the PAVN tightened the noose around ARVN positions in the central highlands. Dak To, once the linchpin of U.S. outposts in western Kontum province fell on the twenty-fourth. The PAVN 320th Division chased the ARVN into Kontum city. Three days later, and further north, the PAVN began a two-pronged push against Dong Ha and Quang Tri city with heavy equipment trucked directly across the demilitarized zone. Dong Ha fell in a day. On May 1 some 8,000 ARVN troops fled Quang Tri and streamed southward on Route 1. Abandoning tanks, trucks, and armed personnel carriers as they went, panicky troops flooded Hue. In desperation, President Thieu fired the corps commander General Hoang Xuan Lam, a political appointee who had led the debacle in Laos the year before, and turned to General Ngo Quang Truong, the hero of Hue's defense in 1968. Truong hastily patched together a last line of defense on the south bank of the My Chanh River about thirty kilometers north of Hue. Fragile ARVN positions everywhere seemed on the verge of collapse.

From Saigon and Washington, it appeared that the Communists were bent on seizing Hue. But the Communists had not prepared to advance so far so quickly. Blaming "strategic commanders" (i.e., the high command in Hanoi) for lack of foresight that prevented "lower echelons" from achieving "certain victory," COSVN's General Iran Van Tra maintained that the ARVN's defeat in Quang Tri left Hue "practically wide open but we did not take advantage of that favorable opportunity."[98] The defense of Hue, however, did draw the ARVN Second Division out of Quang Ngai province, permitting Communist guerrilla forces to recover rapidly across the province.

Farther south, the effort to relieve An Loc sucked up the ARVN reserves including Thieu's Palace Guard. In the Mekong delta communist troop strength continued rising. Estimated at only 3,000 in 1971, Communist forces in the delta would number between 20,000 and 30,000 by September 1972, and half a million civilians came back under Communist control.

Against this background, Kissinger and Le Duc Tho held another secret meeting in Paris on May 2. The United States was now prepared to waive its longstanding demand for total mutual withdrawal of "foreign forces" from the South, but Tho was in no mood to concede anything as long as military victory seemed imminent. Kissinger, thinking he had explored every diplomatic avenue, returned to Washington ready to support Nixon's wish for a massive blow.[99]

Nixon already had concluded that he could not survive politically if he accepted defeat.[100] The fact that it was an election year made it, he thought, more necessary to appear decisive. Moreover, he calculated, it was better to risk cancellation of the Moscow summit than to suffer the humiliation of negotiating with the Soviets at the same time that Soviet arms were crushing a U.S. ally.[101] With Congress debating "end-the-war" bills and withdrawals bringing the U.S. force level steadily down (to 47,000 by June 30), all of Nixon's remaining bargaining leverage was about to evaporate. If he were to end the war without defeat, this was his last chance. Nixon shunned the advice of Laird, who warned of adverse domestic reaction, and of CIA Director Richard Helms, whose agency doubted Hanoi could be forced to withdraw its forces from the South. Instead on May 8, Nixon approved Operation Linebacker to mine the North's harbors, cut all of its communications and rail links, and intensify bombardment of military targets all over the North.

For the first time in the war, newly developed laser and television guidance technology helped "smart bombs" find their targets with unprecedented accuracy.

Just how much the mining and bombing affected the PAVN's ability to sustain its offensive is difficult to say. Hanoi admitted that the blockade forced it to shift most of its import volume from sea to land routes, that is, across the Chinese border.[102] But in the short run it was U.S. airpower in the South that provided the margin of survival for shaky ARVN positions. More dependent than ever on conventional logistic supply that was vulnerable to bombing, the PAVN had difficulty sustaining attacks on such far-flung fronts. During the first week of May, the weather cleared over Quang Tri, permitting U.S. air and naval bombardment to break up PAVN concentrations just north of the My Chanh River. A week later, hundreds of B-52s and fighter-bombers held off a PAVN attempt to penetrate An Loc. B-52s also saw their heaviest use of the war over the Mekong delta, mainly in strikes against PAVN infiltration routes. "[I]t was apparent," wrote an American Air Force general for an official history, "that the ARVN couldn't stand up to the North Vietnamese Army without continuous and massive air support."[103] Considering the ARVN's persistent and pervasive low morale, inadequate training, lack of confidence, defeatism, weak unit solidarity, poor nutrition, graft, corruption, draft avoidance, and alarming desertion rates—all and more detailed in Robert Brigham's unique study of the ARVN[104]—it is surprising that any ARVN units fought as well as they did. Some fought quite well indeed.

By mid-June 1972, the PAVN's offensive had stalled, and on the twenty-eighth, behind a barrage of B-52 bombardments, the ARVN crossed the My Chanh River to inch back toward Quang Tri city (which it retook from a token Communist regional force on September 16). The PAVN remained in control of northern Quang Tri province, and it had demonstrated that Vietnamization depended on the perpetual readiness of the United States to come to the ARVN's aid. But it had failed to dictate the peace. In Hanoi, General Giap, who had warned that such a major offensive might not succeed, took the blame for the disappointing result and lost field command of the army to General Van Tien Dung.[105]

BREAKING THE DEADLOCK

By late summer, both sides were feeling the urge to compromise. Pressures were building in the U.S. Congress to cut off funds for the war, and Nixon knew he would not be permitted many more "savage, punishing blows." He also was increasingly impatient to remove the roadblock that Vietnam placed in the way of other objectives. As for Hanoi, its grasp at "decisive victory" had fallen short, its ports remained blockaded, and its allies had done nothing more than meekly protest. Vietnam, it was painfully clear, was no longer the "front line" against imperialism so far as the Soviet Union and China were concerned. Sen. George McGovern's nomination as the Democrat candidate for president had strengthened Nixon's assurance of reelection. Hanoi evidently concluded that it would get better terms from Nixon before rather than after the November election.

The Kissinger-Tho talks resumed in July. The United States in 1971 already had expressed a willingness to set a timetable for total withdrawal and, later, to let North Vietnamese troops remain in the South. Now, Tho agreed to address military issues first and leave political settlement for later. Gone was the demand for removal of Thieu's regime. Gone was the demand for a coalition government. By October 8 all the elements of agreement were in place: a standstill ceasefire over all Indochina, U.S. withdrawal within sixty days, return of U.S. prisoners but *not* the release of the ten thousand Communist cadres in Thieu's jails, and arrangements for the Vietnamese parties to consult among themselves about elections and the future of South Vietnam. If not quite "the same proposal made by President Nixon himself," as Tho put it, it was close enough to give Kissinger his "most thrilling moment in public service." As far as Kissinger and Tho were concerned the two had made a deal, and it was a better deal for the U.S. than Hanoi had ever offered.

But Kissinger, by his own account, had grossly underestimated America's ally, Nguyen Van Thieu. For years Thieu had taken little interest in the negotiations, believing that Hanoi's intransigence would leave the United States no choice but to go on supporting him. Now, faced with a draft agreement between Hanoi and Washington, Thieu balked, as Kissinger must have anticipated. After all, the draft's requirement that Thieu "consult" with the PRG while Northern troops remained in the South legitimized the threat to his government's existence. Articles that affirmed Vietnam's unity and recognized communist political rights in the South, echoing the Geneva Agreements of 1954, implied that the Communist cause had been just all along. Furthermore, Washington's negotiation of this future for the South, accomplished with as little respect for Saigon's independence as Hanoi showed toward that of the NLF and PRG, placed Thieu in an intolerable position. Acceptance of the draft as written would have proved to himself and to the people he wished to lead that he was indeed a puppet.

Moreover, Thieu knew, as few U.S. leaders or advisers ever recognized, that compromise in Vietnam was a U.S fantasy. In the colonial period, Vietnamese had competed to determine which party would lead Vietnam into the modern world, and the French Sûreté had seen to it that only the most disciplined, unified, secretive, and ideologically implacable of these parties survived. It was hardly realistic to expect the surviving party, now holding the mandate of August 1945 and Dien Bien Phu, to share power with legatees of the colonial past and toadies of imperialism. So Thieu assumed that if he did not eliminate the Communists, they would eliminate him. The third force—or "third segment" as the draft called presumably neutral elements—would have to choose sides. A compromise as envisioned in the draft could only be a prelude to renewed struggle minus the United States, a prospect Thieu lacked the confidence to face.

The draft proved to be divisive for the Communists as well, according to historian Robert Brigham. NLF leaders had not been kept fully informed of what Kissinger and Tho had secretly negotiated and strongly objected to the release of American prisoners without guaranteed release of civilian prisoners from Thieu's jails. To these leaders it seemed that Hanoi was rushing to secure a respite from war without regard for an issue of critical importance to Southern revolutionaries, including the Front's non-Communist members. NLF leaders dug in their heels, going so far as to ask Soviet officials to intercede with Hanoi on their behalf.[106]

As it happened, Nixon himself was having second thoughts. An agreement earlier might have helped his campaign, but a signing only a week or two before the November 7 election, by raising questions about his motives, could create, he said, a "messy situation." Nixon also saw Thieu's intransigence as an excuse to bargain for better terms. Kissinger was sent on another round of negotiations, more with Thieu than with Thuy or Tho, that Nixon may have surmised would result in postponement of the signing.[107] So it was that Hanoi, fearing the United States was backing away from the agreement, publicly revealed what had been secretly negotiated, forcing Kissinger, desperate to keep the negotiations going, to affirm on October 26 that "peace is at hand."

But it was not. When negotiations resumed after the election (which Nixon won in a landslide), Kissinger presented Thieu's demand for sixty-nine changes. Although he quickly withdrew half, which not even he took seriously,[108] the remaining demands were sufficiently substantive to raise doubts in Hanoi that the United States could be held to the October draft of the agreement. In view of congressional obsession with the fate of U.S. prisoners, Hanoi also apparently calculated that it had nothing to lose by postponing settlement. So Tho began introducing his own demands as the price for making changes demanded by Washington. Intensive negotiations brought the two sides very close to what had been agreed in October, but Hanoi's niggling convinced Kissinger that Hanoi was determined "not to allow the agreement to be completed."[109]

As for Saigon, Nixon offered two billion dollars worth of military hardware and "absolute assurances" of "swift and retaliatory action" if Hanoi violated the agreement.[110] He also threatened to sign a separate peace. But to no avail. Thieu could not be budged any more than Hanoi could be pinned down. Pulled between adversary and ally alike, Nixon resolved, as talks came to a close on December 13, to have an immediate final show-down with both.

Such was the background to Nixon's most splenetic decision of the war. After warning of grave consequences if "serious negotiations" did not re-sume within seventy-two hours, Nixon unleashed the full fury of all B-52s stationed in Southeast Asia against previously forbidden targets in Hanoi and Haiphong. (See Map 7.1.) He gave no public explanation. How was he to tell the American people that it was he, not Hanoi, who had reneged on the October agreements and was now bombing Hanoi to make it agree to what it had once accepted?[111]

In the eleven days beginning December 18, with a day off for Christ-mas, U.S. aircraft dropped thirty-six thousand tons of bombs on railroad yards, bus stations, port complexes, factories, radio broadcasting stations, and warehouses—some of them square in the middle of normally densely populated areas. In the operation dubbed Linebacker Two, "smart bombs" made the strikes the most accurate in the history of war. But smart bombs could miss, and not all of the bombs dropped were smart. An entire string intended for the Hanoi railroad yards fell on the adjacent residential and commercial quarter of Kham Thien. Hits on the Cuban Chancery, Hanoi's largest hospital, and civilian housing were due, in the antiseptic language of Washington's military bureaucrats, to "accidents" and "bomb spillover." But the phrase that came to tongues around the world was "indiscriminate carpet-bombing."

Actually, the bombing was as discriminating as bombing could then be, and Hanoi had anticipated it.[112] The government had evacuated more than half the city's population when bombing resumed in April, and on December 3, the day before Tho was to present new counter demands to Kissinger, it had stepped up preparations for disaster relief and relocation of non-essential persons.[113] Kham Thien, an area of one square kilometer housing 30,000 people, contained only a fraction of its normal population when the bombs fell on it. So had An Duong, another bombed neighbor-hood that normally held 6,000 densely packed inhabitants. That so many people had evacuated was their good fortune. That the vast majority of Hanoi's buildings were never touched was plain for visitors to see, too. The destruction was nothing compared to that inflicted on European and Japa-nese cities in World War II. Still, Hanoi on December 30 officially counted 1,318 dead and 1,261 wounded, later adjusting these figures to 2,196 dead and 1,577 wounded as more bodies were pulled out of the rubble.

What did the "December blitz" accomplish? The men who led the raids claimed to have cut the North's resupply—already reduced by the blockade of Haiphong harbor—from 160,000 to 30,000 tons per month. Furthermore, the North fired nearly its total supply of 1,000 SA-2 missiles, expending its

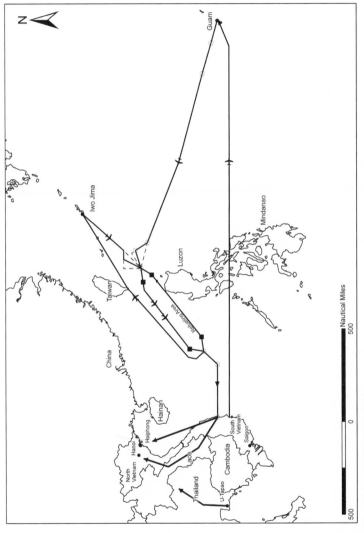

Map 7.1. B-52 Flight Paths

Source: From Brigadier General James R. McCarthy and Lieutenant Colonel George B. Allison, Linebacker II: *A View from the Rock* (Maxwell Air Force Base, Alabama: Airpower Research Institute, Air War College, 1979), p. 3.

Note: Map of the Western Pacific and Southeast Asia. The westbound route shows the general flight path taken by the B-52 forces to arrive at the mainland, from where they dispersed on a variety of routes into North Vietnam. Most sorties recovered to the South and back to Guam. Diversions from these basic routes were sometimes made to meet critical timing requirement or to perform supplemental in-flight refueling.

most effective defense against the big planes. "Why are we stopping now?" the B-52 pilots asked. "'Another week of these missions . . . and the North Vietnamese would have been suing for peace on our terms."[114] But the United States also lost fifteen B-52s (Hanoi claimed thirty-four), or 10 percent of the force it had deployed, and ninety-two crew members. "Another week" may have been all the United States itself could have endured.

Nixon did not depend on the bombing alone to sway Thieu. The day after the bombing began, Nixon sent Thieu an ultimatum to "decide now whether you desire to continue our alliance or whether you want me to seek settlement with the enemy which serves U.S. interests alone."[115] Thieu did drop his objections to the political provisions of the draft agreement, probably because the bombing made Nixon's reassurances credible.[116] But Thieu also restated his opposition to the continued presence of North Vietnam forces in the South and refused to change his position even after Nixon, on January 5, 1973, put into writing his "assurances of continued assistance in the postsettlement period" and of response "with full force should the settlement be violated by North Vietnam." It took a letter from Nixon on the sixteenth threatening "an inevitable and immediate termination of U.S. economic and military assistance" to force Thieu into submission.[117]

Indeed, the December bombing, by completing the alienation of Congress from the president, probably guaranteed that the last credible threat Nixon would ever be able to make regarding Vietnam was to cut off aid to Saigon. Nixon's approval rating for handling the war, 59 percent just before the bombing, fell to 43 percent in mid-January.[118] A poll of the newly elected congressmen and senators, taken as bombs fell, showed that most members now favored immediate legislation to end all U.S. involvement immediately. As Congress returned to session in the first days of January, Democrat Party caucuses of both the House and Senate voted by crushing margins to cut off all funds for military operations in Indochina, contingent only upon the safe withdrawal of the remaining 24,000 U.S. troops and return of U.S. prisoners. Nixon knew he had to wrap up the negotiations quickly, before Congress did it for him.

As for Hanoi, its official reply, which came on December 26 after eight days of bombing, was to accept the gist of what Nixon and Kissinger demanded. Presumably the bombing played a role in Hanoi's decision, but Beijing apparently brought some pressure to bear on Hanoi, too. According to historian Lien-Hang T. Nguyen, China "was no longer willing to aid and support the Vietnamese revolution, especially if Chinese geopolitical interests were at stake," and fear of isolation drove Hanoi back to negotiations.[119] In a cabled briefing for COSVN leaders, Le Duc Tho expressed less concern about the bombing (a "defeat" for the United States, he wrote) than about the strategic fallout from American courting of China and the USSR and from the Indo-Pakistan war. The world and domestic situations were evolving, as Tho put it, in "swift and complicated ways," intensifying Hanoi's need to get the United States out of the war.[120] Talks resumed in early January 1974 on the basis of what had been agreed, except for details, in October 1973. Thus, the United States got what it wanted by being careful not to ask for more than what was already on the table.

The January talks moved swiftly to conclusion. Kissinger extracted wording changes that he claimed gave the United States the right to go on supplying Saigon with military assistance on an "unrestricted" basis. He also claimed to have reduced the National Council of National Reconciliation and Concord—the mechanism for consultation among "three equal segments" on elections and on the South's political future—to "essential impotence."[121] More haggling reaffirmed the demilitarized zone in the precise terms of the Geneva accords of 1954, and though Kissinger expressed satisfaction, those terms defined the demarcation as "only provisional and not a political or territorial boundary," as Hanoi had steadfastly insisted. Joint military commissions were to oversee a standstill ceasefire, and a 1,160-person International Commission of Control and Supervision was set up to report on implementation of the agreement. "Foreign countries" were to end all their military activities in Laos and Cambodia, and a ceasefire was arranged for Laos. Separate talks between the Royal Lao Government and Pathet Lao produced an agreement in February. The "Red Prince" Souphanouvong entered Vientiane to a tumultuous welcome and joined a coalition government dominated by the Pathet Lao a little later. But Hanoi confessed it lacked sufficient control over the Khmer Rouge to bring them to the negotiating table, much less to guarantee a ceasefire. In fact Hanoi's relations with the Khmer Rouge were rapidly deteriorating into a state of armed conflict. By Hanoi's count, 174 military clashes between Vietnamese communist and Khmer Rouge forces occurred between 1970 and 1975, causing 600 Vietnamese deaths.[122]

The ceasefire in South Vietnam went into effect on January 27, 1974, the day the agreement was signed in Paris. The representatives of Hanoi and the PRG signed the first page and the United States and Saigon signed another so that the signature of Tran Van Lam, Saigon's minister for foreign affairs, would not have to appear next to that of Nguyen Thi Dinh, the PRG's minister for foreign affairs. Prisoner exchanges began, the United States signed over its remaining bases, and on March 29, the last U.S. soldier left for home. As far as most Americans were concerned, the war was over, although bombing continued in Laos until mid-April and in Cambodia until August fifteenth, as Congress cut off the last drop of funding.

But it was only a new phase of the war. The ceasefires in Vietnam and Laos—a standstill-in-place leaving hostile forces cheek-by-jowl—invited violation. Hanoi blithely ignored the Agreement's article 20 proscribing "all military activities" by "foreign countries" in Cambodia and Laos. In

Vietnam both sides ordered their armed forces to increase areas of control just before the ceasefire went into effect, enlarging claims that each was sure to contest. As for political settlement, the Paris Agreement proclaimed that "immediately after the ceasefire the two South Vietnamese parties will achieve national reconciliation and concord, end hatred and enmity, prohibit all acts of reprisal . . . assure . . . democratic liberties," as if miracles could be accomplished by decree. The agency of this miracle was to be the National Council of National Reconciliation and Concord, which Kissinger, anxious to avoid the appearance of imposing a coalition government, had worked assiduously to reduce to "essential impotence." Lastly, the Paris Agreement affirmed Vietnam's unity and territorial integrity and ordered North and South to move "step by step" toward reunification, but without obligating the two sides to anything more specific than "peaceful means."

Nonetheless, from the view of the Nixon administration and most Americans the Paris Agreement was satisfactory in that it permitted the United States to complete its withdrawal and left Nguyen Van Thieu in power. Whatever happened next, the U.S. could plausibly claim it had prevented the RVN's collapse and given it the time and resources it needed to defend itself. If things did not go well, American leaders could hope that American credibility would not be at stake. In these ways, the United States, unable to win the war or to end it, arranged an exit from Indochina that sought to keep prestige and reputation intact, much as the French had done nineteen years before.

NOTES

1. Henry Kissinger, *White House Years* (Boston: Little, 1979), 1345.

2. "Bao cao cua Bo chinh tri tai Hoi nghi lan thu 18 Ban chap hanh Trung uong, Ngay 27 thang 1 nam 1970" [Report of the Political Bureau to the 18th Plenum of the Central Committee, January 27, 1970], Dang Cong San Viet Nam, *Van Kien Dang, toan tap* [Complete Party Documents (hereafter cited as VKDTT)], vol. 31, 1970 (2003), 56–60.

3. Richard M. Nixon, "Asia After Vietnam," *Foreign Affairs* (October 1967): 111.

4. Quoted in H.R. Haldeman, *The Ends of Power* (New York: Times Books, 1978), 81.

5. Pham Van Dong speech to the DRV National Assembly, April 8, 1965, Vietnam News Agency, in Wallace J. Thies, *When Governments Collide* (Berkeley: University of California Press, 1980). Appendix 1, 421–422.

6. Kissinger, *White House Years*, 228.

7. Henry Kissinger, "The Vietnam Negotiations," *Foreign Affairs* (January 1969): 211–234.

8. Haldeman, *The Ends of Power*, 83.

9. Christopher E. Goscha, "The Maritime Nature of the Wars for Vietnam (1945–1975)," *Viet Nam Journal* (April 2003), www.vietnamjournal.org/article.php?sid=123&PHPSESSID=447f33e56a6a7ca13f597e6943346e9a (accessed February 6, 2007).

10. Compulsory sales at below market prices and taxation of rice exports were a major source of revenue for the Phnom Penh government. Ironically, it was Vietnamese communist purchases of Cambodian rice to supply troops in South Vietnam that reduced the amount available in the market, forcing the government to use the army to enforce compulsory sales and sparking an armed struggle that Hanoi did not want at that time. See Ben Kiernan, "The Samlaut Rebellion, 1967–68," in *Peasants and Politics in Kampuchea, 1942–1981,* ed. Ben Kiernan and Chanthou Boua (Armonk, N.Y.: M.E. Sharpe, 1982), 166–205.

11. On Vietnamese-Khmer Rouge relations, see Thomas Engelbert and Christopher E. Goscha, *Falling out of Touch: A Study on Vietnamese Communist Policy Towards an Emerging Cambodian Communist Movement, 1930–1975* (Clayton, Australia: Monash University, Centre of Southeast Asian Studies, 1995). See also David Chandler, *The Tragedy of Cambodian History: Politics, War and Revolution Since 1945* (New Haven, Conn.: Yale University Press, 1991); Nayan Chanda, *Brother Enemy: the War after the War* (San Diego, Calif.: Harcourt Brace Jovanovich, 1986); and Ben Kiernan, *How Pol Pot Came to Power* (London: Verso, 1985).

12. The classic account of the bombing and intervention in Cambodia is William Shawcross, *Sideshow: Kissinger, Nixon and the Destruction of Cambodia* (New York: Simon and Schuster, 1979).

13. In a system of "dual reporting," B-52 crews reported striking targets in South Vietnam through regular channels but actually flew over these to strike targets in Cambodia, which they identified in communications through a separate, secret channel.

14. Signs were given to presidential emissary Chester Bowles in January 1968. Just what Sihanouk said to Bowles and whether it constituted an invitation to bomb the sanctuaries is a matter of dispute. Compare Kissinger, *White House Years,* 250, with Shawcross, *Sideshow,* 69–71.

15. Kissinger, *White House Years,* 249. Emphasis is in the original.

16. The "Symington Ceiling" of $350 million on all U.S. aid to Laos was set in 1971. See Timothy N. Castle, *At War in the Shadow of Vietnam: U.S. Military Aid to the Royal Lao Government, 1955–1975* (New York: Columbia University Press, 1993), 99–101, 104–105.

17. David E. Brown, "Exporting Insurgency: The Communists in Cambodia," in *Indochina in Conflict: A Political Assessment,* ed. J. J. Zasloff and A. E. Goodman (Lexington, Mass.: Heath, 1972), 126.

18. *Viet-Nam Documents and Research Notes,* no. 88 (Saigon: U.S. Mission, January 1971).

19. Tran Van Quang, et al., *Tong ket cuoc khang chien chong My, cuu nuoc: thang loi va bai hoc* [Summing Up the National Salvation War of Resistance against the United States: Victory and Lessons] (Hanoi: NXB Ban chinh tri quoc gia, 1995), 236.

20. War Experience Recapitulation Committee of the High-Level Military Institute, *The Anti-U.S. Resistance War for National Salvation 1954–1975: Military Events,* trans. Joint Publications Research Service, JPRS no. 80,968 (Washington, D.C.: Government Printing Office, June 3, 1982), 124.

21. Philip Short, *Pol Pot: Anatomy of a Nightmare* (New York: Henry Holt, 2004), 218.

22. War Experience Recapitulation Committee, *The Anti-U.S. Resistance War*, 117.

23. Robert K. Brigham, *Guerrilla Diplomacy: The NLF's Foreign Relations and the Viet Nam War* (Ithaca, N.Y.: Cornell University Press, 1998), 85–88.

24. Nixon first enunciated this principle during a press conference on Guam, July 25, 1969. The quotation is from his appeal to the "silent majority" during an address to the nation on November 3, 1969. For the speech, see www.presidency .ucsb.edu/ws/index.php?pid=2303. Also see J.L.S. Girling, "The Guam Doctrine," *International Affairs*, vol. 46, no. 1 (January 1970) 48–62.

25. William Burr and Jeffrey Kimball, "Nixon White House Considered Nuclear Options Against North Vietnam, Declassified Documents Reveal," National Security Archive Electronic Briefing Book No. 195 (George Washington University, The National Security Archive, July 31, 2006), www.gwu.edu/~nsarchiv/NSAEBB/ NSAEBB195/index.htm (accessed March 3, 2007).

26. The My Lai massacre, in which soldiers of the American division shot, stabbed, or attacked with hand grenades between 347 and 504 unarmed men, women and children, was the most infamous instance of criminal slaughter by American soldiers, but it was not the only one. A less well known incident involved a platoon of the 101st Airborne Division that had been specially created to find and ambush communist forces in Quang Ngai's Song Ve valley. "Tiger Force," as the platoon was called, slaughtered at least eighty-one and more likely hundreds of unarmed civilians and prisoners while on patrol from May through November 1967. The incident escaped public attention until the Toledo *Blade* revealed it in a lengthy investigative report on October 19–22, 2005. Incidents such as these could be explained if not excused as the actions of stressed individuals serving under incompetent officers. Not so Operation Speedy Express in which the U.S. Ninth Division claimed to have killed, during the first half of 1969, more than ten thousand "VC" while recovering only 748 weapons, a ratio of bodies-to-weapons that could only be explained by the deaths of many unarmed civilians (Guenter Lewy, *America in Vietnam* [Oxford: Oxford University Press, 1978], 142–143). The Ninth Division's commander, Lieutenant General Julian Ewell, encouraged this result using "body count ratios" (U.S.-to-enemy) as a tool for evaluating his division's mid-level officers. Speedy Express, like Tiger Force, also went largely unnoticed until *Newsweek* reporter Kevin Buckley examined the military record and concluded (in *Newsweek*, June 19, 1972, 42–43) that roughly half of the "VC" killed in action had been noncombatant civilians. According to Buckley, U.S. officials estimated that for the entire war up to that time American firepower had caused the deaths of as many as one hundred thousand innocent civilians. If high-ranking officers did not always know what their men were doing in places like My Lai, they understood perfectly the general consequences of their own tactical decisions and management methods. That Communist "people's war" doctrine blurred the distinction between combatants and noncombatants did not justify American strategies and tactics that did the same thing. On Speedy Express and General Ewell, see David H. Hackworth, *Steel My Soldiers' Hearts* (New York: Rugged Land, 2002), esp. 98–99. Hackworth was a Ninth division battalion commander and America's most decorated living soldier.

This is not to suggest that only American soldiers and their allies committed atrocities. In an incident reported by *Time* magazine (December 15, 1967), a Communist force of six hundred attacked the civilian inhabitants of Dak Son hamlet in Phuoc Long province about seventy-five miles northeast of Saigon and killed 252 people. The motive was believed to be retribution against a group of pro-Saigon montagnards that had sought sanctuary in a government-controlled hamlet. Communists were responsible as well for the execution of civilians in Hue during the 1968 Tet Offensive, as discussed in chapter 6. And the Communists "exterminated" village officials and civilians (nearly thirty-seven thousand according to the U.S.) who supported Saigon's cause.

The My Lai and "Tiger Force" massacres were committed by rogue individuals serving in badly officered units; Speedy Express's commander (and how many others?) knowingly counted dead civilians as combatants; Dak Son, Hue and the "extermination of traitors" were selective, purposeful, and premeditated. From both legal and moral perspectives, differences of motive and means absolve none of the perpetrators. A complete weighing of each side's probity would have to include evaluation of the high tolerance exhibited by U.S. forces for "collateral damage" resulting from prodigious reliance on artillery and aerial bombardment in the North, Laos, and Cambodia as well as the South. Taking only "body count" as the measure, U.S. armed forces, by American estimates, did far more harm than revolutionary armed forces to the civilian population. By comparison with other major conflicts of the twentieth century, however, the Second Indochina War was not exceptional in the brutality it inflicted on civilians.

27. *Survey by Gallup Organization, September 1964–February 1973*, iPOLL Databank, The Roper Center for Public Opinion Research, University of Connecticut, www.ropercenter.uconn.edu/ipoll.htm (accessed December 30, 2006).

28. Jeb Stuart Magruder quoting Nixon, in Tad Szulc, *The Illusion of Peace* (New York: Viking, 1978), 158.

29. "Report: Status of Deserters," *Viet-Nam Documents and Research Notes*, no. 56 (April 1969).

30. Author's interview with a PAVN senior captain in December 1972 shortly after his defection in the Mekong delta.

31. U.S. government sources, cited in Guenter Lewy, *America in Vietnam* (Oxford: Oxford University Press, 1978), 191.

32. Combined Intelligence Center Vietnam, U.S. Military Assistance Command Vietnam, J-2, Study ST70-05, "North Vietnam Personnel Infiltration into the Republic of Vietnam" (Saigon, December 16, 1970), 59.

33. Tran Van Tra, *Nhung chang duong cua "B2" -Thanh dong: tap V. Ket thuc cuoc chien tranh 30 nam* [Stages on the Road of the B2-Bulwark, vol. V., Concluding the 30 Years War] (Ho Chi Minh City: NXB Van Nghe, 1982), 64.

34. Vien lich su quan su Viet Nam, *Lich su cong tac dang, cong tac chinh tri chien dich trong khang chien chong Phap va chong My, 1945–1975* [History of Party work and Theater Political Work in the Resistance Wars against France and the United States], (Hanoi: NXB Quan doi nhan dan, 1998), 406–407.

35. Tran Van Quang, et al., *Tong ket cuoc khang chien chong My, cuu nuoc: thang loi va bai hoc* [Summing Up the National Salvation War of Resistance against the United States: Victory and Lessons] (Hanoi: NXB Ban chinh tri quoc gia, 1995), 112, 131.

36. Tra, *Nhung chang duong*, 63.

37. Hoi dong bien soan lich su Nam Trung bo khang chien, *Nam trung bo khang chien (1945–1975)* [The Southern Trung Bo Resistance 1945–1975] (Hanoi: Vien lich su Dang, 1992), 430.

38. Ronald H. Spector, *After Tet: The Bloodiest Year in Vietnam* (New York: The Free Press, 1993), 110–111.

39. James Walker Trullinger, Jr., *Village at War* (New York: Longman, 1980).

40. Eric M. Bergerud, *The Dynamics of Defeat: The Vietnam War in Hau Nghia Province* (Boulder, Colo.: Westview, 1991), 293, 327.

41. Thomas C. Thayer, *War Without Fronts: The American Experience in Vietnam* (Boulder, Colo.: Westview, 1985), 163–164.

42. "Commanders Summary of the MACV Objectives Plan," Saigon, January 1, 1969, 3. Douglas Pike Collection, The Vietnam Archive, Texas Tech University Archive, item #2121211004.

43. Kissinger, *White House Years*, 272.

44. United States Arms Control and Disarmament Agency, "World Military Expenditures and Arms Transfers, 1968–1977" (Washington, D.C.: U.S. Department of State, October 1979), 152. Figures in current dollars.

45. Julian J. Ewell and Era A. Hunt, Jr., *Sharpening the Combat Edge* (Washington, D.C.: Department of the Army, 1974), chart 25, 206.

46. Nancy Wiegersma, *Vietnam: Peasant Land, Peasant Revolution* (New York: St. Martin's Press, 1988), 184–187. Also Laurence I. Hewes, Jr., "Foot-Dragging on Land Reform in South Vietnam," *Center Report* (June 1972): 19. Hewes was an agricultural economist who advised the U.S. government on land reform problems.

47. Roy L. Prosterman and Jeffrey M. Riedinger, *Land Reform and Democratic Development* (Baltimore, Md.: The Johns Hopkins University Press, 1987), 129.

48. A COSVN assessment of the land situation in December 1973 acknowledged that landlordism had almost vanished and middle peasant proprietors were now the center or heart (*trung tam*) of the countryside. These conditions, it correctly noted, were the cumulative result of "struggles" going back to the resistance against France for which the revolution could take much of the credit. It did not mention the Land-to-the-Tiller Law. "Nghi quyet hoi nghi lan thu 12 cua Trung uong cuc, Thang 12 nam 1973" [Resolution of the 12th COSVN Conference, December 1973], VKDTT, vol. 34, 1973 (2004), 478–479.

49. Lewy, *America in Vietnam*, 92.

50. Michael Maclear, *The Ten Thousand Day War* (London: Thames Methuen, 1981), 259.

51. J.A. Koch, "The Chieu Hoi Program in South Vietnam, 1963–1971," Advanced Research Projects Agency (R-1172-ARPA, January 1973), 108.

52. Interview with NTL, Saigon, May 6, 1973, notes on deposit in *Interviews with PAVN and LDP Defectors*, Morris Library, Southern Illinois University Carbondale, 1974.

53. Lewy, *America in Vietnam*, 172.

54. "Chi thi cua Thuong vu Trung uong cuc mien Nam, So 01/CT71, ngay 5 thang 1 nam 1971" [COSVN Directive No. 01/CT71, January 5, 1971], VKDTT, vol. 32, 1971 (2003), 497.

55. See Colby testimony in "Vietnam: Policy and Prospects, 1970," Hearings before the Committee on Foreign Relations, United States Senate, 91st Cong., 2nd Sess. On Civil Operations and Rural Development Support Program (February 17–20, March 3, 4, 17, 19, 1970) (Washington, D.C.: Government Printing Office, 1970), 27.

56. Maclear, *The Ten Thousand Day War*, 260–261.

57. Robert G. Kaiser, Jr., "U.S. Aides in Vietnam Scorn Phoenix Project," *Washington Post* (February 17, 1970).

58. Richard A. Hunt, *Pacification: The American Struggle for Vietnam's Hearts and Minds* (Boulder, Colo.: Westview, 1995), 235–236.

59. Micheal Clodfelter, *Vietnam in Military Statistics: A History of the Indochina Wars, 1772–1991* (Jefferson, N.C.: McFarland, 1995), 236.

60. As suggested by Mark Moyar in *Phoenix and the Birds of Prey: The CIA's Secret Campaign to Destroy the Viet Cong* (Annapolis, Md.: Naval Institute Press, 1997).

61. Hunt, *Pacification*, 226.

62. James Pinckney Harrison, *The Endless War: Fifty Years of Struggle in Vietnam* (New York: Free Press, 1982), 271.

63. See Thomas C. Thayer, "On Pacification," in *The Lessons of Vietnam*, ed. W. Scott Thompson and Donald D. Frizzell (New York: Crane, Russak, 1977), 271.

64. Lam Quang Huyen, *Cach mang ruong dat o mien Nam Viet Nam* [The Land Revolution in South Vietnam] (Hanoi: NXB Ban khoa hoc xa hoi, 1985), 139.

65. "Nghi quyet cua Bo chinh tri ban chap hanh Trung uong, Ve tinh hinh va nhiem vu, Thanh 5 nam 1969" [Resolution of the Political Bureau on the Situation and Tasks, May 1969], in *Mot so van kien cua Dang ve chong My, cuu nuoc* [Some Party Documents on Resisting America and Saving the Nation], vol. II (Hanoi: NXB Su that, 1986), 127–128.

66. Vien lich su quan su Viet Nam, *Lich su cong tac dang, cong tac chinh tri chien dich trong khang chien chong Phap va chong My, 1945–1975* [History of Party work and Theater Political Work in the Resistances against France and America, 1945–1975] (Hanoi: NXB Quan doi nhan dan, 1998), 407.

67. "COSVN Resolution No. 9, July 1969." Douglas Pike collection, Texas Tech Virtual Archive, Item #2121401004.

68. Other researchers have interpreted Resolution 9 as signaling a decision on Hanoi's part to conserve forces and protract the war, but a careful reading of the resolution and related documents leaves little doubt that party leaders composed their differences in a more complex way.

69. For further discussion of this debate, see Ang Cheng Guan, *The Vietnam War from the Other Side: The Vietnamese Communists' Perspective* (London and New York: RoutledgeCurzon, 2002), 138–139.

70. Kissinger, *White House Years*, 441.

71. Le Duc Tho interview with Anthony Barnett, in *Vietnam: Revue d'information et de réflexion sur les réalités vietnamiennes* 1 (December 1980): 70.

72. Kissinger, *White House Years*, 444.

73. War Experience Recapitulation Committee, *The Anti-U.S. Resistance War*, 123–124.

74. Castle, *At War in the Shadow of Vietnam*, 120. See also Clodfelter, *Vietnam in Military Statistics*, 268.

75. Szulc, *The Illusion of Peace*, 242–243; and Shawcross, *Sideshow*, 112–123. Kissinger writes that "We neither encouraged Sihanouk's overthrow nor knew about it in advance. We did not even grasp its significance for many weeks. . . ." Henry Kissinger, *Ending the Vietnam War* (New York: Simon & Schuster, 2003), 132.

76. John J. Tolson, *Airmobility, 1961–1971* (Washington, D.C.: 1973), 215–233.

77. According to Saigon and U.S. officials interviewed by the author in 1973, General Quang headed a group of officers—a "syndicate," one American officer called it—who enriched themselves from ARVN operations in Cambodia.

78. "Code of Conduct" dated April 27 1970, *Viet-Nam Documents and Research Notes*, no. 88 (January 1971).

79. War Experience Recapitulation Committee, *The Anti-U.S. Resistance War*, 129.

80. Engelbert and Goscha, *Falling out of Touch*, 99–100, 112; Kenneth Quinn, "Political Change in Wartime: The Khmer Krahom Revolution in Southern Cambodia, 1970–1974," *Naval War College Review* (Spring 1976): 3–31; Timothy Carney, *Communist Party Power in Kampuchea (Cambodia: Documents and Discussion)* (Ithaca, N.Y.: Cornell University Southeast Asia Program Data Paper no. 106, January 1977), 7–8.

81. See study document on COSVN Resolution 10, *Viet-Nam Documents and Research Notes*, no. 99 (October 1971); and War Experience Recapitulation Committee, *The Anti-U.S. Resistance War*, 123.

82. Colonel Hoang Co Quang, interviewed in Hanoi by the author on April 21, 1984.

83. War Experience Recapitulation Committee, *The Anti-U.S. Resistance War*, 138.

84. Brigham, *Guerrilla Diplomacy*, 61–67.

85. Qiang Zhai, *China and the Vietnam Wars, 1950–1975* (Chapel Hill: University of North Carolina Press, 2000), 170–172, 178.

86. John Garver, "The Tet Offensive and Sino-Vietnamese Relations," in *The Tet Offensive*, ed. Marc Jason Gilbert and William Head (Westport, Conn.: Praeger, 1996), 45.

87. Hanoi later excoriated Beijing for this in a White Book, "The Truth about Vietnam-China Relations over the Past 30 Years" (October 1979), and Beijing replied a month later in *People's Daily* with "On the Vietnamese Foreign Ministry's White Book Concerning Viet Nam-China Relations." See analysis in Garver, "The Tet Offensive. . . ," 52–59. Also see Lien-Hang T. Nguyen, "The Sino-Vietnamese Split and the Indochina War," in *The Third Indochina War: Conflict between China, Vietnam and Cambodia, 1972–79*, ed. Odd Arne Westad and Sophie Quinn-Judge (London and New York: Routledge, 2006), 23.

88. Chris Connolly, "The American Factor: Sino-American Rapprochement and Chinese Attitudes to the Vietnam War, 1968–72," *Cold War History* 5, No. 4 (November 2005): 501–527.

89. "Discussion between Zhou Enlai and Le Duc Tho," 07/12/1972, Cold War International History Project, Virtual Archive, The Wilson Center, www.wilsoncenter.org/index.cfm?topic_id=1409&fuseaction=va2.document&identifier=5034CEB8-96B6-175C-94874FC74022F9D3&sort=Collection&item=The%20Vietnam%20(Indochina)%20War(s) (accessed March 14, 2007).

90. War Experience Recapitulation Committee, *The Anti-U.S. Resistance War*, 138.

91. "Dien So 119, ngay 27 thang 3 nam 1972" [Cable no. 119, March 27, 1972], VKDTT, vol. 33, 1972 (2004), 208–218.

92. See David W.P. Elliott, "NLF-DRV Strategy and the 1972 Spring Offensive" (Ithaca, N.Y.: Cornell University, International Relations of East Asia Project, Interim Report no. 4, January 1974), esp. 39–54.

93. N.C. (pseud.), "Let Us Firmly Grasp This Strategic Opportunity, Intensify Our General Offensive and Uprisings, Defeat the Vietnamization Plan, Achieve a Decisive Victory, End the War, and Move Toward a Complete Victory," *Tien Phong*, no. 4 (internal magazine of the Region 5 party organization), translated in *Viet-Nam Documents and Research Notes*, no. 109 (December 1972).

94. Thayer, *War Without Fronts*, 94–95.

95. Tactical data in this and the following paragraphs are from U.S. Military Assistance Command Vietnam-J2, "The Nguyen Hue Offensive" (Saigon, January 12, 1973).

96. Lien-Hang T. Nguyen, "The Sino-Vietnamese Split," 24.

97. Kissinger, *White House Years*, 1159.

98. Tra, *Nhung chang duong*, 101.

99. Kissinger, *White House Years*, 1173–1174.

100. Seymour M. Hersh, *The Price of Power: Kissinger in the Nixon White House* (New York: Summit, 1983), 510.

101. Szulc, *The Illusion of Peace*, 550.

102. War Experience Recapitulation Committee, *The Anti-U.S. Resistance War*, 149.

103. William W. Momyer, *The Vietnamese Air Force, 1951–1975, An Analysis of its Role in Combat*, USAF Southeast Asia Monograph Series, Vol. 3, Monograph 4 (Washington, D.C.: Government Printing Office, September 10, 1975).

104. Robert K. Brigham, *ARVN: Life and Death in the South Vietnamese Army* (Lawrence: University Press of Kansas, 2006).

105. Cecil B. Currey, *Victory at Any Cost: The Genius of Viet Nam's Gen. Vo Nguyen Giap* (Washington and London: Brassey's, 1997), 283–290.

106. Brigham, *Guerrilla Diplomacy*, 105–110.

107. For a detailed reconstruction of these negotiations, see Hersh, *The Price of Power*, 589–609.

108. Allan E. Goodman, *The Lost Peace: America's Search for a Negotiated Settlement of the Vietnam War* (Stanford, Calif.: Hoover Institution Press, 1978), 152.

109. Kissinger, *White House Years*, 1444.

110. Richard M. Nixon, *RN: Memoirs of Richard Nixon* (New York: Grosset & Dunlap, 1978), 718.

111. Nixon confirmed this in a television interview quoted in Hersh, *The Price of Power*, 619.

112. When talks turned "caustic" (*gay gat*) in late November, the party secretariat ordered cadres in Hanoi, Haiphong and other main centers of communications and industry to prepare for the possibility of expanded warfare and bombing. "Thong tri cua Ban bi thu, So 287-TT/TW, ngay 27 thang 11 nam 1972" [Secretariat Circular, no. 287-TT-TW, November 27, 1972], VKDTT, vol. 33, 1972 (2004), 407, 409.

113. *Hanoi moi* [New Hanoi] (5 December 1972), 1.

114. James R. McCarthy et al., *Linebacker 11: The View from the Rock* (Maxwell, Ala.: Air War College, Airpower Research Institute, USAF Southeast Asia Monograph Series, Vol. 6, monograph 8, 1979), 171–172.

115. Nixon's messages to Thieu are excerpted in Kissinger, *White House Years*, 1459–1460, 1462, 1469.

116. Hersh, *The Price of Power*, 624.

117. Kissinger, *White House Years*, 1459–1460, 1462, 1469.

118. *Survey by Gallup Organization, December 1972–January 1973*, iPOLL Databank, The Roper Center for Public Opinion Research, University of Connecticut, www.ropercenter.uconn.edu/ipoll.html (accessed February 17, 2007).

119. Lien-Hang T. Nguyen, "The Sino-Vietnamese Split," 24.

120. "Dien cua dong chi Sau Manh, So 77, ngay 12 thang 1 nam 1972" [Cable from Le Duc Tho, no. 7, January 12, 1972], VKDTT, vol. 33, 1972 (2004), 1.

121. Kissinger, *White House Years*, 1466.

122. Englebert and Goscha, *Falling out of Touch*, 121.

8

After the Americans

"We sincerely did not want to repeat the grievous naiveté of the 1954–1956 period," wrote Tran Van Tra. Like many Southern party leaders, Tra believed it had been a mistake to make local cadres renounce violence as required by the Geneva accords. Limited to "political struggle" after Ngo Dinh Diem unleashed his troops to exterminate them, recalled Tra, "many comrades had fallen in battle . . . many local movements had drowned in blood."[1] This time the Communists were determined to defend their gains and build on them by whatever means necessary.

The South had changed considerably since 1954, however. The Saigon government was no longer a fragile colonial rump but a fairly stable regime in possession of the world's fifth-largest armed force. Whatever its weaknesses, it was no longer susceptible to overthrow by political turmoil or Southern-based insurgency. Although the Communists had added significantly to their military strength, U.S. withdrawal did not assure them an easy victory, and they knew it. The withdrawal had removed the screen behind which the Saigon regime had been built, but it also had removed a constraint on how Saigon used resources that the United States continued to supply. With the United States gone, the Vietnamese were free, for the first time in a century, to decide without foreign intervention who among them would lead the country into the modern world. Neither side was certain how the subtraction of U.S. power from this contest would affect the balance between them.

In one important respect, however, nothing had changed: the Communists were accustomed to fighting without foreign armed forces alongside them, Saigon was not. Anti-Communists in the South looked as much to the United States as to themselves for defense of the South, partly from habit but also because no leader, party, or government, not even the idea of the "South" itself, commanded their collective loyalties.

FROM CEASELESS FIRE TO POSTWAR WAR

The Paris Agreement recognized two administrations, two armed forces, and two zones of control in the territory of South Vietnam. President Nguyen Van Thieu, however, stood firm on "four no's"—no neutralization (therefore no negotiations), no Communist activity in the South, no coalition government, no surrender of territory. They ruled out implementation of the Paris Agreement's political articles, mocked the idea of compromise, and invited the Communists to respond with equal intransigence. Despite negotiations on a National Council of National Reconciliation and Concord, in gridlock from beginning to collapse in May 1974, it was quickly plain that the purpose of the agreement was to let the United States withdraw and leave the Vietnamese to resolve their irreconcilable differences as they saw fit. Wealthy, educated Vietnamese began asking anxious questions of their foreign friends and arranging study abroad for their children. Others renewed contact with family members on "the other side" and began openly discussing what life would be like under Communist rule. Journalists, artists, writers, and disaffected professionals who for years had admired the Communists for their probity or simply yearned for peace and social reform toyed with the possibility of cooperation. As tension increased, the worldly wags of Saigon dubbed the new conflict "the ceaseless fire" and later, "the postwar war."

The Communists decided to respect the Paris Agreement precisely because they assumed that Thieu was determined to obstruct it. As Le Duan put it in guidelines for Southern regional party committees, "Build the political struggle movement of the masses into a high tide of revolution and force the enemy to implement the agreement, so that peace and revolution may prevail in the South. At the same time, we must vigilantly take precautions and prepare to respond if the enemy stubbornly provokes a resumption of hostilities."[2] By respecting the Paris Agreement, or appearing to do so, the Communists hoped to cast Thieu in the role of peace-breaker and isolate him from a war-weary population, as they had done to Diem with the Geneva accords. But, remembering the 1950s, they were not prepared to rely solely on legalistic demands to achieve their aims.

In early fall 1972, as Le Duc Tho was preparing proposals he felt sure Kissinger would accept, a warning went out to the Communists' Southern commands to brace for a sharpening of the fighting in the period between the announcement of agreement and the ceasefire.[3] The warning assumed that Saigon would try to enlarge its area of control, and the Southern commands were ordered to conduct preemptive uprisings to expand the "liberated areas," break open refugee holding centers, and spark a "return to the village" with the aim of reestablishing revolutionary strongholds before the ceasefire went into effect. By the Communists' own admission, the number of people in "liberated and contested areas" of the South was still below the four million (in a population of 19.5 million) that they had controlled before the 1968 Tet Offensive.[4] That figure, they believed, needed to increase if they were to support their ceasefire claims and win the struggles that were sure to follow.

In anticipation of the ceasefire, both sides attempted to plant their flags on as much territory as possible. In this, the "war of the flags," the Communists took an early lead and succeeded in raising their colors not only in contested areas but in some that had been under Saigon's control for years. They also invaded a portion of Tay Ninh city the day before the ceasefire, provoking the Army of the Republic of Vietnam (ARVN) to counterattack until well after the truce had begun. Each side resorted to "land grabbing" and "nibbling" to consolidate and expand its holdings. But the Communists, eager to make Saigon appear the aggressor, let the ARVN commit most of the transgressions, which the Southern army, flush with new American weapons, proceeded to do. In June 1973 Kissinger and Tho met to reaffirm the Paris Agreement but succeeded in only briefly restoring a very wobbly truce. It was the last time that Hanoi and Washington would discuss ways to make the Paris Agreement work.

Most ARVN operations at first sought to recover areas the Communists had seized from Saigon just before ceasefire, but the ARVN soon encroached upon areas that had long been under Communist control. From January 1973 to mid-1974, Saigon claimed to have placed a thousand additional hamlets under its control; three hundred were retaken from the Communists, who had seized them just before the ceasefire. Ninety had been under Communist control for a long time.[5] According to the Communists' only slightly different assessment, "They [Saigon] retook nearly all of the 394 hamlets we had liberated prior to the signing of the Agreement."[6] Thus began Thieu's drive to establish control over all of South Vietnam. If Communist counterattacks put him in trouble, he believed, the United States would not tolerate the blow to its own prestige.

The Communists had fully anticipated Thieu's strategy but wished to avoid major fighting at that time. Hanoi had sought a halt to the bombing in 1968 partly so the North could support the Southern revolution more effectively, and a similar calculation had figured in Hanoi's decision to sign the Paris Agreement. The North's task, as a directive from the Central Office for South Vietnam (COSVN) noted in March 1973, was "to heal the wounds of war, to build socialism with speed . . . and make a base for the task of liberating South Vietnam and unifying the nation."[7] The North was in no condition in the spring of 1973 to apply the pressure needed to force Thieu to choose between implementing the Paris Agreement or accepting military defeat.[8] For that matter, neither had forces under COSVN's control replaced the arms, equipment, and food supplies consumed in the long spring and summer campaign of 1972.[9] COSVN also acknowledged that the Republic of Vietnam (RVN) had "a firm socio-economic, legal, cultural foundation based on counterrevolutionary ideology and American neo-colonialism."[10] General Tra believed that the ARVN was superior to the People's Army of Vietnam (PAVN) and expressed concern for the morale and equipment of his troops, who had been in combat for years.[11] While Northern recovery temporarily had priority, COSVN's orders to "defend the Agreement" required it to consolidate zones of control, withdraw from contested areas if necessary, abstain from major fighting, and mobilize the people to demand the Agreement's enforcement.[12]

The orders seemed unwisely passive to some of the field commanders. To older cadres in particular, the strategy bore a haunting resemblance to the post-Geneva "political struggle" in which so many comrades had "drowned in blood." "Hanoi," one cadre with the National Liberation Front of South Vietnam (NLF) said later, "'was asking us to return to the pre-NLF days . . . when we were told to avoid the use of armed force altogether. That policy led to disaster, and only the formation of the Front and the reliance on the military struggle saved southerners from complete annihilation.'"[13] In a classical example of commanders far from headquarters taking matters into their own hands, COSVN'S General Tra and the heads of Military Region 9, Vo Van Kiet and General Le Duc Anh, ignored orders and pushed the ARVN out of positions it had established before the Paris Agreement took effect. Tra candidly explained that

> the actions of the military forces of Region 9 were based on the view that there had been no agreement, that nothing had changed, and that it was necessary to keep on fighting. That was an incorrect understanding of the Paris Agreement and of the new strategic phase. But it correctly evaluated the obstinacy of the enemy, just like the Geneva Accords period, and it was resolute in preserving the gains the revolution had won. It was consistent with the actual situation, not illusory or utopian. "Luckily," it was a distant battlefield, so upper-echelon policies were often slow in arriving, and rectification of errors was not always prompt.[14]

Thus some Communist ceasefire violations were also violations of Hanoi's wish. It was "lucky" for Kiet, Anh, and Tra that Region 9's efforts were successful.[15] In a series of debates during mid-1973, their demand for action gained support, and in October, the twenty-first plenum of the Central Committee conceded that Thieu did not intend, and could not be made, to implement the Paris Agreement. The only recourse, the plenum concluded, was a "fierce revolutionary war to defeat the enemy and win complete victory." The plenum authorized immediate retaliatory strikes "based on the specific circumstances of each area" and preparations to resume large-scale warfare in the near future. Authorization also was given on October 24 for the PAVN to form a First Army Corps, the first such unit in the PAVN's history, based in the Tri-Thien zone.[16] (Three more corps would be organized in the next two years.) Formation of army corps, however, did not signify an abandonment of longstanding strategy, only an upgrading of the conventional component of war. In perfectly orthodox fashion, COSVN's instructions continued to emphasize the need to strengthen all forms of armed forces and to develop all forms of struggle, including in the cities.[17]

As 1973 came to a close, the two sides observed an uneasy truce in Quang Tri, Thua Thien, and Quang Nam provinces, where the PAVN held virtually all of the countryside while the ARVN held Quang Tri city, Hue, and a narrow strip of coast. But elsewhere the skirmishing over hamlets disguised maneuvers for strategic position. In the central highlands the ARVN extended its string of firebases to harass PAVN supply lines, and the PAVN began work on a new road, Corridor 613, running north-south through the mountains just inside the Vietnamese border. To cover its western flank, the PAVN left 15,000 troops in Laos to stiffen the Pathet Lao and another 35,000 to man the Ho Chi Minh Trail (in violation of the Paris Agreement), while the Lao Communists peaceably joined the new Provisional Government of National Union. Ostensibly in retaliation for ARVN "land grabbing," the PAVN overran six ARVN firebases in the highlands from September 1973 to April 1974. Eight thousand men died in these battles. North and west of Saigon, the ARVN went on the offensive to break up PAVN logistical bases. In the delta it attacked Communist strongholds in an attempt to interdict infiltration from the Parrot's Beak. The Communists responded in the delta by destroying eighty small outposts between January and May 1974, and daylight ambushes began to occur again. In the first year of "peace," 80,000 Vietnamese, including 14,000 civilians, died in combat or cross fires.

THE MILITARY BALANCE

The Communists considered themselves to be militarily weaker than Saigon, and in terms of military hardware and force levels on the battlefield they were. The ARVN had grown in size and had adequate reserves. It still received substantial U.S. aid, though that aid was decreasing. Thanks to years of stockpiling, the ARVN also had a vast hoard of weapons and ammunition. On the revolutionary side, liberated areas were thinly populated, many party cells were cut off from the people, and irregular forces were weak. Regular forces were not in much better condition. "In continuous action since 1972," noted General Tra, "our cadres and men were tired. Nor had we had time to make up our losses. All our units were in disarray. We lacked manpower, food and ammunition were short, so it was difficult to cope with the enemy's attacks."[18] Tra's predecessor as B2 commander, General Hoang Van Thai, recalled that in late 1973 revolutionary militia and guerrillas "had still not kept up with the requirements;" political organizations and movements in cities, enemy-controlled areas and along the border "were not yet solid." Military aid, "especially with regard to offensive weapons and artillery shells, was not as great as in the past."[19] Coordination of the "three-pronged attacks" (military offensive, proselytization of enemy armed forces, and civilian uprising) was out of the question. "The enemy," said COSVN in February 1974, "temporarily has the upper hand."[20] The Party's Military Commission estimated that it would take "the next several years" to tip the balance decisively in the revolution's favor.[21] To reach that goal, the Communists counted on economic decline and political turmoil in Saigon and the rebuilding of their local and regular forces. A COSVN resolution set a readiness date of late 1977, by which time liberated zones were to be "rehabilitated" and put on the path to socialist development.[22]

In the year following the signing of the Paris Agreement, an estimated 100,000 to 120,000 PAVN troops infiltrated the South,[23] raising their numbers after casualties and rotation to more than 150,000 men. Approximately 30,000 PLAF regulars and 50,000 guerrillas brought the total number of Communist forces in the South to about 230,000. The many tanks lost in 1972 were quickly replaced, and Soviet-built tanks began to appear in Binh Duong province just north of Saigon. The PAVN also sharply increased its supply of 130-mm field guns to the South. Although by the spring of 1974 the PAVN still had only one-fourth as much heavy artillery pieces in the South as the ARVN, its 130s were highly mobile, had longer range than most ARVN guns, and compensated for numerical inferiority with rapid deployment. (The ARVN, however, had tactical air support that the PAVN did not.) The equipment build-up required the PAVN to further improve its logistical facilities in Laos and Cambodia, build a new road linking Route 9 and the central highlands, extend petroleum pipelines into Quang Tri and Quang Tin provinces, and install ground-to-air missiles and large caliber antiaircraft weapons as far south as the Cambodian border of Tay Ninh province. A U.S. congressional staff report concluded in May 1974 that the effect of these developments was "to diminish significantly the logistical advantage which the South enjoyed in the past and to give the North Vietnamese a capability to move and mass troops in a manner hitherto impossible for them."[24]

But the PAVN build-up came nowhere near giving it conventional capability equal to that of the ARVN. The ARVN main force grew from 223,000 to 320,000 in the year following the Paris Agreement. By the spring of 1974, including irregulars, Saigon had more than one million men in arms, or about four times the number of Communist forces in the South and roughly twice as many regulars.[25] Although U.S. aid had declined, the ARVN had huge stocks of equipment and ammunition that the United States had left behind or turned over just prior to signing the Paris Agreement. Last-minute infusions of U.S. aid, known as operations Enhance and Enhance Plus, were valued at $753 million. Two South Korean divisions left behind an additional $250 million worth of equipment.[26] Soviet and Chinese aid to the North in the same period shifted from military to economic. Of some $715 million worth of aid given to Hanoi in 1973, only $270 million was for the military. Although figures on Soviet, Chinese, and U.S. arms shipments are not fully comparable (Communist aid consisted of arms, equipment, and ammunition; U.S. aid included costly operating and maintenance programs), they remove any doubt about Washington's generosity in comparison with that of Moscow and Beijing (see Table 8.1). Contrary to the contention that Hanoi's allies tipped the scales with generous supplies of arms, both the Soviet Union and China sharply reduced their military assistance to Hanoi after the Paris Agreement.[27] Russian sources indicate that reductions in Soviet military aid began even earlier.[28] China shipped Hanoi 69,000 fewer rifles, 3,506 fewer artillery pieces, 25 percent fewer bullets, 37 percent fewer artillery shells and 40 fewer tanks in 1974 than in 1973.[29] General Thai worried that with so much of the PAVN's matériel going to the front practically no heavy artillery shells were left in the North. "What could be done," he wondered, "to have sufficient firepower for the large campaigns" when the time came for the PAVN to attack large enemy bases, cities, and towns?[30]

The great volume of U.S. aid was necessary to sustain an army that had been organized and trained to fight with lavish use of ammunition, motorized transport, air cover, and sophisticated equipment. That was the

Table 8.1. Value of Arms Shipments to North and South Vietnam, 1972–1975 (in millions, current dollars)

	North	South
1972	775	1,300
1973	270	2,700
1974	220	835
1975	130	850

Source: U.S. Arms Control and Disarmament Agency, *World Military Expenditures and Arms Transfers 1968– 1977* (Washington, D.C.: GPO, October 1979), 152.

American way: make contact with the enemy, then rely on artillery and airpower to carry the burden of combat. In 1974 the ARVN fired sixteen times as many artillery shells as the PAVN, a ratio that even U.S. advisers regarded as excessive for defensive forces firing upon a highly mobile, unseen enemy.[31] Within the South, the balance in arms, men, and equipment was heavily in the ARVN's favor.[32] The increasing presence of PAVN anti-aircraft batteries in the South blunted ARVN air support in some places, but material factors were not the sole or even main measure of strength. Saigon's real military vulnerabilities were strategic.

Thieu's effort to extend Saigon's authority took the form of an order for the ARVN to penetrate and hold every corner of the South, which had not been done even with the help of 600,000 foreign troops. Each advance meant defending and holding every point in the "land-grabbing" contest, stretching the ARVN more thinly against an enemy that could choose the time and place of attack. Soon, nearly the entire ARVN was tied down in logistics and static defense. The ARVN thus ceded to the PAVN the ability to concentrate forces for counterattack, to relieve sieges, and to go on the offensive. As the Communists methodically improved their logistical system and conserved equipment, the ARVN began consuming more of its supplies than U.S. aid replaced. Gradually, the military balance began to shift.

THE POLITICS OF DESPAIR

The ceaseless fire was dispiriting to ordinary citizens and soldiers on both sides. But in Saigon despair turned to disgust as the Thieu regime reverted to earlier ways. If the Republic of Vietnam had been finding its feet as a viable state, that progress, if it occurred, stalled as the U.S. prepared to withdraw. Exacerbated by economic decline, and without the United States to cajole or pay for compromise and reform, the divisiveness that had destroyed his predecessors stalked Nguyen Van Thieu.

Thieu was partly to blame. Having wrested control of the military from Nguyen Cao Ky in 1967, Thieu set out to construct an authoritarian state under his tight personal control. In August 1971, the Supreme Court disqualified Ky from the presidential elections. After Duong Van Minh dropped out of the race to protest Thieu's manipulation of the electoral law,[33] Thieu ran unopposed. In 1972, the year of the spring offensive, he declared martial law and installed career police officers as deputy village chiefs to replace civilian security commissioners, effectively ending the pacification campaign's effort to involve villagers in their own security. He also abolished hamlet elections (reversing an earlier reform) and turned the selection of hamlet chiefs and administrative officers over to province chiefs appointed by him. These measures extended Thieu's control down to the level where most Vietnamese had their most direct contact with government while diminishing opportunities for political participation. A decree in the same year raising the price of newsprint, forbidding press criticism of the government, and requiring a $46,500 security deposit from each of Saigon's forty newspapers forced many papers to shut down. In March 1973 after restricting the number of political parties, Thieu inaugurated his own Dan Chu (Democracy) Party. Unlike the other two legal parties, the Dan Chu was the political arm of the government (much as the Can Lao had been for Ngo Dinh Diem), and civil servants felt pressure to join. Thieu unveiled in July an "administrative revolution" that he claimed would transform the "old individualistic mentality" of civil servants into a new "cadre spirit," but which in fact enabled province chiefs to allocate development projects in exchange for political support.[34] Finally, in the August elections for the Senate, the two pro-government slates won all thirty-one contested seats, reducing the opposition to one-quarter of the sixty-member body. Elections for the National Assembly brought a similar result, thwarting a Communist effort to encourage voting for "people who are progressive and inclined toward peace, independence, and neutrality."[35] Five months later the National Assembly voted 153-52 in favor of a constitutional amendment allowing Thieu to run for a third term in 1975.

These moves—toward single-party authoritarian rule in which family relationships, personal connections, and regional and business ties determined entrée into officialdom—were hardly novel for Vietnam nor exceptional for Asia. But they were inaugurated by a man who had never won broad popular acceptance. In a culture that measured legitimacy by the effortlessness of its attainment, he had reached the top with transparent maneuver, sheer doggedness, and the support of a foreign power. His mandate could never be anything but dubious, and so his efforts to create a personal autocracy were resented. Local officials chafed at the intrusive presence of policemen chosen for them as deputy village chiefs. Civil servants resented pressure to join the Dan Chu party and felt demeaned by party-organized "retraining" sessions. The administrative revolution grated on senior civilian officials who regarded Thieu a low-status military upstart. The chronically discontented intelligentsia, antipathetic to the military anyway, grew rebellious at the exclusion of their cliques from the list of approved parties. Where the regime did succeed in establishing its writ in rural areas, old self-destructive practices reappeared. Land reform began to reverse in some secure areas as local officials under pressure from landlords demanded that peasants relinquish titles given them only a few years before.[36] The Hoa Hao Buddhists protested Thieu's efforts to absorb their private militia (which had been a haven for Hoa Hao males evading the draft).[37] In Darlac province, a Jarai tribal leader succeeded in stirring rebellion among montagnards who, previously sheltered by U.S. Special

Forces and aid programs, opposed Thieu's resumption of effort to populate the hills with lowland Vietnamese.[38]

An agonizing economic adjustment to American withdrawal worsened the political tensions. From 1966 to 1972, U.S. troops, contractors, and official agencies spent $2 billion on the local economy, mostly on services. At one time, domestics, repairmen, taxi drivers, bar girls, and guards were earning 35 percent of the South's total income, with public services responsible for another 20 percent.[39] The U.S. presence directly created an estimated 300,000 jobs.[40] Inflation had been controlled—and revenue had risen—by a U.S. agreement (the Commodity Import Program) to exchange dollars for *piastres* and thus facilitate imports. Along with cement and steel for development had come motorbikes, stereos, and cognac to meet the demands of a spreading consumerism. Also to preserve urban tranquility, the regime had held down the price of rice to about half the world level, although this lowered peasant incomes and per capita agricultural production.[41] Little money flowed into savings or investments. What observers saw as wealth (TV antennas, Honda motorbikes) was a fragile bubble. In 1973 U.S. withdrawal combined with rising world prices for commodities (e.g., oil) produced 65 percent inflation and 40 percent urban unemployment in a matter of months. Living standards declined. Several individuals protested the futility of trying to support their families by immolating themselves in the streets. A tripling of patients at a mental hospital near Saigon was attributed to mental stress caused by economic and other war-related difficulties.[42]

With much of the work force on public salaries of diminishing value, corruption became more visible and pervasive. Corruption was not new. Even the puritanical Diem had tolerated corruption. But Thieu found that the loyalty of subordinates depended on it. Some of Thieu's province chiefs bought their posts for thirty to fifty million *piastres* (at a time when the official rate was 118 piastres to the dollar), district chiefs for fifteen to twenty-five million. They recovered many times these amounts from graft. Vast sums were made "taxing" military convoys, scrapping spent artillery shells, and "protecting" gambling dens, whore houses, and smugglers. Under the twin effects of economic decline and the centralization of power, corruption became the glue that held the regime together. A large majority of National Assembly deputies was said to be in Thieu's pay to assure the assembly's complicity in repressing the opposition.[43] At the bottom of the pyramid, petty officials increased their bribery demands to pad their miserable salaries and to meet the demands of superiors. Even policemen operating traffic lights at Saigon intersections turned their tiny domains to advantage, with results that could be seen in their girth. To public criticism, Thieu responded by closing down twenty-four news agencies for operating without government permission and for distributing "libelous stories."[44]

Protest finally broke out behind the unlikely leadership of Father Tran Huu Thanh, a right-wing Redemptorist priest and frequent lecturer at the ARVN military academy. Heading a movement that had gestated in the Redemptorist order, Thanh issued a six-count "indictment" of Thieu's government in September 1974, and three newspapers published it. The indictment charged Thieu with perverting anti-Communism for personal and corrupt purposes. It specifically charged his wife with profiting from a private charity, cited other instances of corruption by his relatives and associates, and hinted at links to the heroin trade. Thieu denied all charges and ordered police to confiscate copies of the three newspapers.

Father Thanh's movement was not the only focus of dissent. Another priest, Father Chan Tin, led demonstrations on behalf of political prisoners and prison reform. Madame Ngo Ba Thanh, a U.S. trained lawyer sympathetic to the NLF, headed a women's movement for peace. Journalists spearheaded attacks on press censorship and on Information Minister Hoang Duc Nha, Thieu's cousin. The regime could not brush off the vociferously anti-Communist Father Thanh as a neutral or Communist dupe as it did the others, and the dissidence gained momentum. Faced with suddenly strong opposition, Thieu in late October accepted the resignations of four cabinet ministers including Nha, dismissed 377 field grade officers for corruption, and transferred three of the four corps commanders. Nothing changed, though. Police continued arresting students and journalists and confiscating newspapers, and opposition leaders continued calling for Thieu to leave office. Around the time that Phu Long province capital was falling to Communist forces in January 1975, Thieu closed more newspapers, Father Thanh accused Thieu of "high treason,"[45] and Duong Van "Big" Minh denounced the regime as "nothing but tyranny."[46]

Significantly, the anti-corruption movement remained predominantly Catholic. Journalists protested against censorship, the Buddhist General Duong Van Minh called Thieu a "great obstacle to peace" in a speech at An Quang pagoda,[47] and non-Catholics expressed sympathy with Father Thanh's aims. But most non-Catholics stood aside, suspicious that the anti-corruption movement disguised a Catholic grab for power. There was quite simply neither the unity nor a personality outside the regime strong enough to present a credible alternative to Thieu. Yet Thieu also was losing his grip. Only after agreeing to give a larger share of power to Premier Tran Thien Khiem was Thieu able, in late November 1974, to reform his cabinet with little-known people, most of whom were Khiem's chums.

The authoritarian trend did not produce a more cohesive, stable, and effective government. Eighty-seven percent of the South Vietnamese electorate in 1971 cast 94 percent of its votes for Thieu in an uncontested election. The figures, however, were not measures of popularity as Thieu's defenders have asserted. The whole point of running unopposed, in Vietnam as anywhere else, was to depoliticize the population by excluding competitors and thus claim legitimacy for one-man (or one-party) rule. To the Vietnamese who cast votes, the election was a public ritual, a spectacle of acquiescence to power, not a referendum on Thieu's fitness to govern. The result signified passive compliance, an outcome without difference from elections in the Communist system.[48] To Americans, however, the election seemed an impudent rejection of what many thought the United States was fighting for. What seemed to them a mockery of American ideals deepened the sense across the country that "our war" was now "their war." As Kissinger delicately put it, "We have succeeded not in guaranteeing necessarily a permanent peace but in moving the decision to a Vietnamese decision."[49]

Meanwhile, the last shred of congressional tolerance for presidential war-making evaporated in July 1973 when Air Force Major Hal Knight, testifying before the Senate Armed Services Committee, revealed the secret bombing of Cambodia. This time the point of contention was not just U.S. policy on the war, but the constitutionally-prescribed checks and balances between the executive and legislative branches of government. The bombing, Congress was incensed to learn, had been conducted on Nixon's orders, and the Pentagon had falsified or destroyed the records. Congress responded by passing the War Powers Act, which prohibits presidents from sending forces into combat without explicit congressional approval or direct attack on the United States. A congressional ban on bombing in Cambodia and a spate of amendments prohibiting any kind of U.S. combat activity anywhere in Southeast Asia quickly followed.[50] Frustrated by Saigon's insatiable dependence on U.S. support, Congress also was averse to a huge, open-ended aid commitment. In May 1974, it cut $474 million from an administration proposal of $1.6 billion for military assistance.

Preoccupied by Watergate, the president was not thinking a great deal about Southeast Asia. According to Kissinger, "Nixon was simply unable to concentrate his energies and mind on Vietnam."[51] Finally, after nearly two years of skirmishing between Nixon and Congress over the scandal, the president resigned on August 9, 1974.

Two days later, President Gerald Ford sent a personal letter to Thieu reaffirming the commitment made by his four predecessors and assuring Thieu that U.S. support would be "adequate."[52] But that was a promise no U.S president, given legislative control over funding, henceforth would be able to keep. Tragically, Thieu and his generals never grasped how weak the U.S. president really was in the face of congressional opposition and went on policing villages, expending supplies, and depleting reserves as if Ford's word was the only one that mattered.[53]

RACE AGAINST THE ENEMY AND HEAVEN

The Communists assessed the prospects of the United States intervening again rather differently—and more accurately. Party Secretary Le Duan said in April 1973, that a defeated United States had withdrawn "never to return."[54] Washington's disarray in the face of recession, the oil crisis, Watergate, Nixon's resignation, and revolutionary advances in Laos and Cambodia further convinced Hanoi leaders that they had little to fear. "The U.S. imperialists would find it very difficult to intervene directly," the Political Bureau concluded in October 1974. "If the puppets are in danger of a complete collapse, we must be on guard against the U.S. intervening with its air force or navy, not to expand the war but to save the Saigon regime. There is little possibility that they will use infantry, but we must continually monitor their plots, be vigilant, and be prepared to react. No matter how they intervene, we will be fully determined and able to defeat them, and they cannot save the Saigon regime from collapse."[55]

By then preparations for another offensive were well under way. Thieu's adamant refusal to implement the Paris Agreement's political provisions in October 1973 supplied Hanoi leaders with a justification to abandon the agreement and begin planning a climactic campaign. Le Duan and Le Duc Tho had laid out guidelines for military cadres in March 1974. PAVN successes later that year—destroying a district capital in Military Region 5 and overrunning ARVN firebases in the highlands—overcame the reservations of some party and military leaders about the PAVN's readiness for a showdown. COSVN, in September 1974, reported that it had fulfilled its objectives for the entire year by restoring liberated zones and contested areas to where they had been in January 1973 but in "more advantageous conditions."[56]

The moment of opportunity, Hanoi sensed, might be brief. Now that the war was no longer bleeding the United States, Moscow's enthusiasm for Hanoi's cause was ebbing. More ominous was the trend in Hanoi's relations with China, which deteriorated as relations between China and the U.S. had improved. Vietnamese and Chinese border guards had taken pot shots at each other in 1973, and in January 1974 China had pushed a South Vietnamese garrison off the Paracel Islands, claimed by Hanoi as well. China, moreover, had taken over the role of big brother to the Khmer Rouge, promoting their alliance with Sihanouk and blunting Hanoi's influence in its own backyard. Why this Chinese assertiveness? The obvious answer, it seemed to paranoid leaders in Hanoi, was that China was preparing to fill the vacuum left by the U.S. withdrawal. If that was China's goal, then China would oppose the emergence of a state—or rather the three states of Indochina under Vietnam's leadership—that could block this design. "China feared that if we won and became stronger we would impede its advance down into Southeast Asia," and in "its status of defeat, the United States was willing for China to expand south, in hopes of stopping the other large countries [i.e., the USSR] from gaining influence," wrote General Thai. The war therefore had to be brought to an end before "any countries inclined toward intervention" could react. [57]

The plan adopted by the Political Bureau at year's end envisioned a two-year, two-step campaign. Main forces were to mount continuous attacks in 1975, paving the way for a general offensive and uprising the following year. The Communists had learned from previous experience not to expect an uprising until the "puppet army" had been smashed. "Only then could favorable conditions be created for uprisings by the urban masses."[58] However, the plan acknowledged that these steps might be compressed into one and victory achieved in 1975 if opportunities were properly exploited. Victory, it was assumed, would more likely take the form of installing a tripartite coalition government (absent Thieu of course) than outright military conquest.

The major role assigned to conventional forces encouraged the high command to plan a military conquest. Generals in the map rooms of Hanoi, given the task of organizing, supplying, and deploying multi-division armies for the first time in their lives, naturally focused on the military dimensions. Many also were skeptical that the "imbalance" between main forces and guerrillas and between the military and political struggle that had emerged since 1968 could be quickly corrected.[59] Such perspectives certainly dominate the account by General Van Tien Dung, PAVN chief of staff and overall commander of the offensive.[60] But at the opposite end of the country, COSVN leaders had somewhat different concerns. A campaign that consisted only of regular forces attacking in the highlands and advancing on Saigon, they pointed out, ran the risk of driving the enemy into Saigon and the richest rice-growing portions of the delta. U.S. air and naval power could easily support such an enclave, exactly as the American General James Gavin had proposed in 1966 and again in 1972. Would that not leave Thieu with control of more than ten million people? Had the French not considered possession of the delta the key to Indochina? Such were the questions that bedeviled COSVN commander General Tran Van Tra, who was more confident with the answers than Hanoi: the political situation could be exploited to bring victory in 1975 and popular uprisings had to play a role. [61]

To preempt an enclave strategy, COSVN requested three to four more divisions for the B2 theater. Supplied with intelligence from agents planted in ARVN headquarters, it also drew up plans to soften Saigon's outer rings of defense and demoralize the ARVN in advance of an attack by the main forces. The theater's plan, said Tra, "was based on the assumption that B2 itself would have to carry out a general offensive and uprising in Saigon and that each military region and province would have to take care of its own battlefield needs without waiting on forces from the upper echelon."[62] To prepare for an uprising, COSVN set a goal of increasing the population in liberated zones of Nam Bo by two million during 1975 and doubling the total in Nam Bo's liberated and contested zones.[63] COSVN also dusted off plans it had carefully revised since the 1968 Tet Offensive and sent out feelers to dissident groups in Saigon and other cities. Only after intense lobbying, however, did COSVN extract authorization to use tanks and artillery from a high command fixated on provinces farther north and on conserving forces for the final push in 1976.

Meanwhile, a massive logistical effort was funneling the PAVN's equipment into the South. "Great quantities of matériel such as tanks, armored cars, missiles, long-range artillery, and antiaircraft weapons, which the U.S. imperialists had sought unsuccessfully to destroy during their twelve-day B-52 blitz against the North, gradually were sent to the various battlefields."[64] Some 30,000 troops and "assault youths" worked feverishly to extend the new road, Corridor 613, from Route 9 to the edge of eastern Nam Bo, 1,000 kilometers to the south. Over this two-lane road, by early 1975, 10,000 trucks were shuttling both ways, fueled by a 5,000-kilometer pipeline that ran from Quang Tri to Loc Ninh. With connecting routes, the PAVN logistical network now had 20,000 kilometers of communications and supply lines, which Dung likened to "sturdy hemp ropes being daily and hourly slipped around the neck and limbs of a monster who would be strangled with one sharp yank when the order was given."[65] (See Map 8.1.) He could have added that Saigon's Air Force had only a fraction of the American capacity to bombard the trail complex. Commando raids on it had almost ceased, and the PAVN had helped to enlarge the "liberated zones" in Laos and Cambodia, with the result that trucks, troops, and equipment now passed from North to South unimpeded. In some years, more than half of transport vehicles using the trail were damaged or destroyed. That number fell to zero in 1974.[66]

Late that year, the Communists thought that the situation had turned decisively in their favor. They had tested themselves against the ARVN in set-piece battles in the highlands, and they had blunted ARVN "nibbling operations" in the delta. Many areas where revolutionary forces had been heavily suppressed between 1968 and 1972 had reverted to their control. As for Saigon, economic troubles, political turmoil, and cuts in U.S. aid were beginning to take their toll. The ARVN's morale was low; desertions were high; and stocks of bombs, ammunition, and petrol were running out. No longer could the ARVN squander supplies in large-scale sweeps, airborne mobility, and the policing of every village. As Dung put it, "Nguyen Van Thieu had to make his army switch to 'poor man's war.'" American aid was by no means meager, but it was inadequate to support the strategy and tactics to which the ARVN was committed.[67]

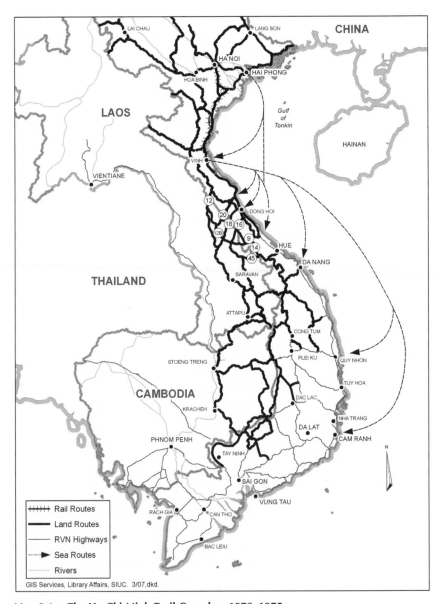

Map 8.1. The Ho Chi Minh Trail Complex, 1973–1975
Source: Senior General Hoang Van Thai, *Nhung nam thang quyet dinh: hoi ky* (Years of Decisive Victory: A Memoir) (Hanoi: NXB Quan doi nhan dan, 1985).

Scanning the South for its first target, the PAVN high command decided against the northern provinces because there the ARVN had concentrated five strong divisions in a small territory.[68] It decided against the ARVN's Third Corps because the three divisions there could be easily reinforced. The Mekong delta was out because it was too far from the main supply lines. This left the central highlands, a vast area over which just two ARVN divisions were thinly scattered. The highlands' relatively open terrain also permitted rapid deployment of tanks and artillery and easy access to the PAVN's much enhanced logistical base in the B3 "western highlands front." If the initial attacks were successful, large forces could move quickly toward the coast and south over existing roads. To the PAVN general staff, the central highlands presented the greatest contrast between thin ARVN defenses and PAVN offensive strengths.

But even as generals in Hanoi were weighing options, mixed regular, regional, and guerrilla forces seized Route 14 and an ARVN garrison overlooking Phuoc Binh city, capital of Phuoc Long province. On January 7, 1975, the province capital, then the whole province, fell to PAVN and PLAF units supported by tanks and a company of 130-mm artillery. The victory suddenly gave the Communists unobstructed access to the lowlands northwest of Saigon. It also vindicated COSVN's persistent demand for a strong attack in the B2 theater, and it resulted in capture of large stores of weapons and ammunition that the PAVN turned on its next targets. Officials in Washington considered diverting a navy task force to Vietnam that was then sailing between Subic Bay and the Indian Ocean. U.S. planes flew over the South, Cambodia, and the North on reconnaissance missions, but administration spokesmen denied any intent to become involved. At the same time, the Ford administration request for $1.3 billion in military aid for Saigon encountered stiff opposition in Congress. A special session of the Political Bureau, meeting in Hanoi since December 18, closed on January 8 with the conclusion that the signs for victory had never been more propitious.

The next day, the Central Military Party Committee, joined by COSVN's Vo Chi Cong and generals Chu Huy Man, Hoang Minh Thao, and Le Trong Tan, met to select the first target. By that time the PAVN had deployed five divisions in the central highlands, compared with two regular divisions, seven Ranger regiments, and one armored brigade for the ARVN. As the ARVN took no steps to reinforce now dangerously vulnerable positions, the committee was sure that PAVN preparations so far had gone undetected. After heated debate, the committee decided to launch the offensive with an attack on Ban Me Thuot, a city of about one hundred thousand, capital of Darlac province, and headquarters of the ARVN Twenty-Third Division. Ban Me Thuot was less well-defended than Pleiku and Kontum, where the ARVN Second Corps command thought that attack was more likely to come. More important, seizure of Ban Me Thuot would isolate the other two cities and connect the PAVN supply lines with roads leading out of the hills.

General Dung left Hanoi on February 5 and traveled to Dong Hoi by air, to Quang Tri by car, up the Ben Hai River by motorboat, and down Corridor 613 to the western highlands to assume supreme command of the campaign. The situation he found was more complicated than he had expected. Large units could not move easily without detection, and information on conditions inside Ban Me Thuot was unreliable. A cadre sent to reconnoiter reported with gee-whiz surprise that the city had bright lights, tall buildings (over two stories!), and was almost as big as Haiphong. Admitting that "to attack a big city was still new to us," Dung decided to use the "blooming lotus" tactic (bypassing outer defenses with sappers to attack the center, then "blooming" outward to meet regiments attacking from outside), which he had concocted for a raid in 1952 on Phat Diem, a Catholic community in the North.[69]

But in all other respects Dung found reason for satisfaction. Major General Pham Van Phu, the ARVN Second Corps commander, had deployed the bulk of his forces to protect his corps headquarters at Pleiku, leaving only one regiment of the Twenty-Third Division and three territorial battalions to defend Ban Me Thuot, despite ample evidence of PAVN intentions. To attack the city, Dung had the entire 316th Division reinforced by one infantry regiment, one sapper regiment, two antiaircraft regiments, two artillery regiments, two engineering regiments, an armored regiment, and a communications regiment.[70] Dung calculated that although in the entire central highlands his forces were "not much superior to the enemy's," at Ban Me Thuot he had 5.5 times as many troops, 1.2 times as many tanks and armored vehicles, and 2.1 times as much artillery. His main concern was to prevent the ARVN from reinforcing the city before he was ready to attack, a fear that was much alleviated by General Phu's deep reluctance to move troops away from his own command post, which was under harassment.[71]

To keep Phu off balance, Dung ordered diversionary attacks north of Ban Me Thuot, destroying two ARVN outposts on Route 19 west of Pleiku. On March 4, the PAVN attacked positions on the same road east and west of An Khe and on Route 21. Although the ARVN moved to clear the roads, the highlands were now cut off. Only Route 14 between Pleiku and Ban Me Thuot remained open, as the 320th Division sought to avoid revealing its position just four kilometers off the road. But encounters with ARVN patrols forced the division to seize that road, too, and by March 9, Ban Me Thuot was effectively encircled. That evening, Dung recalled, officers in his staff could not conceal their "joy and emotion" as "tens of thousands of men moved toward their targets."[72]

At two in the morning, sappers attacked the city's two airfields, a logistic facility, and a storage depot. Long-range artillery opened fire on Twenty-

Third Division headquarters. Tanks left hiding places forty kilometers away with infantry and armored cars falling in behind to converge on the city from four directions. At 7:25 a.m. on March 10, the artillery ceased, and tanks and infantry raced toward the Twenty-Third Division's main installations. A large part of the city was in PAVN hands by late afternoon. Resistance weakened as it became clear that neither aerial reinforcements nor tactical air support could easily penetrate PAVN antiaircraft fire. An airplane with the Republic of Vietnam Armed Forces (RVNAF) mistakenly dropped a bomb on the 23rd Division command post, severing communications and ending organized defense. The division commander, Brigadier General Le Trung Tuong, had already escaped in a helicopter after diverting a Ranger Group to secure a landing zone so he could pick up his family.[73] By 10:30 a.m. the next day, the command post, the division's deputy commander, and the chief of Darlac province were in PAVN hands.

Communist commanders were surprised by the ease of victory at Ban Me Thuot as compared with the hardships of 1968, and they pursued the ARVN cautiously. But Dung demanded speed as any pause risked prolonging the campaign into the rainy season. Now that it was organized like the ARVN into mechanized battle groups equipped with heavy weapons, the PAVN needed dry ground. The rest of the campaign, thought Dung, would be "a race against the enemy and heaven."[74]

Dung's forces could barely keep up with their enemy's collapse. An ARVN attempt to relieve Ban Me Thuot bogged down for lack of helicopters. Worse, the relief force was the Twenty-Third Division's Forty-Fourth Regiment, which had been stationed at Pleiku, although their soldiers' families remained in Ban Me Thuot. When the men of the regiment saw civilians leaving the city, they threw down their weapons to join their wives and children in flight. General Tuong checked into a hospital with a slight facial wound "to avoid responsibility," said a fellow officer, "for [the] certain defeat of his division."[75]

When the United States failed to respond, it became apparent to Thieu that not only would the United States not return to combat, but Congress was unlikely to approve the $300 million supplemental military assistance that Ford had requested ("the minimum needed to prevent serious reversals," Ford had said in January).[76] On March 10, Thieu ordered the airborne division to return from First Corps to defend threatened Tay Ninh (and, some said, to guard against a coup, which indeed had been proposed by Nguyen Cao Ky). On the eleventh, he called a meeting of his chief advisers to discuss what he had vowed never to do, namely, to surrender territory. A general redeployment was ordered to defend Third and Fourth corps, a move Thieu described as "lightening the top to keep the bottom." Lieutenant General Ngo Quang Truong, the First Corps commander, learned on March 13 that he was to keep only Danang. Thieu met General Phu at Cam

Ranh the next day to plan a retreat of ARVN regulars from Pleiku and Kontum to regroup and retake Ban Me Thuot. Montagnard regional and popular forces were to stay behind to screen the move. The United States was not to be told. Phu argued that with reinforcements and supplies he could hold Pleiku for a month but was overruled. To evade Communist forces, he suggested withdrawing by Route 7-B, a narrow unmaintained dirt track from Pleiku to the coast at Tuy Hoa, 225 kilometers away.[77]

Just what Phu's orders were and what he meant to do on his return to Pleiku on March 15 is disputed. Critics accused him of precipitously ordering total withdrawal. Certainly there was no planning.[78] But it hardly mattered. Phu, his senior officers, and their families boarded planes; the Sixth Air Division had its men lifted out by C-130s (leaving sixty-four aircraft on the ground); and army trucks headed out of town. To montagnard irregulars, government administrators, and civilians, the move looked like abandonment. Soldiers bolted to find their families, and a panicky mass streamed out of Pleiku to follow the army convoy down Route 7-B.

The choice of the withdrawal route caught the Communists by surprise, and Dung severely reprimanded the 320th Division commander for having no plan to block the road. But the retreating column was slowed to a crawl by fallen bridges and old land mines, and the division easily overtook it. Regional forces and mutinous montagnards joined the PAVN in raking the retreat with small arms, machine guns, and mortars. One group of refugees, halted by a blown bridge and closely circled by PAVN troops, was bombed by Saigon's air force. On March 22, stunned and starving survivors poured out of the hills with tales of horror, spreading panic to the lowlands.

By that time the PAVN Second Army had retaken Quang Tri city and surrounded Hue. On March 22 PAVN tanks crossed the My Chanh River, where ARVN and U.S. aircraft had successfully halted a similar attack in 1972. Now, without U.S. air support, the elite ARVN First Division disintegrated. Thousands of deserting troops fell back on Hue to join the scramble for transport to the sea. The PAVN entered Hue four days later. Meanwhile, the PAVN Second Division and regional forces had routed the ARVN in Quang Ngai and Binh Dinh provinces and taken possession of the former U.S. Marine base at Chu Lai. Danang was isolated.

Thieu thought Danang was defensible as a coastal enclave. With a population of more than 500,000 (the South's second-largest city), Danang was many times larger than Ban Me Thuot. The ARVN Marine and Third Infantry divisions were stationed there, and thousands of more troops were streaming in from the countryside. Food and ammunition could be supplied by air and sea. But the avalanche of refugees from the highlands had swept through provinces on both sides of Danang and was now rushing into the city. More than one million refugees swarmed in the streets, food reserves dwindled, and deserters turned to looting. The evacuation of U.S. Consulate personnel on March 26 ignited hysterical fury in the huge crowd gathered at the airport. As PAVN artillery began to shell the airfield and military installations on March 28, panicky mobs surged into the center of the city. Communist historiography requires ascribing the seizure of power to "mass uprisings" and the coordination of guerilla attacks with political activity, and guerillas did open the Danang prison,[79] but chaos seems a better word for the assault on Saigon's authority. A despairing General Ngo Quang Truong, his communications cut and staff deserting, ordered his troops to evacuate by sea. Less than half the Marine Division and only one thousand soldiers of the Third Division succeeded in boarding ships; the rest deserted or were left on the beach. Three PAVN divisions and assorted regional and technical units entered the city unopposed on March 29, 1975.

In just two weeks, twelve provinces and nearly eight million people had come under Communist control. The ARVN had lost 35 percent of its troop strength and 40 percent of its weapons. Having expended little of its own supplies and having lost few troops, the PAVN now enjoyed a significant matériel and manpower advantage. But these were not solely the achievements of Communist arms. The ARVN was deployed in far-flung positions that permitted each Communist success to place another ARVN outpost in jeopardy. Fantasizing about U.S. rescue, officers abandoned their troops when reinforcements and air cover failed to appear. Abandoned by their officers, soldiers left their units. Personal ties between superiors and subordinates, so essential to solidarity among Vietnamese, dissolved. Although some units fought bravely and well, many broke up, sometimes without fighting at all. Never planned, retreat turned into panic. Fearing the unknown and not wanting to be left behind, great masses of civilians fled.

As Danang was falling, President Ford dispatched General Frederick Weyand to see what military assistance Saigon needed. Weyand reported that an emergency infusion of $722 million—the value of matériel lost in the retreat thus far—could stave off defeat. But Weyand's over-optimism was obvious. Even the Pentagon's own Defense Intelligence Agency predicted defeat within a month. Ford nonetheless requested the money in a speech that reminded Congress that the $150 billion it had appropriated in past years would have been spent for nothing if it now failed to approve his request, but the words changed few minds. Meeting on April 1, the Political Bureau concluded that "the U.S. has proved to be completely impotent, and even if it increased its aid it cannot save the puppets from collapse."[80] Ford's insistence on the emergency allocation, placed before Congress on April 10, was widely seen as a cynical attempt to hold Congress responsible for the inevitable. The Senate Armed Services Committee rejected the request on the seventeenth. There could be no rescue now, as each day's news confirmed.

Having decided to strike for complete victory by May, the Communists raced to occupy all of ARVN First and Second corps territory and to shift forces southward. A new army corps, the Third, was created. The First Army, dispatched from Ninh Binh province in the North, arrived via Route 9 and Corridor 613 at the southern edge of the highlands in mid-April. The Second Army left Danang in the hands of reserves to advance nine hundred kilometers down Route 1. The PAVN rolled through coastal cities, crushing hastily regrouped ARVN units at Phan Rang on April 16 and reaching Phan Thiet on the nineteenth. Supplies began arriving from the North at Danang, Qui Nhon, and Cam Ranh by sea. Meanwhile, farther south, sizeable Communist units had moved by boat and foot into the Mekong delta and linked up with local forces to menace Route 5, Saigon's main link to delta. At Xuan Loc, a province capital astride a strategic intersection sixty kilometers northeast of Saigon, the ARVN Eighteenth Division, supported by air from nearby Bien Hoa airbase, mounted a valiant defense for eleven days against three PAVN divisions. This time the ARVN division commander had taken the precaution of sending dependents to Bien Hoa and creating strong defensive positions outside the city before the fighting began, and being close to air support certainly helped. But with reinforcements and heavy shelling of the airbase, the PAVN overwhelmed Xuan Loc on April 20, and the way to Saigon was open.[81]

Saigon was not to be the first capital "liberated," however. In neighboring Cambodia, land routes to Phnom Penh had been cut for over a year. Supplies had reached the city by barge up the Mekong River or by air. No longer supported by the Vietnamese, the Khmer Rouge had formed a siege line around the city in early January, and ill-aimed 107-mm rockets had crashed randomly in its streets. Under the desperate illusion that Lon Nol's departure would clear the way to negotiations, government leaders and allies demanded his resignation, and on April 1 the Marshal left for Hawaii by way of Bali. The Khmer Rouge ignored appeals for talks, the U.S. Embassy pulled out on the twelfth, and Khmer Rouge troops entered Phnom Penh on the seventeenth.

In South Vietnam, relentless Communist advances silenced rumors of a second partition or another attempt at "reconciliation." U.S. Embassy dependents quietly departed. Pressure grew on the embassy to begin evacuating staff, Vietnamese employees, and "high-risk" government officials. Ambassador Graham Martin suggested to Thieu that he appoint a premier who could negotiate with the Communists. Then, in the early evening of April 21, police loudspeakers announced that curfew would be set forward one hour to 8 p.m. to herd people before their radio and television sets. For the next hour President Thieu spoke to them in a voice filled with anger, sorrow, and tears. "If the Americans do not want to support us any more, let them go, get out!" The beginning of the end, in Thieu's opinion, had been the Paris Agreement: "Kissinger didn't see that the agreement led the South Vietnamese people to death. Everyone else sees it, but Kissinger does not see it. . . . I said at the time, we must fight. No coalition! If there is a coalition, South Vietnam cannot stand. I never thought a man like Mr. Kissinger would deliver our people to such a disastrous fate." Thieu then announced that he was stepping down ("I resign but do not desert"), taunting those who had called him an obstacle to U.S. aid on the one hand and to a negotiated peace on the other to now do better.[82] His successor, the aged, nearly blind, asthmatic Vice President Tran Van Huong, was immediately pressured to hand over the government to General Duong Van "Big" Minh, whom many believed, or wished to believe, was somehow acceptable to the Communists. Minh's most avid supporter, French Ambassador Jean-Marie Merillon, convinced Ambassador Martin that Hanoi was willing to cut a deal with Minh for a ceasefire and transitional government.[83]

THE HO CHI MINH CAMPAIGN

But deals held no attraction for the Communists. They had firmly believed ever since Ngo Dinh Diem's demise that any successors would be, in General Dung's words, "docile and faithful henchmen" of the United States. "The Huong administration was only the Thieu administration without Thieu."[84] As for General Minh, he was, said Dung, just another "stubborn ringleader."

The Communists moreover were too far advanced with their own preparations and too near total victory to indulge any offer but surrender. Since March, Dung and his staff had been drawing up a plan to attack the city. On April 7, Le Duc Tho had arrived at B2 headquarters to represent the Political Bureau in last-minute discussions, and on the fourteenth, the bureau had given final approval to what it dubbed the Ho Chi Minh Campaign. A special campaign command headed by General Dung and staffed by Pham Hung, Tran Van Tra, and Le Duc Anh was to begin during the last ten days of April.

The PAVN divisions, tanks, and artillery then massing on Saigon's outskirts provided the means of a frontal assault if this proved necessary. But Danang's extraordinary collapse had strengthened faith in the role that political conditions could play in taking a large city. On the other hand, Saigon was five or six times larger than Danang and would have time to prepare a defense. Political upheaval and administrative paralysis, it seemed to the Communists, would certainly help to prepare the way for the entry of main forces. The Communists were particularly keen to avert an ARVN withdrawal into the city, where it might stage a last-ditch defense. The campaign therefore was to be a general offensive and uprising, a combination of political agitation and military thrusts to induce the ARVN to crumble and the "people" to seize power or at least assist in doing so. More concretely, the plan called for cutting off the retreat of ARVN units from the outer perimeter, deep penetration by mechanized units to government "nerve centers," and the emergence of clandestine organs from hiding to lead the people in asking ARVN troops to lay down their weapons. Nguyen Van Linh, COSVN deputy secretary, was placed in charge of organizing mass uprisings, and political cadres joined the throngs of refugees entering the city.

Maneuvering into position took the Communists several days, during which large units had to enter areas long held by Saigon. The region surrounding the city contained "highly populated areas," noted General Tra, "in which supporters of the revolution were not necessarily more numerous than the families of puppet troops. The masses were not awakened. Here was an operation where we had to attack and move, where we had to open a way in order to advance."[85] In other words, armed forces would have to act without the help of popular uprisings. The column assigned to attack Saigon's National Police Headquarters had to "wipe out" forty-five outposts and "liberate" twelve villages on the way to its position. The column commander's aide recorded in his diary: "Passed through a populated area. Most of the people stayed put." Yet at another place he wrote, "When they awoke in the morning and saw the liberation troops everywhere, the people were extremely enthusiastic. One old woman went out into the field and dug up a red flag with a gold star. I don't know when it had been buried, but it looked very new."[86]

By April 26, fifteen Communist divisions and assorted regional and guerrilla forces were set to launch the final attack. Against them, in isolated positions on a tattered perimeter around Saigon, stood about five ARVN divisions. The first assaults cleared roads and bottled up the ARVN Twenty-Fifth Division in Tay Ninh. An attempt to move artillery up to hit Tan Son Nhut airfield ran into stiff resistance, so on April 28, the base was struck by U.S-made A-37 jet fighters recently captured at Phan Rang and led by a defector from Saigon's air force. General Minh assumed the presidency in Saigon the same day. Ordering the troops to keep fighting, Minh announced he would seek "to arrive at a ceasefire, at negotiations, at peace on the basis of the Paris Accords. I am ready to accept any proposal in this direction."[87] But the general offensive went ahead on April 29 as planned. "Our soldiers and people, squashing Duong Van Minh's plot to call for a ceasefire and negotiations to turn over the government, resolutely carried out the order of the Political Bureau and the Campaign command: 'Continue to advance into Saigon according to plan, advance with the greatest possible vigor, liberate and occupy the city, disarm the enemy troops, dissolve the enemy's administration at the various levels, and thoroughly smash all enemy resistance.'"[88] A delegation sent by Minh to parlay with Hanoi's representatives to the Joint Military Commission at Tan Son Nhut (housed there since 1973 under terms of the Paris Agreement to handle ceasefire matters) wound up staying the night in the Communists' bunker as PAVN 130-mm shells fell on the airfield and PAVN columns closed in from five directions.

The PAVN Third Army seized the Twenty-Fifth Division headquarters at Cu Chi on April 29 and sent one division toward Tan Son Nhut. Fifty kilometers north, the First Army surrounded the ARVN Fifth Division at Lai Khe, and a division headed toward the ARVN general staff compound. The Fourth Army took Bien Hoa airbase and ARVN Third Corps headquarters, and its Seventh Division crossed the Dong Nai River. The Second Army closed on approaches over the Saigon River and quickly overcame remnants of the ARVN Eighteenth Division. South of the city, the army-strength 232nd Group broke up what remained of the ARVN Twenty-Second Division.

Where isolated ARVN units resisted effectively, PAVN forces went around them. Others were overrun or simply crumbled at the approach of superior forces. The commander of the ARVN Fifth Division committed suicide. Approaching an ARVN artillery base near Go Vap, General Tra observed that "the puppet troops had lost morale and some had fled, but the 81st . . . airborne Ranger Group continued stubbornly to defend the gates." A Communist regiment attempted unsuccessfully to storm the rangers on April 30. A team finally broke through using a gun from an abandoned tank, seized the post computing center (with everything intact), and turned to staff headquarters. "All enemy troops had fled except a corporal who greeted the team and turned over a bunch of keys with all documents and property. That puppet corporal was comrade Ba Minh, a regional intelligence agent who had been planted in the staff headquarters long before."[89] Behind every military advance, political cadres stepped out to gather supporters, track down ARVN stragglers, and take over administrative offices.

From afar, it looked as if the PAVN was steamrolling the ARVN in a conventional war of movement pitting the North against the South, and it is certainly true that PAVN regulars (and PAVN fillers in PLAF units) played a decisive role. The PAVN, though, was not the only player on the revolutionary side. The strategic plan had called for a "general offensive and uprising," not an exclusively military campaign. Although expectations of what uprisings could achieve had been scaled back after Tet in 1968, neither the concept nor planning for uprisings had been abandoned. And contrary to much that has been written about Northern triumphalism, Hanoi's generals credited political organs and local forces with preparing the ground for victory. As PAVN General Tan pointed out, months before the campaign began, it was *binh van* political cadres (specialists in propagandizing enemy troops) who penetrated the ARVN and undermined its morale, local guerrillas and regional forces that contested control of villages in the "war of the flags," and double agents and citizens who stepped forward to occupy government offices and utilities as the ARVN scattered. In the Communists' zone 9 alone, Tan claimed, local and regional forces compelled Saigon to withdraw from 800 outposts, allowing the Communists to seize full or partial control of sixty-six villages containing over 40,000 people. In zone 8, he said, such forces compelled Saigon to abandon 320 outposts and 193 villages.[90] As for Saigon, in addition to significant sapper and commando elements operating on the city's outskirts, "hundreds" of cadres were in position "to guide the Youth Union and other mass organizations . . . to arise and coordinate when the main-force units attacked," according to General Thai.[91] General Tra, the B2 commander, also described people following local party leaders in seizing police stations and government offices everywhere his forces approached.[92] Even if a fraction of such reports were true, depictions of the offensive as nothing more than a PAVN conquest entirely conventional in form are far too simple.

By the time the PAVN rolled up to the gates of Saigon, most members of the ARVN high command had fled. General Cao Van Vien, the chief of staff, had left on April 28 without resigning. His replacement, General Vinh Loc, broadcast an impassioned speech on the dishonor of flight and then he too had fled. Police Chief Nguyen Khac Binh had taken an armed guard to the airport and commandeered a plane for Thailand. By the morning of April 30, the ARVN Fifth, Eighteenth, Twenty-Second, and Twenty-Fifth divisions had quit fighting or broken up into fugitive groups. Fearing that troops who remained in Saigon might barricade themselves for a futile last stand, General Minh went on radio at 10:20 a.m. and ordered them to lay down their arms. Most obeyed, some turning over their weapons to youthful activists who encouraged surrender. Before PAVN spearheads could reach the city's center, thousands of ARVN troops shed their uniforms and headed for home in their underwear. In government ministries, military headquarters, even the Central Intelligence Organization, small numbers of civil servants and officers revealed to bewildered colleagues, as they took charge, that they always had served the revolution. Resistance sputtered at Can Tho and other points in the delta, but in Saigon the Second Indochina War was over at 10:45 a.m., April 30, when a Soviet-made T-54 tank, the number 843 stamped on its turret, bashed down the gates of Independence Palace.

NOTES

1. Tran Van Tra, *Nhung chang duong cua "B2-Thanh dong": tap V, Ket thuc cuoc chien tranh 30 nam* [Stages on the Road of the B2-Bulwark, vol. V, Concluding the 30 Years War] (Ho Chi Minh City: NXB Van Nghe, 1982), 83.

2. "Dien cua dong chi Le Duan, Nam 1972" [Cable from Le Duan, 1972], Dang Cong San Viet Nam, *Van kien Dang toan tap* (Complete Party Documents [hereafter cited as VKTT]), vol. 33, 1972, 421.

3. "Plan of General Uprising When a Political Solution is Reached," October 4, 1972, in *Viet-Nam Documents and Research Notes*, no. 109 (December 1972). Also see "Directive 20/H," October 15, 1972, in *Viet-Nam Documents and Research Notes*, no. 108 (November 1972).

4. Tra, *Nhung chang duong*, 128, 133.

5. Allen E. Goodman, *The Lost Peace: America's Search for a Negotiated Settlement of the Vietnam War* (Stanford, Calif.: Hoover Institution Press, 1978), 168.

6. Hoang Van Thai, "The Decisive Years: Memoirs of Vietnamese Senior General Hoang Van Thai," *Saigon Giai Phong* (March 13–May 14, 1986), 3, trans. Joint Publication Research Service, JPRS-SEA-87-084, June 23, 1987 (Springfield, Va.: National Technical Information Service, 1987), 8.

7. "Directive 03/CT 73," March 30, 1973, in VNDRNs, no. 115 (September 1973).

8. The Central Committee Report to the Fourth Party Congress in 1978 acknowledged that war damage had nullified ten to fifteen years of growth. Agricultural output increased four percent between 1965 and 1975, but population grew twenty-three percent. Equally disturbing was the loss of control over the economy due to prolonged dispersal of productive assets. See William S. Turley, "Vietnam Since Reunification," *Problems of Communism* (March–April 1977): 45–46.

9. "Nghi quyet, So 01-NQ/74, thang 9 nam 1974" [Resolution no. 01-NQ/74, September 1974], VKDTT, vol. 35,1974 (2004), 367.

10. "Nghi quyet hoi nghi lan thu 12 cua Trung uong cuc, Thang 12 nam 1973" [Resolution of the 12th COSVN Conference, December 1973], VKDTT, vol. 34, 1973 (2004), 474–475.

11. Tra, *Nhung chang duong*, 82-83; Hoang Van Thai, "The Decisive Years," 9.

12. "Directive 02/73," January 19, 1973, in *Viet-Nam Documents and Research Notes*, no. 113 (June 1973); also see Tra, *Nhung chang duong*, 88.

13. Quoted in Robert K. Brigham, *Guerrilla Diplomacy: The NLF's Foreign Relations and the Viet Nam War* (Ithaca, N.Y.: Cornell University Press, 1998), 117.

14. Tra, *Nhung chang duong*, 88.

15. Vo Van Kiet went on to become deputy head of the Saigon-Gia Dinh Military Management Committee in 1975 and chairman of the Municipal People's Revolutionary Committee (in effect "mayor") in January 1976; at the Fourth Party Congress in December, he became an alternate member of the Political Bureau. Le Duc Anh commanded PAVN forces in Cambodia in 1979 and attained a seat in the Political Bureau in 1982. But Tra, after serving as Kiet's superior on the Saigon-Gia Dinh Military Management Committee, faded from view in late 1977 and lost his seat in the Central Committee before the Fifth Party Congress in 1982.

16. War Experience Recapitulation Committee of the High-Level Military Institute, *The Anti-U.S. Resistance War for National Salvation 1954–1975: Military Events*, trans. Joint Publications Research Service, JPRS no. 80,968 (Washington, D.C.: Government Printing Office, June 3, 1982), 160–162.

17. "Nghi quyet hoi nghi lan 12 cua Trung uong cuc, Thang 12 nam 1973," VKDTT, vol. 34, 1973 (2004), 472–549.

18. Tra, *Nhung chang duong,* 54.

19. Hoang Van Thai, "The Decisive Years," 36.

20. "Political Reorientation and Training Materials for Infrastructure Cadres and Party Members," *Viet-Nam Documents and Research Notes,* no. 117 (April 1974).

21. Hoang Van Thai, "The Decisive Years," 37.

22. "Nghi quyet hoi nghi lan thu 12 cua Trung uong cuc," VKDTT, vol. 34, 1973 (2004), 493.

23. These American estimates are not so very different from figures supplied by a communist source after the war. See Appendix A.

24. U.S., Congress, Senate, Richard M. Moose and Charles F. Meissner, "Vietnam: May 1974," 93rd Cong., 2nd sess., August 5, 1974 (Washington, D.C.: Government Printing Office, 1974), 4–5.

25. The Communists estimated revolutionary forces "at most one-third those of the enemy." Tra, *Nhung chang duong,* 55.

26. See T. Christopher Jespersen, "Kissinger, Ford, and Congress: The Bitter End in Vietnam," *The Pacific Historical Review,* vol. 71, no. 3 (August 2002): 443 and fn. 9.

27. Arnold R. Isaacs, *Without Honor: Defeat in Vietnam and Cambodia* (Baltimore, Md.: Johns Hopkins University Press, 1983), 334–335.

28. Oleg Sarin and Lev Dvoretsky, *Alien Wars: The Soviet Union's Aggressions Against the World, 1919 to 1989* (Novato, Calif.: Presidio, 1996), 106–107, 111.

29. Chen Jian, "China in the Vietnam War, 1964–69," *The China Quarterly,* No. 142 (June 1995): 379.

30. Hoang Van Thai, "The Decisive Years," 42.

31. Moose and Meissner, "Vietnam: May 1974," 22.

32. In all of Indochina, the PAVN had 900 tanks to the ARVN's 600, but only 44 armored personnel carriers compared with the ARVN's 1,000. The PAVN's total inventory of 122-mm and 130-mn field guns was nearly 1,200; the ARVN possessed 1,500 105-mm and 155-mm howitzers and 175 self-propelled guns of 175-mm caliber. The North's 200 combat aircraft never dared to venture over the South, which had 500 combat aircraft. The PAVN distributed its equipment along the Ho Chi Minh Trail and across the North as well as in the South, while the ARVN confined its deployments overwhelmingly to the Southern territory that was under its control. International Institute for Strategic Studies, *The Military Balance 1974–1975* (London: International Institute for Strategic Studies, 1974), 60–61.

33. At the NLF's urging, according to Brigham, *Guerrilla Diplomacy,* 99.

34. Jerry M. Silverman, "Local Politics and Administration in South Vietnam," paper presented at the annual meeting of the Association for Asian Studies, Boston, April 3, 1974, 55.

35. "Chi thi cua Thuong vu Trung uong cuc mien Nam, So 06/CT71, ngay 19 thang 5 nam 1971" [COSVN Standing Committee Directive No. 06/CT71, May 19, 1971], VKDTT, vol. 32, 1971 (2003), 534.

36. *The New York Times* (January 14, 1974), 1.

37. *The New York Times* (July 6, 1974), 2; (February 2 1975), 9; and (February 15, 1975), 2.

38. *The New York Times* (November 2,1974), 4. For the background and details of this rebellion, see Gerald Cannon Hickey, *Free in the Forest: Ethnohistory of the*

Vietnamese Central Highlands 1954–1976 (New Haven, Conn.: Yale University Press, 1982), 266–271.

39. Moose and Meissner, "Vietnam: May 1974," 27–29.

40. Allen E. Goodman, "South Vietnam: War Without End?" *Asian Survey* 15, no. 1 (January 1975): 76.

41. Moose and Meissner, "Vietnam: May 1974," 27.

42. *The New York Times* (January 22, 1975), 8.

43. Viet Tran, *Vietnam: j'ai choisi l'exil* [I Have Chosen Exile] (Paris: Editions du Seuil, 1979), 33–34.

44. *The New York Times* (August 9, 1974), 17.

45. *The New York Times* (February 4, 1975), 1.

46. *The New York Times* (February 6, 1975), 10.

47. *The New York Times* (November 2, 1974), 1.

48. Although Vietnam had never been a stable liberal democracy, its people, especially in the South, were not unfamiliar with the concept of competitive elections, having experienced them from national to local levels at various times from the colonial era through the Communist-organized general elections of 1946 that established a coalition government to the experiments in village democracy under Thieu himself. This experience as well as traditional practices of co-optation to village councils had left even rural Vietnamese with a flexible and contingent, not simply "authoritarian," understanding of elections. On the meaning and functions of elections in Southeast Asia (though, unfortunately, excluding Vietnam), see the introduction by R.H. Taylor to *The Politics of Elections in Southeast Asia*, ed. R.H. Taylor (New York: Woodrow Wilson Center Press/Cambridge University Press, 1996).

49. *The New York Times* (January 2, 1974), 24.

50. The War Powers Act, passed over Nixon's veto on November 7, 1973, prohibited the president from committing U.S. troops abroad for more than sixty days without specific congressional authorization. The Cambodian bombing ban was an amendment to an appropriations bill that required the president, who signed the bill on July 1 after a compromise, to discontinue the bombing after August 15. The Military Procurement Authorization passed on November 16, said in part: "No funds heretofore or hereafter appropriated may be obligated or expended to finance the involvement of United States military forces in hostilities in or over or from off the shores of North Vietnam, South Vietnam, Laos, or Cambodia, unless specifically authorized hereafter by Congress."

51. Henry Kissinger, *Ending the Vietnam War* (New York: Simon & Schuster, 2003), 468.

52. Reproduced in Nguyen Tien Hung and Jerrold L. Schecter, *The Palace File* (New York: Harper & Row, 1986), 434.

53. Stephen T. Hosmer, Konrad Kellen and Brian M. Jenkins, *The Fall of South Vietnam: Statements of Vietnamese Military and Civilian Leaders* (New York: Crane, Russak & Co., 1980), 10–11.

54. War Experience Recapitulation Committee, *The Anti-U.S. Resistance War*, 160.

55. War Experience Recapitulation Committee, *The Anti-U.S. Resistance War*, 166–167.

56. "Nghi quyet so 01-NQ/74 . . . ," VKDTT, vol. 35,1974 (2004).

57. Hoang Van Thai, "The Decisive Years," 56–57. Also Le Trong Tan, *May van de ve nghe thuat quan su trong Tong tien cong va noi day xuan 1975* [Some Problems of Military art in the General Offensive and Uprising of Spring 1975] (Hanoi: NXB Quan doi nhan dan, 1985), 41–42.

58. Hoang Van Thai, "The Decisive Years," 167.

59. Communist sources confirm that Southern regional forces and militia and coordination between military and political struggle had remained weak since 1968. See War Experience Recapitulation Committee, *The Anti-U.S. Resistance War,* 162.

60. Van Tien Dung, *Dai thang mua xuan* [Great Spring Victory] (Hanoi: NXB Quan doi nhan dan, 1976).

61. Tra, *Nhung chang duong,* 145.

62. Tra, *Nhung chang duong,* 147–148; on intelligence agents, see 102.

63. "Nghi quyet so 01-NQ/74 . . . ," VKDTT, vol. 35, 1974 (2004), 377.

64. Dung, *Dai thang mua xuan,* 19–20.

65. Dung, *Dai thang mua xuan,* 21.

66. Quan doi nhan dan Viet Nam, *Van tai quan su chien luoc tren duong Ho Chi Minh trong khang chien chong My* [Strategic Military Transport on the Ho Chi Minh Trail in the Anti-U.S. Resistance War] (Hanoi: Tong cuc hau can, 1988), 151, 428.

67. Dung, *Dai thang mua xuan,* 25.

68. The following paragraphs on Communist planning and assault on Ban Me Thuot are based on Dung, *Dai thang mua xuan,* 23–99, unless otherwise indicated.

69. Dung regarded this tactic as a personal hallmark. General Tra's memoir, however, derides the tendency to use the "blooming lotus" everywhere, a tendency based on "the subjective thinking of one person or another." As for Dung's unfamiliarity with attacks on "a big city," Tra implies this was because Hanoi-based commanders lacked the experience of those like himself who had fought for years in the South's more urbanized milieu. Tra, *Nhung chang duong,* 178–179.

70. Hoang Minh Thao, *Chien dich Tay nguyen dai thang* [Great Victorious Western Highlands Campaign] (Hanoi: NXB Quan doi nhan dan, 1977), 56.

71. Hosmer et al., *The Fall of South Vietnam,* 169.

72. Dung, *Dai thang mua xuan,* 79.

73. Hosmer et al., *The Fall of South Vietnam,* 170–171.

74. Dung, *Dai thong mua xuan,* 95.

75. Lieutenant General Nguyen Xuan Thinh, quoted in Hosmer et al., *The Fall of South Vietnam,* 174.

76. *The New York Times* (January 28, 1975), 1.

77. Hosmer et al., *The Fall of South Vietnam,* 182–184.

78. Tran Van Don, in *Our Endless War* (San Rafael, Calif.: Presidio Press, 1978), 224, asserts that Phu "unilaterally ordered the withdrawal of his headquarters with all its supporting forces from Pleiku to Nha Trang." Also see Hosmer et al., *The Fall of South Vietnam,* 177–178.

79. Tan, *May van de,"* 37–38.

80. War Experience Recapitulation Committee, *The Anti-U.S. Resistance War,* 179.

81. For a detailed account of this battle, see George J. Veith and Merle L. Pribbenow, "'Fighting Is an Art,'" The Army of the Republic of Vietnam's Defense of

Xuan Loc, 9–21 April 1975," *Journal of Military History* 68, no. 1 (January 2004): 163–213.

82. Thieu quoted in John Clark Pratt, *Vietnam Voices: Perspectives on the War Years 1941–1982* (New York: Penguin, 1984), 611–612.

83. Don, *Our Endless War*, 249–251, 254; Frank Snepp, *Decent Interval* (New York: Random House, 1977), 324–325.

84. Dung, *Dai thang mua xuan*, 249.

85. Tra, *Nhung chang duong*, 263–264.

86. Tra, *Nhung chang duong*, 270, 271.

87. Quoted in Tiziano Terzani, *Giai Phong: The Fall and Liberation of Saigon* (New York: St. Martin's, 1976), 41.

88. War Experience Recapitulation Committee, *The Anti-U.S. Resistance War*, 182.

89. Tra, *Nhung chang duong*, 288.

90. Tan, *May van de*," 37–38, 78.

91. Thai, "The Decisive Years," 141.

92. Tra, *Nhung chang duong*, 285–313.

9

Of Lessons and Their Price

As South Vietnam was falling, Thieu lobbied Ford and Ford lobbied the U.S. Congress for supplemental military assistance. The two presidents argued that without increased aid the Army of the Republic of Vietnam (ARVN) would be unable to withstand the People's Army of Vietnam's (PAVN) assault. If the supplement were not approved and Saigon collapsed, they averred, it would be the result of insufficient aid, and responsibility would belong to those who opposed the aid. Similar arguments were made for airstrikes against the PAVN's massing armies.

In a narrow military sense, the arguments had merit. For years the U.S. had depended principally on military strategy to secure the Saigon regime, and with the American withdrawal the task of implementing that strategy fell upon the regular ARVN. The ARVN had been trained and organized to rely on firepower superiority, which in turn made the ARVN dependent on a constant flow of equipment, weapons, and ammunition. Because South Vietnam manufactured no military goods, the ARVN required continuing and voluminous U.S. military assistance (roughly $1 billion a year) to sustain combat during Communist offensives (just as the Communists needed substantial, if less, assistance from their allies to mount them). Even with that assistance, it was doubtful the ARVN, due to unwise strategy, could long have withstood a concerted PAVN push without U.S. air cover. That strategy had been to enlarge Saigon's zone of control, with the result that, when the Communists pushed, the ARVN was overextended. Once the PAVN had defeated the ARVN in the highlands, the ARVN's unorganized retreat guaranteed a rout. Without a massive infusion of U.S. aid and combat troops, Saigon was doomed.

In the long run, however, the argument for rescue was vulnerable to severe and compelling criticism. The fact that the argument was made at all simply spotlighted the twenty-five years of U.S. aid that had left Saigon's anti-Communist regimes dependent, seemingly forever, on U.S. support. If emergency aid were given to help stave off defeat in 1975, what guarantee was there that aid would not have to be given again in 1976 and in every year thereafter? The material dimensions of that dependency in fact had grown over the years, not diminished. The DRV, too, was dependent on aid, but it proved more capable of converting that help into battlefield victories. The record provided convincing evidence that the United States, absent an unforeseeable collapse of support for the DRV, had to accept Saigon's defeat if it wished to disengage from Indochina's wars.

COULD THE U.S. HAVE WON?

The question arises from puzzlement that the army of an impoverished state plus some peasant guerrillas could thwart the aims of the world's greatest military power. The all too easy explanation is that the revolutionaries did not in fact defeat the U.S.; rather, the U.S. let itself be defeated when politics at home intervened to snatch defeat from the jaws of victory. This reasoning is simplistic in three ways: first, it exaggerates the efficacy of armed force; second, it disregards the continuum of war and politics; and third, it discounts the enemy's political strengths. Sometimes it is wiser to break off attack than to continue striving for victory, as Pyrrhus, king of Epirus, recognized over two millennia ago. In this war an American victory was beyond attainment at a price that made sense to the majority of senators and congressmen, a substantial proportion of the military establishment, and the American people. This much is obvious, and it is all, really, that needs to be said.

Still, the question will not go away, and so an answer must be given. For most Americans as for their elected officials and military leaders victory meant the attenuation of insurgency and DRV involvement in the South, whether by negotiated agreement or force of arms, to a point that would no longer require the presence of U.S. forces to guarantee the continued existence of the Saigon government, with the DMZ as a *de facto* boundary. This outcome would have been similar to that of the Korean War, a mental template for many Americans at the time, and it might have protected non-Communist governments in Laos and Cambodia as well. This was not in fact the outcome that was sought after negotiations began in 1968 (when Johnson accepted four-party talks including the National Liberation Front of South Vietnam [NLF]), and for that matter every president from Eisenhower onward doubted that American interests required its full achievement. Even so, the war's anatomists ask, could the U.S. have "won" on the Korean model if it had fought without restraint, if it had allocated any resources the military needed to clear and hold all of South Vietnam and perhaps strategic parts of Laos and Cambodia as well? Was there something the United States could have done to avert what, in the end, happened?

American chances of success certainly would have been greater if the U.S. had invaded the North, occupied the Laotian panhandle, and deployed sufficient forces to guarantee a military and administrative presence for the RVN in every village of South Vietnam. Such levels of force might well have sharply reduced the North's capacity to continue the war while allowing pacification programs and institution-building to create a more resilient non-Communist state in the South. However for obvious political, economic, and moral reasons, not to mention the risk of Chinese intervention, these options could not be seriously considered. Aside from the domestic and international opposition such measures would have provoked, the cost in American resources, lives, and attention would have been out of proportion to any conceivable gain for the United States.

More realistically, would it have been sufficient to have given General Westmoreland the 206,000 additional troops and permission for an "amphibious hook" around the demilitarized zone that he requested in 1968? How would the Communists have responded and what would have been the outcome? Although even a PAVN officer would have to reply speculatively, the answers given to the author by a colonel in the PAVN Military History Institute were sobering:

> Look what happened in 1970. Americans and ARVN forces did cross the border into Cambodia, but it was easier for us to fight in Cambodia than in South Vietnam. The fighting showed that the PAVN could adapt to the expansion of the war. In fact, the expansion of war into Cambodia helped us because it laid a basis for us to stage even bigger battles later inside the South. As for an American strike into the North, this would have taken place in an area that had been well-prepared to wage people's war and where our ability to provide material support to the main forces was much greater than anywhere else. So such a strike would have had to deal with popular resistance and then have faced a powerful main force counterattack, like what the Chinese encountered along the northern border in 1979. The PAVN's victories against a strike into the North would have been greater than the ones scored in southern Laos in 1971. A small number of American troops made a difference in Korea, but not in Vietnam where everything is different. So you see, Westmoreland's plan could not have changed the essentials of the strategic situation.[1]

In other words, the Communists had options, ways of "keeping us [the Americans] busy and waiting us out," as McNamara put it to Johnson in October 1966.[2] To be sure, at the time the Joint Chiefs forwarded Westmoreland's request, Hanoi might have felt pressed to compromise.

In the aftermath of the Tet Offensive in 1968, the Communists were in a weakened state. The indigenous Southern forces on which they had pinned hopes for a "general uprising" were in tatters, and Accelerated Pacification was making inroads against their bases of popular support. The PAVN, and therefore the North, faced an increasing burden of conventional combat in which the Americans held a decisive advantage. But considering Hanoi's strategic doctrine and resolve, it is more likely it would have met invasion of the North by withdrawing the PAVN into the hills and from there supported a "people's war" in the lowlands, with China serving as the DRV's strategic rear. This was essentially what Mao Zedong proposed to Hanoi in 1964, and Hanoi's leaders agreed.[3] An invasion would have had to take place in coastal areas where villages had enrolled 10 percent to 40 percent of their populations in the militia. A concentrated American force could have entered the North and crossed the panhandle without difficulty, but any prolonged presence or dispersal of forces would have encountered a vastly better organized resistance than the one the British prepared for the Germans or the Japanese for the Americans in World War II. If the South was a quagmire, then surely the Communists, on home territory and with China supporting them, could have turned the North (and Laos, too) into one as well. And there was the danger of direct Chinese involvement in the form of combat troops.

American strategists had to weigh the costs and risks of winning in Indochina against U.S. interests and obligations outside Asia, too. Almost from the beginning of major U.S intervention the war impinged on U.S. ability to meet commitments in more vital areas, such as Western Europe, where NATO still faced the Soviet threat, or the Middle East, where the USSR supported Israel's enemies. Without mobilizing the reserves, instituting a universal draft, and canceling draft deferments, which no American president thought were politically feasible, the United States could not have expanded its involvement in Indochina significantly without further distracting it from other pressing issues, thinning resources needed elsewhere, and undermining the confidence of important allies.

The American involvement in Indochina also allowed adversaries to assert themselves without fear of consequences, as the Soviet Union discovered when it invaded Czechoslovakia in August 1968. Even if the Johnson administration had been willing to antagonize the Soviet Union and sacrifice Moscow's help in settling the Vietnam conflict,[4] there was not much the United States could have done to help the Czechs. An otherwise belligerent report by a House of Representatives subcommittee noted after a trip to Europe in 1968 that it had "become painfully aware that U.S. forces are spread thin in terms of our global military commitments. Moreover, our forces in Europe and the Mediterranean have suffered as a result of the high priority commitments in Vietnam for both men and equipment."[5]

The strategic dilemma lasted to the end of the war. In late 1972, while berating Thieu for obstructing negotiations, Kissinger pointed out that "We have fought for four years, have mortgaged our whole foreign policy to the defense of one country. What you have said has been a very bitter thing to hear."[6] A further turn of the American screw in Indochina was plausible only in a world where other problems did not exist or the United States chose to take the risk of ignoring them.

The limits on American action were unrelated to American military capabilities. U.S. arms could forestall Saigon's defeat, but they could not alone wean Saigon from its dependency and guarantee its long-term survival. Military might was not relevant to the most fundamental reasons for Saigon's weakness. For the war, contrary to official depictions, required the United States not simply to defend one-half of a divided state from attack by the other (as in Korea), but to defend a specific social and political elite against an ongoing revolution that had begun in all parts of Vietnam decades before. That elite was fractious and disorganized when the United States took over sponsorship of it from France. Tainted by association with colonial rule, its members were mainly from the landowning and urban upper classes. In stark contrast to the Communists, the governing elite in the Republic of Vietnam (RVN) had no background of common effort, sacrifice, or doctrine to lend cohesion; no sensational victories to capture the imagination; no historical touchstones (like the 1945 August Revolution) or personalities (like Ho Chi Minh) to inspire loyalty; and no party system aside from patronage-based cliques and two experiments (*Can Lao* and *Dan Chu*) with cadre parties. Moreover, it was quite isolated—politically and often physically—from the vast majority of the South's population that lived in rural villages, many of which had been bastions of Viet Minh resistance against the French. Although many honorable and capable individuals served the Saigon government, the political class was internally divided and lacked the momentum of its revolutionary rivals. The Saigon government survived the turbulent 1950s only because the Communists, bent on reconstruction in the North and "political struggle" in the South, refrained from exercising their full potential to bring it down. The Communists certainly had no trouble becoming a serious threat almost as soon as they commenced "armed struggle," thanks as much, in the beginning, to a semi-spontaneous popular revolt as to their own organizational efforts.

This is not to say the Democratic Republic of Vietnam (DRV) was a more just, prosperous, or attractive state than the RVN or that the Communist cause was in some abstract sense more just than that of non-Communists. It is simply to observe that the Communists headed a national organization with roots in the South as well as North and possessed cohesion, discipline, and energy that their opponents lacked. Both North and South were heavily aid dependent, but Hanoi had much greater control than Saigon over how it used the aid it received, and it used that aid more effectively. Thanks to their leadership of the August Revolution and the war against France, the Communists in both North and South also were able to tap patriotic feelings and summon their followers to sacrifice at levels their opponents were never able to match. Within the South, the revolution offered an alternative to the social system propped up by the Saigon government that many poor peasants found attractive. About 1970 a more effective state began to emerge around Nguyen Van Thieu, and this state offered people other than those sweltering in refugee camps a greater degree of personal freedom and material well-being than the one in the North. But the institutional deterioration, collapse of confidence, and political unrest after American withdrawal revealed the RVN's enduring fragility and abject dependence on its patron.

Against that unpromising background U.S. involvement must be credited with placing some very major obstacles in the path of Communist victory. U.S. spending significantly increased the number of people who depended on Saigon's war effort for their careers, social advancement, and income. The expansion of the Army of the Republic of Vietnam (ARVN) drew young men into the ranks of Saigon's military, keeping them out of the People's Liberation Armed Force (PLAF). The fighting drove hundreds of thousands of people from contested areas into refugee camps and squatter settlements where they could be kept under watch. The sheer intensity of combat combined with the Communists' overexertion in 1968 increased the risk of supporting the revolution. Perhaps most importantly, Accelerated Pacification and later land and village government reforms finally attacked the Communists' political sources of support.

For a time the proverbial sea in which revolutionary fish were supposed to swim seemed to dry up. Evidence of this "drought" was provided by the Communists themselves in the offensive of 1972, which relied on main forces led by PAVN regulars to restore village political and guerrilla movements to their former strength. But any impression of profound or permanent improvement in Saigon's political resilience was illusory. Also illusory was the perception that popular support for the revolution had dried up. Political cadres were sometimes cut off from access to the people or were themselves exterminated ("hundreds of thousands of cadres and party members sacrificed their lives or were sent to prison," Le Duc Tho told the Fourth Party Congress in 1976),[7] but it is unlikely that the sentiments of several million people whose families had sacrificed for the revolution since the 1940s had changed much. Significant, too, was the growth in party membership in the South from just 5,000 in 1959 to about 200,000 by war's end. Although this was half the number during the 1960s,[8] it was still forty times the total during the party's "darkest days." The war, long by military standards, was too short by political ones to bring about lasting change in the underlying weaknesses of the Saigon side. Only by ignoring these inconvenient facts—not to mention American global obligations, the declining importance of Indochina in American strategic priorities, the war's impact on the economic and political health of the United States, the military options available to the Communists, and the recuperative potential of revolutionary forces in the South—can one argue that the U.S. "won" the war in 1969–1970 and then let victory slip from its grasp by not providing the support to the Saigon government it had promised.[9]

DOMINO THEORY REVISITED

Unable to claim victory in Indochina, champions of intervention sought justification in other kinds of success elsewhere. As Nixon famously put it in his postwar reflections, "We attained part of our goal. We preserved the freedom of our friends and allies for more than a decade. More important, by holding off the North Vietnamese until the mid-1970s, the region's developing countries—some of which became spectacular economic successes—won valuable time to consolidate their own non-Communist governments."[10] In other words, the dominoes did not fall because, and only because, the United States intervened in South Vietnam. One reason American leaders believed this was because prominent Southeast Asians, particularly Singapore's Lee Kwan Yew, told them it was true. "Asian statesmen had good reason for their opinions," wrote Lyndon Johnson, particularly for the view that the 1965 coup which preempted a Communist takeover in Indonesia "probably never would have occurred if the situation to the north, in Southeast Asia had been different—that is, if the United States had not taken a stand in Vietnam."[11]

Nixon, Johnson, and other champions of American policy offered this view unencumbered by doubt or evidence. For a rare attempt to support it one can turn to Mark Moyar's book, *Triumph Forsaken*.[12] The basic facts that Moyar recounts are not in dispute: American presidents from Truman onward believed China and the DRV were determined to extend Communism into Southeast Asia, and they feared that South Vietnam's fall would lead to the fall of non-Communist governments in the region or their appeasement of China, curbing Western access to the region.[13] Southeast Asia's anti-Communist leaders endorsed American intervention in South Vietnam in the belief that this would help to blunt Communist subversion in their own countries. American and Southeast Asian anti-Communists thought this way because Indonesia, Thailand, Malaysia, Burma, and the Philippines had indigenous Communist parties with ties to China. Of these countries, the most important to the strategic interests of the United States, Japan, and the West was Indonesia, which contained half of the region's population and where the Indonesian Communist Party (PKI) had three million members plus a large following in affiliated mass organizations. And finally, although there is disagreement among scholars over the murky details, in 1965 Indonesia's President Sukarno was developing closer relations with the PKI and with China—developments that the coup reversed.

More problematically, Moyar argues that "the dominoes were very vulnerable to toppling." Southeast Asia's anti-Communists were so weak internally, he writes, that South Vietnam's defeat or an American pullout would have forced them to "bow to China or face destruction." Burma, the Philippines, and Malaysia, according to Moyar, all faced dangerous Communist insurgencies in the 1960s that China supported, as did Thailand, which shares a border with Laos and Cambodia. Moyar conjectures that the Thai government, with a tradition of bending before the prevailing wind, almost certainly would have accommodated China rather than face defeat in a Chinese-supported insurgency. After Thailand, other dominoes probably would have fallen as well. The argument echoes Lee Kwan Yew, who predicted that "Thailand would change sides and Malaysia would be put through the mincing machine of guerrilla insurgency. After that, with fraternal Communist parties in control, the Communists would cut our throats in Singapore. The Chinese army would not have to march into Southeast Asia."[14] As for Indonesia, Moyar maintains that American intervention in Vietnam encouraged the generals to stage the coup that destroyed the PKI, preempting a Communist takeover, and he cites statements made by Indonesian leaders years after the coup that are consistent with this interpretation.[15] Last, American intervention exacerbated the Sino-Soviet split and Sino-Vietnamese tensions, further helping to prevent dominoes from falling after 1975.

The argument, while plausible on its surface, crumbles on close examination. Take for example the implicit premise that going to war in 1965 was the only tenable option for the United States because only large-scale intervention in Vietnam could persuade leaders in the "domino" countries that the American commitment to them was reliable. The premise ignores the insight that states generally prefer to "balance" (align with others against the dominant threat) than to "bandwagon" (bend to the will of that threat) if the former is at all possible. The reason is obvious: it is safer "to join with those who cannot readily dominate their allies, in order to avoid being dominated by those who can."[16] In Southeast Asia the alignment least likely to jeopardize the survival of the weak states bordering China was with the United States (or Soviet Union in the case of the DRV), not because the United States was less powerful than China but because it was distant. Is it credible that Thailand's viscerally anti-Communist rulers would have chosen to "bow to China" if the U.S. had offered to defend them rather than South Vietnam? CIA Director Richard Helms did not think so and told President Johnson as much in a memo dated September 1967.[17] In fact Thailand did commit itself more than any other Southeast Asian state to the American project (thus balancing with the U.S.) even before the United States reassured it with the Rusk-Thanat agreement of 1962. Intervention in Vietnam was not needed to establish the credibility of the U.S. guarantee to Thailand, and that guarantee reassured the other non-communist states of Southeast Asia.

A second problem involves the domino theory's confident assertions about China's intentions and capabilities. The intentions of a government are notoriously hard to know, as leaders disagree on goals and means and adjust these in response to events as they unfold. Defining intentions is also a political matter, even in a system as focused on one man as China's in the 1960s. Mao Zedong harbored a desire to see Communism spread, but his country's ability to implement that wish was limited. China in the 1960s was a very poor place, absorbed in its own revolutionary transformation and industrialization. Recognizing China's weakness, preoccupied by domestic affairs and burned by the experience of the Korean War, Chinese leaders were not particularly adventuresome. China studiously avoided provoking American retaliation, counseled Hanoi to do the same, and increased support to other Communist parties in Southeast Asia after 1965 in reaction to American moves. Size disparities, geographic propinquity, and the ethnic Chinese presence across Southeast Asia made China an existential threat to small countries on its border, but the American intervention in Vietnam far exceeded what was needed to deter Beijing from giving anything more than modest support and encouragement to "fraternal parties" outside Indochina.[18]

A third problem is the assumption that Vietnam and China were, and would have remained, collaborators in the spread of Communism in Southeast Asia had the United States not intervened. This ignores Hanoi's distrust of both Moscow and Beijing from 1954 onward, alienation from China's Cultural Revolution in the late 1960s, and dogged effort to maintain freedom of action.[19] It also ignores the contradiction between Hanoi's aspirations in Indochina and the extension of Chinese influence into Southeast Asia. Ideological similarity did not prevent China and Vietnam from parting ways even before the war was over, and Vietnam subsequently regarded China, as it traditionally had done, as the main threat to its security. Over the long run, national interest trumps internationalist sentiment.[20] If stopping Chinese expansionism in Southeast Asia were truly the goal of American policy, the most cost effective American strategy would have been to insist upon implementation of the Geneva Agreements procedures for reunification, even if that resulted in reunification under Communist rule, and then encourage the Vietnamese appetite for independence. Such a strategy was not politically feasible for the United States during the

Cold War, but it no longer looked so shocking an idea when Washington established diplomatic relations with Hanoi in 1997.[21]

What about the effect of the war on the region's economic growth (leaving Indochina aside)? This was almost certainly positive, as American military spending and Cold War-motivated openness to trade and investment stimulated Southeast Asia's economic growth, much as they had done for Europe and Japan.[22] Japan responded to this growth by increasing its investments to take advantage of the region's low production costs. But wartime developments were far from being the only factors accounting for postwar growth. The vaunted boom in Southeast Asia was a phenomenon of the 1980s, and its foundations lay more in political adjustments to economic crisis after the war than in the war period. Thus for example in Indonesia it was the collapse of oil prices in 1980–1981 and again in 1986, and in Thailand a severe downturn in the mid-1980s, not the war, that jarred governments to adopt the export-oriented reforms which fueled the "miracles" of the eighties and nineties.

The war's impact on countries of the region (apart from Laos, Cambodia, and Vietnam) was also much more complicated—and less impressive—than suggested by domino theorists. To start with the critical case, events in Indonesia had a dynamic of their own, independent of what was happening in Vietnam. The PKI owed its influence in the early 1960s more to Sukarno's need of support to counterbalance the military than because of its domestic strength or ties to China. The party, moreover, was ideologically independent, not a "pro-Beijing" party that took orders from China. That distinction belonged to a tiny band of zealots with a following in Indonesia's ethnic Chinese community called Partindo. At least some American officials, closer to the flow of intelligence than the presidents they served, were not very concerned about the PKI because the anti-Communist military was so clearly capable of suppressing it once Sukarno was gone.[23] And indeed when the coup came in 1965 the military wiped out the PKI and orchestrated the slaughter of hundreds of thousands of alleged PKI members, literally exterminating the party and many of its sympathizers in a matter of months.[24] The apparent trigger of that coup was an attempt to assassinate top military leaders by a cabal calling itself the "September 30th Movement," which was led by a battalion commander in Sukarno's bodyguard. The attempt succeeded in killing six generals plus a hapless lieutenant. It stretches credulity to believe that absent American intervention in Vietnam the Indonesian generals would have done nothing in reaction, whether to save their lives and careers or to seize this event as pretext to crush the PKI.

In fact American policymakers, stung by the failure of a coup attempt they had covertly supported in 1958, had been laboring for years to prepare the Indonesian military for a showdown with the PKI. In January 1959 the National Security Council had issued a "Statement of U.S. Policy on Indonesia" that laid down a long-range strategy to make Indonesia "friendly to the West, with the will and ability to resist Communism from within and without."[25] Among the Statement's many recommendations was one to "Give priority treatment to requests for assistance in programs and projects which offer opportunities to isolate the PKI, drive it into positions of open opposition to the Indonesian Government, thereby creating grounds for repressive measures politically justifiable in terms of Indonesian national self-interest."[26] American military aid to the Indonesian army subsequently ballooned (the navy and air force were less cooperative and received much less aid). The Indonesian army high command, spurred by Sukarno's failing health and PKI demands to establish a citizen militia with PKI political officers, began contingency planning for a strike against PKI in January 1965.[27] The September 30th Movement, which assassinated the officers nine months later, was an inept conspiracy of junior officers with connections to a few top PKI leaders, but it provided all the pretext the generals needed to do what they and their American supporters had been preparing to do for years. Undersecretary of State George Ball, writing just six days after the assassinations and obviously aware of the effort that had gone into coaching the generals to act, omitted any mention of Vietnam from a list of factors (military training, technical assistance, explicit assurances, etc.) that "Over past years . . . should have established clearly in minds [of] Army leaders that U.S. stands behind them if they should need help."[28] To assist the army in hunting down its enemies, the U.S. Embassy in Jakarta helped gather the names of PKI senior cadres and made a fifty million rupiah[29] covert payment to the agency it knew was "still carrying the burden of current repressive efforts. . . ."[30]

The outcome (disregarding moral concerns and alternative conceptions of American interests) was unquestionably a huge strategic windfall for the United States. But it was the Indonesian generals' own readiness and the fortuitous bungling of the September 30th Movement, not the American intervention in Vietnam, that caused the generals to strike. American officials with responsibilities in the area understood this. General Bruce Palmer, Westmoreland's deputy in Vietnam and later Army vice chief of staff, wrote that the Indonesian coup did not occur simply because the United States "had committed its power in Vietnam."[31] Richard Cabot Howland, a foreign-service officer in the U.S. Embassy in Jakarta in 1965–1966, later observed in a classified publication that events leading up to and following the coup had a "uniquely indigenous character," and there was "minimal influence on its outcome that could be ascribed to non-Indonesian factors." The idea that Washington's decision to commit troops to South Vietnam "stiffened the spines of the Indonesian officer corps" was, in Howland's word, a "myth."[32] The coup however did make "the fate of South Vietnam less critical to the attainment of United States objectives in Asia," a thought which began to play a part in Washington debates as early as 1966.[33] For with the biggest domino "safely in the hands of the Indonesian army," Vietnam was less important than it had seemed.[34]

As for Thailand, the domino bordering Laos and Cambodia, the Bangkok government during the 1950s worried more about the political loyalties of Thailand's Chinese and Vietnamese minorities than about the Communist Party of Thailand (CPT). The generals who took power in December 1957, though strongly conservative, did not at first share Washington's sense of urgency about a Communist threat. But they soon began playing that card to obtain increases in economic assistance, and in 1960–1961 the Thai quietly allowed the United States to begin using Thai territory for clandestine operations in Laos. This behavior suggests anything but a readiness on Thailand's part to shift allegiance to China and "fall without an insurgency."[35] Thai leaders were nervous and sought reassurance, but if they were of a mind to bend with the prevailing wind they evidently calculated that the wind was American long before the buildup of 1965 in Vietnam.

The CPT moreover did not launch its armed struggle until August 1965, *after* the American buildup in Vietnam had begun. Insurgent numbers and weapons then grew because the DRV and China, having trained a few CPT cadres in the late 1950s, increased support to the insurgency in retaliation for Thai involvement in Laos and support of U.S. intervention. Nonetheless, according to General Saiyud Kerdphol, the founder of Thailand's Communist Suppression Operations Command, "for the first eleven years of the war the insurgents proved unable to expand their operations and influence more than a marginal distance from their jungle redoubts."[36] The development of huge U.S. military bases on Thai soil and the use of Thailand for rest and recreation by American troops meanwhile exacerbated corruption in the Thai government and tensions in Thai society. Popular resentment against the American-backed government of Field Marshal Thanom Kittikachorn, which had authorized the bases, boiled over in a student-led popular rebellion in October 1973, and students fled to the jungles to collaborate with the CPT when the military staged another coup in 1976. "The immediate effect of this strengthening of communist infrastructure [was] . . . the beginning of political infiltration and subversion in several new areas."[37] Upheavals to which the American presence was a contributing factor thus gave the insurgency a new lease on life *after* the Vietnam War's end. How did all this constitute "buying time" for the Thai government to consolidate itself?

Fortunately for the United States, Thailand proved to be much more resistant to the corrosive influences of friends and foes alike than were its Indochinese neighbors. This was because Thailand was utterly unlike South Vietnam in terms of vulnerability to "toppling." It was a united not a divided country; in King Bhumipol Adulyadej it had a monarch with personal prestige sufficient to provide stability despite the coups; the CPT handicapped itself with a largely ethnic Chinese and Sino-Thai leadership; and Thailand had no history of colonial rule for the CPT or any other political movement to exploit for revolutionary purposes. What Thailand lacked, if "lack" is the word, was a public that was willing after 1973 to put up with rule by a corrupt military junta the United States had backed to the hilt. In May 1975, the same month Saigon fell, Thailand's civilian government asked the U.S. to remove all American combat forces and aircraft from Thai soil by 1976. Thai leaders feared Hanoi's retribution for Thailand's collusion in the bombing of North Vietnam, but they soon discovered, as General Kerdphol put it, that "the Vietnamese were really in no position for such a campaign, even had that been their intention, because their own domestic situation proved far more chaotic than earlier supposed."[38]

The Thai insurgency, which peaked in 1978, began collapsing when the Vietnamese invaded Cambodia in 1979, triggering a split within the CPT between its pro-Chinese and pro-Vietnamese factions and the ejection of the pro-Chinese faction from Laos. China also cut back its support of that faction to obtain the Thai government's aid in opposing the Vietnamese occupation of Cambodia. In thus weakening the Thai insurgency China and Vietnam demonstrated influence over its ebb and flow, but equally important causes of its demise were the disillusionment and surrender of student activists who had joined in 1976, the lack of a significant base of popular support for revolution, and a smart, politically-oriented counterinsurgency program devised by the Thai themselves. Ironically, it was American withdrawal from Vietnam and parallel decrease of material support to Thailand that "forced" the Thai to shift from an aid-dependent, "dysfunctional" and "hard" military counterinsurgency program to the ultimately effective one focused on development and political reconciliation.[39] Clearly, Thailand's leaders were determined and able to combat the insurgency rather than to "fall" either to it or to pressures from China.

The other countries of Southeast Asia were even less susceptible to "toppling" than Thailand. In Malaysia ("Malaya" until federation in 1963), the insurgency led by the Communist Party of Malaya (CPM) was, as noted in chapter 3, an essentially ethnic Chinese minority movement, which severely limited its appeal. The "Emergency" as the insurgency was called officially ended in July 1960 and, although a vestigial Communist force survived in the jungle straddling the Thai-Malaysian border, Prime Minister Tunku Abdul Rahman felt sufficiently confident to send "all the arms, war materials and equipment we used against the Communists in Malaya" to South Vietnam.[40] This was five years before the American intervention in Vietnam which, according to the domino theory, saved the Tunku's government from "toppling."

In the Philippines, the Philippine Communist Party's rural-based military wing, the Hukbong Mapagpalaya ng Bayan, was nearly exterminated with American help by 1957. The PCP subsequently turned its attention toward urban students and intelligentsia and enjoyed some success after 1963, but the PCP then split into two groups, one of which, a Maoist faction, formed the New People's Army in 1969. About the same time, a separate conflict flared between Muslims and Christians in southern Mindanao. The spread of violence and lawlessness provided the justification for President Ferdinand Marcos to declare martial law in 1972, a move that accelerated the radicalization of university students and provoked the ire of urban middle classes. The Philippine economy also stagnated, as Marcos fell back on "crony capitalism" to build a political base that stifled growth. Meanwhile, American backing of Marcos and use of Clark Air Base and Subic Bay to support operations in Vietnam provoked a nationalist backlash, which contributed to the rise of "people power" and the overthrow of Marcos in 1986. Post-Marcos leaders struggled with only partial success to reestablish a stable democracy and split over whether to continue the Philippines' "special" relationship with the United States. In 1991, shortly after an eruption of Mt. Pinatubo forced the evacuation of Clark, the Philippine Senate in a 12-11 vote rejected a treaty that would have extended American use of Subic. In brief, the American intervention in Vietnam was largely irrelevant to Philippine security and economic performance. It did however motivate the United States to interfere in Philippine politics in ways that prolonged the country's instability and alienated the nationalistic urban middle classes. One result was to weaken a strategic relationship that had been a linchpin of American ability to project power into the Pacific and Indian Oceans for nearly a century.[41]

To summarize, the thesis that American intervention in Vietnam saved the rest of Southeast Asia from otherwise certain Communist expansion is crude, superficial, and ignorant of Southeast Asian realities. The key non-Communist Southeast Asian states were not the pushovers the domino theory presumed them to be. The United States took steps long before 1965, most notably in Thailand and Indonesia, that proved efficacious in securing the alignment of these states with the West. The economic spillover was favorable but not key to the region's postwar growth, and some side effects were destabilizing. Indeed, by expanding American bases in Thailand and the Philippines to support the war in Indochina the U.S. aggravated political tensions and stoked opposition to American-backed governments in these countries. Thus, just as U.S. intervention imposed a Cold War template on the travails of Vietnam, Laos, and Cambodia, so did it have a polarizing effect on the domestic politics of other countries in the region, causing instability and negative reverberations for American security interests after the war's end. The dominoes that did "fall," Laos and Cambodia, might have done so regardless of American actions, but American intervention in both countries assured the growth of Communist insurgencies in each. Only a "pernicious rewriting of history," as another assessment has put it, sustains the idea that U.S. military intervention helped non-Communist Southeast Asian governments consolidate themselves and establish the foundations of future growth. [42]

THE "LESSONS"

A number of lessons for the United States have been drawn from the Second Indochina War. Regarding the American effort as a failure, Americans generally extracted lessons they believed would avoid similar situations—or bring a better result—in future. In 1984 Caspar Weinberger, Ronald Reagan's secretary of defense, enunciated six "tests" the U.S. should apply when deciding whether to send combat forces abroad. Noting that indiscriminate use of force in pursuit of diplomatic objectives "would surely plunge us headlong into the sort of domestic turmoil we experienced during the Vietnam war," the tests stipulated that the United States should use force abroad only for vital American national interests; with the support of Congress and the American people; when the country is willing to commit itself "wholeheartedly, and with the clear intention of winning; with clearly defined political and military objectives; after realistic assessment of the forces needed to achieve those objectives; and as a last resort." The purpose of the tests was to guard against what many American officials regarded as the key error in Indochina, the "gradualist incremental approach" that had sucked American forces "inexorably into an endless morass" where the U.S. had no vital national interest.[43] Famously restated by General Colin Powell, who had served as a field grade officer in Vietnam before becoming chairman of the Joint Chiefs of Staff and President George W. Bush's secretary of state, the criteria came to be known as the "Powell Doctrine." Powell put an accent on the need for overwhelming force from the start and a clear exit strategy while denying there could be any "fixed set of rules." If "Vietnam" taught the United States anything, Powell wrote, it was that American forces should be sent into "murky, unpredictable circumstances" only after tough questions had been given concrete, thorough, and reliable answers.[44]

More narrowly, American officers who fought mainly PAVN units in conventional combat believed that the root cause of war was North Vietnam. It followed that the United States should have invaded the North or at least have cut the North's access to the South by naval and ground blockade, permitting the protected regimes to resolve their internal problems by themselves.[45] This conclusion suggested what one alternative to the "gradualist incremental approach" might have been. However, officials charged with responsibility for the "other war" as exemplified by "accelerated pacification" and Vietnamization argued that these programs were turning the political tide and should have had higher priority from the beginning.[46] Somewhat different conclusions were drawn by ex-President Nixon, who told NBC's "Meet the Press" in April 1988 "that his greatest mistake as President was . . . his failure to bomb and mine North Vietnam early in 1969 as he later did in 1972." "If we had done that then," he said, "I think we would have ended the war in 1969 rather than in 1973." Critics of the press held that better management of the media was needed to maintain public support. Behind all of these arguments lay the belief that U.S. involvement, if conducted differently, could have brought a favorable, or at least better, result. Contrarily, three-quarters of the people who came to maturity (and, for males to draft eligibility) during the war years believed it had been a mistake to intervene in the first place and remained deeply skeptical of interventionism of any kind.[47] This lesson became encapsulated in the phrase "no more Vietnams."

Strategists in Hanoi naturally assessed the war quite differently. The Communist party's legitimacy hinged on justifying the enormous sacrifices made by the people in not one war but two and in three countries not one. The only permissible broad conclusions were that there had been no alternative to fighting this war or to the way it had been fought. A book published in Hanoi in 1995 for "internal distribution only" devoted 192 pages to "lessons of experience," which were mostly reasons why the Communists won a war they considered unavoidable. [48] The gist of these reasons were evident in the eight categories into which the book organized them: determination to win; a creative, independent and self-reliant strategy; creative conduct of people's war; nationwide organization of forces to strike the enemy; a sturdy rear area and firm revolutionary bases; unity and alliance with the Lao and Cambodian peoples; international solidarity to mobilize the (communist) strength of the era; and reliance on the development of human factors (i.e., motivation). Along with praising what the party leadership had done right the book acknowledged "errors and shortcomings" of a "subjective" nature, or failures of resolve or judgment. The party, it said, underestimated the damage done to revolutionary forces in the South in 1955–1958 and in the two years following the 1968 Tet Offensive. The party made a similar but less harmful error in assessing the balance on the eve of the 1972 spring offensive and again was slow to adjust. In each of these episodes an inaccurate assessment of the balance of forces caused the party to be slow in formulating an effective response.[49] These errors might suggest a structural bias toward over-optimism in party decision-making, but if that was a lesson drawn in Hanoi the book did not say so. A different kind of error was the failure to appreciate sooner what "ruinous results" the "wicked" Pol Pot clique would bring to Cambodia.[50] Sometimes rocky relations with Moscow and Beijing reinforced the lesson first learned at Geneva in 1954 that "every communist party has prime responsibility for the destiny of its own people," a discrete way of saying that great power allies could be trusted only insofar as interests coincided although their support was indispensable.[51] But overshadowing all was the axiom that there had been no choice but war: "Only if the South were liberated from the violent repression of American imperialism and its puppets could we put an end to the sorrow and anger of our people, protect the North, and bring the revolution to all of the country. . . . There was no other path than this path. There was no possibility of 'hiding underground' in wait for an opportunity to come from outside; nor was there a possibility that 'peaceful competition' between the two systems might in time liberate the South."[52] The lessons drawn by the Vietnamese Communists were thus applicable to the war they had fought and none other. They therefore had no lessons to guide them, or perhaps were misguided by what seemed confirmation of their invincibility, when they sent ten PAVN divisions into the "murky, unpredictable place" that was Cambodia in December 1978.

Whether lessons from this war were worth applying elsewhere is properly the subject of a different book. The sorting out of factors that are unique from those that may be duplicated in other times and places is in any case an endless task. The present work more modestly suggests that in Indochina the United States made commitments out of proportion to its interests. This was done in the belief that maintaining the credibility of commitments required defending them everywhere. But placing credibility at stake in a region that was not vital to U.S. interests undermined the conviction of the American people that the commitment had to be kept. Neither U.S. enemies, U.S. allies, nor its own people believed that the United States, for the sake of Indochina, would long sacrifice its effectiveness in other parts of the world. Thus, an appearance of unconditional commitment to the Saigon regime—to which the United States was never bound by formal treaty or alliance—actually undermined U.S. credibility.

The United States also exposed itself to the charge of hypocrisy by declaring support for the South's self-determination but then opposing the referendum that would have allowed South Vietnamese to express themselves on the question of reunification. And the U.S. trapped itself by supporting governments in Saigon that lacked the confidence of their own people. Unstinting support of such groups required the United States to involve itself in stabilizing fragile governments and in "nation-building," which cast the United States in a quasi-colonial role in the eyes of the Vietnamese and of the world. Having adopted chronically weak clients to fight a long-established, well-organized, deeply entrenched adversary, the United States had to substitute its own resources and purpose for those of the regimes it purported to defend. These in turn were robbed of initiative and stigmatized by dependency. Under the circumstances, the United States could not intervene without perpetuating conditions that U.S.

leaders believed required them to intervene in the first place. Finally, for reasons that lie outside the scope of this study, a succession of U.S. leaders grossly miscalculated the weight of the first war on the trajectory of the second, the efficacy of military power, the relevance and transformative capacity of American advice, and the skill, adaptability, and determination of the enemy.

THE COST

The cost was extremely high. For the United States, the direct budgetary cost of the war has been variously estimated at between $112 billion and $155 billion. This spending was about 9 percent of the American gross domestic product (GDP) at the height of the war, moderate compared with the 37 percent of GDP spent during the peak of World War II and 14 percent during the Korean War but over twice the 4.4 percent allocated for the Iraq War in 2008.[53] Other and future costs (e.g., sacrificed earnings, veterans benefits, war-related recession) have been estimated to bring the grand total as high as $925 billion.[54] Damaging in a different way was the political cost of rancor between the executive and legislative branches over the war-making powers of the president and the alienation of a generation from its government. And the United States had its dead: 47,406 killed in action and 10,787 dead from non-combat causes—a total of 58,193. The U.S. also had 2,477 soldiers missing in action, who with exceedingly few exceptions could be presumed dead.[55] (With discovery of remains since war's end, the number of MIAs still unaccounted for as of December 2006 had dropped to 1,791). Also dead were 4,407 troops from South Korea, 468 from Australia and New Zealand, and 351 from Thailand. Among Hanoi's allies, about 15,000 Soviet armed forces personnel had served in Indochina,[56] mostly servicing the Soviet Union's military assistance program. After the Cold War, U.S. investigators found evidence in Russian archives that twenty-one Soviet military personnel were still missing in action as of 2000.[57] China, which sent a total of some 320,000 military-related personnel to work on transportation lines and antiaircraft batteries, lost 1,100 killed and 4,200 wounded.[58]

These losses pale beside those suffered by the countries of Indochina.[59] U.S. government sources estimated the total number of Vietnamese Communist troops killed in action from 1961 through 1975 at 1,027,085,[60] a figure Pentagon officials suggested may be inflated as much as 30 percent. Yet Hanoi's Ministry of Labor, War Invalids and Social Affairs estimated Communist military deaths from 1954 to 1975 at 1.1 million.[61] Post-war estimates of ARVN casualties indicate 254,257 dead, giving a total Vietnamese combatant deaths of 1,281,342 or more. In addition, the Pentagon estimated 65,000 civilian war deaths in the North and 522,000 in the South for a total of 587,000,[62] which would imply a Pentagon estimate of total Vietnamese war dead, civilian and military, of 1,868,342. A study using the analytical tools of modern demography, however, estimated total civilian and military war deaths from 1965 to 1975 for all of Vietnam in the range of 791,000 to 1,141,000,[63] yielding a mid-point of 966,000, half the Pentagon estimate and less than one third of the 3.1 million total (two million civilians and 1.1 million military, counting from 1954) claimed by the Vietnamese government. Still, a loss of one million was "proportionally 100 times greater than that suffered by the United States."[64]

Given the uncertain reliability of global figures, slivers of data sometimes provide more telling snapshots: RVN and U.S. military hospitals admitted an average of 57,000 civilian war-related casualties per year from 1968 to 1972,[65] a toll of wounded that left the South at war's end with 83,000 amputees. Dead parents left 800,000 orphans.[66] This, the second war, was much more lethal than the first, too: in the eleven provinces of southern Trung Bo, 5.6 times as many combatants on the revolutionary side alone died fighting the U.S. as died fighting France.[67]

Needless to say, both the Communist and non-Communist sides had countless thousands missing in action as well, of whom a full and accurate accounting can never be made. Hanoi has claimed 300,000 MIAs on the revolutionary side, without clarifying what it means by "MIA" or how these have been counted. Not even a crude estimate is available for the number of ARVN troops who should be considered missing in action and presumed dead not deserted, but there were undoubtedly many. Roughly 150,000 South Vietnamese, mostly former RVN officials, military officers and their dependents, fled within weeks of Saigon's fall to live in exile abroad.

In addition to the human cost the physical destruction was horrendous, though distributed differently between regions. In the North the bombing made railroads impassable and turned its roads into cratered tracks, at least for short periods. Hanoi and Haiphong were spared, but twenty-nine of thirty provincial capitals were heavily damaged, and nine were completely leveled.[68] Power stations, bridges, and petroleum storage tanks were favorite targets. In the South bombs and artillery fell mostly in rural areas rather than on cities, roads, and facilities needed for postwar reconstruction, leaving the South in better position than the North to recover when the war was over. But it was in the South that heavy use was made of chemical defoliants. Agent Orange, the highly toxic chemical linked to cancer and birth defects, was sprayed on 3.2 percent of the South's cropland and 46.4 percent of the forest. It was in the South, too, that the U.S. dropped 400,000 tons of napalm.[69] Though not on a par with the world wars or China's civil wars in terms of absolute severity, the period from 1965 to 1975 for Vietnam alone has been judged the fourth most severe in proportional impact on the society involved of all such wars since 1816. In battle deaths per capita, this war ranked sixth, while the period 1960 to 1965 ranked seventh among civil wars.[70]

The death and destruction were the price Vietnam paid for its reunification, which came swiftly once the war was over. Hanoi leaders themselves had not anticipated making this decision so soon. Le Duan told Zhou Enlai in June 1973 that whatever government was agreed to in negotiations "can exist for ten or fifteen years. And then the name can be changed. So we are not in a hurry to turn South Vietnam into a socialist entity." Pham Van Dong chimed in to say that meanwhile Hanoi would "highlight" the role of the NLF and the Provisional Revolutionary Government of South Vietnam (PRG) without compromising the party's leadership.[71] But that was before the Communists' total triumph in 1975 swept aside all obstacles to reunification at Hanoi's pleasure. Instead of installing the PRG as the government of the South—a task that vastly exceeded the PRG's administrative capabilities—the party placed the larger towns and cities under military management committees in accordance with a plan drawn up shortly before Saigon fell.[72] The party secretariat sent a directive to Southern party organs in April 1975 explaining how People's Revolutionary Committees dominated by party cadres were to take over in other "newly liberated areas" and use existing RVN personnel to run essential services.[73] In mid-1975 the party decided to erase all remaining barriers between North and South forthwith. The South, party leaders believed, needed to commence "socialist transformation" immediately to narrow inter-regional differences, address urgent economic needs of both regions, and gird the country for confrontation with China.[74] The NLF, the Vietnam Alliance of National Democratic and Peace Forces (VANDPF) and lesser front organizations merged with the Vietnam Fatherland Front, the national front headquartered in Hanoi. Elections for a National Assembly with 492 seats almost equally divided between North and South took place in April 1976, and formal unification as the Socialist Republic of Vietnam (SRV) followed in July. At its Fourth National Congress in December, the Lao Dong Party ceremonially took its Southern branch, the People's Revolutionary Party, back into the fold and renamed itself the Vietnam Communist Party.

The rapid pace of reunification displeased non-Communist Southerners who had taken the NLF's ten-point program at face value ("a largely liberal and democratic regime," an "independent and sovereign economy," etc.). Truong Nhu Tang, the NLF's disillusioned ex-minister of justice, went into exile to write *A Viet Cong Memoir*, evidently surprised to learn that one had to be a Communist party member to hold high position in a Communist state. Most non-Communist leaders of the NLF and PRG who made peace with the new order were given sinecures or comfortable retirement. Party members of the NLF and PRG, however, suffered no loss of status for their service in the South. On the contrary, they did rather well from it: Nguyen Huu Tho, founding president of the NLF, became vice-president of the SRV; Madame Nguyen Thi Binh, PRG foreign minister, served as SRV education minister before following Tho into the vice-presidency; Huynh Tan Phat, ex-NLF general secretary and PRG premier, became SRV vice-premier; Nguyen Van Hieu, also an ex-NLF general secretary and a chief NLF diplomat, became SRV minister of culture; PLAF officers adopted PAVN insignia; and so on. The party, not "the North," won the war in Vietnam.

As for Laos, information is too fragmentary to do more than suggest damage proportional to that experienced by Vietnam.[75] The heavily bombed Ho Chi Minh Trail, after all, passed through eastern Laos, and the area was not unpopulated. One survey of data on war deaths in all wars since 1945 notes that

> It may at times be difficult for readers to grasp the meaning of the mid-range level of deaths when the numbers do not appear to be extremely high. The following example is helpful. Between 1967–68 and 1972, deaths in Laos caused by local combat and daily U.S. bombing from the air averaged 30 people per day, or around 11,000 per year. That level of killing was maintained for at least four years. However, if one compares the size of the Laotian population and that of the United States and applies a proportionate rate of deaths to the U.S. population at the time, that would amount to 3,000 people per day, or 4.38 million people in four years.[76]

But Laos was spared a cataclysmic last offensive by the ceasefire and neutral coalition government of 1973. The transition to Communist rule was relatively peaceful, as the Pathet Lao promoted local seizures of power by "people's committees" and elections to engineer the abdication of King Savang Vatthana and the installation of a People's Democratic Republic on December 2, 1975. By that time over 25,000 ethnic Lao and 30,000 Hmong had fled across the Mekong River into Thailand, starting an exodus that would continue for years.[77] Guided and nurtured by North Vietnam in war, the Pathet Lao became a docile client of Hanoi in peace.

In Cambodia the victorious Khmer Rouge, vengeful toward former enemies, distrustful of former friends, and unsure of their hold on power, launched a reign of terror that shortened the lives of perhaps a quarter of Cambodia's seven million people. Estimates of deaths directly attributable to the Khmer Rouge vary widely, from the Khmer Rouge's own admission of 20,000 to more than three million claimed by the Vietnamese. But there is great uncertainty about the number of deaths due to execution compared with war-related mortality due to American bombing, civil war, famine, overwork, collapse of health care, etc. Cambodia specialists estimate that for the entire decade of the 1970s the number of "excess deaths" (by unnatural causes) was from 740,000[78] to 1.7 million.[79] A more recent demographic accounting using 1992 electoral lists to "reconstruct" the Khmer population estimates 2.2 to 2.8 million excess deaths in 1970-79, of which 60 percent were violent.[80]

Suspecting the Vietnamese of seeking dominion over Cambodia, the Khmer Rouge rebuffed Vietnamese efforts to find a basis for postwar cooperation and turned for help to China. The Khmer Rouge also demanded the return of territories Vietnam had occupied during its "southward march" in the eighteenth and nineteenth centuries. The Second Indochina War was only days over when the Khmer Rouge seized several Vietnamese-held islands and sent military probes into the Mekong delta. The Vietnamese quickly beat back these challenges, but in 1977 the Khmer Rouge resumed attacks along the border and slaughtered hundreds of Vietnamese civilians, and the fighting escalated during 1978. Hanoi, closely aligned with the Soviet Union, moved to terminate the threat of a Chinese-backed regime in Phnom Penh by sponsoring a Cambodian resistance organization to cover an invasion, which took place in December. China in turn mounted a punitive attack on Vietnam in February 1979 and began a long campaign, with the approval of the United States and Thailand, to "bleed" Vietnam by means of diplomatic isolation and arms supplies for Khmer resistance forces, which included the Khmer Rouge. Thus, for a third time since World War II, Indochina was swept into a vortex of conflict with Vietnam at the center.

NOTES

1. Interview with Colonel Hoang Co Quang, Hanoi, April 21, 1984.

2. Quoted in Robert S. McNamara, *In Retrospect: The Tragedy and Lessons of Vietnam* (New York: Random House, 1997), 262.

3. Mao Zedong and Pham Van Dong, Hoang Van Hoan, Beijing, October 5, 1964, in "77 Conversations between Chinese and Foreign Leaders on the Wars in Indochina, 1964–1977," ed. Odd Arne Westad et al. (Washington, D.C.: Cold War International History Project, Working Paper No. 22, May 1998), 76.

4. Which Johnson was loathe to do. See Ilya V. Gaiduk, *The Soviet Union and the Vietnam War* (Chicago: Ivan R. Dee, 1996), 176.

5. U.S. House of Representatives, Special Subcommittee on National Defense Posture, "Review of the Vietnam Conflict and Its Impact on U.S. Military Commitments Abroad" (August 24, 1968), 54.

6. Henry Kissinger, *Ending the Vietnam War: A* History of America's involvement in and Extrication from the Vietnam War (New York: Simon & Schuster, 2003), 365.

7. Radio Hanoi broadcast, December 17, 1976, in Foreign Broadcast Information Service, *Daily Report: Asia and the Pacific,* December 26, 1976.

8. Alexander Casella, "Dateline Vietnam: Managing the Peace," *Foreign Policy,* No. 30 (Spring 1978), 172. The official figure for Southern party membership in 1978

was 273,000. *Los Angeles Times*, October 18, 1978. Total party membership in 1976 was 1,533,500.

9. As argued by historian Lewis Sorley, "Could the War Have Been Won?," in *The* Real *Lessons of the Vietnam War: Reflections Twenty-Five Years After the Fall of Saigon*, ed. John Norton Moore and Robert F. Turner (Durham, N.C.: Carolina Academic Press, 2002), 413–418.

10. Richard Nixon, *In the Arena: A Memoir of Victory, Defeat, and Renewal* (New York: Simon and Schuster, 1990), 339–340.

11. Lyndon Johnson, *The Vantage Point* (New York: Holt, Rinehart and Winston, 1971), 357. Also see Kissinger, *Ending the Vietnam War*, 561; and Lee Kwan Yew, *From Third World to First: The Singapore Story: 1965–2000* (New York: HarperCollins, 2000), 452–459, 467.

12. Mark Moyar, *Triumph Forsaken: The Vietnam War, 1954–1965* (New York: Cambridge University Press, 2006), xx–xxi, 375–391. Also see Moyar's comment at hnn.us/roundup/comments/30490.html (accessed August 15, 2007).

13. Not everyone beneath the presidents subscribed to the domino theory, however. For analysis of the "intrabureaucratic battle" over the validity of the theory, see Gareth Porter, *Perils of Dominance* (Berkeley: University of California Press, 2005), 243–254.

14. Lee, *From Third World to First*, 457.

15. In presenting these generals' statements, Moyar does not take into account the high value Indonesian culture places on maintaining interpersonal harmony and the reasons that Indonesian generals might have to please American ears.

16. Stephen M. Walt, *The Origins of Alliances* (Ithaca, N.Y.: Cornell University Press, 1987), 18.

17. Helms's "best guess" about what might follow a Communist victory was that "the present Thai leadership would continue to seek US support. . . . In Malaysia, Burma, the Philippines, and Indonesia, non-Communist political forces now have a clear ascendancy. The will of the present ruling groups to maintain themselves in power, to assert full national independence, and to resist internal subversion would persist despite Communist success in Vietnam. None of these four states would be destined inevitably to fall under Communist control or to be pressured into a vassal relationship with China." Memo from Helms to Johnson in *Lyndon B. Johnson's Vietnam Papers: A Documentary Collection*, ed. David M. Barrett (College Station: Texas A&M University, 1997), 472–473.

18. American desire to spread capitalism and democracy mirrored Mao's dream for Communism, but the U.S. had vastly greater resources of both "hard" and "soft" power than China to materialize its desires. Why should China have succeeded where the U.S. has repeatedly failed?

19. On Hanoi's efforts to keep great power allies at arms length, see W. R. Smyser, *The Independent Vietnamese* (Athens: Ohio University Center for International Studies, 1980). Smyser was an assistant to Kissinger.

20. In March 1971 Zhou Enlai, speaking to Le Duan and Pham Van Dong about weapons supplied via Vietnam and Laos to the Communist Party of Thailand, said, "We hold that support to the people's revolutionary struggles cannot be sacrificed for the sake of relations between governments. Only traitors do that." Yet in 1979

that is exactly the sacrifice China made when it curtailed support to the CPT to gain access through Thailand to supply the Khmer Rouge resistance against the Vietnamese in Cambodia. "Discussions between Zhou Enlai, Le Duan and Pham Van Dong," 03/07/1971, Cold War International History Project, Virtual Archive, The Wilson Center.

21. As Marc Jason Gilbert suggests in his "Introduction," in *Why the North Won the Vietnam War*, ed. Marc Jason Gilbert (New York: Palgrave, 2002), 12–13.

22. This was pointed out to me by Adam Fforde and Markus Taussig in personal communication, December 12, 2006.

23. Gareth Porter, *Perils of Dominance: Imbalance of Power and the Road to War in Vietnam* (Berkeley: University of California Press, 2005), 239, 247.

24. The Indonesian Parliament in 2004 authorized a Truth and Reconciliation Commission modeled after that of South Africa to investigate this slaughter and other human rights abuses. The Constitutional Court declared the law unconstitutional in December 2006. Indonesian military leaders, not surprisingly, preferred to bury the past.

25. NSC 5901, February 3, 1959, in Department of State, *Foreign Relations of the United States, 1958–1960, Volume 17 Indonesia* (Washington, D.C.: U.S. Government Printing Office, 1994), 341–342.

26. NSC 5901, 343.

27. John Roosa, *Pretext for Mass Murder: The September 30th Movement and Suharto's Coup d'État in Indonesia* (Madison: University of Wisconsin Press, 2006), 188–189. My interpretation in this paragraph is similar to the far more detailed account in Roosa, 176–201.

28. Telegram from Department of State to the Embassy in Indonesia, October 6, 1965, in Department of State, *Foreign Relations of the United States, 1964–68, Volume 26: Indonesia; Malaysia-Singapore; Philippines* (Washington, D.C.: U.S. Government Printing Office, 2001), 309.

29. This took place just days before the issuance of a New Rupiah and amidst financial upheaval, so the sum's value could have been five hundred or half a million dollars depending on the exchange rate. Ambassador Green's memo to Assistant Secretary of State Bund on December 2, 1965, described the amount as a "comparatively small sum."

30. See National Security Archive bulletin "CIA Stalling State Department Histories," July 27, 2001, with links to the supporting documentation at www.gwu.edu/~nsarchiv/NSAEBB/NSAEBB52 (accessed September 17, 2007).

31. General Bruce Palmer, Jr., *The 25-Year War: America's Military Role in Vietnam* (Lexington: University Press of Kentucky, 1984), 6.

32. Richard Cabot Howland, "The Lessons of the September 30 Affair," *Studies in Intelligence* 14, no. 2 (Fall 1970): 13–29.

33. R. B. Smith, *An International History of the Vietnam War, Vol. III: The Making of a Limited War, 1965–66* (London: Macmillan, 1991), 208, 210.

34. Roosa, *Pretext*, 15.

35. Moyar, *Triumph*, 139.

36. Saiyud Kerdphol, *The Struggle for Thailand: Counter-Insurgency 1965–1985* (Bangkok: S. Research Center Co., Ltd., 1986), 132.

37. Kerphol, *The Struggle for Thailand*, 132.

38. Kerdphol, *The Struggle for Thailand*, 123.

39. Kanok Wongtrangan, "Revolutionary Strategy and Tactics of the Communist Party of Thailand: Change and Persistence" (Bangkok, ca. 1983) ms. in author's possession.

40. Tunku Abdul Rahman Putra, *Looking Back: Monday Musings and Memories* (Kuala Lumpur: Pustaka Antara, 1977), 141. The gift violated the Geneva Agreements, as the Tunku admits in this memoir.

41. Closure of Subic Bay and Clark Field, Filipinos soon realized, left the Philippines exposed to China's expansive claims in the South China Sea. These claims extend into the Philippines' two hundred nautical mile maritime Exclusive Economic Zone and motivated Manila to negotiate a Visiting Forces Agreement with the U.S. The agreement, which facilitates military cooperation but provides no base rights, became effective in 1999. The "China threat" thus caused the Philippines to strengthen its security relationship with the U.S. rather than to appease China.

42. Gareth Porter, "Dominos, Dynamos, and the Vietnam War," *Current History* 94 (December 1995), 411.

43. Caspar Weinberger, "The Uses of Military Power," speech to the National Press Club, Washington, D.C., November 28, 1984. /www.pbs.org/wgbh/pages/frontline/shows/military/force/weinberger.html (accessed September 2, 2007).

44. Colin Powell, "U.S. Forces: Challenges Ahead," *Foreign Affairs* 71, no. 5 (Winter 1992), 38–39. Powell's thoughts were expansion of similar points that had been made by president Ronald Reagan's Secretary of Defense, Caspar Weinberger.

45. The classic statement of this view is Harry G. Summers, Jr., *On Strategy: The Vietnam War in Context* (Carlisle, Pa.: Strategic Studies Institute, U.S. Army War College, April 1981).

46. See for example Robert Komer, "Was There Another Way?," in *Lessons of Vietnam*, ed. W. Scott Thompson and Donald D. Frizzell (New York: Crane, Russak, 1977), 211–223.

47. A Gallup poll for *Newsweek* magazine in 1985 indicated that 63 percent of a national sample and 76 percent of college graduates in the 30–39 age bracket believed the war to have been a "mistake." In answer to the question whether the United States should make greater use of military force abroad, 75 percent of the national sample and ninety percent of the Vietnam era college graduates answered no. See *Newsweek*, April 15, 1985, 37.

48. Tran Van Quang, et al., *Tong ket cuoc khang chien chong My, cuu nuoc: thang loi va bai hoc* [Summing Up the National Salvation War of Resistance against the United States: Victory and Lessons] (Hanoi: NXB Ban chinh tri quoc gia, 1995), 117–309. This volume summarizes the conclusions of the Politburo's War Review Leadership Committee.

49. Tran Van Quang, et al., *Tong ket*, 131.

50. Tran Van Quang, et al., *Tong ket*, 237.

51. Tran Van Quang, et al., *Tong ket*, 250, 254.

52. Tran Van Quang, et al., *Tong ket*, 138.

53. *The Economist*, February 10, 2007, 28.

54. Robert Warren Stevens, *Vain Hopes, Grim Realities: The Economic Consequences of the Vietnam War* (New York: New Viewpoints, 1976), 187.

55. Because of the attention given in the United States to the U.S. missing-in-action (MIAs) and to reports that some were still alive, many Americans believed the number of missing in Vietnam was large by comparison with previous wars. The facts are these: The 78,751 MIAs at the end of World War II represented 27 percent of that war's U.S. battle deaths and 0.4 percent of the sixteen million servicemen in the military during it. The 8,177 MIAs of the Korean War equaled 15.2 percent of the U.S. battle deaths and 0.14 percent of the era's 5,720,000 U.S. servicemen. In Vietnam, the 2,477 MIAs equaled just 5.4 percent of the war's U.S. battle deaths and 0.028 percent of the eight million persons who served in U.S. armed forces from 1964 to l973 and 0.095 percent of the 2,594,200 who were actually sent to South Vietnam. By comparison with other major conflicts in which the United States had been involved, the Indochina War produced by far the fewest MIAs in both absolute and proportional terms—0.3 per cent of the number that resulted from World War II and less than one-third the number from Korea. As for POWs, the House Select Committee on Missing Persons in Southeast Asia concluded in December 1976 that "no Americans are still being held alive as prisoners in Indochina, or elsewhere, as a result of the war in Indochina," and no credible evidence has subsequently been adduced to show otherwise. It must be remembered, too, that for many cases there was evidence of death or reason to presume death (e.g., the 436 air force pilots who were shot down over the sea and 647 cases, mostly dead or wounded, who could not be recovered from the battlefield). Figures on servicemen and battle deaths are from Department of Defense, Office of the Assistant Secretary of Defense (OASD) (Comptroller), "Selected Manpower Statistics," March 1979, 83. For figures on MIAs in other wars and discussion, see James Rosenthal, "The Myth of the Lost POWs," *The New Republic*, July 1, 1985, 15–19; and Bill Herod, "America's Missing: A Look Behind the Numbers," *Indochina Issues*, no. 54, (February 1985). For history and statistical update, see Defense Prisoner of War/Missing Personnel Office, Department of Defense, http://www.dtic.mil/dpmo.

56. Oleg Sarin and Lev Dvoretsky, *Alien Wars: The Soviet Union's Aggressions Against the World, 1919 to 1989* (Novato, Calif.: Presidio, 1996), 94.

57. U.S.-Russia Joint Commission on POW/MIAs, "Working Group Summaries, 17th Plenum" (November 14–15, 2000).

58. Brantly Womack, *China and Vietnam: The Politics of Asymmetry* (New York: Cambridge University Press, 2006), 176, citing Guo Minh, *Zhong Yue quanxi yanbian sishi nian* (Nanning: Guangxi Renmin Chubanshe, 1992), 69–71.

59. The rate of war deaths if applied to the American population at the time would have exceeded fifteen million or, on a daily basis for fifteen years, a toll equal to more than one September 11, 2001, per day. The Second Indochina War accounted for about 16 percent of all deaths suffered in war from 1945 to 2000. Calculated with data from Table 2, Milton Leitenberg, "Deaths in Wars and Conflicts in the 20th Century" (Ithaca, N.Y.: Cornell University, Peace Studies Program, Occasional Paper no. 29, 3rd. ed., 2006), 76–79.

60. Micheal Clodfelter, *Vietnam in Military Statistics: A History of the Indochina Wars, 1772–1991* (Jefferson, N.C.: McFarland & Company, 1995), 257.

61. Agence France Presse, April 4, 1995; Associated Press, April 3, 1995; Xinhua News Agency, April 3, 1995.

62. Clodfelter, *The Vietnam War*, 256.

63. Charles Hirschman, Samuel Preston, Vu Manh Loi, "Vietnamese Casualties During the American War: A New Estimate," *Population and Development Review*, Vol. 21, 4 (December 1995), 807.

64. *Ibid.*, 809.

65. Louis A. Wiesner, *Victims and Survivors: Displaced Persons and Other War Victims in Viet-Nam, 1954–1975* (New York: Greenwood, 1988), 229.

66. Clodfelter, *The Vietnam War, 256.*

67. Hoi dong bien soan lich su Nam trung bo khang chien (Editorial Council on the History of the Southern Trung Bo Resistance), *Nam trung bo khang chien (1945–1975)* [The Southern Trung Bo Resistance, 1945–1975], (Hanoi: Vien lich su Dang, 1992), 538.

68. See "Report of the United Nations Mission to North and South Viet-Nam," March 1976, in U.S. Congress, Senate, *Aftermath of War: Humanitarian Problems of Southeast Asia*, Staff Report for the Subcommittee to Investigate Problems Connected with Refugees and Escapees, Committee on the Judiciary, 94th Cong., 2nd sess. (May 17, 1976), 153, 163.

69. Clodfelter, *The Vietnam War,* 237.

70. Melvin Small and J. David Singer, *Resort to Arms: International and Civil Wars, 1816–1980* (Beverly Hills, Calif.: Sage Publications, 1982), 102, 238.

71. "Discussion between Zhou Enlai, Le Duan, Pham Van Dong and Le Thanh Nghi," 06/05/1973, Cold War International History Project, Virtual Archive, The Wilson Center.

72. "Dien cua Ban bi thu, So 178, ngay 21 thang 4 nam 1975" (Cable from the Secretariat, no. 178, April 21, 1975), in Dang Cong San Viet Nam, *Van Kien Dang toan tap, tap* 36 (Complete Party Documents, vol. 36), (Hanoi: NXB Ban chinh tri quoc gia, 2004), 157–162.

73. "Dien cua Ban bi thu, So 17, ngay 19 thang 4 nam 1975" (Cable from the Secretariat, no. 17, April 19, 1975), Dang Cong San Viet Nam, *Van Kien Dang toan tap* vol. 36, 152–156.

74. William S. Turley, "Hanoi's Domestic Dilemmas," *Problems of Communism* (July–August 1980), 44, 55.

75. See U.S., Congress, Senate, "Humanitarian Problems in Indochina," Hearings before the Subcommittee to Investigate Problems Connected with Refugees and Escapees, Committee on the Judiciary, 93rd Cong., 2nd sess. (July 18, 1974).

76. Milton Leitenberg, "Deaths in Wars and Conflicts in the 20th Century," 80.

77. W.R. Smyser, *Refugees: Extended Exile* (Washington, D.C.: Center for Strategic and International Studies, 1987), 61.

78. Michael Vickery, *Cambodia, 1975–1982* (Boston: South End Press, 1984).

79. Ben Kiernan, *The Pol Pot Regime* (New Haven: Yale University Press, 1996).

80. Patrick Heuveline, "'Between One and Three Million': Towards the Demographic Reconstruction of a Decade of Cambodian History (1970–79)," *Population Studies* 52, No. 1 (March 1998), 60.

Appendix A

Annual Troop Movement from North to South and Casualties en Route, May 1959 to April 1975—Group 559 and American Estimates

Table A.1. Annual Troop Movement from North to South and Casualties en Route, May 1959 to April 1975—Group 559 and American Estimates

	Group 559 Official Figures*								American Estimates			
Year	Divisions	Regiments	Battalions	Companies	Numerical Strength	Wounded	Killed	% killed, Wounded	Confirmed	Probable	Possible	Numerical Strength
5–12/1959			2		569			0.0				
1960	1	1	3	14	876	5	7	1.37	**4,556	**26		**4,582
1961		2	4	16	3,400	12	9	.62	4,118	2,177		6,295
1962		2	4	18	4,601	9	6	.33	5,362	7,495		12,857
1963		2	9	31	6,997	5	12	.24	4,726	3,180		7,906
1964		2	11	42	7,970	74	60	1.68	9,316	3,108		12,424
1965		8	28	91	16,706	115	157	1.63	23,770	1,910	8,050	33,730
1966		12	52	308	32,391	533	899	4.42	44,300	10,500	30,000	84,800
1967		12	65	343	33,281	1,148	973	6.37	***20,700	****5,100	***14,100	***39,900
1968		16	74	476	38,127	1,779	1,310	8.10				
1969		18	98	579	51,588	3,414	1,548	9.62				
1970	1	26	119	722	62,992	3,336	1,587	7.82				
1971	7	16	73	795	82,499	4,617	2,087	8.13				
1972	7	50	217	819	92,514	4,565	2,450	7.58				
1973	8	55	166	940	100,495	1,250	886	2.13				75,000
1974	8	55	181	934	97,690	636	355	1.01				
1–4/1975	7	55	160	983	94,506	284	141	0.45				
Total	38	332	1,266	7,111	727,202	21,802	12,487					
Average	2.2	19.5	74.5	418.3	42,777	2.99%	1.73%	4.72%				

Sources: Quan doi nhan dan Viet Nam, *Van tai quan su chien luoc tren duong Ho Chi Minh trong khang chien chong My* [Strategic Military Transport on the Ho Chi Minh Trail in the Anti-U.S. Resistance War] (Hanoi: Directorate of Logistics, 1988), p. 424; *Viet-Nam Documents and Research Notes*, Nos. 36–37 (Saigon, U.S. Embassy, June 1968), p. 19. American estimates to 1967 are the ones given by U.S. Ambassador W. Averill Harriman to the DRV delegation in Paris on May 27, 1968. Column eight, "% killed, wounded," is calculated and does not appear in the source table.

Notes: The figures for Group 559 include only those troops for which the Group was responsible. An unknown additional number of troops were infiltrated by sea.
*Group 559 was not responsible for all of the troops that made the trip south. The figures for the Group thus do not include forces that moved by sea (very few) or in whole units across the DMZ, as in 1972.
**1959–1960 combined.
***First half of the year.

Appendix B

Revolutionary Armed Forces and Population in the B2 Theater

Table B.1. Revolutionary Armed Forces and Population in the B2 Theater

	Reinforcements			Troop Levels (thousands)				Situation of the People		
								Population (millions) living in:		
	Supplied by the Great Rear*	Recruited In-Place	Ratio Supplied ÷ Recruited	Main Forces	Regional Forces	Popular Self-Defense Forces	Ratio of Forces** We = 1 Enemy = n	Liberated Zones	Contested Zones	Liberated Villages
1961	1,410	8,316	.17	7.5	8.2	69.5	10	4.100	0.995	122
1962	3,225	10,618	.30	16.8	18.8	72.0	5.3	4.076		
1963	1,036	24,300	.04	25.6	29.0	73.0	4	4.000		162
1964	1,364	18,160	.08	34.9	37.6	135.0	5.1	4.368		285
1965	7,621	14,918	.38	54.0	45.5	129.8	4.2	5.103		545
1966	9,809	6,351	1.54	63.7	44.3	147.3	5.4	4.360	1,229	425
1967	31,760	1,000	31.76	89.8	45.2	139.0	4.4	2.660	0.775	327
1968	67,667	16,763	4.04	129.0	44.7	118.0	3.7	3.304	1,229	465
1969	43,219	100	432.19	146.2	38.5	50.1	3.8	1.460	2,108	213
1970	26,062	1,860	14.01	139.9	34.0	51.2	3.8	0.988	1,920	107
1971	28,020	1,772	15.81	136.7	38.8	39.9	3.4	0.229	1,492	139
1972	34,275	7,203	4.76	150.0	36.7	62.2	2.1	0.719	2,209	185
1973	24,780	2,300	10.77	160.6	39.8	70.6	2.1	0.698	2,212	199
1974	28,612	2,974	9.62	169.1	38.8	79.5	1.9	1.681	2,236	235
1975	66,696	9,424	7.08	209.0	62.0	79.5	1.4			
Total	375,556	126,059						13.600		1,475

Source: Quan doi nhan dan, *Tong ket cong tac hau can chien truong Nam bo-cuc Nam Trung bo (B.2) trong khang chien chong My* [Review of Logistical Work on the B2 Battlefield in the Anti-U.S. Resistance War] (Hanoi: Tong cuc hau can, 1986), pp. 546–547. This volume is stamped "Secret: internal army distribution." The third column, "ratio of "supplied" to "recruited," is calculated and does not appear in the source table.

*"Great Rear" is a euphemism for the North.

**A note in the original sources states: "The ratio of forces between us and the enemy does not include the popular self-defense forces." The Vietnamese term for "popular self-defense forces" is *dan quan tu ve.*

Further Reading

The readings below represent but a small fraction of the vast and growing literature related to the Second Indochina War. I have deleted some works from the list in the first edition and replaced them with a larger number of more recent titles.

BIBLIOGRAPHIES, DICTIONARIES, ENCYCLOPEDIAS

Edwin E. Moise's *Historical Dictionary of the Vietnam War* (Lanham, Md.: Scarecrow Press, 2001) and *The A to Z of the Vietnam War* (Lanham, Md.: Scarecrow Press, 2005) are authoritative guides by a prominent historian of the war. An excellent historical dictionary by a leading historian is William J. Duiker, *Historical Dictionary of Vietnam* (Lanham, Md.: Scarecrow Press, 1998). The mother of all bibliographies is Moise's constantly updated "Vietnam War Bibliography" on the internet at www.clemson.edu/caah/history/facultypages/EdMoise/bibliography.html.

Stanley I. Kutler, ed., *Encyclopedia of the Vietnam War* (New York: Scribner, 1996) provides balanced coverage of the Vietnamese and American participants in articles that are longer, more original, and more scholarly than in other works of this kind. For a scholarly compendium of information that includes a section of incisive answers to critical questions, weighted toward American concerns and actions, see David L. Anderson, *The Columbia Guide to the Vietnam War* (New York: Columbia University Press, 2002).

PRIMARY SOURCES

Since documentation on American politics and policy related to the war is so vast and scattered (e.g., five presidential libraries), I will only mention a few easily accessible collections here. The forty-seven-volume study known as *The Pentagon Papers* that was commissioned by Secretary of Defense Robert McNamara, photocopied surreptitiously by Daniel Ellsberg, and synopsized in *The New York Times* is a gold mine of U.S. government internal documents. The official version, Department of Defense, *U.S.-Vietnam Relations, 1945–1967*, 12 vols. (Washington, D.C.: Government Printing Office, 1971) is a disjointed compendium of documents and staff papers. Senator Mike Gravel tidied up a large portion of these for publication as the *Senator Gravel edition, The Pentagon Papers*, 5 vols. (Boston: Beacon, 1971). Casual readers can get the flavor of these multi-volume collections in the one-volume work compiled by Neil Sheehan et al., ed., *The Pentagon Papers* (New York: Quadrangle, 1971) as serialized in *The New York Times*. More recently, the documentary deluge has continued with the release of State Department Central Files, National Security Council classified histories, transcripts of the Paris peace talks, and CIA Research Reports through the "Indochina Research Collections" microfilm series (Frederick, Md.: University Publications of America, various dates). For a single volume of intelligence estimates with a searchable CD tucked in the sleeve, see National Intelligence Council, *Estimative Products on Vietnam, 1948–1975* (Washington, D.C.: Superintendent of Documents, 2005).

Of course, U.S. government-generated documents reflect the views, assessments, and decisions of American policymakers and agencies. The nearest equivalent for the "other side" is the huge trove of Communist documents captured by United States, South Vietnamese, and allied forces and gathered together as the CDEC (Combined Documentation Exploitation Center) Collection of Captured Enemy Documents. The CDEC collection consists of roughly three million images on 110 ten-inch reels of microfilm, and copies are held at the National Archives, University of Massachusetts–Boston, and Texas Tech University, but the huge number of documents, not to mention uneven image quality and storage format, limit its use. Much smaller but still valuable collections are those of Douglas Pike (Chicago: Center for Research Libraries, items 1–850, 1966; and Ithaca, N.Y.: Cornell University Library, items 856–1120, 1967) and Jeffrey Race (Chicago: Center for Research Libraries, 1968). Digitization of the CDEC, Pike and a good many lesser collections by Texas Tech University will vastly improve access to these materials, and work is underway to make them available on the internet at www.vietnam.ttu.edu. Selected translations of captured documents released by the U.S. Information Service as *Viet-Nam Documents and Research Notes*, nos. 1–117 (Saigon: U.S. Mission, 1967–1972) may be found in most large university libraries. A few of these documents along with an extensive selection of materials mainly from U.S. official sources are arranged chronologically in Gareth Porter, ed., *Vietnam: The Definitive History of Human Decisions*, 2 vols. (Stanfordville, N.Y.: Coleman Enterprises, 1979).

For documents from the Communist side one does not need to rely exclusively on captured materials or heavily edited excerpts in official histories, as was the case up to the mid-1980s. Various institutions in Hanoi began releasing documents from the war period around that time while allowing piecemeal access to archives. Currently the most comprehensive collection of official Communist party documents is Dang Cong San Viet Nam, *Van Kien Dang, toan tap* [Complete Party Documents] (Hanoi: Chinh tri quoc gia, 2003), whose 48 volumes (and counting) begin in 1927 and encompass the war years and beyond. The collection is of course not literally "complete," only the documents are, but it is nonetheless an extraordinary compendium for such a generally secretive government. Readers lacking command of Vietnamese can get a taste of the "complete" collection in *75 Years of the Communist Party of Viet Nam (1930–2005): A Selection of Documents from Nine Party Congresses* (Hanoi: The Gioi Publishers, 2005), a single volume of more than one thousand pages. The defunct non-Communist regimes are very poorly represented in the war's publicly available records and are likely to remain so, although this may change as scholars obtain access to RVN records that remained in Vietnam after 1975.

BACKGROUND HISTORY

Readers who want to deepen their grasp of the historical background should consult Alexander B. Woodside, *Community and Revolution in Modern Vietnam* (Boston: Houghton Mifflin, 1976); Hue-Tam Ho Tai, *Radicalism and the Origins of the Vietnamese Revolution* (Cambridge, Mass.: Harvard University Press, 1992); Mark Philip Bradley, *Imagining Vietnam and America: The Making of Postcolonial Vietnam, 1919–1950* (Chapel Hill: University of North Carolina Press, 2000); David G. Marr, *Vietnam 1945: The Quest for Power* (Berkeley: University of California Press, 1995); Kim N. B. Ninh, *A World Transformed: The Politics of Culture in Revolutionary Vietnam, 1945–1965* (Ann Arbor: University of Michigan Press, 2002); and Neil L. Jamieson, *Understanding Vietnam* (Berkeley: University of California Press, 1993). On Vietnamese nationalism, see William J. Duiker, *The Rise of Nationalism in Vietnam, 1900–1941* (Ithaca, N.Y.: Cornell, 1976) and David G. Marr, *Vietnamese Tradition on Trial, 1920–1945* (Berkeley: University of California Press, 1981). The most authoritative study of the "indigenization" of Communism in Vietnam remains Huynh Kim Khanh, *Vietnamese Communism 1925–1945* (Ithaca, N.Y.: Cornell, 1982).

GENERAL HISTORIES

George C. Herring, *America's Longest War: The United States and Vietnam, 1950–1975* (New York: Wiley, 1979) focuses on U.S. policies, politics, and perspectives, as the title implies. Still the best "read" and one of the most devastating descriptions of Americans in Vietnam is Frances Fitzgerald, *Fire in the Lake* (Boston: Atlantic Monthly Publications, 1972), although her interpretation of Vietnamese society and culture strikes scholars as eccentric, precious, and out of date. Gabriel Kolko's *Anatomy of a War: Vietnam, the United States, and the Modern Historical Experience* (New York: Pantheon Books, 1985), by a scholar deeply familiar with Marxism, is a work of remarkable breadth and durability despite its age. In scope and detail nothing beats veteran journalist Arthur J. Dommen's thousand-page epic, *The Indochinese Experience of the French and the Americans: Nationalism and Communism in Cambodia, Laos, and Vietnam* (Bloomington, Ind.: Indiana University Press, 2001), which is one of the few histories that truly does cover all of Indochina, with Dommen's antipathies to the Communists on display. Mark Moyar's, *Triumph Forsaken: The Vietnam War, 1954–1965* (New York: Cambridge University Press, 2006), a richly documented account of the war to 1965, mines the evidence to support a hard-line revisionist interpretation. The ten essays by leading historians of the war in Marc Jason Gilbert, ed., *Why the North Won the Vietnam War* (New York: Palgrave, 2002) find grounds for a synthesis of "orthodox" and "revisionist" interpretations, though leaning toward the former. For essays with a strongly revisionist bent, see John Norton Moore and Robert F. Turner, ed., *The Real Lessons of the Vietnam War: Reflections Twenty-Five Years After the Fall of Saigon* (Durham, N.C.: Carolina Academic Press, 2002).

JOURNALISTS AND MEDIA

To the consternation of U.S. diplomats and generals, most journalists were poor team players compared with correspondents in previous wars. The note of skepticism is struck early by David Halberstam, *The Making of a Quagmire* (New York: Random House, 1965). Robert Shaplen's *The Lost Revolution* (New York: Harper & Row, rev. ed., 1966) and *The Road from War* (New York: Harper & Row, 1970) record copiously what a veteran correspondent considered to be missed opportunities for the United States. Bitter indictments of both the United States and its South Vietnamese allies can be found in Gloria Emerson's award-laden *Winners and Losers* (New York: Random House, 1976). Jonathan Schell, *The Military Half* (New York: Knopf, 1968), clinically describes the destruction by American forces of hundreds of hamlets in two provinces, while his *The Village of*

Ben Suc (New York: Knopf, 1967) is the classic account of a "search-and-destroy operation," specifically Operation Cedar Falls. Don Oberdorfer, *Tet!* (Garden City, N.Y.: Doubleday, 1971) is a blow-by-blow account of the 1968 offensive; and Robert Pisor, *The End of the Line* (New York: Norton, 1982) provides a detailed account of the siege of Khe Sanh based on U.S. sources and interviews with some of the non-Communist participants. An excellent retrospective, filled with the anecdotes that journalists excel at telling, is Arnold R. Isaacs, *Without Honor: Defeat in Vietnam and Cambodia* (Baltimore, Md.: Johns Hopkins, 1983). Veteran correspondent A. J. Langguth looks back in *Our Vietnam: The War 1954–1975* (New York: Simon & Schuster, 2000), a work strongly focused on personalities and story-telling, which makes for good light reading, but pretty much devoid of argument, analysis, or interpretation.

As for the impact of the media, former journalist Peter Braestrup, *Big Story*, 2 vols. (Boulder, Colo.: Westview, 1977; abridged ed., New Haven, Conn.: Yale, 1983), blames the media for making Tet 1968 seem a defeat, thus turning military victory into political defeat for the United States and Saigon. David F. Schmitz rebuts Braestrup's thesis, arguing there was no media bias and no sudden change of public opinion, in *The Tet Offensive: Politics, War, and Public Opinion* (Lanham, Md.: Rowman & Littlefield, 2005).

THE TET OFFENSIVE

The puzzle of Tet 1968—in what sense it was a surprise and how (or whether) it shaped American policy thereafter—is sufficiently beyond definitive solution to assure that it will remain controversial (see Journalists and Media, above). James J. Wirtz argues in *The Tet Offensive: Intelligence Failure in War* (Ithaca, N.Y.: Cornell University Press, 1991) that pre-existing belief systems caused the American failure to correctly interpret the evidence of impending attack. Ronnie E. Ford, *Tet 1968: Understanding the Surprise* (London: Frank Cass, 1995) comes to a broadly similar conclusion but adds fascinating insight into the military doctrines and intelligence failures on the Communist side as well. The argument that skewed intelligence and claims of progress made the offensive appear to the American public as bigger and more effective than it really was is developed in Jake Blood, *The Tet Effect: Intelligence and the Public Perception of the War* (London: Routledge, 2005). The thoughtful, balanced collection of essays in Marc Jason Gilbert and William Head, ed., *The Tet Offensive* (Westport, Conn.: Praeger, 1996) weigh the reasons to consider 1968 the pivotal year. Ronald H. Spector's pithy description of the fighting in the wake of the offensive, *After Tet: The Bloodiest Year in Vietnam* (New York: The Free Press, 1993), is a rich source of fact and insight relevant to the entire war, mostly as experienced by American troops.

THE RVN AND THE ARVN

The Republic of Vietnam's government and army evaporated in May 1975 and public attention moved on to other things. Scholarly interest is destined to remain thin, except perhaps for the person and fate of Ngo Dinh Diem. Published just before Diem's death, journalist Denis Warner's *The Last Confucian* (New York: Macmillan, 1963) contained two chapters on the man, his regime and his family that popularized the image of Diem as a traditionalist out of touch with his times and people. A later account, more sharply focused on events leading up to the coup and on international context, also by a journalist, is Ellen J. Hammer, *A Death in November: America in Vietnam, 1963* (New York: Dutton, 1987). A more penetrating but neglected gem by a disenchanted ex-member of Diem's government is Nguyen Thai, *Is South Vietnam Viable?* (Manila: S.N., 1962). Thai's answer to his own question was "maybe," but only if Diem stepped aside. Seth Jacobs, *Cold War Mandarin: Ngo Dinh Diem and the Origins of America's War in Vietnam, 1950–1963* (Lanham, Md.: Rowman & Littlefield, 2006) is an American historian's conventional interpretation of the man and his times. Philip E. Catton, *Diem's Final Failure: Prelude to America's War in Vietnam* (Lawrence: University Press of Kansas, 2002) and Edward Garvey Miller, *Grand Illusions: The Making and Unmaking of America's Alliance with Ngo Dinh Diem, 1954–1963* (Ph.D. dissertation, Harvard University, 2004, and forthcoming as a book) take issue with "last Confucian" orthodoxy by emphasizing Diem's patriotism, independent spirit, and conservative modernist ideas about socio-economic development. Miller had access to many official documents from the Diem era now archived in Vietnam.

The government and politics of the Republic of Vietnam (RVN) can be seen as an experiment in state-building under inauspicious conditions. Allan E. Goodman, *Politics in War: The Bases of Political Community in South Vietnam* (Cambridge, Mass.: Harvard, 1973) is a systematic and, in retrospect, optimistic analysis of Saigon's efforts to develop effective representative institutions. Also see Howard R. Penniman, *Elections in South Vietnam* (Washington, D.C.: American Enterprise Institute, 1973). Thich Nhat Hanh, one of the more thoughtful leaders of the Buddhist protest movements, puts his pain, rage, and patriotism on display in *Lotus in a Sea of Fire* (New York: Hill and Wang, 1967). Robert J. Topmiller, *The Lotus Unleashed: The Buddhist Peace Movement in South Vietnam, 1964–1966* (Lexington: University Press of Kentucky, 2002) is a rare study of politics under the RVN that concentrates on the "Buddhist crisis" and regional secessionism of 1966. The highland minorities, or "montagnards," mobilized to fight by the Green Berets only to be abandoned at war's end, are the subject of Gerald Hickey, *Sons of the Mountains* (New Haven, Conn.: Yale University Press, 1982) and *Free in the Forest* (New Haven, Conn.: Yale University Press, 1982), two monumental ethnographic histories of cultures the war destroyed.

The religious sects that caused so much trouble for Diem have remarkably few chroniclers in English of their involvement in the war. Nguyen Long Thanh Nam, *Hoa Hao Buddhism in the Course of Vietnam's History*, trans. Sergei Blagov (New York: Nova Science Publishers, 2003) is a Hoa Hao leader's account of this Buddhist group's rocky relations with political authority of any kind. Sergei Blagov, *Caodaism: Vietnamese Tradition and its Leap into Modernity* (New York: Nova Science Publishers, 2001) surveys Cao Dai history, doctrines, and political role. Sergei Blagov's *Honest Mistakes: The Life and Death of Trinh Minh The (1922–1955): South Vietnam's Alternative Leader* (Huntington, N.Y.: Nova Science Publishers, 2001) sifts the conflicting stories, rumors, and evidence concerning this elusive Cao Dai military leader (or terrorist, depending on one's point of view) and confirms that the French assassinated The in retribution for the killing of a French officer. Jayne Werner, *Peasant Politics and Religious Sectarianism: Peasant and Priest in the Cao Dai in Viet Nam* (New Haven, Conn.: Yale University Southeast Asia Monograph Series, no. 23, 1981) is a scholarly analysis of Cao Dai as a social movement.

Mark Moyar, *Phoenix and the Birds of Prey: The CIA's Secret Campaign to Destroy the Viet Cong* (Annapolis, Md.: Naval Institute Press, 1997) argues that the Phoenix program, despite some defects, was highly effective and not a blank check for "hit squads" as claimed by antiwar pamphleteers. But a lot hinges on whose testimony and which documents an author considers most reliable. Dale Andrade, *Ashes to Ashes: The Phoenix Program and the Vietnam War* (Lexington, Mass.: Lexington Books, 1990), like Moyar, puts a generally positive spin on Phoenix; Douglas Valentine, *The Phoenix Program* (New York: Morrow, 1990) a negative one.

While Western scholars are exploiting RVN documents only recently made available by the Vietnamese authorities, memoirs by the South's anti-Communist leaders give some voice to Saigon's side. Tran Van Don, *Our Endless War* (San Rafael, Calif.: Presidio, 1978) is a relatively dispassionate memoir by one of the generals who organized the coup against Diem. In the largely ghost-written *Twenty Years and Twenty Days* (New York: Stein and Day, 1976) Nguyen Cao Ky offers his explanation of why the U.S. and South Vietnam lost the war, while in the memoir *Buddha's Child: My Fight to Save Vietnam* (New York: St. Martin's Press, 2002) Ky blames just about everything that went wrong on Nguyen Van Thieu, who died in September 2001 without producing his own self-serving tract. Lam Quang Thi, one of Saigon's better generals, analyzes the causes of the South's fall in *Autopsy:*

The Death of South Viet Nam (Phoenix, Az.: Sphinx Publishing, 1986) and follows up with a thoughtful career autobiography in *The Twenty-Five Year Century* (Denton: University of North Texas Press, 2001). A number of studies of specific campaigns by ARVN officers have been published under the auspices of the U.S. Army Center of Military History, most notably Cao Van Vien and Dong Van Khuyen, *Reflections on the Vietnam War* (Washington, D.C.: Center of Military History, 1980); Cao Van Vien, *The Final Collapse* (Washington, D.C.: Center of Military History, 1982); and Hoang Ngoc Lung, *The General Offensives of 1968–69* (Washington, D.C.: Center of Military History, 1981). Excerpts from interviews with these and other Saigon figures are quoted at length, with insightful commentary, in *The Fall of South Vietnam: Statements by Vietnamese Military and Civilian Leaders*, ed. Stephen T. Hosmer, Konrad Kellen, and Brian M. Jenkins (New York: Crane, Russak, 1980). Robert K. Brigham's social history of Saigon's army, *ARVN: Life and Death in the South Vietnamese Army* (Lawrence: University Press of Kansas, 2006), uses extensive interviewing and primary documentation to explore the weaknesses of the losing army.

THE SOUTHERN REVOLUTION

Jeffrey Race, *War Comes to Long An: Revolutionary Conflict in a Vietnamese Province* (Berkeley: University of California Press, 1972), is the classic account of how the Communists, starting from a position of weakness, gained ascendancy over Saigon forces in the Mekong delta. Decades after it was published, American counterinsurgency strategists were still reading and trying to absorb the lessons of *War Comes to Long An*. David W. P. Elliott, *The Vietnamese War: Revolution and Social Change in the Mekong Delta, 1930–1975*, 2 vols. (Armonk, N.Y.: M.E. Sharpe, 2003) is a massive and massively detailed account of life in Dinh Tuong province that mines hundreds of interviews conducted by the RAND Corporation during the war plus other documentation. A "concise edition" of a mere 500 pages (M.E. Sharpe, 2006) makes this micro analysis of one province accessible to the general reader. Utilizing a subset of the RAND interviews used by Elliott, David Hunt brings the skills of a social historian to bear on the everyday realities of village life during war in *Into the Maelstrom: Vietnam's Southern Revolution, 1959–1968* (Amherst: University of Massachusetts Press, forthcoming). Hunt makes a powerful argument for crediting peasants with far more agency than other scholars—and the communist party—have done. Harvey Meyerson, *Vinh Long* (Boston: Houghton Mifflin, 1970), is neither as schematic as Race nor as penetrating as Elliott but at least brings one more Mekong delta province under the lens. Yet another province study from the delta, Eric M. Bergerud, *The Dynamics of Defeat: The Vietnam War in Hau Nghia Province* (Boulder, Colo.: Westview Press, 1991), focuses on pacification and its ultimate failure. Robert L. Sansom contests the thesis that tenancy and unequal land distribution drove peasants into the arms of the Communists in *The Economics of Insurgency in the Mekong Delta of Vietnam* (Cambridge, Mass.: MIT Press, 1970). For portrayal of a different war in a different region, see James Walker Trullinger, Jr., *Village at War* (New York: Longman, 1980), based on the author's observations while a voluntary aid worker near Hue. Samuel L. Popkin analyzes the political economy of peasant society in Vietnam from colonial times onward in *The Rational Peasant* (Berkeley: University of California Press, 1979), a work that takes issue with the "moral economy" approach advanced by James C. Scott in *The Moral Economy of the Peasant* (New Haven, Conn.: Yale University Press, 1977). While not focused on the war, Scott and Popkin sparked a debate among specialists over the appropriate methodology for studying peasant mobilization into revolutionary politics. Douglas Pike, an official of the U.S. Information Agency, probably did more than anyone to popularize the term "Viet Cong" with his book *Viet Cong* (Cambridge, Mass.: MIT Press, 1966), an early description of the Communist organizational structure and methods. More systematic in approach and more narrowly focused on Communist armed forces (the PLAF) are Paul Berman, *Revolutionary Organization* (Lexington, Mass.: Heath, 1974) and William Darryl Henderson, *Why the Vietcong Fought* (Westport, Conn.: Greenwood, 1979). Southern Communist militant and colonel in the PLAF, Madame Nguyen Thi Dinh describes the origins of revolutionary armed struggle in the Mekong delta in the translation of her memoir, *No Other Road to Take* (Ithaca, N.Y.: Cornell University Southeast Asia Studies Program, 1976).

For no reason based in logic or fact, critics of American policy often felt obliged to accept much of Hanoi's depiction of events as true, including the fiction that the NLF emerged from a congress of "former resistance fighters" and non-Communists held in 1960. The most influential early statement of the thesis that Hanoi merely sanctioned developments it could not control was George McT. Kahin and John W. Lewis, *The United States in Vietnam* (New York: Dial, 1967). In a later work, *Intervention: How America Became Involved in Vietnam* (New York: Random House, 1986), Kahin presented a more nuanced view of the party's role in organizing and guiding the movement. (On American policy, Kahin is on surer ground and witheringly effective.) For detailed, authoritative treatments of the NLF's founding by specialists capable of exploiting Vietnamese language materials, see Carlyle A. Thayer, *War by Other Means: National Liberation and Revolution in Viet-Nam 1954–60* (Sydney, Allen & Unwin, 1989); William J. Duiker, *Sacred War: Nationalism and Revolution in a Divided Nation* (Boston: McGraw-Hill, 1995); and Robert K. Brigham, *Guerrilla Diplomacy: The NLF's Foreign Relations and the Vietnam War* (Ithaca, N.Y.: Cornell University Press, 1998).

Brigham had access to Vietnamese archives and conducted interviews with some of the principals to confirm that NLF leaders often asserted a Southern point of view but always through the party's chain of command. NLF Minister of Justice Truong Nhu Tang's *A Vietcong Memoir*, with David Chanoff and Doan Van Toai (New York: Harcourt Brace Jovanovich, 1985) is a widely read account of the astonishingly slow discovery by a non-Communist that the Communists were really running the show.

THE NORTH

A number of journalists visited the North during the war and wrote accounts that are best forgotten. One exception is Gerard Chaliand, *The Peasants of North Vietnam* (Baltimore, Md.: Penguin, 1969). For scholarly studies of DRV politics and society that include commentary on the impact of war, see *Vietnamese Communism in Comparative Perspective*, ed. William S. Turley (Boulder, Colo.: Westview, 1980). Hanoi's attempt to remain neutral between Moscow and Beijing while preserving the support of each is analyzed in Donald Zagoria, *Vietnam Triangle* (New York: Pegasus, 1967) and W. R. Smyser, *The Independent Vietnamese* (Athens, Ohio: Ohio University Center for International Studies, 1980). Ang Cheng Guan, *The Vietnam War from the Other Side: The Vietnamese Communists' Perspective* (London and New York: RoutledgeCurzon, 2002) is an incisive survey of the view from Hanoi which makes effective use of Vietnamese sources that became available in the 1980s and 1990s. An authoritative secondary source on the evolution of Hanoi's strategy is William J. Duiker, *The Communist Road to Power in Vietnam* (Boulder, Colo.: Westview, 1981). The only biography of Giap that gets the story about right is Cecil B. Currey's *Victory at Any Cost: The Genius of Viet Nam's Gen. Vo Nguyen Giap* (Washington and London: Brassey's, 1997), which portrays Giap as a dominant influence on Hanoi's military strategy who nonetheless was sometimes sidelined by other leaders. Currey had one interview with Giap and subsequently corresponded with him.

Of course, Hanoi has its own spokesmen. The ablest writer for foreign audiences was Nguyen Khac Vien, *Tradition and Revolution in Vietnam* (Berkeley, Calif.: Indochina Resource Center, 1974) and *The Long Resistance 1958–1975* (Hanoi: Foreign Languages Publishing House, 1975), both of which emphasize the continuity of Vietnam's anti-colonial and reunification struggles with its previous struggles against foreign rule. As for military strategy, it must be remembered when reading Vo Nguyen Giap, *People's War, People's Army* (New York: Praeger, 1962) that this work anthologizes articles about the war with France; it is not necessarily the blueprint for the war with the United States. Giap's later *Big Victory, Great Task* (New York: Praeger, 1968), written on the eve of the Tet Offensive, attempts in the manner of generals everywhere to apply the lessons of the past. Giap tacitly conceded in 1969 that the Southern revolution was "temporarily" on the defensive in, *Banner of People's War, the Party's Military Line* (New York: Praeger, 1970), which also contains an insightful introduction by French scholar Georges Boudarel. Articles by several PAVN commanders, in which a debate over military strategy can be discerned, are translated and analyzed in *Visions of Victory*, ed. Patrick J. McGarvey (Stanford, Calif.: Hoover, 1969). An account of the 1975 offensive as seen by the PAVN Chief-of-Staff is General Van Tien Dung, *Our Great Spring Victory* (New York: Monthly Review, 1977). The account by COSVN's military commander who none too subtly criticizes the high command in Hanoi is General Tran Van Tra, *Vietnam: History of the B2-Bulwark Theatre, vol. V, Concluding the 30 Years War* (Springfield, Va.: Joint Publications Research Service, translation no. 82,783, 1983), a work that was withdrawn from Vietnam's book stalls almost immediately upon publication.

The Cold War's end made it possible for Ilya V. Gaiduk to use Soviet archives in writing *The Soviet Union and the Vietnam War* (Chicago: Ivan R. Dee, 1996) and *Confronting Vietnam: Soviet Policy Toward the Indochina Conflict, 1954–1963* (Stanford, Calif.: Stanford University/Woodrow Wilson Center Press, 2003). Qiang Zhai, *China and the Vietnam Wars, 1950–1975* (Chapel Hill: University of North Carolina Press, 2000), and Chen Jian, *Mao's China and the Cold War* (Chapel Hill: University of North Carolina Press, 2001) make clear on the basis of copious documentation from Chinese archives that Beijing was determined to meet any American threat to the DRV's survival or to China's own security with great force, despite irritation at Hanoi's warming relations with Moscow. Ralph B. Smith's *International History of the Vietnam War* (London: Macmillan, 1983) deserves mention for putting his subject in a truly global perspective though without the benefit of documents released since the Cold War's end.

THE AIR WAR

The North's internal response to U.S. bombardment is described in mind-numbing detail in Jon M. Van Dyke, *North Vietnam's Strategy for Survival* (Palo Alto, Calif.: Pacific Books, 1972), which should be read in conjunction with the bombing study by the Air War Study Group, Cornell University, *The Air War in Indochina* (Boston: Beacon, rev. ed., 1972). For a theoretically-informed analysis of the bureaucratic politics and process behind bombing policy by a disillusioned ex-Pentagon official, see James Clay Thompson, *Rolling Thunder: Understanding Policy and Program Failure* (Chapel Hill: University of North Carolina Press, 1980). Mark Clodfelter, *The Limits of Air Power: The American Bombing of North Vietnam* (New York: The Free Press,

1989) is another authoritative study that situates the bombing in the wider context of the war and the history of bombing. Covering the air war in all of Indochina, Ronald B. Frankum Jr.'s *Like Rolling Thunder: The Air War in Vietnam 1964–1975* (Lanham, Md.: Rowman & Littlefield, 2005) is a good update based on U.S. military documents released since war's end. Although not about the air war, Adam Fforde and Susanne H. Paine's *The Limits of Liberation* (New York: Methuen, 1987) is a rigorous analysis of the North's economic performance that discusses how the DRV adjusted its economic structure during it, with lastingly negative effects.

CAMBODIA

Amidst the dearth of work on Cambodia in English, David P. Chandler, *A History of Cambodia* (Boulder, Colo.: Westview, 1983) stands out as the essential introduction. Milton E. Osborne, *Before Kampuchea* (Boston: Allen Unwin, 1979) is a retrospective tour of the horizon on the eve of war by a former Australian diplomat. The ultimate insider source on the regime of Prince Sihanouk up to the time of its overthrow is, of course, Norodom Sihanouk, *My War with the CIA* (New York: Pantheon, 1973), to which the chastened follow-up is Sihanouk, *War and Hope* (New York: Pantheon, 1980). The classic account of Cambodia's slide into war and the "secret bombing" is William Shawcross, *Sideshow: Kissinger, Nixon and the Destruction of Cambodia* (New York: Simon & Schuster, 1979), to which Kissinger responds at length in his memoirs (see below). Also see Peter A. Poole, *The Expansion of the War into Cambodia* (Athens, Ohio: Ohio University Center for International Studies, 1970) and the leftist perspective of Malcolm Caldwell and Lek Tan, *Cambodia in the Southeast Asian War* (New York: Monthly Review, 1973). François Ponchaud, a Catholic priest who observed the Khmer Rouge takeover of Phnom Penh, records the war's ominous end in *Year Zero* (New York: Henry Holt, 1977).

Study of the Khmer Rouge used to suffer for lack of access and documentation, making the adjective "shadowy" for once seem deserved. Timothy Carney ably surveyed what little was known about the Khmer Rouge up to the year after they came to power in *Communist Party Power in Kampuchea (Cambodia)* (Ithaca, N.Y.: Cornell University Southeast Asia Studies Program, 1977). *Peasants and Politics in Kampuchea, 1942–1981*, ed. Ben Kiernan and Chantthou Boua (New York: Sharpe, 1982) shed substantially more light in this collection of articles and documents, including items by Khmer Rouge leaders whom Pol Pot liquidated. Attempt at systematic interpretation of the revolution in Cambodia by scholars with appropriate experience and linguistic training begins with *Revolution and Its Aftermath in Kampuchea*, ed. David P. Chandler and Ben Kiernan (New Haven, Conn.:

Yale University Southeast Asia Studies Monograph Series no. 25, 1983) and Michael Vickery, *Cambodia: 1975–1982* (Boston: South End, 1984). Craig Etcheson, *The Rise and Demise of Democratic Kampuchea* (Boulder, Colo.: Westview, 1984) was the first serious history of Khmer Communism from 1930 to the present. Ben Kiernan's *How Pol Pot Came to Power: a History of Communism in Kampuchea, 1930–1975* (London: Verso, 1985) was the second and more thoroughly grounded in primary materials. David P. Chandler, *Brother Number One: a Political Biography of Pol Pot* (Boulder, Colo.: Westview Press, 1999) does as much to uncover the inner workings of the Khmer Rouge as it does to analyze Pol Pot's personality, political thought, and crimes. Journalist Anthony Short's *Pol Pot: Anatomy of a Nightmare* (New York: Henry Holt, 2004) is a well-researched, even handed, and highly readable account.

The Vietnamese Communists virtually created the Khmer Rouge and later disowned them. To understand why, see Thomas Engelbert and Christopher E. Goscha, *Falling out of Touch: A Study on Vietnamese Communist Policy Towards an Emerging Cambodian Communist Movement, 1930–1975* (Clayton, Australia: Centre of Southeast Asian Studies, Monash University, 1995); David Chandler, *The Tragedy of Cambodian History: Politics, War and Revolution Since 1945* (New Haven: Yale University Press, 1991); and Nayan Chanda, *Brother Enemy: the War after the War* (San Diego: Harcourt Brace Jovanovich, 1986).

LAOS

Arthur J. Dommen, *Laos: Keystone of Indochina* (Boulder, Colo.: Westview, 1985) is an update of Arthur J. Dommen, *Conflict in Laos* (New York: Praeger, rev. ed., 1974). Early writings by Dommen and others, mostly journalists, tend to focus on the themes of intrigue in Vientiane and the unattainability of neutrality. Bernard Fall, *Anatomy of a Crisis* (Garden City, N.Y.: Doubleday, 1967) thoroughly dissects the U.S. role in the events of 1960–1961. Marek Thee, *Notes of a Witness* (New York: Random House, 1973), records the impressions of a member of the International Control Commission who worked in Laos during the Kennedy administration. British scholar Hugh Toye's *Laos: Buffer State or Battleground* (New York: Oxford, 1968) is an authoritative survey of the diplomacy and politics of the war's early stages. *Laos: War and Revolution*, ed. Nina S. Adams and Alfred W. McCoy (New York: Harper & Row, 1970) is a collection of articles on a wide range of topics written from an "antiwar" perspective. For a now outdated but nonetheless careful analysis of U.S. policy toward Laos from 1954 to about 1970 based on a Harvard Ph.D. dissertation, see Charles A. Stevenson, *The End of Nowhere* (Boston: Beacon, 1972). Australian journalist Wilfred Burchett, *The*

Furtive War (New York: International Publishers, 1963) discusses the collapse of neutralism from a point of view that is sympathetic to Hanoi and the Pathet Lao. A work that makes effective use of interviews and the vast hoard of documents in military archives and presidential libraries to expose the "secret war" is Timothy N. Castle, *At War in the Shadow of Vietnam: U.S. Military Aid to the Royal Lao Government, 1955–1975* (New York: Columbia University Press, 1993).

The Lao Communists attracted attention from oddly few serious analysts. The standard works, all having one old hand in common, are Paul F. Langer and Joseph J. Zasloff, *North Vietnam and the Pathet Lao* (Cambridge, Mass.: Harvard, 1970); Joseph J. Zasloff, *The Pathet Lao: Leadership and Organization Eight Essays* (New Haven, Conn.: Yale University Southeast Asia Studies, 1983); and MacAlister Brown and Joseph J. Zasloff, *Apprentice Revolutionaries: The Communist Movement in Laos, 1930–1985* (Stanford, Calif.: Hoover Institution Press, 1986), which sums up about everything anyone in the West could possibly have known about the Pathet Lao as of the mid-1980s. Even more then the Republic of Vietnam, the Royal Lao Government has been thinly studied and is likely to remain so. For a rightist view, but very dated, see Sisouk Na Champassak, *Storm over Laos* (New York: Praeger, 1961). On the later military campaigns from a Royal Lao Army perspective, see Soutchay Vongsavanh, *Royal Lao Government Military Operations and Activities in the Laotian Panhandle* (Washington, D.C.: U.S. Army Center for Military History, 1981).

AMERICAN POLITICS AND DIPLOMACY

The problem here is not dearth but surfeit. Kahin's *Intervention: How America Became Involved in Vietnam,* cited above, is an important extension and update based on new documentation of the earlier *The United States in Vietnam* with John Lewis. Wallace J. Thies, *When Governments Collide* (Berkeley: University of California Press, 1980) demonstrates that (and to a certain extent why) coercion was ineffective against Hanoi in the period 1964–1968. In contrast to the conventional view that Cold War ideology and a sense of insecurity impelled the U.S. toward intervention, Gareth Porter argues in *Perils of Dominance* (Berkeley: University of California Press, 2005) that national security bureaucrats pressured Kennedy and Johnson, against the two presidents' better judgment, to take aggressive military action while the U.S. enjoyed strategic superiority over the Soviet Union. Robert J. McMahon's *The Limits of Empire* (New York: Columbia University Press, 1999) takes a broad view of the U.S. role in Southeast Asia since World War II to argue differently from Porter that U.S. ambitions exceeded its capacities. Robert D. Schulzinger utilized archives in presidential libraries, among other things, to write a well-documented exploration of American perceptions and policy-making in *A Time for War: The United States and Vietnam, 1941–1975* (New York: Oxford University Press, 1997). Allan E. Goodman, *The Lost Peace* (Stanford, Calif.: Hoover, 1978) contrasts the U.S. search for compromise with Hanoi's refusal to make concessions. Gareth Porter interviewed officials in Hanoi for *A Peace Denied* (Bloomington: Indiana University Press, 1975) and is considerably more sympathetic than Goodman to Hanoi's point of view. The sage observations of an early State Department dissenter can be found in Paul M. Kattenburg, *The Vietnam Trauma in American Foreign Policy, 1945–1975* (New Brunswick, N.J.: Transaction Books, 1980). Other American diplomats' accounts are Townsend Hoopes, *The Limits of Intervention* (New York: McKay, 1969); Chester L. Cooper, *The Lost Crusade* (New York: Dodd, Mead, 1970); Frederick Nolting, *From Trust to Tragedy: The Political Memoirs of Frederick Nolting, Kennedy's Ambassador to Diem's Vietnam* (New York: Praeger, 1988). Ex-CIA analyst Frank Snepp, *Decent Interval* (New York: Random House, 1977) vividly recounts Saigon's collapse and accuses U.S. officials of perfidy and incompetence. Michael Charlton and Anthony Moncrieff, *Many Reasons Why* (New York: Hill & Wang, 1978) quotes principal actors at length from interviews conducted for a BBC radio program. For a vigorous defense of U.S. involvement and military conduct based on an analysis of copious U.S. statistics, see Guenter Lewy, *America in Vietnam* (New York: Oxford, 1978). A more sober retrospective by prominent figures in the planning and execution of the war is W. Scott Thompson and Donald D. Frizzell, ed., *Lessons of Vietnam* (New York: Crane, Russak, 1977). By helping Diem's government to survive for six years, the Eisenhower administration simply postponed the day of reckoning, according to David L. Anderson, *Trapped by Success: The Eisenhower Administration and Vietnam, 1953–1961* (New York: Columbia University Press, 1991). David L. Anderson, ed., *Shadow on the White House: Presidents and the Vietnam War, 1945–1975* (Lawrence: University Press of Kansas, 1993) is a collection of crisp essays on presidential leadership by prominent historians of the war. Many military officers counseled caution and gave other good advice but were just as inconsistent and irresponsible as civilians when it came to taking it, according to Robert Buzzanco, *Masters of War: Military Dissent and Politics in the Vietnam Era* (Cambridge: Cambridge University Press, 1996), a study of American civil-military relations.

Joseph G. Morgan's *The Vietnam Lobby* (Chapel Hill: University of North Carolina Press, 1997) describes the American Friends of Vietnam, a lobby group consisting of people who worked for Diem's appointment as premier and supported the Republic after his assassination. Seth Jacobs argues in *America's Miracle Man in Vietnam* (Durham, N.C.: Duke University Press, 2004) that religion and racism shaped the perceptions of American policymakers in ways that made Diem seem a more attractive ally than any non-Christian South Vietnamese alternative. Howard Jones, *Death of a Generation: How the Assassinations of Diem and JFK Prolonged the Vietnam War* (Oxford: Oxford University Press, 2003) discerns "a pattern of withdrawal . . . in the making" at the time Diem and Kennedy were assassinated. Fredrik Logevall, *Choosing War: The Lost Chance for Peace and the Escalation of War in Vietnam* (Berkeley: University of California Press, 1999) finds no such pattern, only rigidities in thought, perception and decision-making that resulted in Johnson's decision to escalate the war. H.R. McMaster argues and richly documents in *Dereliction of Duty: Lyndon Johnson, Robert McNamara, the Joint Chiefs of Staff, and the Lies That Led to Vietnam* (New York: Harper-Collins, 1997) that politics, lying, and deceit in the Johnson administration produced the "wrong" decision to apply graduated pressures rather than the "right" decision for overwhelming military force. Francis X. Winters, *The Year of the Hare: America in Vietnam January 25, 1963–February 15, 1964* (Athens: University of Georgia Press, 1997) focuses on Diem's resentment of dependence on American advice and the emerging consensus in Washington to remove him. It is also a strong statement of the thesis that Diem's overthrow doomed subsequent efforts by the United States to secure the independence of South Vietnam.

Something approaching obsession with this war is evident in the memoirs of wartime presidents Lyndon Johnson, *The Vantage Point* (New York: Holt, 1971), and Richard Nixon, *RN: The Memoirs of Richard Nixon* (New York: Grosset, 1978). With pithy prose and self-deprecating wit, Henry Kissinger's *White House Years* (Boston: Little, Brown, 1979) and *Years of Upheaval* (Boston: Little, Brown, 1982) examine the diplomacy and politics of the war on the American side from the perspective of the ultimate insider and bogey man to opponents of Nixon's policies. Kissinger has gathered and revised his writings on Vietnam to rebut his critics with sometimes slippery argumentation into a single volume, *Ending the Vietnam War: A History of America's Involvement in and Extrication from the Vietnam War* (New York: Simon & Schuster, 2003), which bitterly criticizes Congress for obstructing the rational pursuit of an outcome more favorable to Saigon and to American strategic interests. Robert McNamara admits mistakes ("I was wrong," he says) in *In Retrospect: The Tragedy and Lessons of Vietnam* (New York: Times Books, 1995). Harvey Neese and John O'Donnell (eds.), in *Prelude to Tragedy: Vietnam, 1960–1965* (Annapolis, Md.: Naval Institute Press, 2001), gather original articles by some interesting people with on-the-ground experience of the war. The best commentaries on the presidents are Doris Kearns, *Lyndon Johnson and the American Dream* (New York: Harper & Row, 1976); Tad Szulc, *The Illusion of Peace* (New York: Viking, 1978); Seymour M. Hersh, *The Price of Power* (New York: Summit, 1983); Herbert Schandler, *The Unmaking of a President: Lyndon Johnson and Vietnam* (Princeton, N.J.: Princeton University Press, 1983), and George C. Herring, *LBJ and Vietnam:*

A Different Kind of War (Austin: University of Texas Press, 1994). Herring is particularly good on Johnson's distrust of the military and the makeshift nature of policy-making during his administration.

The length, documentation, and divisiveness of the war are rich terrain for the student of the United States. Against the "quagmire hypothesis" that the United States could not easily back out of a war it had stumbled into, Daniel Ellsberg, *Papers on the War* (New York: Simon & Schuster, 1972) argues in a chapter on "the stalemate machine" that the war was prolonged by the need of successive presidents to get elected. Robert L. Gallucci, *Neither Peace Nor Honor* (Baltimore, Md.: Johns Hopkins, 1975) plumbs *The Pentagon Papers* to analyze the impact of bureaucratic procedures and infighting. Leslie Gelb and Richard Betts, *The Irony of Vietnam* (Washington, D.C.: Brookings, 1979) comes to the ironic conclusion that the policymaking system "worked" in the sense that it fulfilled the wish of six administrations to prevent the loss of Vietnam to Communism. Larry Berman, *Planning a Tragedy* (New York: Norton, 1982) uses documents from the LBJ Library to examine Lyndon Johnson's halting steps toward escalation in 1965. Former pacification chief Robert Komer, *Bureaucracy at War* (Boulder, Colo.: Westview, 1985), indicts organizational constraints for inhibiting adaptation to an atypical conflict, with costly consequences for the United States. The definitive study of the war's impact on executive-legislative relations, commissioned by the Senate Committee on Foreign Relations, is William Conrad Gibbons, *The U.S. Government and the Vietnam War*, 5 vols. (Princeton, N.J.: Princeton University Press, 1986–).

Was it legal in international law? One might think the answer should be simple and straightforward, but it is not. Essential background is provided in Robert Randle, *Geneva 1954—The Settlement of the Indochinese War* (Princeton, N.J.: Princeton University Press, 1969). The Lawyers Committee on American Policy Toward Vietnam, *Vietnam and International Law* (Flanders, N.J.: O'Hare, 1967) and Richard A. Falk, comp., *The Vietnam War and International Law*, 4 vols. (Princeton, N.J.: Princeton University Press, 1968–1976) find the U.S. in violation, while John Norton Moore, *Law and the Indo-China War* (Princeton, N.J.: Princeton University Press, 1972) defends the legality of American intervention. Peter D. Trooboff, ed., *Law and Responsibility in Warfare: The Vietnam Experience* (Chapel Hill: University of North Carolina, 1975) reveal the ambiguities in the application of the laws of war to an unconventional conflict.

On the broader effects of the war on U.S. society and politics, see John E. Mueller, *War, Presidents, and Public Opinion* (New York: Wiley, 1973); Robert Warren Stevens, *Vain Hopes, Grim Realities: The Economic Consequences of the Vietnam War* (New York: New Viewpoints, 1976); and Pulitzer Prize-winning *They Marched into Sunlight* by David Maraniss (New York: Simon & Schuster, 2003) bounces back and forth between the U.S. domestic scene and Indochina but is by far best when it comes to detailing the anxieties of student demonstrators and anxious officials in Washington.

Writing on U.S. armed forces, strategies, and experience has been left largely to people who served in the armed forces or government. The official summary of U.S. strategy and operations through the Tet Offensive is Admiral U.S.G. Sharp and General William C. Westmoreland, *Report on the War in Vietnam* (Washington, D.C.: Government Printing Office, 1969), which can profitably be compared with the acid-tinged memoir by General Westmoreland, *A Soldier Reports* (Garden City, N.Y.: Doubleday, 1976). Phillip B. Davidson, *Vietnam at War, The History: 1946–1975* (Novato, Calif.: Presidio, 1988), by the chief of U.S. intelligence under Westmoreland and then Abrams (1967–1969), covers the first two Indochina wars in a more thorough and detached manner than Westmoreland's final reports, providing an informative view of how things looked from inside the U.S. high command. Other personalized accounts from the command level and composed with some detachment are General Bruce Palmer, Jr., *The 25-Year War* (Lexington: University of Kentucky, 1984) and D. R. Palmer, *Summons of the Trumpet* (San Rafael, Calif.: Presidio, 1978). Stuart A. Herrington, *Silence Was a Weapon* (Novato, Calif.: Presidio, 1982) and *Peace with Honor* (Novato, Calif.: Presidio, 1983) recount the personal experiences of a U.S. Army intelligence officer in the period 1970–1975. The first volume in the U.S. Army's own history of the war is Ronald H. Spector, *Advice and Support: The Early Years 1941–1960* (Washington, D.C.: Government Printing Office, 1985); the second is Jeffrey J. Clarke, *Advice and Support: The Final Years, 1965–1973* (Washington, D.C.: Center of Military History, 1988). David H. Hackworth, America's most decorated officer, castigates his superiors in *Steel My Soldiers' Hearts* (New York: Rugged Land, 2002). Readers will find all they can stomach about the My Lai massacre in Seymour Hersh, *My Lai 4* (New York: Random House, 1970), and, by the officer who conducted the official inquiry, W. R. Peers, *The My Lai Inquiry* (New York: Norton, 1979).

In the category of lessons, regrets and recrimination in the U.S. military, Douglas Kinnard, *The War Managers* (Hanover: University Press of New England, 1977) analyzes what the war meant to army general officers who commanded in it. Douglas Blaufarb, *The Counterinsurgency Era* (New York: Free Press, 1977) finds performance falling short of doctrinal claims. Andrew F. Krepinevich, *The Army and Vietnam* (Baltimore, Md.: Johns Hopkins University Press, 1986), a major in the U.S. Army at the time of publication, deflates the idea popular among his superiors that all the U.S. needed to win the war was more men and hardware. Pacification has sturdy defenders in Richard A. Hunt and Richard H. Shultz, Jr., *Lessons from an Unconventional War* (New York: Pergamon, 1982), but the way it was actually conducted comes in for sustained critical analysis in Hunt's *Pacification: The American Struggle for Vietnam's Hearts and Minds* (Boulder, Colo.: Westview

Press, 1995). John Paul Vann's story as a sharp critic of American strategy while an army colonel and later as a civilian pacification chief is told in Neil Sheehan's classic, *A Bright Shining Lie* (New York: Random House, 1988). Lewis Sorley, *A Better War: The Unexamined Victories and Final Tragedy of America's Last Years in Vietnam* (New York: Harcourt Brace, 1999) argues that the "better war" was the one General Abrams was winning until budget cuts and troop withdrawals turned victory into defeat. C. Dale Walton, *The Myth of Inevitable US Defeat in Vietnam* (London: Frank Cass, 2002) claims to expose the "numerous (often gross) strategic errors on the part of the United States" which caused it to lose the war, but he does not analyze why these errors were made. James H. Willbanks, *Abandoning Vietnam: How America Left and South Vietnam Lost Its War* (Lawrence: University of Kansas Press, 2004) argues that Vietnamization contributed to Saigon's defeat in two ways: it did not become official policy until too late to be properly implemented, and shaping the ARVN in the image of the U.S. military made it overly dependent on firepower.

Thomas C. Thayer, *War Without Fronts: The American Experience in Vietnam* (Boulder, Colo.: Westview Press, 1985) provides an eye-opening search for patterns in the mountains of statistical data produced by MACV that lays the blame for defeat mainly at the feet of the South Vietnamese. Another numbers-based analysis is Micheal Clodfelter, *Vietnam in Military Statistics: A History of the Indochina Wars, 1772–1991* (Jefferson, N.C.: McFarland & Company, 1995). The work that has had by far the most, and some would say baneful, influence on thinking inside the U.S. Army, however, is Colonel Harry G. Summers, Jr., *On Strategy* (San Rafael, Calif.: Presidio, 1982), which pins the blame for defeat on failure to respect Clausewitz's rule about taking the battle to the enemy's base. Pacification's advocates disagree.

Index